THE 12 METRE CLASS

THE 12 METRE CLASS

The History of the International 12 Metre Class

from the First International Rule to the America's Cup

LUIGI LANG AND DYER JONES

ADLARD COLES NAUTICAL
London

Published 2001 by Adlard Coles Nautical
an imprint of A&C Black (Publishers) Ltd
37 Soho Square, London WID 3QZ
www.adlardcoles.co.uk

Copyright © 2001 Yachting Library S.r.l.
C.so Monforte, 16 - 20122 Milano

ISBN 0-7136-6179-8

A CIP catalogue record fo this book is available from the British Library.

TEXT:
Luigi Lang
with the cooperation of Dyer Jones, President of International Twelve Metre Association (ITMA)

TRANSLATION:
James Taylor

ILLUSTRATIONS:
page 10 (drawing): Archive of John Lammerts van Bueren
pages 16, 17, 20, 23, 25, 28, 37, 42, 48, 74-75, 76: Archive of Yachting Library; © Carlo Borlenghi - See & Sea, Milan
pages 19, 31, 33, 35, 58-59: © Studio Faggioni
pages 21, 26, 47: © Beken of Cowes
page 29: Archive of The Herreshoff Marine Museum, Bristol, Rhode Island, USA
page 39: Archive of Henrich Wehrmann
pages 40, 65 (drawings), 67, 71: Archive of AIVE
pages 41, 43, 50, 53, 54-55, 56, 57, 63, 64, 66, 68, 69, 71, 77, 78: © Carlo Borlenghi - See & Sea, Milan
pages 51, 61: © Mystic Seaport, Rosenfeld Collection, Mystic, Connecticut
page 60: © Tony Dixon
page 74: Archive of Cantiere Navale dell'Argentario
page 77: Archive of Chris Ennals

ART DIRECTION:
Roberta Grossi

REPRO HOUSE:
Esseci, Milan; Italy

PRINTING:
Graficarta, Segrate, Milan, Italy

CONTENTS

PREFACE BY OLIN STEPHENS   11

INTRODUCTION   13

THE 19TH CENTURY:
the SEARCH FOR A RATING RULE   16

THE INTERNATIONAL RULE   30

THE FIRST VERSION OF THE RULE: 1907-1920   36

THE SECOND AND THIRD VERSIONS
of the INTERNATIONAL RULE   44

THE 12 METRES OF THE SECOND AND
THIRD RULE   60

RESTORING A TWELVE METRE   72

APPENDICES   79
    1. TWELVES AND THE AMERICA'S CUP
    2. THE TWELVE METRE REGISTER
    3. INDEX OF YACHTS NAMES

BIBLIOGRAPHY   171

DAVO

Designer	Max Oertz
Year of build	1907
L.W.L.	11.28 m
Max beam	3.85 m
Sail area	2.30 m

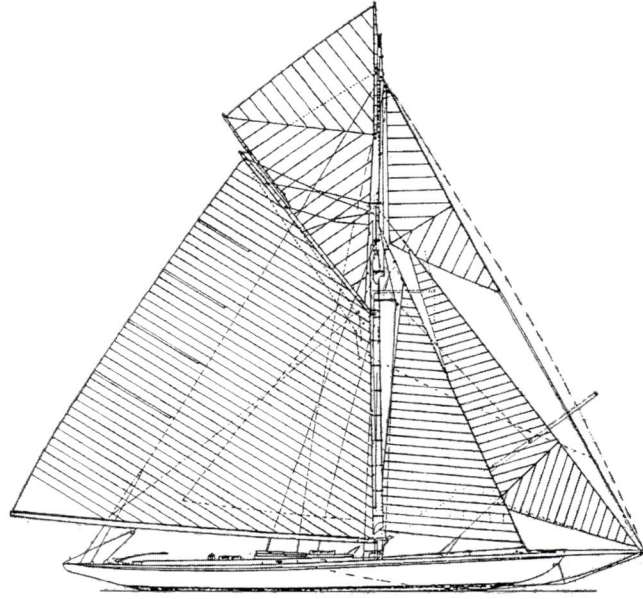

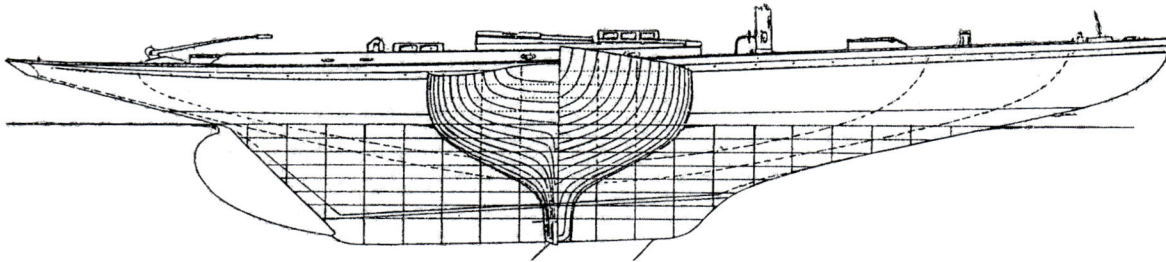

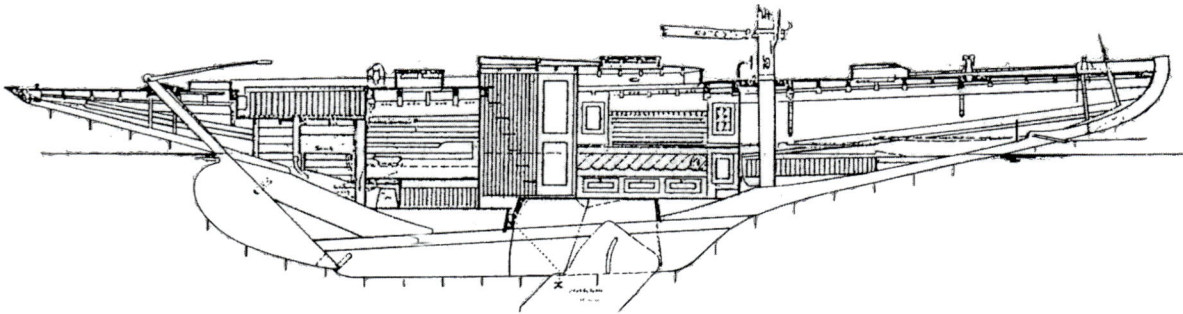

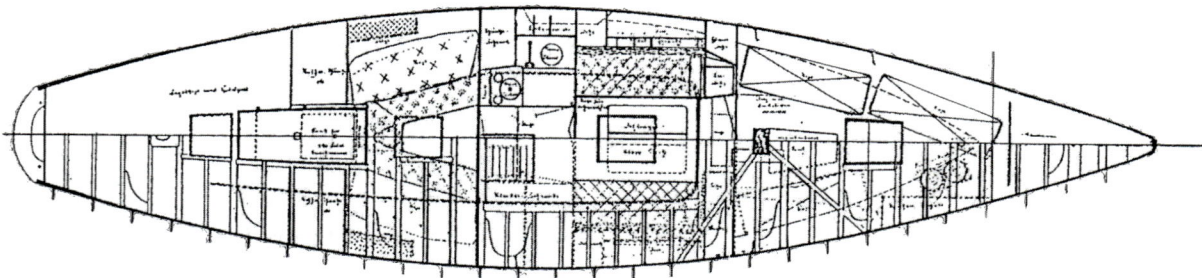

PREFACE

*O*ver the years the 12 Metre Class has anchored the yacht racing community. In the era of the largest yachts the 12s found their place as the smallest of the largest, and when the trend turned smaller they became the biggest of the smaller classes, filling many and varied demands. Whether in good times or bad, 12s have been there, fitting the times and rewarding the owners with prestige and good sailing. The authors, calling on their association with the class, have now filled a gap in the story of yachting with a full class history.

It is a class that has been blessed with stability. Breakthrough changes, such as the separation of the keel and rudder and the use of the wing keel, have occurred, but only at intervals. Structural requirements have changed but have been kept strong. Since the acceptance of the Second International Rule, the coupling of the fairly generous displacement with the waterline length has set a stable class character with the power to be fast to windward and roomy below with good headroom under a flush deck.

Happy in a long life, I can relate to the class back as far as 1928, soon after the introduction of the class to America. That May, as a young designer and an enthusiastic sailor, I made the trip from New York to Halifax, Nova Scotia. In compliance with American customs requirements, a group of German built yachts, 8 Metres and 12s, had been unloaded from a freighter and rigged to sail in the U.S. I was to crew in an 8 but I admired the beauty and power of the large Burgess designed 12s, the first of the class I had seen. The new boats raced on Long Island Sound and on the New York Yacht Club Cruise, but in the financial depression following 1930 the class was less active. It so happened that, prior to the 1934 season, Drake Sparkman, my partner, had arranged the sale of the British 12, Mouette, to an American client who feared that he *might have no competition during the difficult summer. Accordingly he chartered one of the Burgess boats which my partner and I raced against him and a scattering of others. It was a summer of easy sailing in a professionally crewed yacht. Our wives as well as us thoroughly enjoyed it and when we were able to beat the newer boat, as we did to win the Astor Cup of the NYYC, we felt it was a triumph.*

Our authors will tell us more of the widespread growth of the class as it prospered in Europe and Scandinavia up to the time of the war. In America the first locally designed and built 12s were, in 1935 and 1937, those designed by Clinton Crane for himself and by his friend Van S. Merle-Smith. They were followed by Bill Strawbridge's Francis Herreshoff designed Mitena. *Later, in 1938, I came to know the class through three designs, one of which was Harold Vanderbilt's* Vim. *He sailed her successfully in England in 1939, the last season before the Second World War.*

After the war inflation made the 12 Metre class, in its medium sized character, seem a better choice than the big Js for the renewal of the America's Cup. By then the International Rule was common to Britain and America. The class was chosen after some legal work made that possible by modifying the previously required dimensions. In America four new boats were built for the 1958 revival. Columbia, *an S&S design, became the successful defender, bringing me back to the class. The class continued as the vehicle for the Cup until 1987. My association with the 12s continued until I retired in 1980. They proved themselves a good choice by opening, for a number of countries, the door to the Cup. The class grew and spread. The authors will describe in these pages how the boats, their history and their wide popularity has continued over the years.*

Olin J. Stephens II

INTRODUCTION

*O*ne of the most important influences on yachting in the 20th century was surely the International Rule for measuring and rating yachts. The greatest marine architects worked within the confines of the International Rule; boatyards all over the world received metric class commissions for a century and most of the modern innovations in techniques and materials of yacht construction derived from the development of these classes, which contributed some of the most glorious pages in the history of yachting.

Further, the International Rule is not simply a rating rule. For the first time, the authors of the Rule created a system which took into account ratings, the rules for measurement, construction regulations (the scantling rules drawn up by Lloyd's), and the racing rules. This complex mix of rules and regulations, thanks to successive updates, is still in force and approaching the end of its first century. Notwithstanding its age, the Rule is still in force and new boats are produced in the 5.5, 6, and 8 Metre Classes. Every year World Championships or Continental Championships are held with wide and intense participation, indicative of the widespread interest in these classes. In the Twelve Metre Class World Championship in 2001 thirty-five boats were entered, more than for any past Championship. Yachts representing the history of the class from 1909 to the last America's Cup contenders were present.

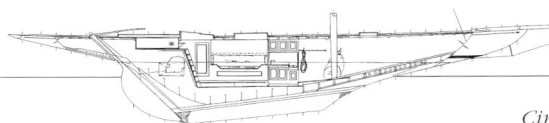

Cintra

Many metric yachts are also present at classic yacht regattas. In an age marked by a constant search for new solutions, it seems significant that there are so many projects reconstructing or rebuilding the great boats of the past: "J" class, 23 M International, or the "Big Boats"; projects which proceed from the talking stage to designers' tables. Probably the sheer beauty of the older boats, their speed, and finally the desire to step back a moment from the modern world and its frenzy, inspire these projects.

Of all the older classes, perhaps the Twelves are the most fascinating, and certainly the most long-lasting. Being the principal class for nearly thirty years of America's Cup racing certainly gave new youth to a class which already had a splendid history. The Twelves are not only the protagonists of the most famous cup in yachting history; if one takes the time to read this book and some of the descriptions in the Register of all those designed (even those not even built) Twelves, one will be caught up in the events and traditions of the past century. These yachts and their bigger brothers ("J" class, "Big Boats", 15, 19, and 23 Metre International Classes) were at the forefront in the evolution of technique and construction, great races, and social encounters which, on some occasions, brought together royalty and high society. Equally important, they were the passions of owners who lived and raced on and for their yachts.

Some points may make it easier to understand the development of the class: the hundred years of the International Rule can be divided into four distinct periods:

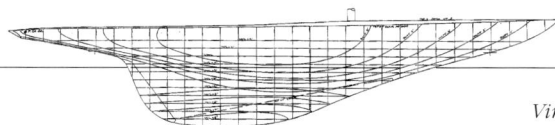

Vim

1907 - 1914: *this is the period of the First Rule, the first experiences with the Formula, the first races, the Olympic Games; here the 12 is the little sister of the 15 and 19 Metres;*

1922 - 1939: *the season of great races, famous owners, grand society events connected with the races;*

1958 - 1987: *America's Cup period; the Twelves represent the cutting edge of sailboat technology;*

1988 - today: *after a long interlude the class is again in fervent activity; attention is given both to racing and to the restoration of older Twelves dating from before the last war.*

If there were a dozen nations active in the design and construction of Twelves, it was England and Norway which dominated the first fifty years, with the US dominant in the last fifty years. These three nations produced the largest number of designs, from the drawing tables of several important designers: William Fife III, Johan Anker, Alfred Mylne, Charles E. Nicholson and Olin Stephens.

There were also important owners, often members of the same family, and often, contrary to more recent times, the skippers of their boats. Among these let us cite the Coats, Charles MacIver, Henry Horn, the Larsens, the Olsens, the von Erpecoms, John Payne, Richard Fairey, William Burton, Arthur Connell, Thomas Sopwith, Ralph Gore, Hugh Goodson and Harold Vanderbilt. All made splendid contributions to the history and tradition of yachting.

Luigi Lang and Dyer Jones

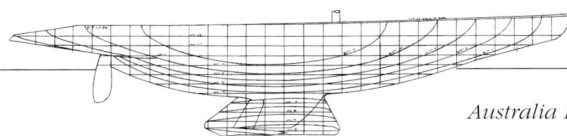

Australia II

THE 19TH CENTURY:
THE SEARCH FOR A RATING RULE

The following salient points of 19th century yachting history, paying special attention to rating formulas, will give us a deeper understanding of the environment that created the International Rule, the measurement rule to which all 12 Metre yachts have been designed and built. The birth of the Rule was not simply the brilliant idea of a single designer, nor an isolated occurrence. The lack of space must necessarily limit us to the Thames, the Solent, the Clyde, and the northeastern coast of the United States. Influences from other European countries, specifically Scandinavia, will be mentioned, but if we are to deal with the development of formulas the most important changes in yachting took place in Great Britain and the United States.

The first traces of yachting as such are recorded halfway through the 1600s in Holland, while the first "competition" seems to have taken place in July 1749. The term "regatta" was first used in England on the 28th of June 1775, when "several respectable gentlemen proprietors of sailing vessels" decided to race each other while escorting the competitors of a rowing race at Battersea.

That same summer members of the Cumberland Society created the Cumberland Fleet, which later became the Royal Thames Yacht Club. Here we already had the first subdivisions among yachts: the tonnage limited between 2 and 100 tons, and the separation of the competitors into two classes: "below Bridge" for the larger yachts with the sea keeping qualities necessary for the Thames estuary and the Channel, and "above Bridge" for the smaller, undecked yachts. Bear in mind that the then current definition of yacht referred not to specially designed vessels, but rather to already existing vessels modified for recreation from the fastest successful fishing and trading designs.

Gradually this new form of recreation moved south from London to the Solent and the town of Cowes, already renowned for summer vacationing. This was the period following the Napoleonic wars, and Britain entered a century characterised by heady expansion and splendour. The Clyde in Scotland and the Solent in the Channel became the centres of British yachting and inspired the development of this new activity among the other European nations.

H.R.H. Henry Frederick Duke of Cumberland, founder of the Royal Thames Yacht Club, 1775.

(10) Advertisement for steamer *Nile* to watch RTYC races, 1841.

Top: Notice of the race of 1835.
Left: Advertisement for a RTYC regatta in 1841. On July 6th 1775 the London newspaper, The Public Advisor, published the following race instructions: "A silver cup, the gift of His Royal Highness, The Duke of Cumberland, is to be sailed for on Tuesday, the 11th Instant, from Westminster Bridge to Putney Bridge and back, by Pleasure Sailing Boats from Two to Five Tons burthen, and constantly lying above London Bridge. Any gentleman inclined to enter his Boat may be informed of particulars by applying to Mr. Roberts, Boatbuilder, Lambeth, at any time before Saturday Noon Next".

The 1st of June 1815 was the birth date of another great English club: fortytwo gentlemen created the local yacht club in Cowes, shortly after renamed the Royal Yacht Club, and finally the Royal Yacht Squadron.

Modern yachting had now taken form, and racing proliferated, as did the need to find a system that would allow the large variety of designs to compete against each other while giving an even chance of victory to all: the first rating problems were born. The first solutions were orientated towards racing rules and allowances, rather than ratings related to design parameters. Many experiments were carried out: real time racing with the yachts divided by tonnage or by rig; handicaps according to distance, with the variation in rating calculated at the finish line or determined by a staggered starting time.

In yachting, "tonnage" is a measure of volume, not a measure of weight. The term originally came into use during the XIV century, defining as a "tun" a barrel holding not less than 252 gallons of wine. The number of "tuns" that a vessel could stow therefore determined the vessel's "tonnage". Over time the exact value of a "tun" became increasingly precise, but today "ton" remains a definition of volume, and is used as a tax parameter on cargo carrying capacity.

In the late 1820s the prevailing system finally divided the yachts by tonnage; in the same class racing is on elapsed time, while between different classes a time allowance is awarded, calculated by the dimensions of the largest yacht. This system, laid down in Cowes in 1829, was known as the Tonnage Rule. The rule divided the yachts into four classes with the following handicaps: the 1st class must give the 2nd class 1/2 mile, the 3rd class 1 1/4 miles, and 2 1/4 miles to the 4th class. Two years later the classes were increased to six, and the first official recognition of the Tonnage Rule

Tons	Diff. of Time	h.	m.	s.	Tons	Diff. of Time	h.	m.	s.
Under 1	75 seconds per tons	10	28	45	Under 16	60 seconds per tons	10	46	15
2		...	30	0	17		...	47	15
3		...	31	15	18		...	48	15
4		...	32	30	19		...	49	15
5		...	33	45	20		...	50	15
6	70	...	35	0	21	55	...	51	15
7		...	37	10	22		...	52	10
8		...	38	20	23		...	53	5
9		...	39	30	24		...	54	0
10		...	40	40	25		...	54	55
11	65	...	41	50	26	50	...	55	50
12		...	42	55	27		...	56	40
13		...	43	0	28		...	57	30
14		...	44	5	29		...	58	20
15		...	45	10	30		...	59	10

This is the first handicap table, and was given its creator's name: Askers Graduated Scale. The cutters are then divided into four groups: from 30 to less than 50 tons, from 50 to less than 75 tons, from 75 to less than 105, and over 105 tons. The schooners are only divided into two groups: over and under 140 tons. An allowance based on one mile is given to each group.

One of the essential elements of the Tonnage Rule was the famous 1773 "Builder's Measurement Rule". Although modified in 1836, it was still known as the "B.O.M. - Builder's Old Measurement":

$$\text{Tonnage (Rating)} = \frac{L - 3/5B \times B \times 1/2B}{94}$$

where L is the length of the keel (length of keel or the length which is in contact with the ground), and B is the beam.

occurred in 1834 when King George IV ordered that from then on the King's Cup would use the new system. But the system was too simple; it did not take into account enough of the variables that differentiated one vessel from another. New methods were needed.

In 1838 the distance handicap was changed to a time handicap. In 1843 George Holland Askers, owner of the 217 ton schooner *Dolphin*, perfected

Right: Thistle, G.L.Watson, 1887. She was designed as a challenger for the America's Cup. Later she became Meteor and was bought by the Kaiser.

There were no penalties for waterline length, freeboard, draft or sail area.
In George Watson's words: "...gradually the boat builders realise that, by increasing draft and ballast, beam can be reduced and that a yacht with the same nominal displacement as before can be built with a longer waterline and increased sail area."

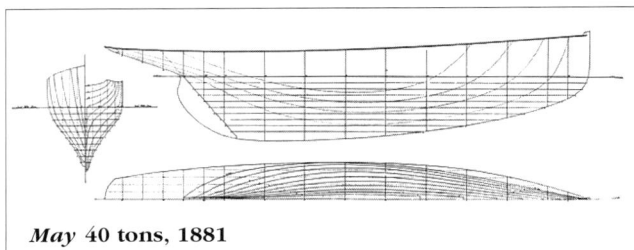

May 40 tons, 1881

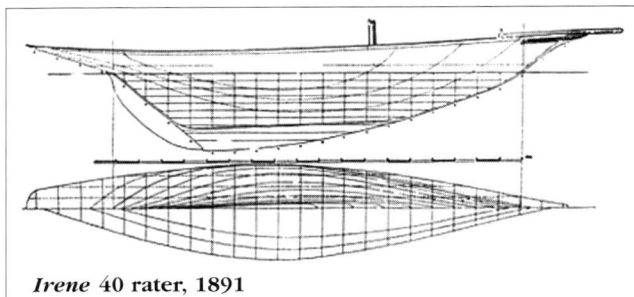

Irene 40 rater, 1891

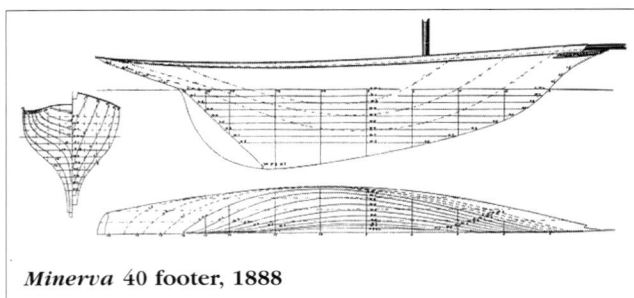

Minerva 40 footer, 1888

Development of the sheer lines on British cutters.
From the top: May (*T.M.R.*); Irene (*L & S Area Rule*); Minerva, *an evolution of Kemp's Rule.*

his own system of groups and handicaps. The yachts were divided into two categories: cutters and schooners. Although progress had been made, the importance of a rating handicap, as opposed to a racing handicap, was not yet fully understood. In fact, one of the essential elements of the Tonnage Rule was the famous 1773 "Builder's Measurement Rule", which took only hull length and beam into account. This rule was created to calculate the cargo carrying capacity of a merchant ship, made by an 1834 Act of Parliament and shortly thereafter adopted internationally. It necessarily fell quite short of indicating the possible displacement or performance of a modern yacht.

With the approach of 1850, yachting as a sport was becoming increasingly important.

There were now are at least 16 yacht clubs in England, and the Royal Yacht Squadron counted a fleet of approximately 100 yachts, while the Royal Thames Yacht Club fleet numbered approximately 130. Yacht owners must deal with the new reality of complex formulas that attempted to make vastly differing yachts competitive against one another. Acker's Scale and the Tonnage Rule (also known as the Old 94 Rule) were carefully studied, and the yachtsmen soon realised that to win, a lower displacement would give a higher allowance.

The fact that builders took into consideration keel length brought about the first designs with an inclined stern post: a shorter keel favours a lower rating with a higher allowance, while increased waterline length gives greater speed.

However, we shouldn't think of a rapid revolution in design; awareness is as gradual as evolution in new designs. When the schooner *America* arrived at Cowes, the yachts that were waiting for her were as modern as could be expected, yet still of traditional design.

The spread of "tonnage-cheating" - looking for loopholes in the rating formulas to better one's own rating - carries on to the present day. It is not necessarily true that new designs are better than the preceding ones; they simply have a better rating. This results in extreme new designs and non-competitiveness for the older designs; a rule must intervene to keep owners satisfied and keep competition alive.

So work began on displacement formulas. The Builder's Measurement Rule was finally deemed outdated for yachting's needs. After specifying that the L of the formula no longer applied to the length of the keel but to the length of the hull, in 1854 the Royal London Yacht Club, followed by the Royal Thames Yacht Club, proposed the first formula specifically conceived for yachts - the famous Thames Measurement (T.M.):

$$\text{Tons (Thames Measurement)} = \frac{(L-B) \times B \times 1/2B}{94}$$

where, finally, L is the length measured on deck from the stem to the stern post, and B is the beam. Despite initial criticisms (Vanderdecken's famous, though never built, project to decrease L by bringing the stern post half way forward), the new formula obtained the desired effect: older yachts were competitive again and the "tonnage-cheaters" penalised.

The yacht *America's* success in the 100 Guinea Cup, combined with the new formula, ignited ideas and enthusiasm in English yachting, setting off a quarter century of heady splendour.

Owners, designers, and shipyards were all very active, launching the large schooners with famous names which incorporated the lessons garnered from the design of *America*. Designers and shipyards began a period of intense activity, while highly experienced fishermen, hardened by winter fishing in the northern ocean, became the excellent seamen and captains running the large new yachts during season after season of highly competitive racing. But even this formula was far from perfect:

Ever narrower, ever more sail area: T.M. yachts sail almost on their beam ends. They exhibit a sudden, though fast, movement through the water. "Plank on edge" construction is born, accompanying an ever-increasing length/width ratio: from a value of 4 when the Thames Measurement was first applied in 1854, in 1882 the Spankadillo's *ratio was an incredible 7.2 (with a LWL of 11 metres and only 1.90 metres of beam). Galatea,* the America's Cup challenger in 1886, *was a typical "plank on edge" cutter.*

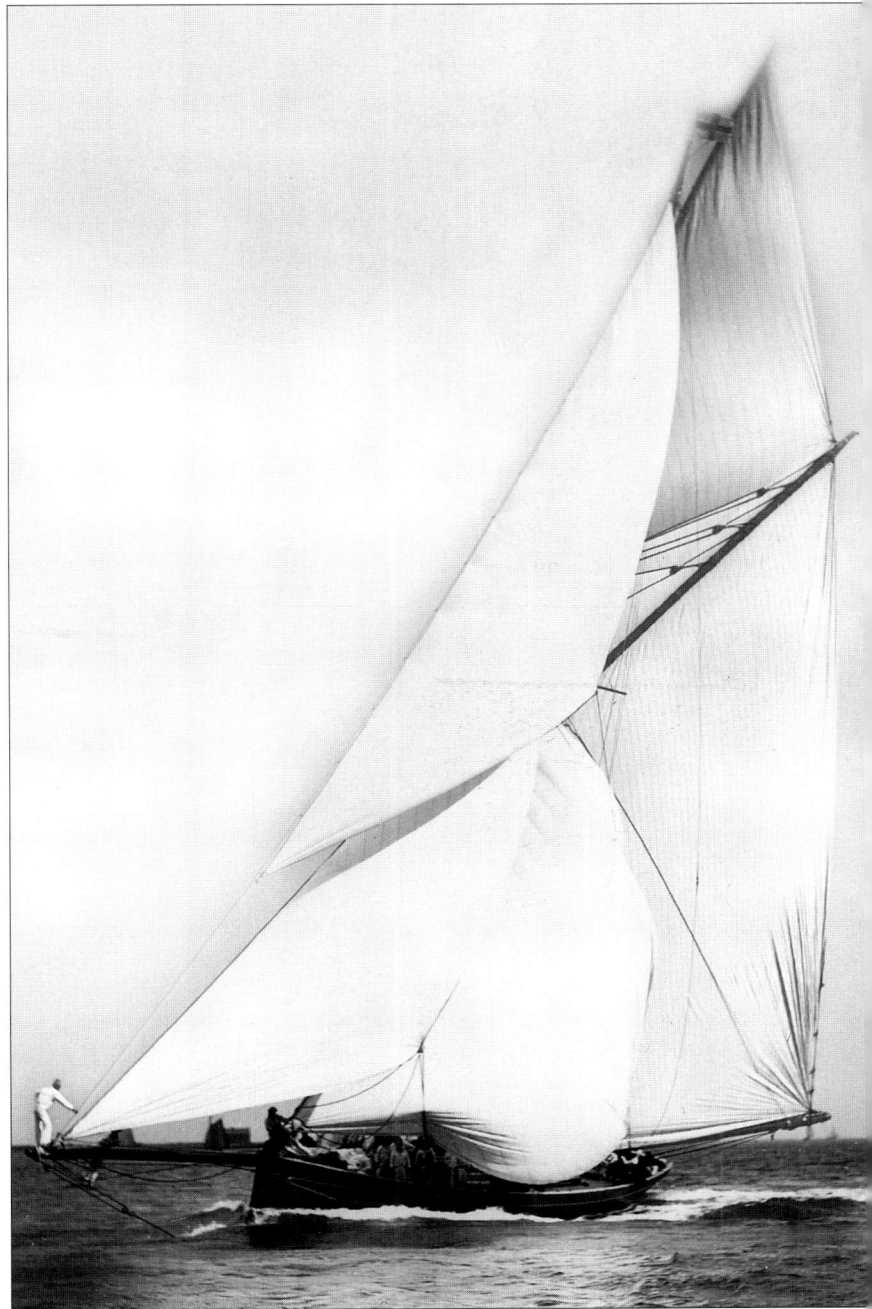

once again beam was excessively penalised, creating yachts designed with a very narrow beam. Stability was not completely sacrificed, as the Rule allows only internal ballast, yet quite soon it became evident that the T.M. gives a very long and fine hull. Nor are any sail area restrictions contemplated. The most extreme case was *Oona* in 1886: her LWL was 10.33m, beam 1.67m, displacement 12 tons, and a sail area of 185 square metres.

Her first voyage was never completed as she foundered with all hands (including her designer, Payton) in a storm off Ireland. The Thames Measurement, even after the period when it was actively used as a racing handicap, continued to be used to identify yachts. The 1980 edition of Lloyd's Register of Yachts still had a T.M. column for a considerable number of entries.

The extreme designs caused disillusionment among yacht owners. Each yacht club had its own racing rules: it became complicated to race among clubs, let alone internationally. The time was ripe for new changes.

Two interesting developments came about in 1875: the first was the launching of *Jullanar*. Designed by her owner, farm machinery manufacturer Ernest H. Bentall, *Jullanar's* lines were innovative: fine entries to reduce waves, the longest possible waterline length combined with the least possible wetted surface to increase speed. She won everything for the next three seasons.

The second, and far more important development, was the founding of the British Yacht Racing Association (Y.R.A.) on the 17th of November.

Due to increasing discontent with the Thames Measurement (in May, a race on the Thames River was characterized by all the yachts lowering their club pennants in protest), the Y.R.A.'s first secretary Dixon Kemp immediately addressed the two major issues that had given rise to the protests; new scantling rules to avoid the further construction of unseaworthy yachts, and the definition of a handicap rule which would be accepted by all the clubs and resolve the series of problems that had emerged over the last fifty years. Many yacht clubs promptly joined the new association, although the two most important, the Royal Thames and the Royal Yacht Squadron, delayed entering until 1881 when the Prince of Wales became president of the Y.R.A. The last barriers to their membership fell, and the Y.R.A. became truly representative of English yachting as a whole.

The Thames Measurement is first modified by redefining L, from length measured on deck from the stem to the stern post, to length at the waterline (LWL).

Although progress was made, the race for narrower hulls continued. In 1877 the first yacht with external ballast, *Hilda*, was built.

There are limits to what can be expected from a poorly conceived rule, and it appears that successive changes in a rule cannot correct its intrinsic defects. This was borne out in 1881 by the Y.R.A.'s "1730 Rule", an attempt to increase maximum beam. The formula is:

$$\frac{(L+B)2 \times B}{1730}$$

Unexpectedly, yacht designers did not follow the "suggestion" which was intended to increase beam with increasing length, and the race towards "longer and thinner" continued.

In 1880 Dixon Kemp proposed a new rule, for both sides of the Atlantic and it was adopted immediately in the United States. The Y.R.A. only agreed to its use in 1886. Displacement tons were abandoned, beam was no longer an element, dimensions were no longer limited: only factors relating to a hull's speed and power were considered - the product of waterline length and sail area divided by a constant.

Satanita, built following Dixon Kemp's formula, which proved itself technically valid and innovative, bringing designers back to fuller waterline forms, less wetted surface, bow overhangs, and above all a more normal beam without excessive ballast.

The new formula was called the "Length and Sail Area Rule":

$$\frac{L \times S}{6000}$$

The constant was chosen as a factor which would keep the new rating's value close to its predecessor in tons. Even though the product of length and area gives a result in square feet or tons, the yachts were divided or "rated"; hence the name "raters": 20, 40 or 50 Raters and so on. Together with the new formula the Y.R.A. published the "Rules of the Yacht Racing Association", a conversion table to calculate the rating in minutes per mile.

The formula was embraced promptly by the smaller yachts; there are many 40 and 20 raters, and even smaller (1, 2, and 5.5 raters). With the larger yachts, hampered by the Tonnage Rule's heritage and fiercely critical of all aspects of the new rule, the Y.R.A.'s most recent formula was slow to catch on. Even if the 1887 G.L. Watson designed America's Cup challenger *Thistle* was defined as a 120 rater, by 1891 only three other large yachts had followed: *Valkyrie* (77 rater), *Iverna* (117 rater), *Yarana* (62 rater), with widely different ratings. 1893 was the turning point, with Watson's *Valkyrie II*, commissioned by Lord Dunraven for an

America's Cup Challenge. *Valkyrie II* was to be designed with the American rating in mind, but competitive in English waters too. The usual criticisms changed to eager impatience when it became known that the Prince of Wales had ordered a similar yacht from Watson, designed according to the "Length and Sail Area Rule": *Britannia. Callunna* by Fife, and Soper's *Satanita* soon followed, the latter the largest "rater" built, with a LOA of 40 metres and LWL of 29.8 metres. Numerous smaller raters, designed to the latest criteria, soon followed. The American yacht *Navahoe* crossed the Atlantic

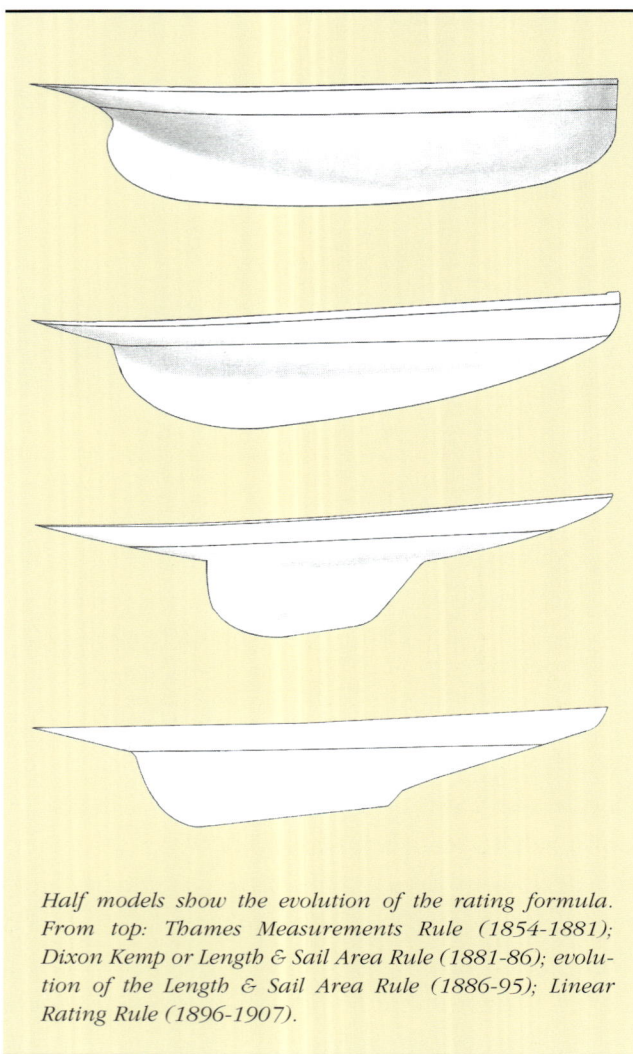

Half models show the evolution of the rating formula. From top: Thames Measurements Rule (1854-1881); Dixon Kemp or Length & Sail Area Rule (1881-86); evolution of the Length & Sail Area Rule (1886-95); Linear Rating Rule (1896-1907).

in 1893, followed shortly after by *Vigilant*, and they raced in English waters for three seasons against *Britannia, Satanita, Valkyrie II, Callunna, Meteor* and *Ailsa*. The racing, run under the "Length and Sail Area Rule", proved highly competitive, for Dixon Kemp's formula had revitalised the languid English yachting scene of the 1890s.

The formula's weak point was its devaluing of for length. Reducing LWL as much as possible, sail area can be increased without affecting the rating, and long overhangs will optimise speed; with all this canvas lateral stability is obtained by increasing beam, narrowing the stations, and deep bulb keels. In smaller vessels, the hulls are very light and difficult to steer, with no headroom or accommodation below decks.

If the Thames Measurement produced plank on edge yachts, the Length and Sail Area Rule produced skimming dishes and fin keels.

Once again it became obvious that the Rule was still inadequate; in 1892 the most important designers wrote to the Y.R.A. asking to revise the formula with the aim of limiting the current extremes in design.

A new solution was found in 1896 with Froude's Formula, elaborated by R.E. Froude, son of the famous yacht designer William Froude.

It became known as the first "Linear Rating Rule":

$$\frac{L+B+3/4G+1/2\sqrt{S}}{2} = \text{Rating in feet}$$

The formula is quite similar to the Length and Sail Area Rule, with two important additions: first, the value G (skin girth) measured vertically, from one waterline to the other, along the outside of the position 60% of waterline length from the bow; second, that the rating is expressed in feet, instead of the traditional tons, therefore giving the denomination "linear" to the formula. The rating should correspond to the LWL in feet. It was hoped that by introducing beam, girth, and by diminishing the importance of

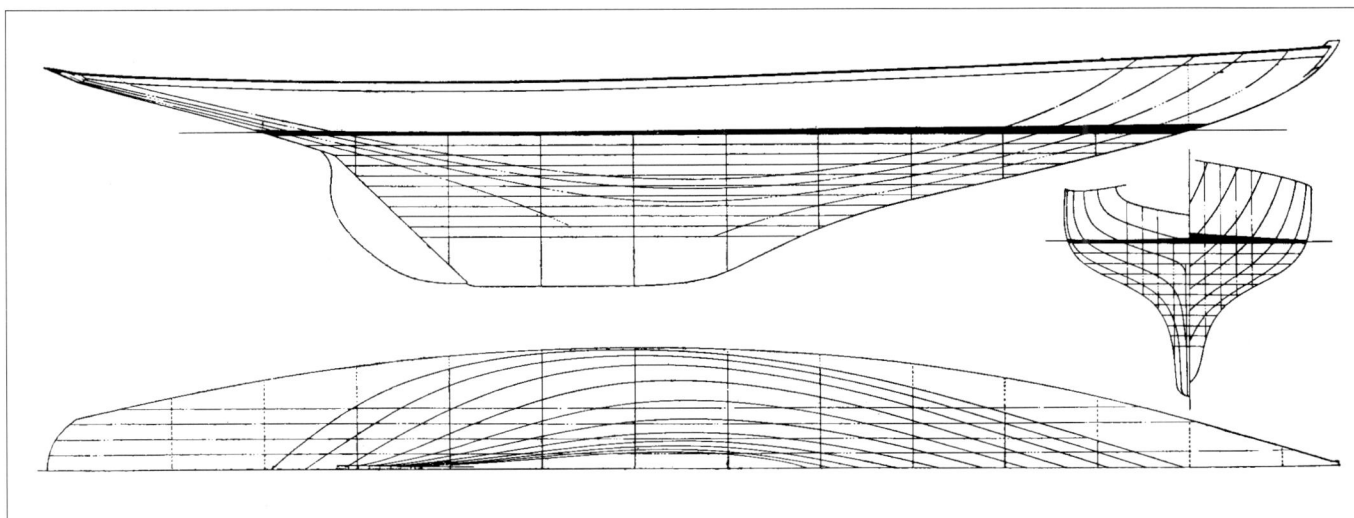

Top: Watson's Britannia *was such a revolutionary design, that never "such a balanced and better built yacht has ever crossed a starting line". In designing her he applied his fundamental beliefs on how a vessel should be built and act: lightness combined with strength and a hull that will slip over the water and not cut through it.*
Below: Jullanar, *1875.*

sail area, the inadequacies of the previous formula could be corrected. Almost immediately critics of the new formula pointed out that, instead of resolving previous defects, the Linear Rating Rule exacerbated them. Yacht designers continued to design lighter and more over-canvassed boats since no limit was placed on minimum displacement, and the decreased importance given to sail area tended to cause their increase.

The new formula's impact in the smaller classes was explosive, hulls became even wider with shorter waterline, excessive sail area, and flat bottoms with deep torpedo fin keels. The new racers had a very short life and soo became old fashioned. They were superceded in their first season by the newer designs (the Duke of York's Sibbock-built 1-rater *White Rose* was commissioned under the condition that she was to be built in eight days, to be sure that she would be the latest fashion at Cowes that year). The difficulties with the formulas had at least one important consequence: to avoid early obsolescence and exaggerated spending, owners and

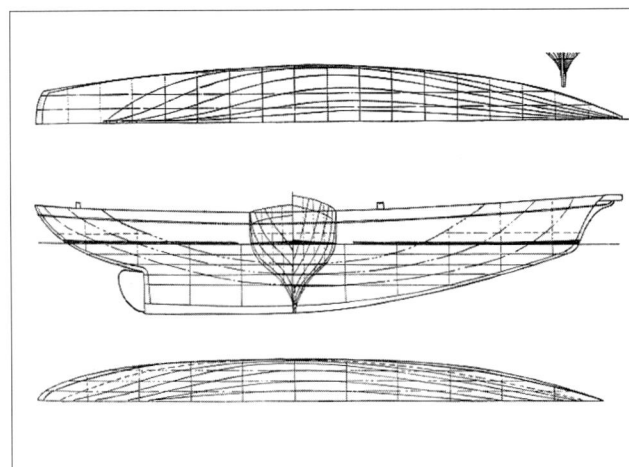

designers spent more effort on developing one-designs like the Solent 8 tonner, the first English one-design. And the "Big Class" also had its share of problems.

Meteor II, the new Watson designed yacht for the German Emperor and built expressly to beat *Britannia* and *Ailsa*, had the same waterline length as *Britannia*, but with a lighter displacement and 200 square metres more sail area as now allowed by the formula, balanced by greater beam and increased ballast. By lowering the bottom limit of the "big class" to allow the ex 40 Raters to race against their larger cousins, giving preference to yawls over cutters and recalculating the time on distance handicap, the Y.R.A. took revolutionary decisions that led to the disappearance of the class. *Britannia* was put up for sale, while *Ailsa, Bona,* and *Satanita* moved to the Mediterranean to race; there the newest formula had not been adopted. Heckstall-Smith wrote in his "*Britannia* and Her Contemporaries" that: "In 1897, as a result of these modifications, the "great class" created by *Britannia* and her contemporaries in 1893 fell into decline and gradually became extinct... The result of the Y.R.A.'s ruling was a complete disaster. The Y.R.A. destroyed the racing of the most important class." The great cutters disappeared from the racing scene, to reappear only in the 1920s under the 23 Metre International Rule. After this poor showing, the Y.R.A. applied the second "Linear Rule" in 1901.

Rating in feet =

$$\frac{L+B+3/4G+4d+1/2\sqrt{S}}{2.1}$$

The innovation was the introduction of "d", a new factor created by the Danish chemist Alfred Benzon and successfully integrated into the Copenhagen Formula, widely used by the Scandinavian countries. The value of "d" is the difference between "G" and the new measurement "Chain" or "chain girth", where Chain is the length of a chain led from one side of the hull to the other, passing below the waterline. This value (not a fixed value, it may fluctuate as the need arises) was incorporated as an attempt to limit the skimming dish effect in hull design. To avoid the continuous formula changes that had characterised the last twenty years it was also established that the formula would remain in effect and unmodified for at least seven years.

This version of the Linear Rule was no luckier than the others. The ever-present loop-holes in the formula still allowed for extreme overhangs, shallow draft, exaggerated sail area and fragile construction.

In France the Cèrcle de la Voile de Paris, the Yacht Club de France (with the Caillebotte formula) and the UYF-Union des Yachts Français (with the Godinet formula) created interesting formulas during the 1880s and 1890s.

The Godinet Formula was particularly useful when applied to small hulls and was used, with a few minor changes, on Lake Geneva. The Baltic countries were also very active during the 1890s when Denmark, Sweden and Norway created the "Baltic Rule", and as we noted above, Benzon (later an important member of what became the IYRU) introduced the "chain" concept.

The United States, while following a route parallel to England, was the other pole in the development of yachting rules. While the International Rule was most certainly born out of a wide European collaboration, we cannot deny the influence of American ideas on that rule.

Given the great distances involved and the lack of a central governing body (the North American Yacht Racing Union wasn't created until 1926), the American protagonists were the East Coast yacht clubs, principally the New York Yacht Club and the Seawanhaka Corinthian Yacht Club. The winner of the first race organised by the NYYC in 1845 appears to have been the yacht *Cygnet*. Racing was governed by local handicaps (Old Custom Measurement, Custom House Measurement) based on tonnage and customs regulations; handicaps were adjusted often and awarded in seconds per ton per mile. In the 1850s the NYYC experimented with several short term solutions. In 1853 their formulas were based on displacement; after realising the impracticality of measuring tonnage, in 1856 the formula moved to measuring sail area, with the yachts split into three classes. For the first challenge for the America's Cup of 1870, it was back to length times beam. For the 1871 Cup the new "Displacement Rule" came into effect; it took into consideration the sum of three hull stations and LWL:

$$\text{Rating} = 100 \times (A \times L/4)^{1/3}$$

Rating research here took a different direction from English practice. Displacement is a factor and beamy craft were favoured, contrasting with the narrow English designs. Low freeboard, generous overhangs, flat hull shape and lots of canvas characterised the American racers. Though undergoing a few minor adjustments, the Displacement Rule was to last until the early 1880s. For the 1876 and 1881 America's Cup matches the NYYC, slightly modified the Displacement Rule, creating the "Cubic Contents Rule".

But the search for ever faster yachts led to extreme consequences even in America. The lack of a limit to sail area created beamy, shallow and over canvassed vessels. These factors lowered stability, and several important yachts capsized. In 1876 the schooner *Mohawk* (45.7m LOA, 9.2m beam, only 1.8m draft) capsized at anchor when hit by a gust and sank, with the loss of the owner William T. Garner (Vice Commodore of the NYYC), his wife and their guests. Enough was enough, and the dramatic accident deterred further construction of these unseaworthy craft.

When Dixon Kemp and the American yacht designer Edward Burgess began to correspond, the Americans showed great interest in Kemp's formula (though not yet officially approved by the Y.R.A.). The Seawanhaka Corinthian Yacht Club adopted it, and after slight modifications used it for their 1882 season; fully satisfied, Seawanhaka suggested that the NYYC should adopt it on a larger scale. The famous Seawanhaka Rule was approved by the principal American yacht clubs meeting the year after:

$$\text{Rating} = \frac{L+\sqrt{S}}{2}$$

Though inspired by Kemp, the Seawanhaka Rule made important changes: L and S were now summed, sail area was brought to a linear value, and the result was expressed in feet; for the first time sail area was calculated by actually measuring mast, boom, and gaff lengths.

The Seawanhaka Rule lasted for twenty years; the NYYC abandoned the "Cubic Contents Rule"; the America's Cup was run by integrating the Seawanhaka Rule and the NYYC's norms. Some of the most beautiful yachts were launched under this rule: A. Carey Smith, W. Gardner, Edward Burgess, and Nat Herreshoff were the protagonists of the era. Yet 'rule cheating' persisted with fin keels and skimming dishes plus scows and the first catamarans on the North American coast.

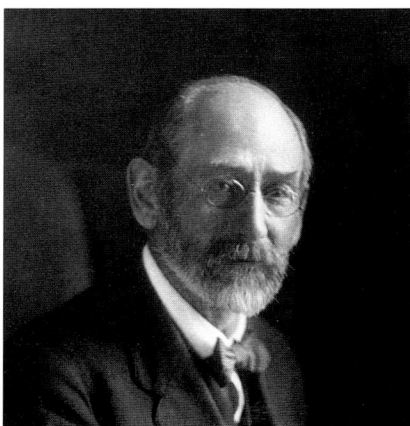

The yacht designers Burgess and Herreshoff.

Once again, the current rule began to show its age. Herreshoff himself proposed a new rule. In 1902 the NYYC sent a letter to the best-known designers in America, Europe, and Australia proposing a revision to the rule and welcoming suggestions. Many contributions were made, however the NYYC adopted Herreshoff's proposal. Any hope of approving a single formula for international use was dashed. In 1903 the NYYC and the Seawanhaka Corinthian Yacht Club discarded the Seawanhaka Rule and adopted Herreshoff's proposal, which took the name "Universal Rule" in 1904. Two years later the Universal Rule was adopted by all American yacht clubs and would be used for all the America's Cup challenges until 1937. The 1909 (and latest) version was the following formula:

$$\text{Rating} = 0{,}18 \frac{L \times \sqrt{S}}{D^{1/3}}$$

The square root of the sail area and the cube root of displacement ("D") caused all the measurements to be expressed as linear, and therefore in feet. Herreshoff contributed new ideas both for measuring "L" and for calculating displacement. In addition, completing the formula, he gave the NYYC (by revising a previously commissioned calculation used to determine allowances) the "Time allowance tables for every mile in seconds and tenths of seconds"; he then divided yachts into classes according to their rating, identifying each class with a letter: S, R, Q, P, M, L and J.

Right: Herreshoff's Gloriana *was a profoundly innovative design. Sweetening her lines, Watson created* Britannia.

THE INTERNATIONAL RULE

In the early nineteen hundreds, nearly eighty years had gone by since the first serious attempts had been made to regulate handicap yacht racing. And although the situation on both sides of the Atlantic had improved considerably, no definitive solution had been arrived at.

The disappearance of the large racing yachts and the proliferation of one-designs were symptomatic of the dissatisfaction and confusion reigning among owners (England at the time had 23 different one-design classes!), and new yacht construction concentrated primarily on cruising designs.

A new racing design, drawn according to a current rule, would only be competitive for one season.

As important regattas multiplied in Europe's most elegant venues, Brooke Heckstall-Smith gave life to a series of initiatives supporting the owner's desire to race not with infinite variations of the rules found on the local level, but with an internationally valid, clear-cut rule.

After having first verified that the various national rating rules were not so different from one another, and that all the rules (except for the French one) expired in 1907, Heckstall-Smith wrote to the Yacht Club de France asking if they would extend their rule's expiration date, and participate in the creation of a new, internationally valid rating rule. When the French accepted, the invitation was then sent to the other yachting nations (including the United States); the proposal was welcomed by all. In May 1905 the Y.R.A. officially invited the representatives of the major yacht clubs to an

NUMBERS OF REGISTERED EUROPEAN YACHTS IN 1906	
Britain	2959
English Domains	311
Austria and Germany	599
France	363
Norway and Sweden	300
Belgium and Holland	191
Denmark	107
Italy	76

PARTICIPANTS IN THE CONFERENCE AT LONDON'S LANGHAM HOTEL ON THE 15TH OF JANUARY 1906

Austria: Lieut. Baron von Preuschen (Royal Austrian Navy)
Denmark: F. Hegel, Alfred Benzon
England: R.E. Froude, W.P. Burton
France: Louis Dyèvre, M. Blanchy
Germany: Admiral Burmester (Deutscher Segler-Verband), Professor Busley
Holland and Belgium: Jonkeer W. Six, M. von Bernuth (President Royal Nautique Anversoise)
Italy: Conte Eugenio Brunetta d'Usseaux (Regio Yacht Club Italiano)
Norway: Johan Anker, Finn Knudsen
Sweden: Vice Admiral Jacob Hagg, Theodore Alpen
Switzerland: Jean Mirabaud
H.M. the Prince of Wales, President of the Y.R.A., nominated the Y.R.A.'s Vice-President Augustus Manning chairman of the conference, and Brooke Heckstall-Smith secretary.

The 15 I.R. Tuiga *was designed by William Fife in 1909.*

**THE INTERNATIONAL RULE
FOR MEASURING AND RATING YACHTS**

Validity 10 years (from January 1st, 1908, to December 31st, 1917).
Rating formula (expressed in linear units - feet or metres):

$$\text{Rating} = \frac{L + B + 1/3\,G + 3\,d + 1/3\sqrt{S} - F}{2}$$

L = waterline length (LWL)   d = difference between girth and chain
B = beam   S = sail area
G = chain girth   F = freeboard

- *the rule defines precisely where and how each term is to be measured.*
- *no crew is to be on board the yacht while measuring; level marks will be placed on the hull in a clearly visible location, sail area measurements will be indicated (as in America) by black stripes on the yards.*
- *cabin location and dimensions.*
- *hollow metal masts are not allowed, nor are hollow wooden masts on yachts over 10 metres.*
- *all yachts must have a certificate from either Lloyd's Register of British and Foreign Shipping, Germanischer Lloyd or Bureau Veritas. When a yacht has been classified, International Rule yachts will then be given an "R" rating.*

CLASSES

Classes	English feet	Max. crew
Class A (over 23M)	over 75.4	no limit
Class R International Classes		
23 m.	75.4	no limit
19 m.	62.3	20
15 m.	49.2	14
12 m.	39.4	10
10* m.	32.8	8
9 m.	29.5	6
8* m.	26.2	5
7 m.	23.0	4
6* m.	19.7	3
5 m.	16.4	2

* particular attention to be paid to these classes

- *handicaps allowing older yachts to race with their corresponding Metre class will be given until December 31st, 1909.*
- *older yachts can be remeasured with the new formula and race in class until December 31st, 1909.*
- *each yacht must have a valid measurement certificate.*
- *actual measurements must be carried out in accordance with the relevant thirty-three articles and two appendices.*

international conference in London, planned for early 1906. The agenda for the meeting contained the following three points:
- verify the possibility of creating a new general rating rule that might be adopted by all the world's yachting nations;
- if this possibility existed, how should the new rule be formulated;
- define the structure of the rule.

The NYYC sent a representative to the London Conference as an "observer".

This individual was George A. Cormack, Secretary of the NYYC; his trip was paid for by J.P. Morgan. Subsequently, NYYC hosted the "Atlantic Coast Conference" on 29 January 1908 at its New York clubhouse. This meeting of leading American yacht clubs was called to discuss changes to the measurement, handicap, scantling, and racing rules, some of which were similar to the proposals made in London.

It would be several years, however, before American yachtsmen would embrace the International Rule, preferring to stay with the Universal Rule (originally the "Herreshoff Rule").

The representatives of eleven countries met at London's Langham Hotel on January 15th 1906. H.R.H. the Prince of Wales, President of the Y.R.A., nominated the Y.R.A.'s Vice-President Augustus Manning Chairman of the conference, and Brooke Heckstall-Smith, Secretary.

The delegates were all convinced that just creating a new rule would not solve the problem; a complete and articulated system was needed that would be able to deal with each new situation as it arose.

Given their vast experience and direct knowledge of the problems involved, Froude, Benzon, Busley and Anker were the main players.

A five-day schedule and a fifteen-point agenda were agreed upon. A precise summary of the current situation showed that all the participants had common rating rule problems, and that the differences that existed between the various rules were fairly minor.

France was the only country to put forward (at the last minute) a different proposal, very similar to the American Universal Rule.

The fifteen-point agenda was approved at the conference's conclusion; each participating country was to verify and confirm it, and all were to meet again in June.

All the countries involved approved the agenda, except for France, which limited the application of the formula to 52 Raters and above, and at the same time asked for substantial modifications to the rule for smaller yachts.

The June conference examined the French proposal and rejected it by nine votes to five; it also approved the new rating formula, dividing yachts into classes, and delegated the application of the formula to a committee made up of Manning as President, Benzon, Busley, Le Bret (France), Burton, and Heckstall-Smith as Secretary.

This committee met in Berlin from the 18th to the 20th of October 1906 and issued very precise and detailed instructions on how the rule was to be applied. It nominated the national measurers and authorised them to issue measurement certificates. The success of the London meetings convinced the delegates to continue.

At the next conference, held in Paris on October 14th, 1907, the racing rules were officially approved and an organisation was founded to unite all the European nations with interests in yachting - the International Yacht Racing Union (I.Y.R.U.).

In two years the yachting world was revolutionised and the basis for 20th century yachting was laid.

The International Rule is divided into the following three sections: the International Rule for Measuring

10 I.R.: the Class will maintain its position within the International Rule in 1921.

and Rating Yachts (see facing page), Scantling Regulations and Sailing Rules.

Scantling Regulations

Since one of the more important decisions taken during the 1906 conference was the issue of a Scantling Rules certificate, Lloyd's Register of British and Foreign Shipping, Germanischer

Lloyd, and Bureau Veritas (Norsk Veritas was included later) were asked to draw up an agreement in merit.

This agreement was entitled "Rules for the Building and Classification of Yachts of the International Rating Classes", better known as Lloyd's Scantling Rules.

The Scantling Rules were made up of 44 articles; 22 tables in feet and 22 tables in metres.

These rules were precise, yet liberal; many types of materials were allowed, as long as the yacht was granted certification by one of the three institutes above.

These certificates divided yachts into two classes;

TECHNICAL SPECIFICATIONS
UNDER DIFFERENT RULES

LWL	1881-86	1886-95	1896-1907	1907 onwards
50 ft	20 tons	20 rater	52 ft rating	15 M
60 ft	40 tons	40 rater	65 ft rating	19 M
80 ft	85 tons	140 rater	75 ft rating	23 M

Rater, 1901.

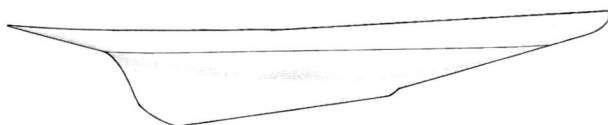

The girth 'd' is included for the first time

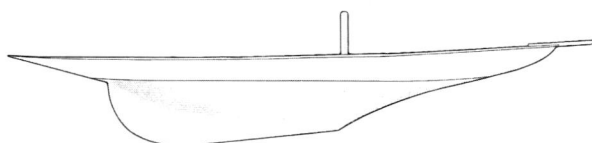

15 Metre S.I.

Development and evolution of the linear rated yachts.

---

the "A" class for yachts of 23 metres or longer and the "R" class for the International Classes. The application of the Scantling Rules gave positive results.

A yacht could now be well built and still highly competitive and a vessel's seaworthiness returned to normal levels.

The Rules were accepted by all, with designers making only a few requests for modifications, primarily to the smaller classes (Linton Hope was an example, with his work on the 6 Metres).

Sailing Rules

This section contains the 53 articles that deal with race organisation, starts, sailing, protests and handicaps. They were approved at the Paris meeting and then by the newly born I.Y.R.U., and although modified and updated over the years, they still form the basis of today's I.S.A.F. (International Sailing Federation) "Racing Rules of Sailing". And finally, a 1908 meeting set down a handicap, in seconds, for the "A" class yachts when racing against "R" classes.

The new International Measurement Rule was an immediate success. 771 yachts (including 328 Six Metres and 35 Twelve Metres) were built in Europe between 1907 and 1914.

There were several reasons for this success: the boats were better balanced with less extreme overhangs and sail area. The freeboard as a negative factor in the formula led to increased freeboard, producing boats which were drier and more seaworthy.

The chain measurement and measurement of the difference between girth and chain developed greater displacement and fuller hulls; the closer the values of the two factors became, the rounder hulls became, the lower the rating, and the more sail area and LWL as speed factors could be developed.

Sheer lines and plans of a beautiful 23 Metre yacht.

In conclusion, hulls were very different from before; much more seaworthy and safer. Finally we were on the right path.

The Rule would be updated twice, in 1919 and in 1933, and in the second half of this century changed into fractions of metres as the boats did likewise (e.g. 5.5 Metre yachts).

But the direction had been set and would last the whole century. But all the older European rules didn't just disappear: one-designs are still built and cruising yachts still use the old *Thames Tonnage* rule.

Only the success of offshore racing would bring new solutions (the RORC and CCA formulas) complementary to the International Measurement Rule.

THE FIRST VERSION OF THE RULE
1907-1920

The first Twelve Metres were launched in 1907, the last for the America's Cup races in 1987, and the Measurement Rule has been updated to 2001.

Throughout these 90-odd years Twelve Metre design, construction and competition have contributed to the most important chapters of international yachting and made it the most successful of the Metre classes.

A Twelve Metre was considered a medium sized yacht that did not have too high a price, "an ideal middle ground between the larger 23, 19 and 15 metres and the smaller classes which were inshore raced or day sailed". *Mouchette* was described by Gael in the June 1908 issue of Yachting World as:

"like the other vessels in her class, a beautiful, small ship, well equipped under all aspects to race brilliantly but at the same time to be a medium sized cruiser. The hull is much roomier than the taxable dimensions would suggest [the Thames Measurement has apparently not been forgotten!] and the below decks layout has been designed with the owner's and his guests' comfort in mind..."

Using the Thames Measurement a 12 Metre measures 27 tons while a 15 Metre measures 50: almost twice the displacement with only three metres difference in rating. In this case the Thames Measurement, based on a yacht's volume, is a great help in differentiating the two types. A Twelve is a very competitive yacht, but at the same time has enough accommodation below decks to guarantee the owner pleasant cruises while transferring his yacht in comfort from one race to another.

While the first two Twelves were built for the Dutch (the Max Oertz designed *Davo II* for C. Vermeer) and the French (the Duperron designed *Cygne* for G. Lacroix), it was the English designers and shipyards, followed closely by the Norwegians, who dominated the class. Out of 40 Twelves built between 1909 and 1917 (to the first version of the Rule), 17 were of English design and construction, 14 Norwegian, 8 German and 1 French.

While French interest in the Twelves lasted only one season (*Cygne* was converted to a cruising yawl with an auxiliary motor), their value as an international class was confirmed by their spread beyond the Clyde to the Baltic, Holland and even Argentina.

The class was formed initially on the Clyde thanks to Major Andrew Coats. He commissioned a new design from his nephew T.C. Glen-Coats, a brilliant amateur designer who collaborated with Alfred Mylne's office. *Heatherbell* raced against the raters *Kelpie* and *Eileen*, and immediately demonstrated the superiority of a vessel built to the new rule, even when raced against well sailed Raters.

SKEAF II

Designer	G. Barg
Year of build	1908
L.O.A.	16.85 m
L.W.L.	11.48 m
Max beam	3.51 m
Draft	2.30 m
Sail area	186 m²

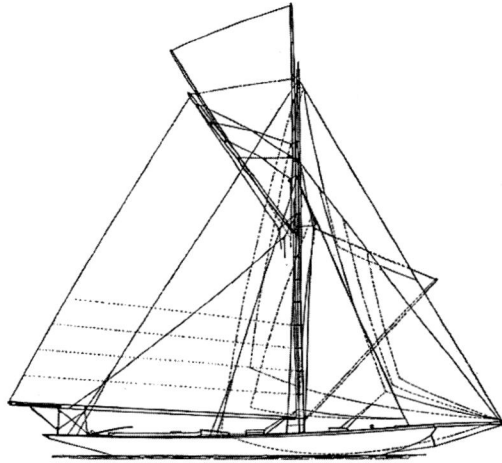

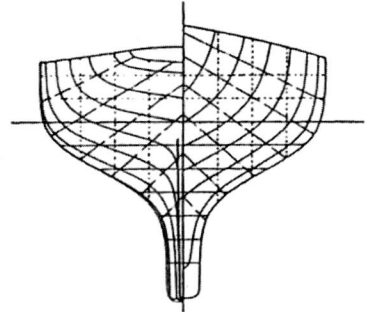

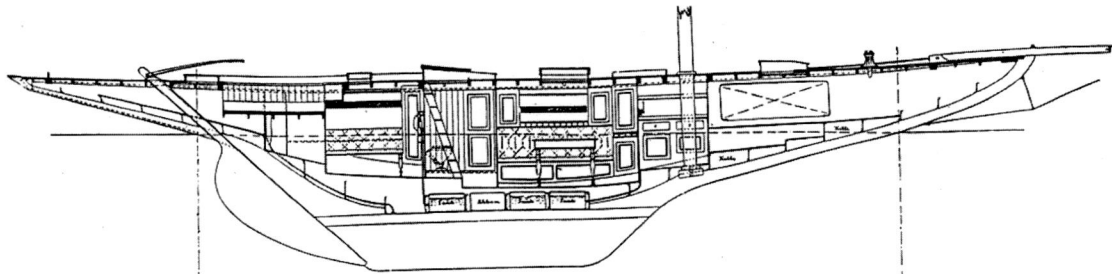

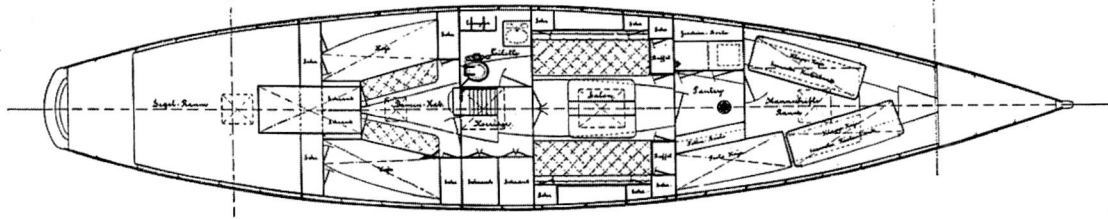

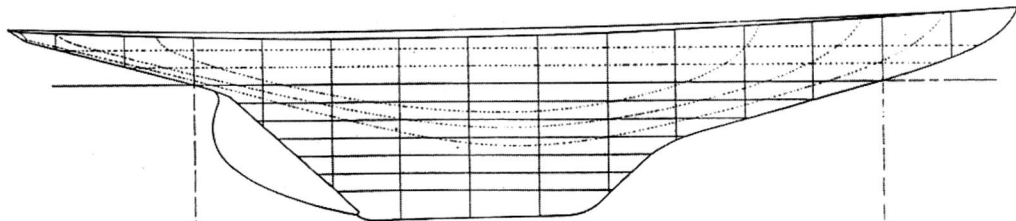

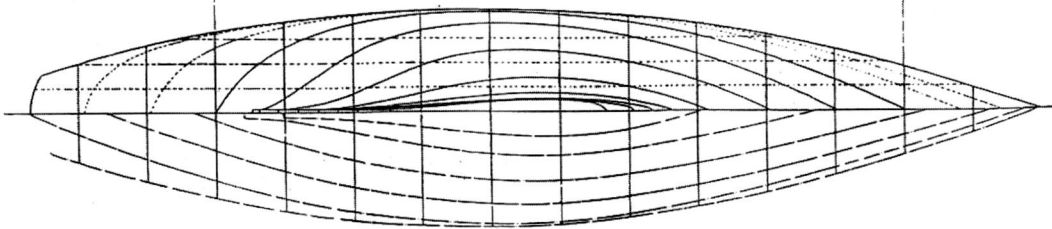

In 1908 *Alachie, Hera, Mouchette* and *Nargie* were the next boats to be launched, followed by *Cintra, Cyra* and *Javotte* in 1909 and *Ierne* in 1911 - all were built on the Clyde in Scotland. *Cintra* sailed best in light winds, and *Javotte* and *Mouchette* in moderate breezes whereas *Alachie* and *Hera* sailed well in all conditions. *Cintra* was the most successful of them all, coming first in 1909, 1910 and 1911.

The Clyde was the centre of 12 Metre yachting activity in early period - it was not until 1910 that six yachts were delivered to the Solent. Camper and Nicholsons built only two 12 Metres during this period.

Two great designers were responsible for the major part of the new class: the intuitive and creative William Fife III drew the lines of *Alachie, Cintra, Magnolia, Erna Signe, Ierne* and *Skeaf* (now *Mariline*); the more mathematically inclined Alfred Mylne *Mouchette, Nargie, Cyra* and *Javotte*.

The Scandinavian designers weren't to be left behind, with Bergen and the Baltic as the centres of activity for the Twelves. The most successful designer was Johan Anker and his yard, Anker & Jensen. Anker, an influential participant of the London and Paris conferences, designed *Brand IV* in 1909. Nine other Twelves, together with successive designs under later versions of the Rule and those of the other Metre classes made Anker the greatest designer ever of Metre classes.

The other Baltic designers were Max Oertz, with three designs to his credit, and G. Barg with four, while the St. Petersburg area of Russia was also active in the 12 Metres. Argentina, in addition to its interest in Six and Eight Metres, was also interested in Twelves. A member of the Argentina Yacht Club commissioned *Ráfaga* from Charles E. Nicholson.

Ráfaga was one of two Twelves designed by Nicholson under the first version of the Rule. Soon both *Alachie* and *Mouchette* were sold to members of the Argentina Yacht Club.

The following owners made an important contribution to the history of this class in the last century.

In Great Britain, the brothers Andrew (*Heatherbell, Cintra*) and George (*Alachie*) Coats, along with their nephew, Thomas Glen-Coats and Charles McIver (*Mouchette* and *Gavotte*) took part with great success in all the regattas up until 1912 when their interests started turning towards the 15 Metres.

The war then curtailed their activities for a few years. In Germany, an important wood merchant, Henri Horn, became famous throughout the regattas in the Baltic Sea thanks to *Skeaf,* and, at the same time, Alfred Larsen with *Magda* and Thomas Olsen with *Figaro* were pre-eminent in Norway.

The growing interest in the Metre classes caused an intense racing season on the Clyde and in continental Europe at Kiel, Oslo, Le Havre, Copenhagen, Amsterdam and the 1914 European Week in Norway. The predominance of Cowes Week was yet to come.

The "European Week" regattas were also extremely important; they were high level races which drew interest from the yachtsmen and, at the same time, were a fashionable event. Thought out by the IYRU, the European Week was organised each year by a different country. The first time it took place in Cowes in 1911, then in Kiel in 1912, Le Havre in 1913 and Oslo in 1914. Once again these regattas

Top: William Fife III, one of the most popular designers of this time. Right: Traum *(ex* Heti) *designed by M. Oertz. She's now undergoing a refit in Hamburg.*

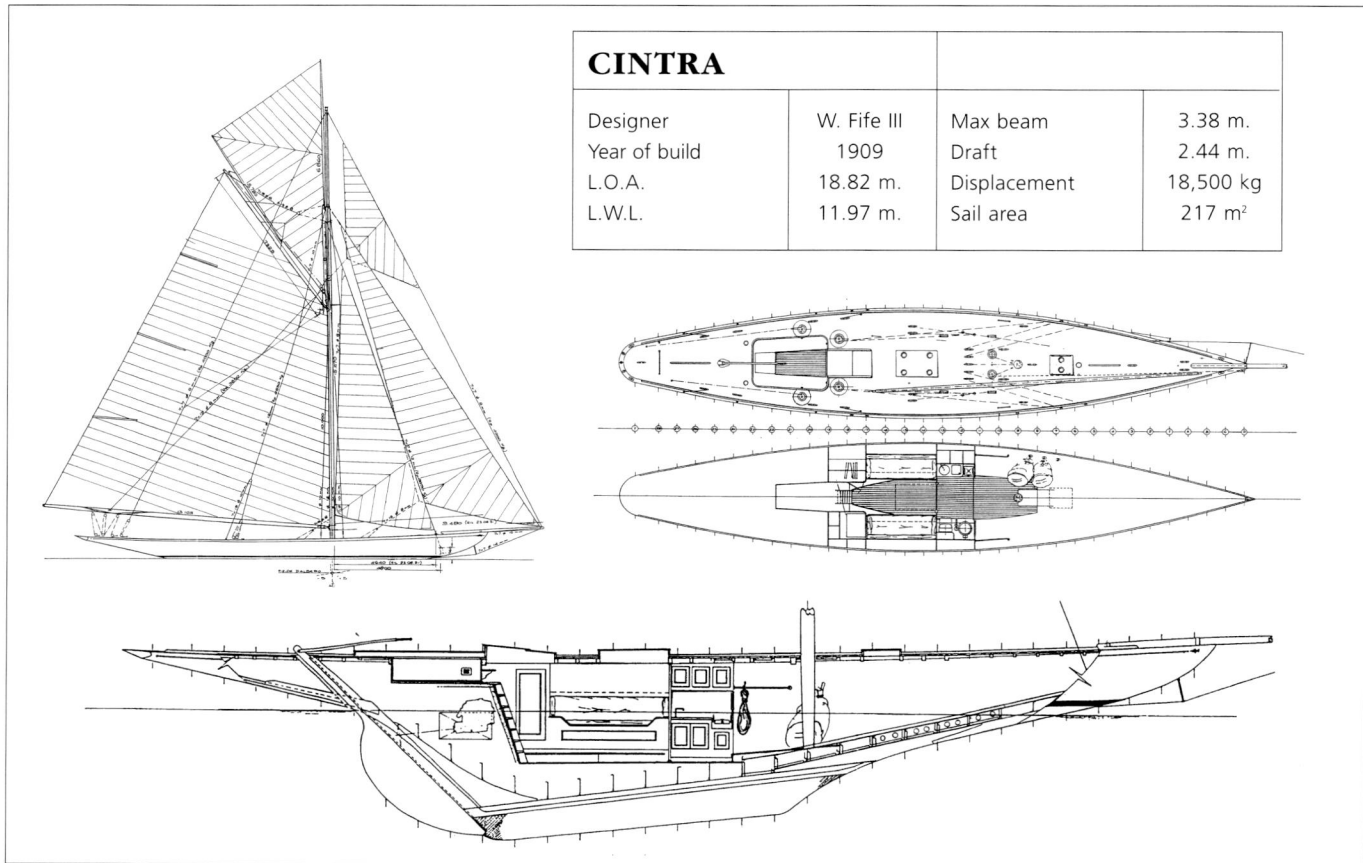

CINTRA			
Designer	W. Fife III	Max beam	3.38 m.
Year of build	1909	Draft	2.44 m.
L.O.A.	18.82 m.	Displacement	18,500 kg
L.W.L.	11.97 m.	Sail area	217 m²

CINTRA

Cintra *is a fine example with which to illustrate the main features of the First International Rule. She was a winner in the Twelve Metre category, particularly with light winds, has fine elegant lines and has been renovated perfectly.*

She also illustrates very well the limitations of the First Rule which led to its revision and changes in the Second Rule.

While the Twelve Metre boats constructed according to the Second and Third Rule do not differ greatly from each other, those constructed in accordance with the First Rule are notably different

The hull: *is shorter; usually the overall length is less than nineteen metres; the formula of tonnage penalizes the width and the keel, consequently you have long thin hulls with a limited draft.*

The topsides are restricted thus the hull sits low in the water and the displacement is less. The hull usually has mahogany planking on oak frames; the stem and sternpost, the keel and the rudder are in oak or teak, and the deck in pine.

Rigging: *it has gaff sails and being lightly penalized, the sail area is of particular importance with a large mainsail of about 120 – 130 square metres and a topsail of about 30.*

The boom extends beyond the stern; it is obligatory to have a bowsprit to balance the sail area considering that the mast is positioned well forward.

The bow has three smaller sails; the inner and outer jib and a small jib top with a total sail area of 70/80 square metres. The formula closely binds the sail area to the waterline length; the larger the former the shorter the latter. The stays are Atlantic steel.

Sails: *are cotton.*

Layout of the deck: *there are no winches so all manoeuvres are done by hand or hoists; the sheets are hemp and the halyards are steel with the final part in hemp. There is a tiller.*

Interior: *there were no precise rules as there would be in the future; the quarters are adequately comfortable with a spacious saloon and two berths in the stern, a heads, a small galley and a large space forward for sail stowage.*

stopped taking place during the years of the war. The 19 and 15 Metres were the "toys" of a short lived moment, but the great designer's innovative experimentation was concentrated on these classes. This caused a slack period in the Twelves from 1912 until 1922, but didn't prevent an intense 1912 season with some 30 starts for *Cintra*, *Hera* and *Ierne*, including racing in the Baltic where *Ierne* met with considerable success against a large fleet

(Mylne's 1908 Project N°148) cost £1850, of which £1650 were construction costs and £250 went for the sails. The designer received 15 Guineas.

An early Twelve had a very elegant hull with pronounced, though not excessive, overhangs. Freeboard was higher than on earlier designs, but less important than it would become under later versions of the Rule. Beam and length over all were both less than those coming later; LOA grew from

of German and Scandinavian Twelves.

These prewar races were also important social events, not just among the yachting enthusiasts, and the presence of European royal families kept the season lively and brought in crowds of sightseers at the various venues. But what was a Twelve built to the first International Rule like? Certainly different from the linear Raters that came before, and different too from those built after 1920.

The cost was between one and two thousand pounds. In his book Chris Freer noted that *Nargie*

15-18 metres to 20 under the revised Rule.

The sail numbers were given only during the first years of the 1920's; the classes were defined with letters whilst the numbers could change at each regatta. The letter "E" belonged to the 12M I.R.

A pre-1920 Rule Twelve was fore and aft rigged with a mainsail and a main topsail. The fore triangle was divided into three small jibs; total sail area was about

Top: Interior of Cintra; *the sumptuous upholstery, combined with white bulkheads and deckhead give a clean and elegant feel.*

THE TWELVE METRES AND THE OLYMPIC GAMES

Magda IX, *with Johan Anker at the helm, won the gold in the 1912 Olympics.*

The Twelves were an Olympic class for the 1908, 1912 and 1920 games. Their presence at the Olympics was never numerous for various reasons, and although the Eight Metres were an Olympic class until the Second World War, the Twelves' last presence was in 1920. The Twelves' 1908 Olympics took place with exclusively English participants from the 11th to the 13th of August, not on the Solent with the other Olympic classes but on the Clyde where the Twelves were normally based.Three races were planned, over a thirteen mile, twice-around course. Racing were *Heatherbell* (the 1907 season's winner), *Alachie, Nargie, Mouchette* and *Hera*.

The selection winners were *Mouchette*, designed by Mylne, fitted out by Charles MacIver, with an all English crew from Liverpool; and *Hera*, designed by Glen-Coats, fitted out by his uncle Major Andrew Coats, with an entirely Scottish crew.

The first race was very intense, with 30 tacks on the first beat. *Hera* was definitely faster, beating *Mouchette* by 1m 37s. She won the second race by a larger margin and was awarded the 12 Metre class's first Olympic gold medal. The 1912 Olympics had more of an international flavour, even though only Scandinavian yachts participated.

The Norwegian *Magda IX*, with Johan Anker at the helm, won the gold, Nils Persson's *Erna Signe* took the silver for Sweden, and the bronze went to *Heatherbell*, now in Finnish hands with Ernst Krogius.

In the 1920 Olympics two gold medals were awarded: one for the Twelves designed according to the first version of the Rule, and the other for those designed after the new 1919 Rule revision. Only two Twelves raced, however, one in each category, and both were Norwegian.

True victory would be hard to find here, except for Johan Anker who built both yachts, *Atalanta* and the new *Heira II.*

220 square metres of which 120 was just for the mainsail. All sails were cotton and there were no winches aboard; the foresails were manageable enough without winches, though the main must have required considerable trimming skill. Shrouds and stays were of Atlantic steel while running rigging was manila. The wooden main-mast was solid while the other yards were hollow to save weight, and a long bowsprit pointed the way.

A pre-1920 Twelve was built strictly to Lloyd's Scantling Rules.

The frames were almost always composite, with one galvanised steel frame to every two wooden frames, though there are cases where all frames were wooden, with the principal frames in oak. Floors were of galvanised iron, stem and stern posts in oak, elm or teak. Planking below the waterline was usually 38-40mm pitch-pine, above the waterline 30mm mahogany. The deck, of 32mm pine, was beautiful and uncluttered: a cockpit, two hatches and two companionways. There were no lifelines. She had a tiller and not a wheel; and one can imagine the skill required of a helmsman and the difficulty of controlling a yacht of this size when hit by a puff. Though much lighter than more recent Twelves, they went about with more difficulty, with a centre of gravity very far forward to compensate for the size of the mainsail; an older Twelve was difficult to handle. The accommodation was comfortable, simple, and elegant. There was standing room below and the layout was built according to the Rule and included the owner's cabin aft, a heads, a large saloon, a small galley and a roomy forepeak for the sails and the

Composite structure of the hull of Cintra.

crew. The effect was spacious and elegant.

The crew was normally made up of seven or eight, including the owner, skipper and crew, the latter being paid either by the season or by the race. Often they were local fishermen who had found a new job for the summer. The owner was often capable enough to helm his yacht while racing.

A pre-1920 Twelve was absolutely beautiful under sail, especially if designed by a great master like Fife. Under towering canvas, the hull threw itself through the waves and the long boom followed the boat's movements skimming the waves.

Forty Twelves were built; after 80 years more have survived than would have seemed possible.

Cintra: In perfect condition, she is the only Twelve to have kept her gaff rig; lying in Italy.

Danseuse III: Lying in Norway.

Desirée (ex *Sybillan*): Transformed into a ketch rigged cruiser; lying in Italy.

Erna Signe: Refit completed in 2000; lying in Norway.

Heti (ex *Romeo*): In very poor condition, she is now undergoing a refit in Hamburg; there is no scheduled completion date, though she will return to her original gaff rig.

Le: Lying in Norway.

Magnolia: Her refit was completed in 2000; Bermuda rigged; lying in Norway.

Mariline (ex *Skeaf*): Awaiting a complete refit; lying in Portugal.

Varuna (ex *White Heather*): Undergoing refit in Imperia (Italy), scheduled to be ready in 2002.

Vineta (ex *Figaro*): Lying in France, in wreck condition.

THE SECOND AND THIRD VERSIONS OF THE INTERNATIONAL RULE

Two years after the first application of the Rule (in 1907), its weak spots became evident and the first criticisms appeared. The situation, however, differed from that of the preceding formulas whose faults, as we have seen, caused owners

The famous yacht designer Charles E. Nicholson.

not to build new yachts but to turn their attention to one-design racing. The large number of boats built in the different Metric classes is indicative of the success of the Rule and of owners' interest. However, by 1909, critical considerations began to appear and new ideas developed which were to revolutionise the shape of things to come in yachting.

There was a point regarding the smaller boats; although the International Rule included a 5 Metre class, this was the least popular and was active only in Germany.

As a consequence each country developed national rules for smaller boats, especially in France and Scandinavia, which extended their influence into the Mediterranean and the Swiss lakes.

The English 18-footer class was adopted in all of Europe.

Another criticism was directed towards the Scantling Rules, considered too strict for small craft, and responsible for an unreasonable increase in both cost and weight for boats destined to race in sheltered waters. Linton Hope, among others, urged successfully for a revision of the rules for classes smaller than the Eight Metres.

On the other hand, the fact that the formula gave little weight to sail area had led to an increasing number of sails and sail area, this while new studies and experiments regarding sails were going on and the concept of 'aspect ratio' developed. Supported by aerodynamic research, yachtsmen on both sides of the Atlantic began to realize that a tall, narrow sail plan was more efficient than those then current.

In 1907 Nathaniel Herreshoff had observed the increase in power given by a taller sail plan. However, the effort to extend sails upward brought with it topsails, topmasts and gaffs that were extremely hard to handle, especially going to windward.

In 1919 Herreshoff had begun to experiment with the Bermuda rig and observed its efficiency compared to the gaff rig. A good example of this is the Herreshoff "S" Class designed by N.G. Herreshoff in 1919 and built by Herreshoff Manufacturing Company until 1942.

In Europe, Charles Nicholson attacked the problem with an innovative design, the 15 Metre *Istria*. She was the first yacht to use a one-piece mast with a topsail set on it. To keep the tall mast straight, Nicholson had developed such a web of stays and shrouds that it looked like a radio antenna, and so became known as a "Marconi" rig.

Today we use the terms "Marconi" or "Bermuda" rig interchangeably, but strictly speaking they are not the same thing. The Marconi rig had a one-piece mast, but set both mainsail and topsail on it, and it was not until the Twenties that the Bermudan mainsail replaced this arrangement. In the Twenties, Nicholson still insisted that the proper term for the mainsail was "jib-headed mainsail" and for the topsail "jib-headed jackyard topsail".

Istria was a turning point for the International Rule. Nicholson put into her design all the innovations permitted by loopholes in the Formula; once more there was a risk of turning class development into a race for ever more expensive novelties, with older boats made obsolete by newer designs.

Istria, *was the first European 15 Metre I.R. to have a Marconi rig. She was designed by Charles E. Nicholson and was a very successful racer before the Great War.*

Already in 1913, the owners of large yachts began to turn away from the 15 and 19 Metre classes, favouring the revival of handicap racing. In 1914 the Great War put a stop to racing in England but not in the Scandinavian countries which remained neutral.

There the building and racing of sailboats continued, but the time was ripe for a revision of the International Rating Rule which was in any case due to expire in 1917.

Consequently a meeting was convened in February 1916 to discuss new proposals. The principal speakers were again Benzon and Anker; the latter, basing his proposal on his experiences with different rules then extant, made a long speech which began with a proposal to change the Rule.

JOHAN ANKER'S PROPOSAL FOR AN INTERNATIONAL RULE OF MEASUREMENT

The International Rule is, I think, the one which best answers the purpose. In spite of its errors, it has in the large classes provided us with boats which have ample space below deck, and which are excellent boats at sea; and this is not my experience only. But the rule is incomplete. It could be improved. We must have the sail area diminished and the beam increased; but I think it would be an error to discard all the experience we have had with this rule in order to experiment with something which has not been tried.

Finally, I come to what owners demand of a rule of measurement.

It does not suffice for a rule to provide good boats. It must give owners the greatest possible facility for competition. It can never be sufficient for our men to be the best at Stromstad, Grenata or Flekkefjord: we must have higher aspirations. Only in this way shall we be able to induce our youth to devote themselves to sailing.

The advantage of the International Rule lies only in the fact that it is international.

In all countries it has afforded owners the same problems to solve. Competition has been as keen as possible, and our own racing owners have thereby become experienced sailors to an extent never reached before.

My wishes for the new rule I can summarize in the following words: let it not demand less of our skill and foresight than the old one. The road to the promotion of yacht racing leads through difficult problems and keen competition.

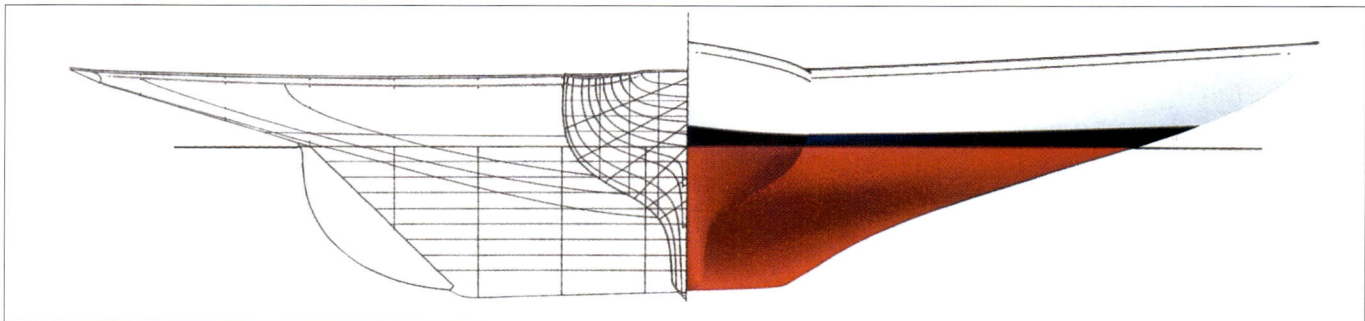

Sheer lines, plans and sections of a 12 I.R.

This and other conferences led to the development of the "S Formula", valid in Scandinavia.

Its success was limited and only a few yachts were built to this rule: *Santa* (later *Thea)*, *Tatjana* (later *Noreen)* and *Heira II* which were subsequently rated as 12 Metres.

The need was for a renewal of the Rule which would meet the following criticisms: excessive and unaesthetic overhangs, too light displacement, excessive sail area, a tendency toward unstable hull shapes, with shallow draft and round barrel-shaped sections.

In October 1919 delegates from Argentina, Belgium, the Netherlands, Denmark, France, Norway, Great Britain, Spain, Sweden and Switzerland met in London to revive the I.Y.R.U. (Italy joined them in February 1920), and approved the new rule known as the Second International Rating Rule.

The Second International Rating Rule, like the First, contains instructions for the measurers, references to the Scantling Rules (which were to be revised in 1921), and racing rules. There is also a section regarding handicaps when racing between different classes.

There are some important points to be made regarding the innovations in the formula.

The 15 and 19 Metre classes, important in the First Rule both for the designers and for the great racing seasons of the past, disappeared. The most important class became the 23 Metres which produced some of the most beautiful boats in the history of yachting.

The 9, 7, and 5 Metre classes also disappeared; the last of these produced a long search for a replacement which ended in the Fifties with the creation of the 5.5 Metre I.R. class.

The basic formula was that of the First Rule, with some important changes.

The dominant element of the formula is the relation between rated length and sail area. Beam was no longer considered (but reappeared as Minimum Beam) and the importance of the chain measurement was reduced ("G" and "g"). With the elimination of the beam measurement ("B") it was the intention of the Rule to favour wider boats by eliminating the benefit of narrow hulls which produced a lower rating.

The coefficient of 2.5 was calculated to bring the new ratings value near to that of the preceding formula and thus permit earlier boats to remain competitive.

Numerous specific limits, which were intended to discourage the search for 'blind spots' in the rules and exaggerated designs conceived to exploit such 'blind spots', were also included.

The Rule was drawn up in a meeting of the I.Y.R.U. in February 1920, with the adoption of new sail numbers which were composed by the number of the class (e.g. 12) over the letters identifying the nationality of the boat and followed by a progressive identification number.

THE SECOND INTERNATIONAL RATING RULE

The rule was to be in force for six years, beginning January 1st, 1920.

$$\text{Rating} = \frac{L + 0.25G + 2\,d + \sqrt{S} - F}{2.5}$$

Rating is expressed in linear units (feet or metres)

L = length
G = chain
d = difference between girth and chain
S = sail area
F = freeboard

- *Limitations and important clarifications, some valid for a single class, are expressed in the articles of the Rule;*
- *In calculating sail area the fore triangle is considered at 85% of its measured value;*
- *The maximum height of the sail plan above the waterline may not exceed twice the waterline;*
- *Hollow masts are not permitted except for the part above the jib halyard.*

CLASSES

Classes	English feet	Max. paid crew
> 20 m.	> 65.60	no limit
20 m.	65.60	14
17 m.	55.76	10
14 m.	45.92	5
12 m.	39.37	4
10 m.	32.80	3
8 m.	26.24	2
6 m.	19.68	2

- *There is no limit to unpaid persons aboard.*

Tomahawk was designed by Camper & Nicholson in 1939. She was considered the most successful 12 I.R. in British waters. She was only beaten by the American Vim.

Thanks to the experience acquired during the twelve years of the First Rule, the Second Rule was a success and the formula, with slight modifications, remains valid today. It made the Twenties a high point in the history of yacht racing.

The large boats once again had the well-proportioned elegance of *Britannia* and some of the most famous yachts in history were built and launched in this period.

It was an exciting time for the smaller classes as well; architects and builders had a chance to compare their innovations at the Olympic Games, the French and Italian Cups, race weeks at Kiel and Le Havre and at the Scandinavian Gold Cup.

There were new developments across the Atlantic as well. In 1925 a group of associations and yacht clubs created the North American Yacht Racing Union - NAYRU - and adopted a single rule for American Racing.

In 1942 the New York Yacht Club and the Eastern Yacht Club, the only two important clubs which had declined to join in 1925, voted to join the NAYRU which thus became the legitimate representative of American yachting.

The birth of the NAYRU was encouraged by a group of important American naval architects: Starling Burgess, Clinton Crane and Frank Paine. They favoured the introduction of the

---

THE THIRD INTERNATIONAL RATING RULE

The new formula was as follows:

$$\text{Rating} = \frac{L + 2d + \sqrt{S} - F}{2.37}$$

Rating is expressed in linear units (metres or feet)

L = length   S = sail area
G = chain   F = freeboard
d = difference between girth and chain

The various articles were substantially unchanged but there was a precise ruling regarding masts and their dimensions; the larger classes no longer appear and the new International classes are 14, 12, 10, 8, 6 Metres.

International Rating Rule which the Herreshoffs had bitterly opposed.

Informal contacts began across the Atlantic.

Some American owners had been present unofficially at IYRU meetings and from 1925 on, their presence was a constant. In 1920 a group of 6 Metre owners began discussions to organize races on both sides of the Atlantic.

The result was the British-American Cup and by the mid-Twenties they were racing one another at the One Ton Cup, Seawanhaka Gold Cup, the Scandinavian Gold Cup, and at the Olympic Games.

In February 1927 the first official joint meeting of the IYRU and the NAYRU was held at the Royal Thames Yacht Club. The IYRU agreed to modify the Rating Rule, including some elements of the Universal Rule: hollow masts, maximum mast height, maximum freeboard, and, as a concession to the Scandinavians, some internal changes which increased living accommodation, including the addition of a small deckhouse.

In 1930, on the occasion of the America's Cup, Brooke Heckstall-Smith reached an agreement with the New York Yacht Club to adopt the Universal Rating system, leaving in force the International Rating Rule for the Twelves and the smaller classes.

Large yachts would be marked "J" for those having a rating of 76 feet, "K" for those rated 65 feet and "L" for those rated 56 feet. The "M" class was not included in the agreement, although yachts of the "M" class were only slightly larger than the 12 Metre class. The smaller classes were comprised of the 12 Metres, 8 Metres and 6 Metres.

The interest of the Americans was manifested in a commission to Abeking & Rasmussen to build 13 Ten Metres, followed by 11 Eight Metres and 6 Twelve Metres, all designed by Starling Burgess between 1927 and 1929.

The meeting of the IYRU in 1933 approved the Third International Rule whose formula remained essentially unchanged except for the elimination of the chain measurement.

The new Rule was to be in effect from October 1, 1933 until December 31, 1939 while the preceding Rule might be applied until December 31, 1936. Since then, the formula has been unchanged.

With the adoption of the Second International Rating Rule there began one of the most interesting periods in the history of the Twelves. It was a

Cotton Blossom III, *ex* Waiandance (US 1), *is one of the six 12 I.R. built by A & R under Burgess' design.*

moment of great creative fervour, of important technical innovations, with numerous races and social occasions.

This was true for all the metric classes, but the Twelves became the most important; the attention of the sailing world was focused on them and on the large yachts: 23 Metres, "J" Class and the other "Big Boats". It is evident that in the succeeding period in which the Twelves became the chosen boats for the America's Cup Races races that the greatest efforts in design, construction, and generally of technical development, together with abundant financial resources, were concentrated on the class.

It is equally true that the post-WWII Twelves were out-and-out racing machines, built for a single race, highly specialized and used in a very different way to comparable boats of the Twenties and Thirties. Let us first describe the characteristics of a Twelve according to the Second and Third Rule; as we

have seen the two formulas are similar, while the innovations with regard to the First Rule are substantial.

In essence, the formula of the Third Rule is based on two fundamental factors: speed, which is expressed with the conventional measurement of length, and power, the driving force necessary to produce speed which is given by sail area.

The "d" of chain and freeboard have much less importance in the formula, their presence being principally to limit variations in design. Thus, the sum of the length and the square root of sail area, combined with two other factors of less importance divided by a constant, must equal 12.

The hull

An innovation with respect to the first Rule establishes that length is measured 18 cms above the waterline; the "L" of the formula is the sum of "L" and the total of the various chains and the free-

---

THIRD INTERNATIONAL RATING RULE'S MAIN RULES

Compared to the First Rule, a Twelve is longer, with long but not excessive overhangs, and beamier, with fuller sections. Other restrictions to the designer's freedom come from the regulations contained in those articles of the Rule whose violation brings heavy penalties:

- keel depth may not exceed a determined value (approx. 2.75 m, with a tolerance of only a few cms.)

- freeboard is deductible to a maximum value proportional to the rating

- beam may not be less than 3.6 m (this restriction was approved by the Permanent Committee at its meeting in London on November 26th, 1936 and confirmed by the International Conference in September 1937)

- displacement may not be less than a value strictly proportional to the waterline length. For example, a LWL of 13.72 m

corresponds to a minimum displacement of 25 tons, while the minimum displacement becomes 26.25 tons when the LWL is increased to 14.17 m. The penalties related to the differences in the chain measurement discouraged hulls with skimming dish or wineglass shapes

- accommodation must follow the requirements of the Scantling Rules both in layout and equipment. From the spartan interiors dictated by the First Rule, the Third Rule prescribed comfortable interiors permitting an agreeable life aboard.

Rig and sail area

Here the two rules (Second & Third) are quite different, the Third being much more restrictive and detailed.

The total sail area is given by the sum of the mainsail area plus 85% of the fore triangle; the fact that they are expressed

as square roots limits the impact of sail area on the rating. The sail plan may not exceed a given height (the criteria vary from one rule to another); the fore triangle must be less than 3/4 of said height; for spinnakers and balloon jibs the maximum measurements of "I" and "J" are prescribed.

The battens may not be more than six in number and their length may not exceed a value proportional to the rating.

Masts may be in wood or metal and must correspond to certain measurements which relate to their diameter, weight (minimum 453.3 kg) and the position of the mast's centre of gravity.

While in the Second Rule masts must be solid, the Third Rule, at the request of Johan Anker, permits hollow masts from 300 mm. above the deck, but with a minimum thickness of 25 mm.

Trivia showing the characteristics of a typical 12 Metre at the end of the 1930s, after the International Conference of 1937 introduced the final changes of the Third Rule, are as follows:

LOA:	*approx 21m.*
LWL:	*from 13.70 m. to 14.20 m.*
Beam:	*approx 3.60 m.*
Draft:	*approx 2.75 m.*
Displacement:	*approx 25-27 tons*
Sail area:	*approx 170 -190 sq.m.*
Mast height above deck:	*approx 25 m.*

Interiors must be constructed under Lloyd's Scantling Rules.

A maximum of six battens.

The mast, in wooden or metal construction only, must have a minimum weight of 453.5 kg. Hollow masts are allowed 30 cm up from the deck.

Max beam cannot be less than 3.60 m.

The fore sail area is calculated as 85% of the total sail area.

board, measured at its extremes. Compared to the preceding version, this definition of "L" results in a hull which is longer over-all with well-proportioned overhangs and sections at the bow and stern, as excessively short overhangs are penalized. Sections overly full result in a penalty reducing the length at the waterline and consequently lower boat speed.

The resulting Twelve is quite different from its predecessors built according to the Second Rule, particularly because of the consequences brought about by the Bermuda rig and its progressive development as naval architects became familiar with its characteristics. Its increased power and greater efficiency to windward made possible greater speeds and consequently a greater waterline length.

The lowered centre of gravity and consequently different hull balance, imply greater weight in the keel, more than twice that of the first Twelve

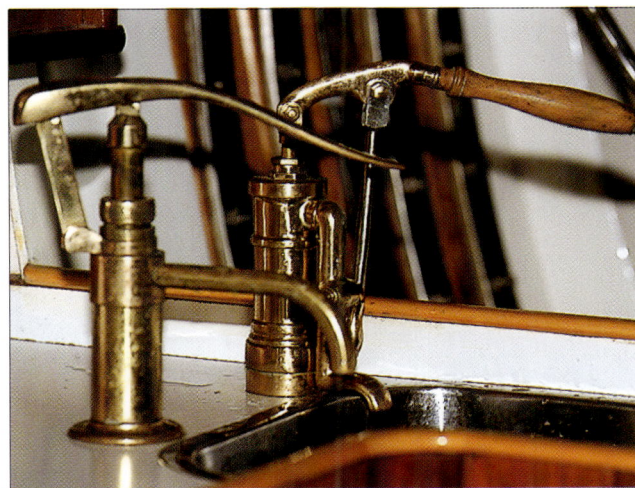

DETAILS AND INTERIORS OF A TWELVE PROPERLY RESTORED.
Below decks: Min. height 1.70 m, an ample owner's cabin with two berths, a large saloon with at least one other berth and a table of at least 0.45 sq.m, a toilet compartment with a head, washbasin and running water, a galley with a cooker (alcohol or paraffin) sufficient for at least six persons, three crew berths, hanging lockers of at least 0.2 sq.m, other lockers and storage space for at least 0.5 sq.m, a water tank of at least 115 litres capacity.

Top: *Coffee grinder on board* Nyala. *Right:* Vim, *one of the most famous and successful Olin Stephens' designs.*

Metre boats. This affects the hull structure which must be more rigid and at the same time as light as possible. Lighter woods were used, while in the United States at the end of the Thirties double-planked construction was employed, giving lighter and stronger hulls.

Let us keep in mind that these were boats used also for long cruises and thus built to criteria very different from modern Twelves which are pure racers.

The greater forces developed by a more modern rig dictated the eventual replacement of the tiller with wheel steering; in 1939 only *Westra* still had a tiller.

Changes of equal importance took place in the sails and rigging. It became apparent that a larger foresail was more efficient than a number of small jibs; after the first trials in Italy at the 1926 Genoa races, the "genoa" jib became popular, requiring the

shortening of the spreaders to permit the genoa to overlap the mainsail. The sails were cotton, at least for racing; in navigation between races linen sails were still used, being cheaper and less delicate. In racing sails the search was for tightly woven and more resistant cotton canvas. Increased rig efficiency brought the end of sheet tackle and the use of winches which began about 1925 and soon became widespread; *Vim* was the first Twelve to mount coffee-grinders.

The increased hull length dictated the end of the bowsprit and required stronger rigging overall. Aerodynamic principles were applied to the design of sails with implications for the form and construction of masts; for shrouds galvanized steel cable was produced which had twice the breaking strength of past shrouds and the mast design was reconsidered in the light of ever-greater loads. The first oval shroud cables appeared and the first halyards in steel cable.

Shapes were tested in wind tunnels at Gottingen and at the NACA, influenced by the research done for "J" class boats which competed for the America's Cup and by the fact that the two principal airplane manufacturers in England, C.R. Fairey and T.O.M. Sopwith, owned Twelves and made their labs available for research.

The mast remained a weak spot in spite of the development of new construction techniques. The limits dictated by the Rule regarding weight, dimensions and sections were insufficient for the increased loads they had to support and dismastings were the order of the day.

There were two rigs which led to a change: Mylne's rig for *Marina* and Stephens' for *Vim*. The first had a height above deck greater than the norm (25.3 m as opposed to the usual 25 m) and Mylne used three sets of spreaders to give stability and sufficient angle to the shrouds. Further, the mast was the first to use a diamond spreader, which stiffened the upper part of the mast, permitting the elimination of the mast head stay fitting and consequently a better set of the genoa and greater ease in handling the spinnaker.

The rig of *Vim* was considered revolutionary, not so much for the numerous little improvements as for the construction material, aluminum, which for an equal weight was more rigid and stronger. But what a difference!

If the cost of a wooden mast had increased over the years to two or three hundred pounds for the most sophisticated masts, the cost of *Vim*'s mast was £1500.

How much did a Twelve cost? Freer's book gives the cost of *Marina*, Alfred Mylne's design No.368 in 1935. The yacht sold for £ 4,850, total cost to build £3,573 of which £1,800 for labour, £441 for wood, £951 other materials and £380 for sails.

The gross margin thus was £1500, £1,000 expenses and £500 profit. That this was the going price is confirmed by the price of *Iyruna* which a few years earlier cost its owner £4,800.

In any case, these figures are far removed from the cost of a "J" class yacht which in 1932 cost about £25,000 for construction and £5,000 annual maintenance, including £1,000 to update equipment. Expenses for the crew were not insignificant even if most of the crew members were hired only for the season which lasted from mid-June until the beginning of September.

There is record of a meeting of owners in which the question of salaries for skippers and crew members was discussed and a reduction of 10% voted, which meant that a sailor would earn two pounds and fourteen shillings.

The hope was that this would lead to increased hiring following an increase in construction commissions to the yards.

The twenty years from 1920 until 1940 were the time of glory for the class: nearly seventy Twelves were built.

Many factors contributed to this success: the favourable economic situation (notwithstanding the crash of 1929); the important races which

brought people together for socialising and parties, thus increasing people's desire to participate; the ever increasing cost of the big yachts and their resulting crisis.

The principal reason for the success of the Twelves is to be found in a sensible, logically evolved rating rule. Yachts built at the beginning of the period would remain competitive despite the launch of new designs.

In addition, thanks to the innovations introduced in 1927, the Twelve was considered a reasonably priced yacht, comfortable for racing or cruising, sufficiently strong and seaworthy to permit navigation in the Channel, the North Sea and the Baltic. In contemporary documents we find evidence which supports this view.

At Cowes Week in 1934 there was great expectation because the Twelves of the Second Rule (*Flica, Iyruna, Veronica, Zelita* and *Zoraida*) were to race for the first time against boats built to the Third Rule (*Miquette* and *Westra*). The differences were slight; *Flica's* rating, launched in 1929 according to the Second Rule, was 39.35 and according to the Third Rule was 39.45.

Yachting World wrote:

"The figures surely prove that a yachtsman building a boat to the new rule may build her like either of the two new boats, *Miquette* or *Westra*, or like *Flica*. He may in fact take his choice. The eminent designers themselves will doubtless assume 'the new boats are better', the public, however, will be inclined to declare in favour of the boat which comes in first the greatest number of times in the course of the season, and particularly perhaps during Cowes Week."

The Races were won in turn by *Westra* and

Veronica; the season acclaimed *Westra* as the winner, followed by *Flica, Miquette* and *Veronica*. Finally, we must include the declaration of Uffa Fox:

"This is the largest class in the International Yacht Racing Union rule, and there is no doubt the speed, seaworthiness and cabin accommodation of the 12 Metre racers makes them very dear to the seaman's heart.

In 1928, when we sailed the 14-footer across Channel to Havre for the regatta there, we came upon the *Vanity* anchored inside the breakwater, ready for the morrow's race, and filtering up through the cabin skylight came the sweet strains of music from a violin, for her owner, Johnny Payne, was below whiling away an hour with his fiddle.

That picture of comfort and contentment always rises before my eyes as I think of the 12 Metres, and with it another picture, that of the 12 Metre *Clymene* converted to a yawl beating the ocean racers in their own hard weather and under their own racing rules. The photograph of *Clymene* taken that day by Beken gives a good idea of a 12 Metre in action and illustrates the speed and seaworthiness of the class. It must be remembered that in the race that day were the finest ocean racers, *Dorade* and *Mistress* of America, and *Neptune* and *Lexia* of this country, were ranged against the *Clymene*, and yet she beat them under their own rule and weather conditions.

The picture of her flying along in that race is the finest argument I know for the 12 Metre class, especially when beside it rises the picture of restful content *Vanity* made in Havre, with her owner living aboard and enjoying the life."

Top: Uffa Fox.
Right: Mouette *easy sailing on a flat, smooth sea.*

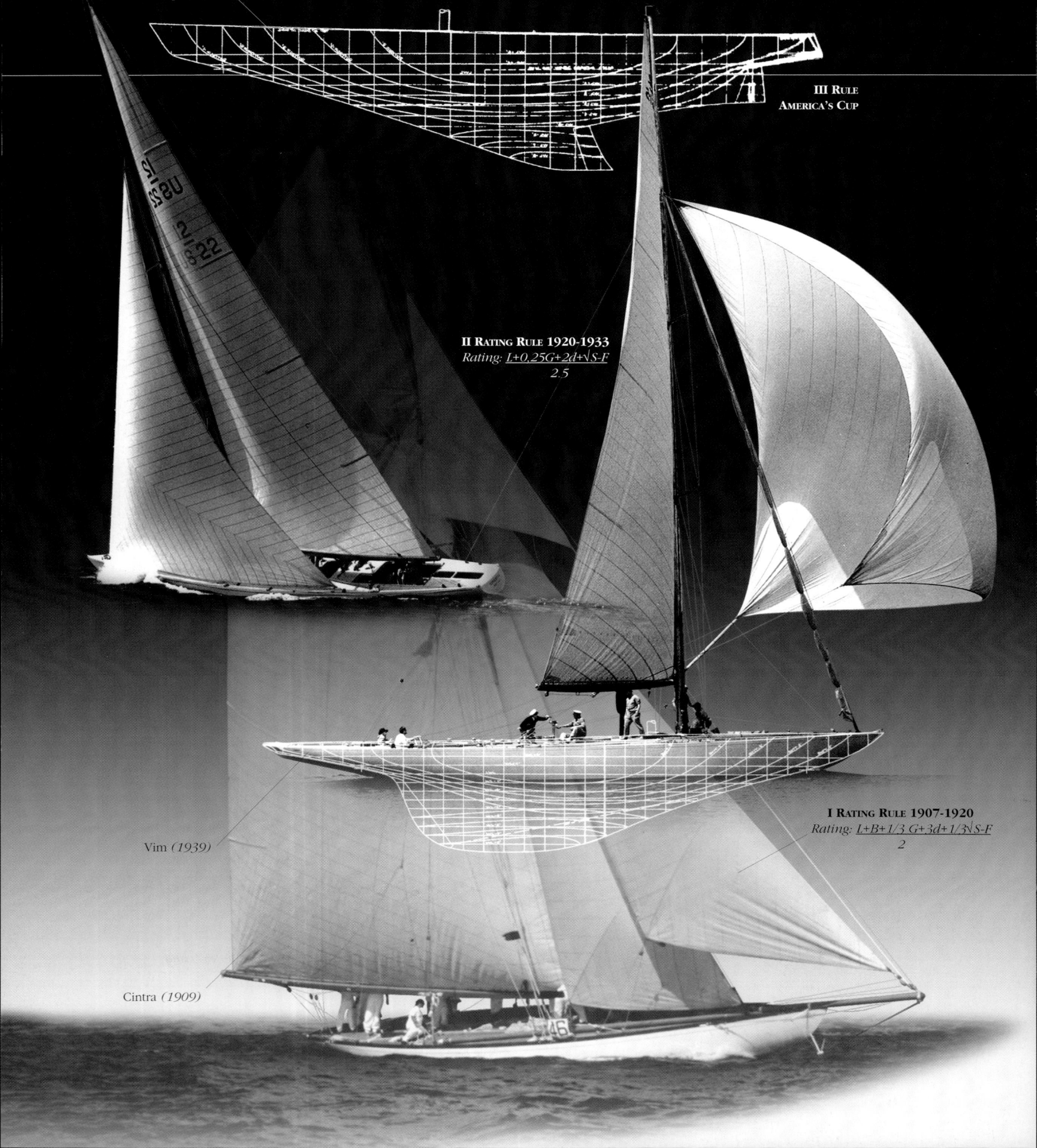

III **R**ule
America's **C**up

II Rating **R**ule **1920-1933**
Rating: $\dfrac{L+0.25G+2d+\sqrt{S}-F}{2.5}$

I Rating **R**ule **1907-1920**
Rating: $\dfrac{L+B+1/3\,G+3d+1/3\sqrt{S}-F}{2}$

Vim *(1939)*

Cintra *(1909)*

Australia II (1983)

III RATING RULE 1933-1939
Rating: $\frac{L+2d+\sqrt{S}-F}{2.37}$
*Since 1956 the Rating Rule has been fitted to the
America's Cup Deed of Gift.*

*The plate shows the evolution of the
ratings formula through the lines of
four famous yachts:* Cintra *(1909) and*
Vim *(1939) are still classical in their
shape while* Intrepid *(1967) and*
Australia II *(1983) look much more
aggressive and modern.*

THE 12 METRES
OF THE SECOND AND THIRD RULE

Sixty-seven Twelves were built to the Second and Third Rule to which we can add three designs never built. The two lists below include the best of European and American boat design and construction at the time. Clearly the Twelves were not easy to design or to build if the list includes only seventeen architects and only eleven shipyards, all large ones. Were there problems of organization in realising efficiently such demanding constructions? Or knowledge of the clients who could afford such costly projects? Or production capacity? Or capable workmen?

Probably these were all factors. For the other metric classes there were many architects and many

THE 12 I.R. SECOND AND THE THIRD RULE

DESIGNERS		BUILDERS	
Charles E. Nicholson	17	Camper & Nicholson	17
William Fife III	12	W. Fife & Son	13
Johan Anker	9	Anker & Jensen	9
Alfred Mylne	4	Abeking & Rasmussen	9
Henry Rasmussen	3	Henri B. Nevins	5
Burgess	6	Bute Slip Dock	5
Stephens	3	Aresa, Baglietto, Burmester,	
Crane	2	Herreshoff, Skalurens	
Baglietto, Burell, Costaguta,		Skibsbygg and Stockholms	
Eslander, Giles, Glen-Coats,		Båtbyggeri (Plym),	
Gruber, Jensen, Robert,		Costaguta, Holmens,	
Skalurens	1 each	Soon Slip	1 each
L. Francis Herreshoff	1		
Boyd, Morgan Giles and Uffa			
Fox (never built) 1 each			

boatyards who tried their hands, for the Twelves as for the 15M, 19M and 23M, only three designers, with their yards, dominated, the scene: William Fife III, Johan Anker and Charles E. Nicholson; to these names we can add Alfred Mylne whose every design was a leader in its period.

There were 110 Twelves designed to the three Rules: twenty by C. Nicholson, nineteen each by William Fife and J. Anker, eight by A. Mylne. At the end of the 1930s the Twelves ended their first long season and the Second World War ended their racing for nearly twenty years.

With only one exception the principal figures of this first period died during this period: Anker in 1940, Fife in 1944, Mylne in 1951 and Nicholson in 1954. With their deaths the yards closed, or at any rate, ceased construction of Twelve Metres. The single exception is Olin Stephens who made his debut in the 1930s and continued to play an important role through the 1980s.

For a list of the Twelves built please refer to the Appendix. Here we shall comment on the most important designs, together with the principal designers and owners from those two amazing decades.

Norway

World War I brought an end to yacht racing in Europe except in Scandinavia which, being neutral,

Right: The 12 I.R. Trivia *racing in the Mediterranean.*

could continue to design and build. We have already mentioned the activities of Anker and Benson, the "S" class, and the Norwegian victories in the third and last pre-war Olympics with the Twelves *Atalanta* and *Heira II*.

Two interesting designs came from Anker's drawing board, both initially conceived according to the "S" rule: *Tatjana* (later *Noreen*) and *Santa* (later *Thea*). *Tatjana*, built for a Danish owner, had a long and successful career due to her conception as pure racer, which paid off both in the class races and in the many handicap races in England in which she participated. *Santa* (later *Thea*), although less successful in the past, has survived in good condition and is expected to race again in 2001 after a complete restoration. Anker also drew up the plans of *Vema III*, another Twelve which dominated racing in the Thirties; she had a long career in

England and Norway and continues to race after a recent restoration.

Britain

The first British design to the Second Rule appeared in 1923: *Vanity*, plans by William Fife III, owner John Payne. She had many successes during her career, which ended when she sank in the Caribbean in 1992. From the beginning of the century, Payne was a respected skipper, especially of 12 and 15 Metre boats. An accomplished sailor and violinist, he lived aboard *Vanity* and sailed her to all the races, winning frequently. Her career continued in 1958 when she was restored by her new owner, Capt. Boyle and served as trial horse for *Sceptre* during the America's Cup Challenge of 1958. Towards the end of the Eighties she was completely restored by Camper & Nicholson, although not much of the original material survived.

Unquestionably one of the designs that influenced the development of the Twelves was a Charles E. Nicholson design launched in 1929 for the airplane manufacturer Sir Richard Fairey. Designed to win, it was one of the first boats to use an aeronautical research lab to develop the design and study wind flow over the sail surfaces. It was considered the fastest Twelve in light airs, and the ability of her owner-skipper played an important part. In 1933, five years after her debut, it was written:

"We consider Mr. C.R. Fairey's *Flica* the best of the Twelves. No yacht could be handled better; her owner is one of our leading helmsmen."

Flica remained for many years the boat to beat, even under her new owner Hugh Goodson. She is still in existence, although in need of restoration.

Sir Richard Fairey's name is linked to another important Twelve designed by Nicholson, *Evaine*. She was, with *Trivia*, one of the leading boats of

Left: Rig details on a vintage 12 I.R.; wooden tackleblocks are in the foreground.

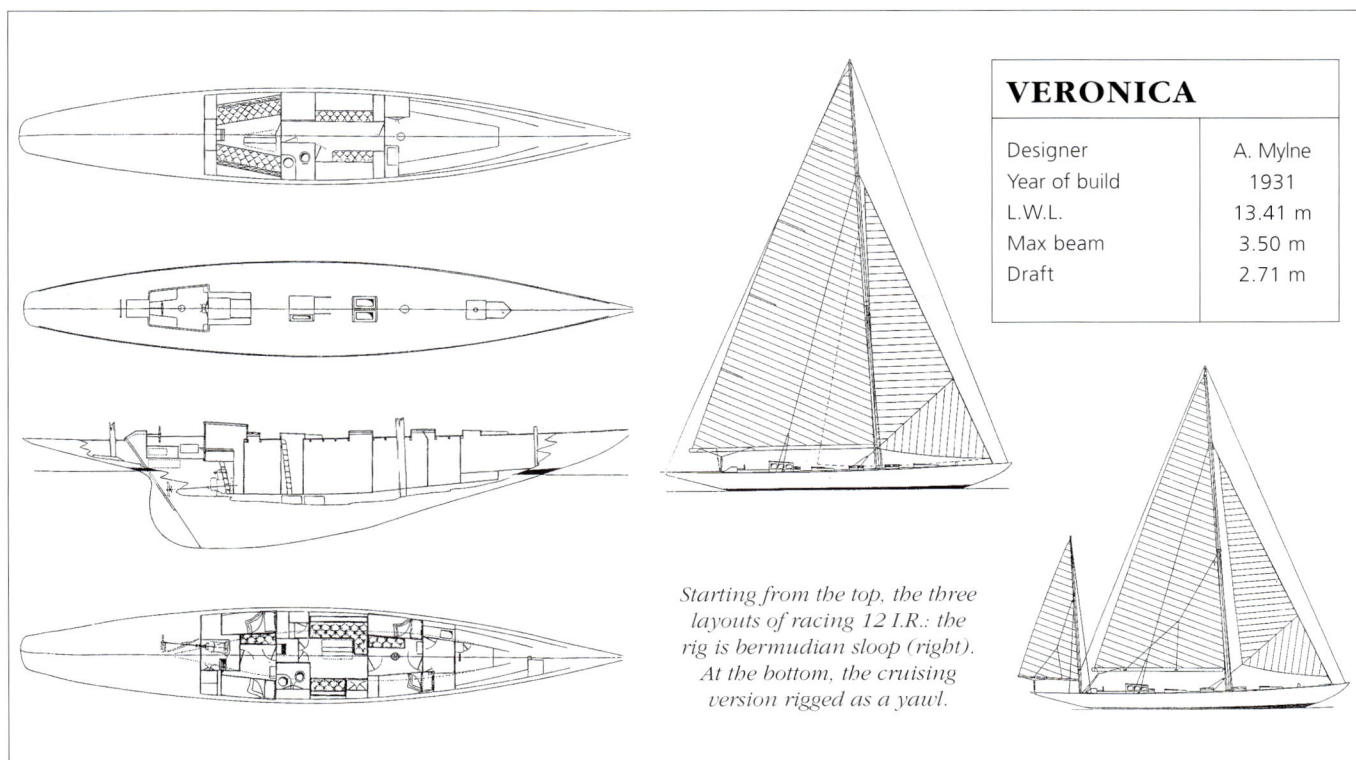

VERONICA	
Designer	A. Mylne
Year of build	1931
L.W.L.	13.41 m
Max beam	3.50 m
Draft	2.71 m

Starting from the top, the three
layouts of racing 12 I.R.: the
rig is bermudian sloop (right).
At the bottom, the cruising
version rigged as a yawl.

VERONICA K10

Veronica *was one of the key yachts in the
history of the Twelve Metre class under the
Second Rule, having battled against* Flica
*for supremacy in the ratings in the English
regattas in 1932 and 1933.
This is also why there was interest in
converting the racing yacht to a cruising
yacht. The work was carried out by Mylne,
her original designer, demonstating
the yacht's flexibility.
The owner of* Veronica *was Sir William
Burton, president of the Y.R.A. and other
English yachting institutions and also the
owner of several Twelve Metre boats.
As well as* Veronica, *he also owned*
Noresca, Iyruna, Marina *and* Jenetta.
The hull: *is in wood with mahogany
planking on an oak frame with each third
rib in steel (compostite construction). The
building techniques of the hull are no different from those used previously. However,
the waterline is radically different; the
overall length is more than that permitted
by the First Rule and there would be no
change with the subsequent rules, remai-
ning between, according to different designs, twenty and twenty one metres; the
modifications introduced with the formula
of tonnage meant a wider hull with deeper
draft. Compared to a Twelve Metre boat of
the Third Rule the waterlines are fuller and
the wetted surface is greater and the bow
and stern are more streamlined.*
Rigging: *it is Bermudan rigged with a sail
area of about 180 square metres; the first
experiments with the shape and
material of the stays had begun; the mast
was not hollowed, at least as far up as the
jib halyard.*
Sails: *are in cotton for regattas and linen
for transfers. In the first years twin foresails
were used but by the end of the 1920s it
was more common to use a genoa. On the
sails are the new sailing numbers.*
Layout of the deck: *there is still a tiller
and in 1925 the first halyard and sheet
winches appear.*
The interior: *is defined in a very precise
manner by the Rule which states the
dimensions allowed precisely.
The quarters are reasonably comfortable
with a large saloon, a main cabin in the
stern, a heads, a galley and a large space
forward for sail stowage.*
Alterations: *on the orders of her new
owner Robert Dunlop, the designer
Mylne supervised the project which
transformed the yacht into a cruiser.
The mast was shortened by about 3.60 m
and the main boom by about 2.20 m.
It is rigged as a Bermudan yawl.
The interior was completely refurbished
and fitted with every comfort.
An engine was also installed.*

the closing years of the Thirties; the two faced each other in race after race in 1937 and 1938 .

Trivia managed to win overall; but only by a narrow margin. Fairey was very fond of this boat, and kept her until the end of his life. She later appeared on the scene as pacesetter for *Sceptre*, first challenger for the America's Cup after the war. The match races between the two were invaluable for tuning *Sceptre* and she beat *Trivia* in the final races by a narrow margin. A similar situation occurred in the American camp, where *Columbia* had to struggle to beat *Vim* for the nomination as defender. The design of Twelves had reached its peak on both sides of the Atlantic; further progress could only be made by developing new materials for the hull, rig, and sails.

Sir William P. Burton was owner of Twelves and a major player in the story of British yachting. A well-known businessman, he was one of the creators of the International Rule, having been the English delegate to the London Conference in 1906, and president of the Y.R.A. for many years. Capable and enthusiastic, he was one of the few amateurs who could skipper a yacht like a professional. His first Twelve was *Noresca* (1924) followed by *Iyruna* (1927), *Veronica* (1931), *Marina* (1935) and (1939), all except *Noresca* were designed by Mylne.

Every one of his boats presented innovations, especially in the rigging.

Marina gave him first place in the class in the 1935 and 1936 seasons, after two years in second place with *Iryuna*.

Veronica is also worthy of mention both for her results (second place in 1932 and 1933) and for the conversion to a cruising yawl by Mylne: an exam-

Top: Detail of Trivia*'s mainsheet block.*
Below: Nyala*'s binnacle.*

ple of how a Twelve can be easily transformed into a comfortable and elegant cruising boat.

Burton launched *Jenetta* in 1939 but the approaching war prevented her realizing her great promise; at the opening of the season, she was recognized as a fast and powerful yacht, the best design Mylne had drawn up to that time.

Arthur C. Connell, another owner from a family of yacht owners around the turn of the century, was an excellent helmsman, although occasionally unpredictable. He owned five Twelves: *Zinita*, *Zoraida*, *Zelita*, *Westra* and *Ornsay*. The first three were all from the drawing board of Fife, as family tradition dictated. However, after he commissioned a boat from Charles E. Nicholson, he began to win races. *Westra* was first in her maiden season, 1934, and second in the two successive seasons. Connell commissioned a new yacht, *Ornsay*, twin sister to *Tomahawk*, but health problems in the family allowed him to take part in only a few races. During the war both *Ornsay* and *Westra* were laid up ashore at Camper and Nicholson's yard and were destroyed by a bomb.

T.O.M. Sopwith, after Lipton a principal in the English challenges for the America's Cup, was also an owner of Twelves. All of his Twelves produced mediocre results for him, but brilliant results for succeeding owners. This, was true for *Mouette*, who did well after her transfer to the U.S., and for *Blue Marlin*, which remained Sopwith's for only one disappointing year. In the hands of her new owner, W.R. Westhead, *Blue Marlin* had a succesful season, ending in third place overall and the only victory of an English Twelve over *Vim* (by thirteen seconds !).

BLOODHOUND	
Designer	C. Nicholson
Year of build	1936
L.O.A.	19.26 m
L.W.L.	13.72 m
Max beam	3.81 m
Draft	2.77 m

Bloodhound, *one of the Twelve Metres designed for ocean races.*

Vim, owned by Vanderbilt, didn't give *Tomahawk* a chance. Sopwith had commissioned *Tomahawk* in the hope of beating his friend in English waters. She was, however, the best of the English Twelves, and once *Vim* had gone home, she won most of the races that followed. This was the last Twelve designed by Nicholson, and she is still afloat in splendid condition.

Two more Twelves were important in the final years of the decade before the War: *Trivia* and *Flica. Trivia* was built for V.W. McAndrew and was one of Charles E. Nicholson's best designs; she was in the forefront during the seasons of 1937 and 1938, together with *Evaine*, which she finally defeated by a narrow margin. The appearance of *Vim* and *Tomahawk* pushed her out of the limelight, but she was considered the best of the Twelves after

these two. *Trivia* had a long racing life after the war, and renamed *Norsaga*, she won many races in Northern Europe and in America, and was pacesetter for *Sceptre* during her preparation for the America's Cup challenge of 1964. Beautifully restored, she nowadays sails in the Baltic.

Flica II is remembered not so much for her results, the 1939 season being a disappointment, as for her design and construction. Hugh Goodson, the enthusiastic young owner, decided to build a new Twelve which he commissioned from Laurent Giles when he realized that *Flica* was no longer competitive. Giles made five models and tested them at the Stevens Institute; the model which was chosen was then given to Fife's yard to be built and featured numerous innovations: interior bulkheads in plywood with balsa wood core, deck hardware in aluminum alloy, rigging of stainless steel rod with an oval section. The tuning was demanding, and although *Flica II* aroused much curiosity, results were not up to the owner's expectations. Her post-war career was more satisfying and *Flica II* served as a pacer for *Sceptre* in her preparation for the America's Cup challenge in 1958.

The history of British Twelves would not be complete without mention of *Foxhound*, *Bloodhound* and *Stiarna*. They are similar designs in which Charles E. Nicholson demonstrated the adaptability of a Twelve to the requirements of ocean racing. These boats are considered Twelves, but are less extreme than the last boats built to the Rule; shorter overhangs, displacement is greater and the sail plan less extreme. With these modifications they are more comfortable in a seaway and are still able to win races as did *Bloodhound* in the Fastnet of 1939.

Mediterranean & the Baltic

Class activity in the Mediterranean was practically nil excepting one boat in Spain (*Yatset*, 1933) and two in Italy (*Corsara*, 1929 and *Emilia*, 1930). The first Italian project, originally named *La Spina*, came about because Marchése Spinola hoped to establish a class of Twelves in Italy. She was followed by *Emilia* but for personal reason; the owner converted her to a Bermuda schooner before launch. The following year Marchése Spinola, seeing that no one had followed his lead, had *La Spina* converted to a yawl.

Surprisingly in Sweden there was only one construction during this period, *Princess Svanevet*, which survives in England as *Barranquilla*.

Germany started by building eight Twelves to the First Rule and continued with six Twelves built by Abeking & Rasmussen for American owners, in the period between the wars built only four Twelves for German owners.

Three were drawn by Henry Rasmussen and all are still afloat: *Anita* (1938), *Westwind* (1938, ex *Inga*)

and *Ostwind* (1939, ex *Sphinx*). *Aschanti III*, designed by H. Gruber and built by Burmester in 1939, burned after a brilliant career as a racer.

During this period the activity of Twelves in Europe was limited to the Baltic, especially to Kiel Week.

U.S.A.

In the Twenties interest in the International Rule revived in the U.S.A. and the NAYRU was created, to facilitate communications with the IYRU.

The first American designer to design to the Metric rule was Starling Burgess, who made an agreement with Henry Rasmussen to build fourteen 10 Metre yachts. As a result, a group of owners came to Burgess, Rigg & Morgan to commission the design and to Abeking & Rasmussen to commission the construction of six identical boats, which would race in Long Island Sound. Built to the Twelve Metre Rule, they were 21 metres long, their hulls elegant yet powerful, with a large uncluttered deck and comfortable cabin arrangements.

In 1928 *Waiandance*, *Isolde*, *Tycoon*, *Iris*, *Anitra* and *Onawa* arrived as deck cargo in Halifax N.S. where they were delivered to their owners, launched and rigged, and taken to Long Island Sound on their own hulls. Of the six, only two are still afloat: *Anitra* and *Onawa*.

The American fleet was enlarged by two European Twelves: *Cantitoe* (ex *Magda XI*) designed by J. Anker, and *Mouette*, a Charles Nicholson project which dominated the English championship in 1928 and 1929. At this time the English boats were clearly superior and the English press wrote:

"...in this Class we lead …. But Americans have not been in the first flight. I am told that the English 12-metre *Mouette*, Nicholson's best boat racing in America, has given the yankees such a hiding that they never had since old James Coats sent over the Watson 10-tonner *Madge* from the Clyde, or Fife's 20-tonner *Clara* went there. *Mouette* has proved the high standard of our designs."

Vanity V and *Trivia racing head to head in the Mediterranean.*

Mouette was built for T.O.M. Sopwith, Vanderbilt's rival in the America's Cup races. Sopwith was also the owner of *Tomahawk* which was beaten in English waters by *Vim*, owned and skippered by Vanderbilt during his successful season of 1939. Probably because of English superiority, repeated American proposals for an International 12 Metre Cup to be raced in American waters were never accepted, just as the Cup offered by Fairey, owner of *Flica*, was not taken up by the Americans as they would have had to race in English waters.

An American response soon arrived because the Third Rule developed by the IYRU and the NAYRU stimulated the interest of American yacht designers;

Details on the deck of Vim; *the coffee grinder is in the foreground. On the following pages:* Zio *and* Nightwind, *1939.*

in 1935 the first Twelves entirely designed and built in the U.S.A. were launched: *Seven Seas* and *Mitena*. The latter was a Francis Herreshoff design, with an elegant canoe stern, but not very fast. In fact, she never won a race and it is hard to tell if this was due to her idiosyncratic lines, to an LOA of nearly 22 metres which was out of line with other Twelves, or to the sail area of only 165 square metres. *Seven Seas* by Clinton Crane, was more successful and in the races on Long Island Sound in 1936 and 1937 was fast enough to beat *Mouette*. Meanwhile, Professor Kenneth S. M. Davidson of the Stevens Institute of Technology, inspired by the English use of wind tunnels in sail development, was attempting similar experiments in hull design, testing models in tanks. The first results were very promising, and were used by Clinton Crane and Olin Stephens. In 1937 Crane launched for his own use his second design, *Gleam*, which made use of the testing tank data and produced a hull which was faster than *Seven Seas* but did not equal her results on the course. He made his data available to the Class and, while Herreshoff ignored them, Olin Stephens used the data while designing *Northern Light* and *Nyala*. *Northern Light* was fast and very successful during her first season; *Nyala* won the American championship in 1939. In 1937 *Gleam* won the Astor Cup, beating the "J" boats over a short course. In

1938 Harold Vanderbilt raced on *Seven Seas* and was so enthusiastic that he decided to order a new Twelve from Olin Stephens; the result was *Vim*, a milestone in the history of the class. She was a development of *Nyala*, the design which owed much to the 6 Metre *Goose*, and utilised the results of tank testing.

Like the recent English designs *Trivia*, *Evaine*, *Flica II*, *Jenetta*, *Ornsay* and *Tomahawk*, *Vim* was slightly longer than preceding Twelves, but very different. Tank tests had led to an aggressive hull design, optimized to cut through the water with a minimum of resistance, particularly going upwind; the hull was fuller especially where the stem meets the keel, the overhangs were shorter, the maximum beam slightly greater. She was perhaps less beautiful than *Tomahawk* but surely more powerful.

After her launch, *Vim* was shipped to England where her arrival was eagerly awaited. Served by a first-class crew, including the Vanderbilts, the Stephens brothers, Rod and Olin, and the expert helmsman Briggs Cunningham, *Vim* lost the first race due to a navigational error but won the next two "leaving her rivals practically dead in the water". It was thus for the rest of the season which ended with 19 victories in 28 races.

English superiority in the Twelves was over. *Vim* returned to the U.S.A. and continued to race in 1940 against *Nyala* and *Northern Light* with alternate results; in the end, the championship was won by *Nyala*. In 1958 she fought to the bitter end in the defender's selections for the America's Cup and was narrowly defeated by *Columbia* after five closely fought races head to head. *Vim*'s victories ended the long season of the Twelves between the wars which brought down the curtain on a particularly lively scene. Nearly twenty years went by before the Twelves entered a third period of development. But everything had changed: owners, designers, boatyards, and a new racing context: the America's Cup.

VIM

Designer	Olin Stephens
Year of build	1939
L.O.A.	21.13 m
L.W.L.	13.71 m
Max beam	3.66 m
Draft	2.67 m

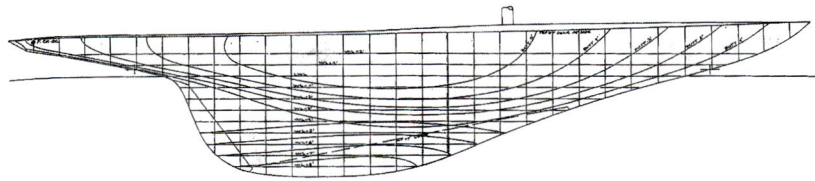

VIM US 15

Design: Olin J. Stephens – design no. 279

In 1939, Vim *dominated the regattas in which she participated in England, and until 1967 she continued to be a reference point for the America's Cup Twelves, her lines inspiring* Columbia, Constellation, Gretel *and* Gretel II.

The hull: Vim *is a "great" 12M; she is 21.13 m in length with the waterline length being 13.71 m. The bottom of the boat follows traditional lines but with details showing refinements with particular attention being given to the front section which is full and joined to the keel, and the stern section which is designed in such a way as to minimize drag. The hull has double planking and the inner hull, in cedar, is crossed.*

The framing is in oak and the deck is in pine. This building technique is lighter but above all makes the hull stronger. There is a small trim tab on the outer part of the rudder.

Rigging: *an aluminium mast was used, which for the same weight allowed by the rules, was stronger and more rigid. The halyard of the mainsail and the jib run on the inside of the mast. The shrouds are conventional but double: a shroud at the top of the mast and another on the highest crosstree.*

Sails: *these are made of ordinary cotton but are cut in such a way as to take into account the improved angle when sailing close-hauled which the new mast allowed.*

Layout of the deck: *two capstans were*

mounted: the cockpit is dry and very spacious compared with English standards. The wheel and the binnacle form one simple but efficient unit; particular care has been taken to simplify all manoeuvres.

Interior: *the interior is the minimum necessary to provide for the comfort of the owner and guests. In the stern is a cabin with two bunks with another two berths immediately adjacent to them; the toilet and galley are in the bow area while the space in the centre of the boat is reserved for the sails and for the rigging so as to maintain the weight at the centre and also give the crew ample space to move around.*

The interior remains very comfortable and luxurious.

RESTORING A TWELVE METRE

Towards the end of the 1980s, in America and Italy, yachtsmen took a new look at the pre-war Twelves and saw beautiful boats with good sea-keeping qualities, still usable for cruising and racing. In the U.S. *Gleam* and *Northern Light* were experiencing a second childhood; in Italy a group of owners began to search out and buy older Twelves to restore.

More than fourty years had gone by since the last great races of the Pre-War Twelves; many had been destroyed in accidents or by neglect, some had been converted to cruisers and continued to sail, others were used as trial horses for America's Cup boats in training.

In 1987 *Tomahawk*, after years of neglect was purchased and restored, with the intention of making a comfortable cruiser rather than restoring her as a racer and, in rapid succession, the naval architects Giorgetti and Magrini undertook the restoration of *Cintra* and *Vim*, for the same owner, and *Trivia* and *Flica II* for other owners.

The enthusiasm took hold, and in following years *Sovereign*, *Nyala* and *France II* underwent restoration. More recently *Erna Signe, Evaine, Magnolia, Vema III, Vanity V, Zinita, Onawa* got the same treatment; *Wings* and *Anitra* are awaiting restoration.

It's like reading 1930s yachting magazines! A.I.V.E. (Associazione Italiana Vele d'Epoca, the Italian Vintage Yacht Association) played an important part in these developments and many owners of Twelves joined up. A.I.V.E. has organised races at the request of its members and developed rules to permit Twelves of different periods to race together. These rules, through penalties and allowances within the ratings, encourage owners to restore yachts to the original design and construction. Now this rule has been replaced by the New 12 Metre Class Rule published in 2001 by the I.T.M.A. (International Twelve Metre Association), which has, in part, adopted the ideas of American owners of Twelves. The Rule specifies that for older boats the Class Rule in force at the time of construction is to be respected and encourages owners to restore yachts to the A.I.V.E. standards. Twelves built to the Class Rule before the America's Cup races can never compete with boats designed for those races. Therefore it is foolish to try to bring an older Twelve up to date; the only result would be to compromise a boat which has important historical value. The pre-war Twelves were born to voyage and to race, with sea keeping

Left: Cintra *under sail.*
Right: Varuna *being restored.*

qualities that were demonstrated in numerous crossings between England and the Continent.

The Twelves that raced for the America's Cup were built for match racing in special conditions dictated by the venue. The design of Twelves during the first 35 years of the International Rule developed according to the technology then available. The last boats launched before the war, like *Vim* and *Tomahawk,* manifest an equilibrium of all the elements involved; spars, hull, rig and sails, using the most advanced technology then available. Modernising a classic Twelve means compromising this harmony and destroying a classic boat.

Many pre-war Twelves or America's Cup boats are now being restored or have already been restored. Of the more recent boats, we have little to say other than to express congratulations that someone keeps these boats alive and sailing.

Let us mention three interesting restorations of America's Cup Twelves. *Sovereign* and *Columbia* which had been in the past converted for cruising were restored to their original racing trim; *France II,* on the other hand, though still a fast sailor, had been given a luxurious interior.

However, when we speak of restoration, we refer to pre-war Twelves. Two schools of thought prevail: on the one hand, a scrupulous rebuilding to the original design using original materials; on the other hand, a less orthodox restoration using modern materials and techniques.

If changes of rig, use of modern cloth and cut for the sails, and more powerful winches may be judged fairly harshly, there is no doubt that the use of epoxy resins to cover the hull, or the reconstruction of planking with moulded wood or with technologies entirely alien to the era are to be condemned. Many such errors are often found together, and one wonders why they bothered with the original boat and didn't go ahead and build a replica rather than render a classic unrecoverable?

Nyala. *Top: the original coffee grinder has been used as a model to make a new one, faithful to the original.*
Right: Composite structure with wooden and metal frames.

Cintra

Cintra, with *Magnolia,* is the oldest Twelve still in existence and the only one with her original gaff rig. She was found in 1990 in terrible condition, converted to cruising, with a two level deckhouse excessively compared to the freeboard, her stern cut off and a big inboard engine installed. The restoration was supervised by the Studio Giorgetti and Magrini and done by Cantiere La Bussola at Fiumicino. Those few elements found were used in the reconstruction: some photos, the original sail plan, an overall drawing and sketches of the mast made by William Fife. Roughly 50% of the original planking in Honduras mahogany was in reasonable condition while the knees and ribs of galvanised iron, typical of construction at that time, were in bad condition.

Fortunately the acacia ribs were in excellent condition, so that it was possible to work on the planking without risk of deforming the hull. The elm deck beams, the keel, the stem and stern post were also in excellent condition. The upper part of the rudder and the rudder housing were in oak, equally in excellent condition.

After partial removal of the hull planking, the deck was rebuilt: sheets of 20 mm marine plywood covered with planks of 15 mm yellow pine (like the original decking) and by mahogany partners,

stringers, carlins and hatches. The hull was then planked and caulked and afterwards treated with modern products. The lack of original plans led to an intense search among old photos and books in order to reconstruct the mast and rigging. The only modern concessions were six small winches for two halyards, the main sheet and the lower running back stays. The interior was restored to its original smaller volume. Moving forward, we have the engine compartment with the batteries, fuel tanks and the small auxiliary motor; the companionway steps separate the chart table to starboard from the oilskin locker to port, two facing leather couches, a bulkhead dividing the living area from the working area, the galley to port, heads to starboard, and the sail locker in the bow.

Nyala

Nyala needed work to eliminate past modifications and sloppy workmanship. Regarding the construction techniques of the era and especially those of the Nevins yard where the double planked *Nyala* was

built, the original drawings were fortunately available for consultation, as were those from Sparkman & Stephens. At the time the use of glue in marine construction was limited and greater reliance was placed on the accuracy of the woodwork while pegs and screws in silicon bronze, together with the caulking, held the structure together and watertight. The hull was rebuilt using the original timber and techniques. In order to work on the structure of the boat the interior was removed. A large part was the original Eastern White Pine, which was saved and reinstalled after the other work was finished. The double planking below the waterline was replaced, some of the oak ribs were replaced, the bronze and steel knees were all replaced. The mast step was put back in its original position, having been moved about a metre aft some time earlier. A 62 HP engine with a drive shaft length of over 5 m was installed under the cabin sole to lower the centre of gravity. The deck was rebuilt with 35 mm planks of Sitka Spruce, using the traditional method of cotton caulking covered with black rubber. The mast part-

Vintage details: from the left, hand pump; fore companionway; bowsprit and some details of the deck. Right: a Twelve Metre is waiting, helpless, to be broken up or restored.

ners were replaced. The deck beams, after removal, were partially replaced. The stern and transom were rebuilt. The cockpit was rebuilt as originally designed. The deck hardware is composed of the restored originals, including the original coffee grinders constructed by the Nevins yard.

The hatches, apart from the centre hatch, were rebuilt following the original plans. The same American woods used during *Nyala's* construction were procured for the restoration. All the screws are of silicon bronze.

But one important detail remains to be discussed: the mast and the rudder. Considering the care taken overall to reconstruct faithfully, it seems strange that carbon fibre was chosen as the material for the mast and rudder. The intention was to improve her sailing performance, but the result was contrary to expectations. The natural rigidity of carbon fibre added to the excessive thickness required by the minimum weight requirement resulted in a mast which impaired performance. Added to this were the difficulties with the rudder, which was a source of turbulence. Adding insult to injury, *Nyala* was disqualified from racing on account of the above mentioned modifications.

The following year the rudder and mast were changed: the rudder was rebuilt in wood following the original plans and was better integrated with the hull lines, the mast was rebuilt according to the model made by Sparkman & Stephens in 1939 to replace the original wooden mast, using the experience of *Vim*. *Nyala* gained a half-knot and went back to racing with her original balance, with great success.

APPENDICES

Twelves and the America's Cup

12 Metre Register: alphabetical list of names

Index of Yachts Names

1. TWELVES
AND THE AMERICA'S CUP

In 1939 a world war once again interrupted yacht racing.

This was a long period of inactivity for the Twelves; eleven years would go by before another Twelve was built. Only a few Twelves were kept in racing trim; most were stored ashore or converted to cruisers.

In 1956 a new era was assured for the Twelves when it was the class chosen for the 1958 America's Cup races.

The Twelves that raced for the Cup had little in common with their predecessors although the basic formula stayed the same, with small changes like freeboards and limitations on deck openings.

In the preceding two decades the boats were fast and manoeuvrable but also comfortable and habitable.

The Cup Twelves are a different breed: they are derived from seagoing thoroughbreds, but destined for racing around the buoys, on courses which are always the same and defined by the Deed of Gift which requires "mutual consent" or the consent of the Supreme Court of the State of New York if it is to be modified.

They are designed to perform best in the sea conditions where they will race: Newport for the first challenges and Perth for the last in 1987.

If the matches maintained an appearance of comfort, such appendages were soon eliminated.

The boats, pure racers, were nonetheless rich in innovations and technical solutions which were soon applied to ordinary yachts.

The Twelves continued to attract the greatest designers of the century.

From 1946 on, John Illingworth, as the English representative, got in touch with DeCoursey Fales, Commodore of the New York Yacht Club, to discuss new challenges with new rules for the Cup. Both agreed on the desirability of using boats smaller and less costly than the "J" class.

As for the type of boat to adopt, the discussion was between ocean racers and the Olympic classes; the Americans favoured a specialised boat whose use would, in effect, be confined to the Cup races. Agreement was reached finally in 1956 by Henry Sears, Commodore of the New York Yacht Club and Sir Ralph Gore, a well-known helmsman of Twelves before the war and now President of the YRA.

This agreement modified the original Deed of Gift of the Cup and had to be ratified by the Supreme Court of the State of New York as none of the original signatories of the Deed were still alive. Changes naturally followed in the International Rule.

The new Deed of Gift provided that the LWL for single-masted vessels be reduced from 65 ft to 44 ft and thus permitted the International Twelve Metre Class to be chosen for the Cup races.

The rule that the challenger had to arrive on her own bottom was repealed. (Note that this rule had contributed to keeping the English "J" boats alive until recent times as they were of much stronger construction than the American "J"s which were intended to last only for the time of a Challenge).

As for previous matches, a set of "conditions" and race instructions supplement the Deed of Gift.

Of special importance are the articles from 10 to 14 which establish the rating rules, the obligation to race in real time, that the rating may not exceed Twelve Metres, as well as selection of the Challenger and the Defender.

Article 10 confirms the International Rule of 1939 as modified in 1950, including the Instructions to Measurers.

Interior arrangements, equipment and dimensions of anchors, chains and lines must be those of the International Rule of the Twelve Metre Class.

Highly specialised Twelves are permitted, but the hulls must be of wood. Metal masts are permitted and structural elements not prescribed by the rules may be in any material. The Certificate of Construction was that of Lloyd's Register as revised in 1949; said revisions would not

The opening picture of the Appendices is Australia II. *Right,* Dame Pattie *and* Columbia *brush before the 1967 match. Both were admonished by the NYYC.*

be applied to yachts already certified.

The Third International Rule was applied to all Cup Challenges until 1987 and is still in force with updates made from time to time regarding its "application".

In June 1957 the Royal Yacht Squadron issued a challenge in the name of a syndicate of members headed by Hugh Goodson.

The Board of Trustees of the New York Yacht Club accepted the challenge and a race between two Twelves was set for September 1958 at Newport, R.I.

The Royal Yacht Squadron invited four of the best English designers - David Boyd, James McGruer, Charles Nicholson Jr, and Arthur Robb to present two models each: one of a conventional Twelve Metre and the other of an innovative Twelve.

The eight models were tested in the tank of Saunders-Roe at East Cowes against a model of *Flica II*, which was considered the fastest pre-war English Twelve.

The Boyd model was chosen; the yacht was named *Sceptre* and the Alexander Robertson and Son boatyard at Sandbank, where Boyd was a director, was commissioned to build her. However, his experience with larger boats was limited to the design of the Twelve Metre *Caledonia* in 1939, a project which was never built.

The testing tank was used more to choose between the models than to try new ideas; the nine models were tested in 48 hours although the Stevens Institute considered that time sufficient only to test two models. After the races it became known that the testing of the three defenders had lasted almost a year for each.

It was not until her launch in April 1958 that *Sceptre* revealed her secrets. In the end these did not amount to much: there was nothing very innovative about the hull, which was wood on steel frames; the lines were traditional, quite full forward and narrower towards the stern; displacement was over thirty tons, three

Briggs Cunningham, Columbia *'s skipper.*

more than the defender.

Boyd could apply his experience designing 6 Metres and came up with a series of brilliant solutions which enlarged the cockpit and extended it almost to the base of the mast. The weight advantage of a smaller deck permits more weight in the keel which in turn increases stability and power. The crew stays in the cockpit and can work better while the crew weight serves to lower the centre of gravity even more. While the winch drums are on deck, the mechanical parts are under the deck; giving greater access and again a lower centre of gravity. The helmsman and navigator have an unobstructed view because the deck is free of crew.

Another modification for match racing is the reduction of accommodation to the minimum required by the Rule. Berths are small and flimsy while the heads is located under the cockpit. Lightweight materials are used wherever possible and every gram saved goes into the keel.

Evaine was chosen as a trial horse and refitted by her owner Owen Aisher with a new aluminium mast. *Evaine* was a good Twelve and performed well, but decidedly less well than those launched in 1939 (*Flica II* and *Tomahawk*) and was much inferior to *Vim*.

Hugh Goodson refused to be skipper and left the place to Graham Mann, Bronze Medallist at the Olympic Games in Melbourne in 1956 but without experience in Twelves.

The sails made by Herbulot were tried and a gigantic spinnaker was chosen, with a base longer than the boat (the Rule gives no limit for the base of spinnakers).

The Americans feared the English challenge and mounted a very serious defence of the Cup. Three syndicates were formed to build three new Twelves and to these was added *Vim*, restored to racing condition by her owner John Matthews. Olin Stephens was called to help with the restoration, which had to do mostly with equipment. But especially important was the crew, which included Bus Mosbacher, Ted Hood, Dick Bertram and Matthews' two sons, Don and Dick. Hood took advantage of the occasion to experiment with sails made of Dacron, at that time a novelty.

The high costs of a defence created problems for Henry Sears, who was forming a syndicate of the New York Yacht Club to build *Columbia*. Just to give an idea, *Columbia* and *Weatherly* ended up costing about $300,000 each, roughly the cost of *Ranger* in 1937.

Olin Stephens was commissioned to draw the plans; he tested six variations of the original design of *Vim* at Hoboken.

Columbia was to be an all-round boat, adapted to the conditions expected at Newport in early September. She was slightly longer than *Vim* and therefore, to stay in the formula, had a slightly reduced sail area. This was compensated for by the increased efficiency of the new sail cuts and, later, by the Dacron sails that Hood supplied after the defender was selected. The greater length brought increased displacement and wetted surface, thus greater resistance in light airs but also greater power with fresh breezes and rough seas.

COLUMBIA

Designer	O. Stephens
Year of build	1958
L.O.A.	21.15 m
L.W.L.	13.93 m
Max beam	3.55 m
Draft	2.73 m
Displacement	28,350 kg
Sail area	173 m²

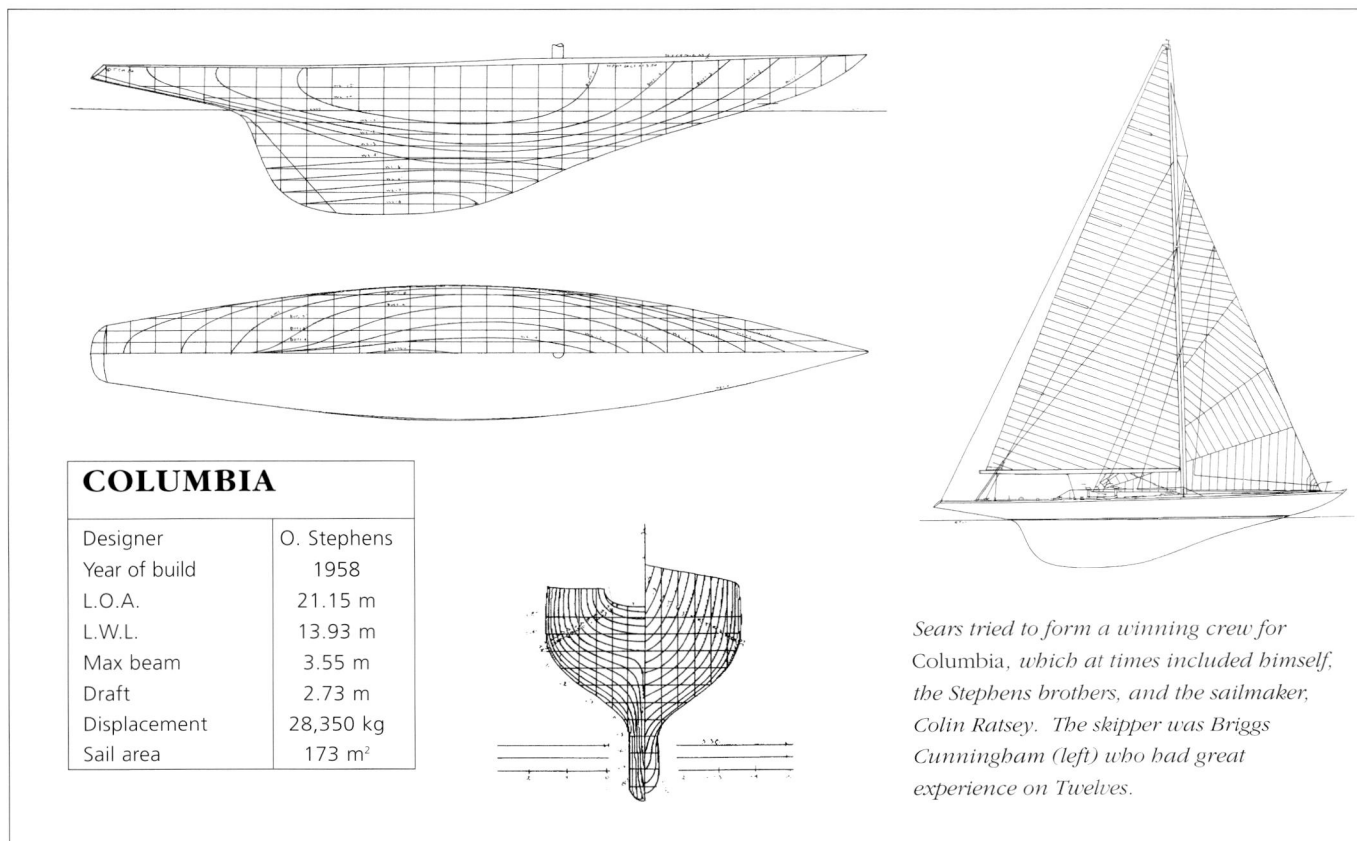

Sears tried to form a winning crew for Columbia, *which at times included himself, the Stephens brothers, and the sailmaker, Colin Ratsey. The skipper was Briggs Cunningham (left) who had great experience on Twelves.*

Columbia was built by Nevins, and despite some problems suffered by the yard, was launched on June 3, 1958. Rod Stephens was responsible for the running rigging and equipment and, as usual, acquitted himself well, finding solutions which speeded up the handling of the sails. The two coffee grinders were placed close together, making it possible to pass the genoa sheet over both winch drums and speed up trimming.

The sails were by Ratsey & Lapthorn; if Ted Hood had the best Dacron available, Ratsey used Terylene and the selection races contributed to a better understanding of the use of these new synthetic fibres in sailcloth.

The new fibres resulted in a lighter and more rigid sail, thus lowering the centre of gravity and, at the same time, giving a more efficient and smoother aerofoil.

Columbia usually carried one main, seven jibs and ten spinnakers.

Henry D. Mercer, along with Cornelius S. Walsh and Arnold D. Frese formed the Weatherly Syndicate and hired Philip L. Rhodes to design the boat (although he had no experience with metric yachts) and manage the entire defence effort. The boat was built by Luders and launched in June 1958. Solidly built, with extensive use of laminated mahogany in the keel, the stem and stern pieces, the result was a very pretty boat, on the heavy side, and consequently not at her best in light airs. The skipper was Arthur Knapp, Jr.

The most beautiful Twelve is considered to be *Easterner*, launched in late June 1958. Her topsides were varnished and the deck painted a light green. She belonged to the dean of American yacht-

ing, Chandler Hovey, who, at the age of 78 built a new boat to add to the "J" class yachts *Yankee*, *Weetamoe* and *Rainbow* which he had owned previously.

Designed by Raymond Hunt and built by Graves Yacht Yard, her chances were compromised by the fact that the crew was chosen mainly from the owner's family. The result was that *Easterner*, although well designed and built, never won a race.

The defender's selection trials comprised three series of races. The first series was at the beginning of July; the final one began on September 1.

On September 3 it was decided to run one last race between *Vim* and *Columbia*, which finally beat *Vim* by thirteen seconds and was named defender of the America's Cup for the first defence in Twelve Metre boats.

Sceptre carrying the enormous Herbulot spinnaker, longer on the foot than the yacht's overall length. Below: Columbia.

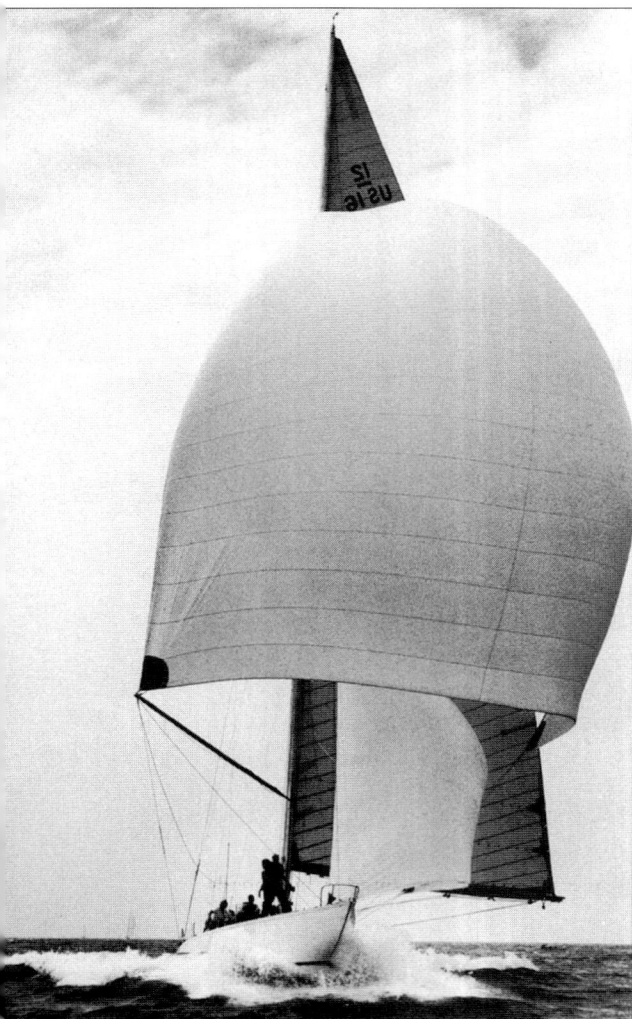

Columbia's edge was particularly in the upwind legs with a fresh breeze.

The American superiority in Twelve Metres was confirmed when *Columbia* defeated *Sceptre* in four straight races.

The defeat of 1958 did not discourage the English from presenting new challenges; *Sceptre* was purchased by a group of seven people intending to use her as a point of departure for a new challenger. Another group, the Red Duster Syndicate, was formed under the aegis of the Royal Thames Yacht Club and purchased *Trivia*, renamed *Norsaga*.

In April 1960 the New York Yacht Club announced that it had accepted a challenge presented by the Royal Sydney Yacht Squadron in the name of the Sir Frank Packer Syndicate.

As a start, Packer (an oil and press baron) chartered *Vim* for four years and commissioned Alan Payne, a young Australian architect whose career was on the rise, to design a new Twelve. *Gretel*, named after Packer's late wife, was to be built by Lars Halvorsen & Sons.

Payne got permission from the New York Yacht Club to test models at the Stevens Institute which also had the data for *Vim*. The defenders also authorised the use of some non-Australian components: Barient winches and Hood sails.

Gretel was launched in February 1962; the Australians were enthusiastic and optimistic because she was faster than *Vim*.

The design was a good one, elegant and powerful, with full sections adapted to fresh breezes and moderate seas; the bow was narrow while the stern was wide and flat so as to lengthen the waterline when heeled.

The deck, free from obstacles, was in fibreglass covered with teak. DeHavilland made the three-part mast with elliptical sections.

The coffee grinders were placed on deck as the Class Rule had been changed to eliminate large cockpits and could be linked together. The sails were cut and sewn in Australia of American Dacron whose use had been authorised by the Defender.

The defender selection trials for the New York Yacht Club were between four yachts, only one of which, *Nefertiti*, was new while modifications were made to the other three.

Columbia had a new owner and some changes were made to her keel, her weakness was the crew, and she was soon eliminated.

Easterner, sailed by the family of the owner, had the same results as before.

Weatherly, purchased by Henry Mercer's syndicate, was much improved by her designer, Philip Rhodes, and the Luders yard: the stern was cut back, weight reduced above deck and the wetted surface reduced by remodeling the hull. The boat increased her speed, but the decisive element was the new skipper, Bus Mosbacher.

Nefertiti was built by a syndicate headed by Ross Anderson, Commodore of the Boston Yacht Club who felt that the U.S. ought to have a new Cup defender. Ted Hood drew the plans aided by Britton Chance, Jr. who did tank tests.

Nefertiti was built by James E. Graves and was important in the development of the Twelves. The first Twelve to have a rudder with a wide base, she was the largest yet built and had a light displacement (almost a ton lighter than *Columbia*); she had a large wetted surface and a large keel which made her fast in fresh breezes but less so with light airs and calm seas, despite the large fore triangle.

Nefertiti started out well in the trial races to choose the defender, winning ten of twelve races, but due to light airs, lost the final races and *Weatherly* was chosen to represent the NYYC.

The Cup races of 1962 are remembered as among the most exciting. The final 4-1 result did not give an accurate picture of *Gretel*'s capabilities.

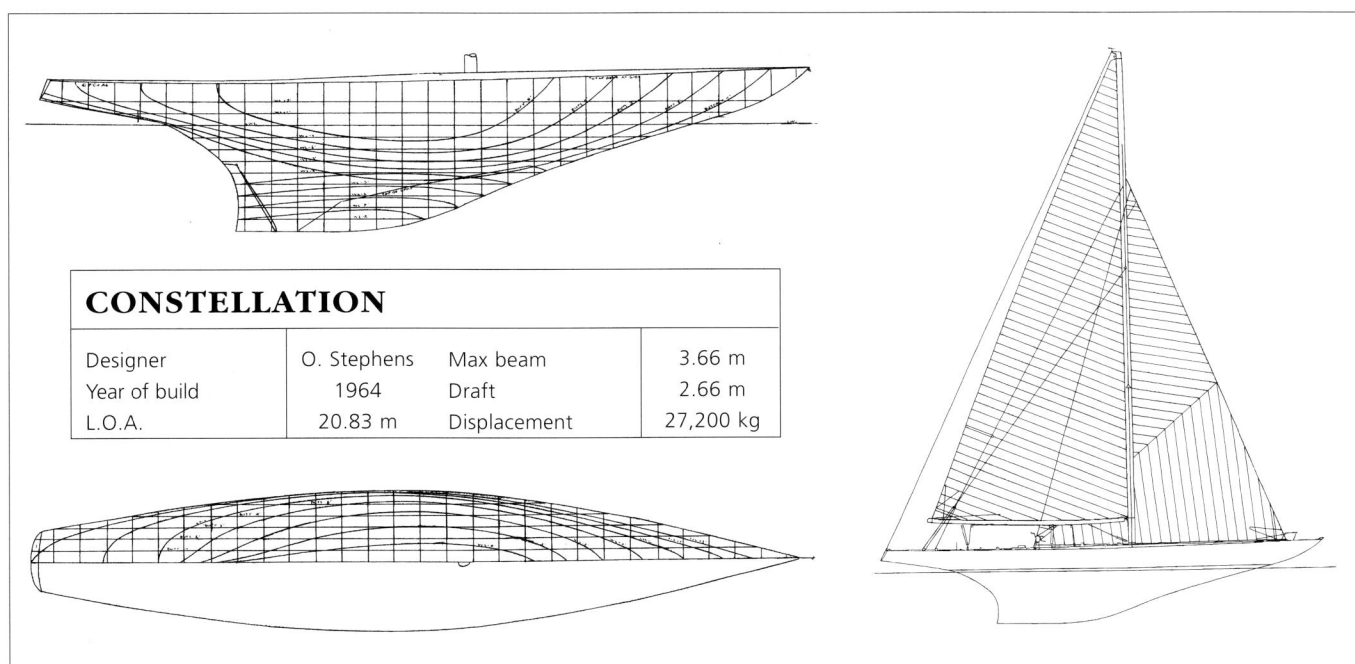

CONSTELLATION

Designer	O. Stephens	Max beam	3.66 m
Year of build	1964	Draft	2.66 m
L.O.A.	20.83 m	Displacement	27,200 kg

Constellation, *designed by S & S for Walter Gubelman in 1964, won very easily against the British challenger,* Sovereign.

Four new Twelves were present at the races in 1964: *Sovereign, Kurrewa V, American Eagle* and *Constellation.* The Americans were impressed by *Gretel's* results and convinced that only Mosbacher's experience had saved the Cup. Therefore they changed important points in the Rules: the contenders must be produced entirely in the country which they represent, particularly sails and sailcloth; the course would be of the Olympic type, with more legs on the wind and more turns around the buoys than formerly, consequently more difficulty for crews and designers.

The challenge of 1964 was presented by the Royal Thames Yacht Club and in June 1963 the new challenger *Sovereign* was already training on the Clyde. The owner was J. Anthony J "Tony" Boyden, who once again chose David Boyd and Alexander Robertson & Sons to design and build the boat. Boyd could test models at the Stevens Institute which the Americans had not yet put off-limits, and

he produced a hull with nice, classic lines: a sharp bow and a narrow stern. The first tests took place on the Clyde against *Sceptre* which had been renovated and made faster by her new owner; as the tests went on, the new boat established her superiority. However there were contrary indications at Cowes Week, where *Sovereign* was regularly beaten by *Norsaga* which, together with *Flica II*, helped tune the challenger.

Kurrewa V was commissioned by the Australian brothers Frank and John Livingstone in order to have another modern Twelve with which to make comparisons and choose the English challenger. To save time and money, they asked Boyd and the Robertson yard to design and build the new boat, using the moulds which had served in the construction of *Sovereign.* Therefore, *Kurrewa V* was a twin to *Sovereign,* with a slightly modified keel and a stiffer mast. After nineteen races in English waters and seven more against *Kurrewa V* in the waters off Newport,

Sovereign was selected for the challenge. Her skipper was Peter Scott.

The NYYC chose the defender from the following: *Nefertiti,* whose keel and underbody had been modified, skippered by Ted Hood; *Easterner,* with the Hovey family aboard and *Columbia.* In addition the Aurora Syndicate headed by Pierre S. "Pete" Du Pont ordered a new boat designed by Bill Luders Jr. and built by his yard, Luders Marine Construction. The mast heightened by a deck elevation known as "Mount Luders".

Olin Stephens also designed a new boat, *Constellation,* which was built by the Minneford Yacht Yard for the Gubelmann syndicate. The mast and boom were flexible, the rudder, fine and deep, shaped like a scimitar. Stays and shrouds were made from elliptical steel bars and the search for lower weight led to interior bulkheads made of aeronautical aluminium honeycomb panels.

The races to select a defender were dominated by *Constellation* and *American*

INTREPID			
Designer	O.J. Stephens	Max beam	3.68 m
Year of build	1967	Draft	2.78 m
L.O.A.	19.66 m	Displacement	27.9 t
L.W.L.	14.27 m	Sail area	164 m²

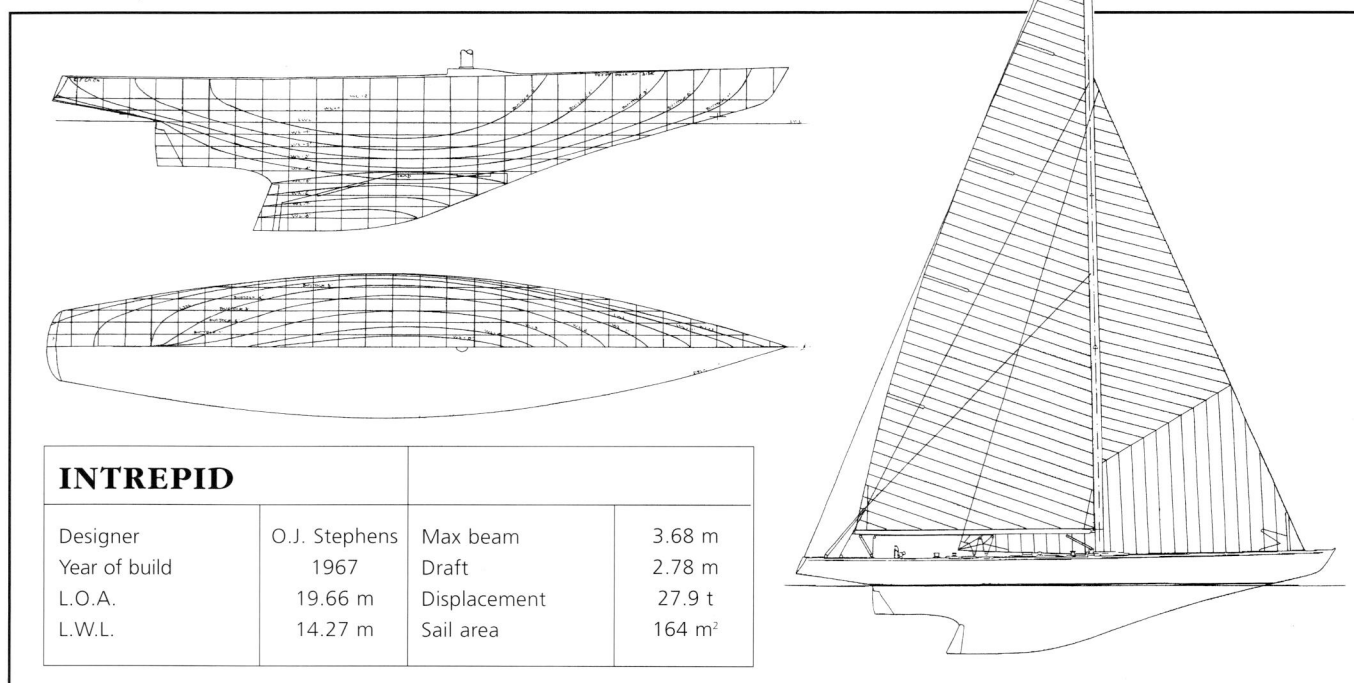

INTREPID US 22

Design: *Olin J. Stephens*
Shipyard: *Minneford Yacht Yard, Inc.*
Launched: *May 1967*
Owners: *Syndicate formed by: J. Burr Bartram, John T. Dorrance Jr., Patrick E. Haggerty, Eleanor B. Radley, William J. Strawbridge, Harold S. Vanderbilt, Gilbert Verney*
Club: *New York Yacht Club*
Skipper: *Emil "Bus" Mosbacher, Jr*
America's Cup: *defender and winner of the 1967 match (against* Dame Pattie *by 4 to 0) and 1970 (against* Gretel II *by 3 to 2).*

Intrepid *marks a turning point in the design of the Twelve Metre boat. She was the first to detach the rudder from the keel. However, this was not the only reason she was a revolutionary design.*

The hull: *The rudder being separated from the keel meant that the keel could be reduced and made more efficient than previous designs with a smaller wetted surface area. Seven models were made and tank tests led to an ever greater reduction in the length of the keel which ended in a trim tab while the rudder was placed nearly at the end of the waterline at a distance of nearly three metres, thus increasing its efficiency. The trim tab can be connected to the main rudder to increase the efficiency or can be locked in the desired position so that it functions as a flap.*

Layout of the deck: *This was completely revolutionized. The large cockpit design pioneered on* Sceptre *was subsequently prohibited, and a return to conventional designs was made. Copying from* Sceptre, *but keeping to the regulations of the Cup, the deck was positioned over the space reserved for the crew. The entire crew, except for the helmsman, the tactician and the two responsible for trimming the sheets of the jib and spinnaker, is placed under the deck in the central part of the hull. Here, as well as the rigging, are all the mechanisms for the winches and capstan winches. Four handles can be linked on a single winch allowing four men to easily sheet in the genoa when sailing close-hauled. This design also allows the centre of gravity to be lowered because it reduces to a minimum the internal space permitted by the regulations. The berths are of balsa wood and are designed in such a way as not to take up any room needed for manoeuvres. The boat is lined with terylene material instead of wooden bulkheads. The cockpit is on two levels: the higher one is for the helmsman and the tactician, while those responsible for the sheets are in the front part and have only their head and shoulders above deck .*

Rigging: *This is very innovative. The boom and the upper half of the mast is in titanium. The boom is flexible and placed very low on the deck so as to improve the performance of the mainsail especially when sailing close-hauled. The rigging is steel rods and elliptical in form.*

Sails: *Ted Hood, responsible for the sails, introduced innovations in their cut, material and warp. To better understand the technical evolution of the new materials it is enough to remember the work done on* Columbia *to reduce the weight at the top of the mast. They had to take into account a mainsail made of material weighing fourteen ounces while the mainsails of* Intrepid *used new materials weighing nine and a half ounces.*

Eagle, *Constellation* won the final and the nomination as defender. Once again the English took a beating: four to zero.

The second Australian challenge arrived in 1967 from a syndicate of fifteen Melbourne businessmen headed by Emil Christiansen. They engaged Warwick Hood, a student of Alan Payne, to design *Dame Pattie*, which was built by W.H. Barnett. LWL was 14.30 m, almost thirty centimetres more than the boats built for the preceding challenge and consequently the boat had a smaller sail area; to reduce the wetted surface and the chain girth, the bow sections were U-shaped, the main section was reduced as was the keel length (after the first tests the keel was lengthened again by adding a heel piece). The rudder had a new shape and was wider in the upper part than in the lower, the overhangs were shorter, and the sails were made in Australia of a specially produced cloth, called KAdron; the rigging was made of round rods.

Sir Frank Packer presented a challenge too and engaged A. Payne to modify *Gretel* which improved, but not enough to beat *Dame Pattie*.

The real innovations came from the U.S., and once again, from Olin Stephens who designed *Intrepid*. The Intrepid Syndicate, directed by Bill Strawbridge and headed by J. Burr Bartram was given the opportunity to defend in the name of the N.Y.Y.C. Among the syndicate members was Harold Vanderbilt; the skipper was Bus Musbacher. As for the races, there is little to tell: *Intrepid* beat them all, losing only two races; once because of a tactical error and once because she was dismasted. As for the Cup races, the story was the same; *Intrepid* defeated *Dame Pattie*, four to zero.

The races of 1967 were barely finished and already new challenges arrived at the N.Y.Y.C. from Australia, France, Great

Crewmen hang on the windward rail to increase stability.

Britain and Greece. The latter two nations withdrew their challenges and France and Australia, by agreement with the N.Y.Y.C. as Trustee of the Deed of Gift, prepared to race in a challenger selection series in the waters off Newport.

As usual Sir Frank Packer reserved himself a place onstage ordering a new Twelve from Alan Payne.

Gretel II was built by William Barnett and launched in February 1970. James Hardy was appointed skipper.

There were many innovations in *Gretel II*: twin steering wheels (which later became the norm), folding spreaders (so that the lee spreaders would not interfere with the genoa when close-hauled) and a profiled mast placed aft of the norm in order to have a larger fore triangle.

It was the best boat of this America's Cup, but handicapped by crew problems. In France, Baron Bich opened his pockets wide and, having created the A.F.C.A. (Association Française pour la Coupe de l'Amérique), had proceeded to purchase *Kurrewa V, Sovereign* and *Constellation*. He then ordered a boat designed by the American Britton Chance and built by Hermann Egger (named *Chancegger*, a combination of the two names) whose role was to act as trial horse for his challenger *France*, designed by André Mauric. *Chancegger*, although destined never to compete for the Cup due to the Deed of Gift, was a laboratory of new ideas, of which Mauric made only partial use in designing *France*.

The LOA of the challenger was little more than her LWL; with her maximum displacement towards the stern to augment the laminar flow while the fore sections were full and flattened to increase speed while running before the wind.

In the USA two new boats were built to compete with *Intrepid* for the role of defender. Neither *Valiant*, the new Stephens design, nor *Heritage*, designed and built by Charles E. Morgan, were successes. *Valiant* was slow and hard to steer with a turbulent wake, *Heritage* was very pretty but her results were not.

Consequently, the methods of tank testing were brought into question; both boats had undergone extensive testing as models, and the results full scale were disappointing. Perhaps it was necessary to change the system of testing and of analysis of the results.

Intrepid was present for the same owners, but changes had been made both to the hull and rigging by Britton Chance. It was not clear that the boat had been improved.

Mosbacher was unable to participate, and Bill Ficker was named skipper.

Selection races were held as in the past, and *Intrepid* was chosen as defender. On the challenger's side, *Gretel II* easily beat *France*.

The 1970 America's Cup races were hard fought, and after two races each boat had won twice, with winning margins counted in seconds; *Intrepid* won the last two races by narrow margins.

1974 saw the first aluminium hulls, and the birth of *Courageous*. The war in the Middle East and the resulting oil crisis, as well as the development of scantling rules for aluminium 12 Metre construction, caused a year's postponement of the Cup. When it took place, it was a rerun of the previous match: the French competed with *France* against the Australian's new boat *Southern Cross*, with a predictable French defeat, and in the match itself, *Courageous* beat *Southern Cross* four to zero.

More important than the racing was the innovation in construction material, which brought about significant changes in the design of Twelves. Lloyd's Register approved the participation of aluminium hulls, and *Courageous, Mariner*, and *Southern Cross* were all built of this new (for 12 Metre yachting) material.

Designers could now build hulls that were stiffer (and thus better able to with-

Weatherly *was choosen to defend in the Cup series of 1962. She beat the Australian challenger* Gretel *4-1.*

stand the stresses imposed by modern sails and rigs) and, at the same time, lighter, giving the possibility of more weight in the keel (Stephens calculated that the difference was slightly less than four tons). Another important advantage of aluminium construction was the ease with which modifications could be made compared to wood.

Courageous was ordered from Sparkman & Stephens by a N.Y.Y.C. syndicate, now headed by Bob McCullough after Strawbridge's resignation.

Olin Stephens, aided by David Pedrick, conducted tests with models one-third full size, LWL 4.5 metres, displacement nearly one ton, and clearly much more expensive. The boat was built at Minneford Yacht Yard and Ted Hood was ultimately chosen as skipper, but with Dennis Conner at the wheel for starts, after the elimination of *Mariner* freed him for the task.

Courageous was not as novel as *Valiant* and *Intrepid* had been, but had very elegant lines, with long overhangs and a short keel.

Mariner had been designed by Britton Chance, after tank tests and computer-aided modelling had resulted in a revolutionary underbody characterised by a stern transom below the waterline, which meant that the hull did not become progressively narrower towards the stern as was usual.

The theory was fascinating but in practice the boat was a disappointment and *Mariner* was rapidly eliminated despite the skill of her two helmsmen, Dennis Conner and Ted Turner, both getting their first taste of America's Cup racing.

Two newcomers to the Australian team were to be active in future Cup racing: Alan Bond, head of the Southern Cross Syndicate, and Bob Miller, the designer (who later changed his name to Ben Lexcen).

In the 1974 season, the most exciting moments were the finals of the N.Y.Y.C.

An elegant Olin Stephens and, below, Alan Payne, designer of Gretel I *and* II.

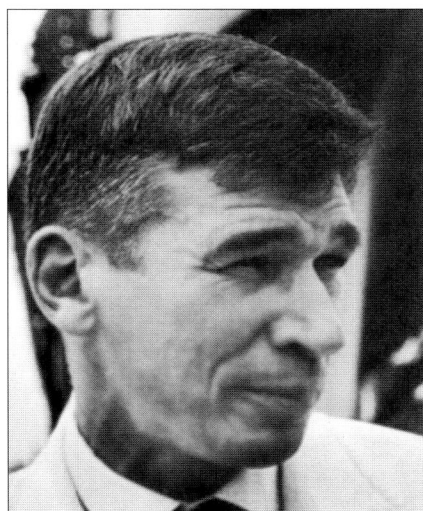

selection trials with *Courageous* opposing *Intrepid,* rebuilt by Driscoll Boats of San Diego to a design by Stephens similar to her original lines. *Courageous* won by a score of three races to two.

At the Cup races of 1977 the Swedes presented their first challenge, while the English withdrew.

The Australians presented two challenges from two different clubs.

Only *France II* was of wood (moulded); all the others were of metal, and all complied with the new Cup rules published by the N.Y.Y.C. requiring self-draining cockpits of specified dimensions.

France II's design was dated; the boat was so slow that she was replaced during the challenger selection trials by *France I*, which was defeated by *Australia*, 4-0.

The Swedish syndicate, comprising forty industrialists and the King of Sweden, presented a novel design by Pelle Petterson, the fruit of concerted efforts by the syndicate. *Sverige* had a low wetted surface and an original stern section. At the centre of the yacht she had double wheels which controlled both rudder and trim tab; winches were cross-linked, and driven by bicycle pedals. *Sverige* was very fast tacking, and defeated *Gretel II* after seven exciting races, only to be eliminated in the challenger selection finals by *Australia*.

Australia was the evolution of *Southern Cross*; the design was by Ben Lexcen and young Johan Valentijn. Compared to her predecessor, she was about three tons lighter, faster when tacking and spread more canvas. She did very well in the selection trials, and won all her races.

The defenders had two new Twelves. *Independence* was designed practically by trial and error; Ted Hood developed his ideas as construction advanced, changing keels and rudders until he was satisfied with the result. At sea, trials were held against *Courageous*, which Hood had modified and made faster.

Enterprise was born on the drawing board and in the test tank; conceived as a development of *Courageous*, Stephens hoped to improve on his earlier boat and did extensive testing with one-third size models as before. She tuned up racing against *Intrepid*, which, although not updated for lack of money, was still hard to beat in strong winds and heavy seas. At the beginning of the defender selection trials, Ted Turner was asked to take the helm of *Courageous*, although she had been assigned the role of trial horse. *Courageous* won the defender selection

Long hired David Pedrick to prepare a defender to be called *Clipper*, using equipment from *Independence*. The skipper was Russell Long, Huey's son. In light airs *Clipper* was faster than *Freedom* but her crew did not have the experience to compete at these levels.

Freedom, Olin Stephens' last Cup boat, was built for another NYYC syndicate and skippered by Dennis Conner. Funds were short, and tank testing very limited.

The hull resembled *Enterprise*, but had the lowest freeboard of any Twelve, which in theory increased stability and lowered air resistance.

After trials of both boats, Conner chose *Freedom* for the defender eliminations against *Courageous*, skippered by Ted Turner, and *Clipper*. *Freedom* won the selection trials and the Cup defence, beating a revamped *Australia*, four victories to one.

Seven yachts competed for the 1983 challenger trials: *Australia II, Challenge 12, Advance, Victory '83, Azzurra, Canada* and *France III*. Additionally, yachts built for testing purposes included *Spirit of America, Magic* and *Victory '82*.

For the first time in the 12 Metre era, Canada issued a challenge and arrived with a boat designed by Bruce Kirby, designer of the Laser dinghy. *Canada* was a traditional Twelve with a well trained crew; they came fourth in the challenger selection trials.

Italy also challenged for the first time. *Azzurra* was financed by Consorzio Sfida Italiana America's Cup and flew burgee of the Yacht Club Costa Smeralda.

The Italian Twelve was a descendant of *Enterprise*, which had been purchased by the Consorzio and studied by Vallicelli in the test tank of the Italian Navy.

Surprisingly, *Azzurra* did well because of the qualities of both the design and the crew, and ended third among the challengers. Great Britain's syndicate, headed by Peter de Savary, presented two Twelves: *Victory '82* and *Victory '83*. The

Marcel Bich, helmsman of France, *on board his 12 I.R., together with his crew.*

and subsequently the Cup races, defeating *Australia* 4-0.

In 1980 four nations were challenging; Australia, Sweden, France and Great Britain, whose syndicate, headed by Tony Boyden, hired the young architect Ian Howlett to design *Lionheart*.

The boat went into the Twelve Metre history book because her designer discovered and used a loophole in the Class Rule, which permitted the mast to be flexible (in its upper part) and thus set a larger mainsail (roughly 20 sq.m). This made *Lionheart* hard to beat in light airs. However, she was defeated by *France III*, giving Baron Bich, after all his effort, the pleasure of one victory in Cup racing. In any case, this newly discovered loophole was exploited by the Australians in the final races.

France III was a new design by Johan Valentijn; similar to *Australia*, she first had two trim tabs, but the excessive complexity caused the idea to be shelved. *France III* got as far as the challenger finals, where she was eliminated by *Australia* at which point Baron Bich announced his retirement from further Cup Racing.

In the USA, a syndicate headed by Huey

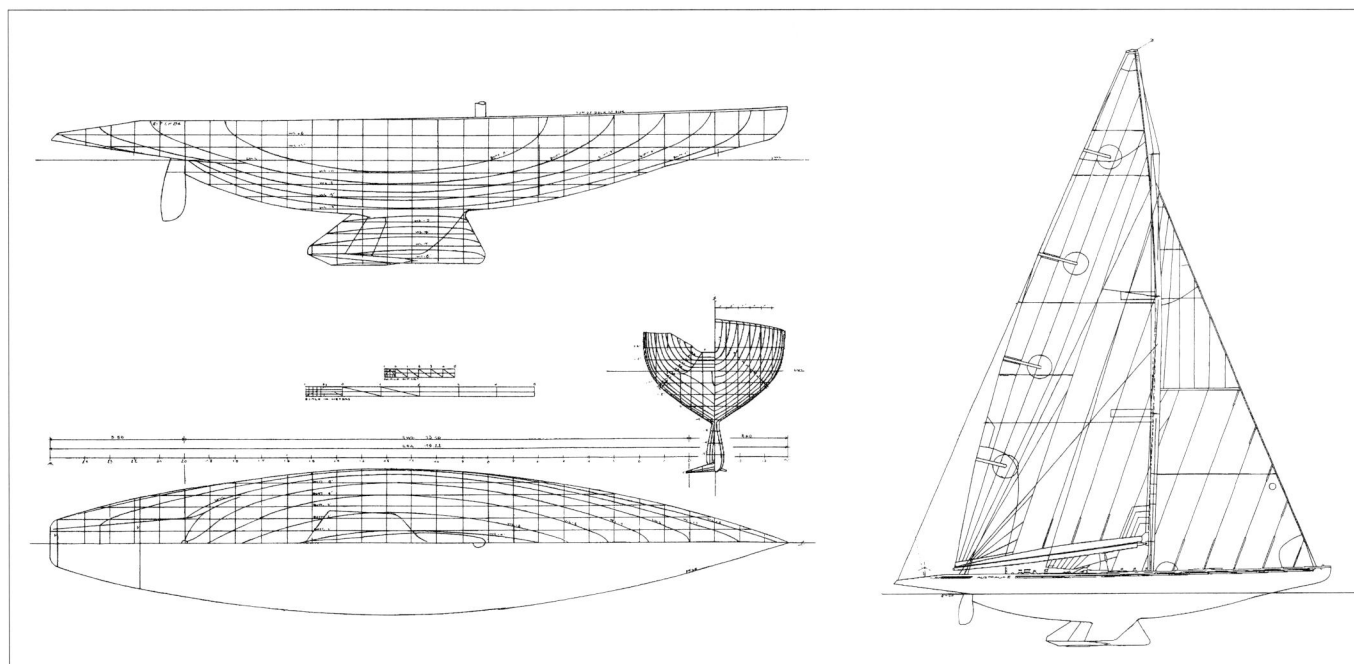

AUSTRALIA II KA 6

Design: *Ben Lexcen*
Shipyard: *Steve E. Ward & Co.*
Launched: *June 1982*
Owner: *America's Cup Challenge 1983-Alan Bond*
Club: *Royal Perth Yacht Club*
Skipper: *John Bertrand*
America's Cup: *winner of the 1983 series against* Liberty *by 4 to 3*

Australia II *and Ben Lexcen are two names which go into the pages of yachting history after one hundred and thirty two years of undisputed American supremacy.*
Australia II *should not only be remembered for this sensational event but also because, like other projects which added to the development of the 12 Metre boat, such as* Vim *and* Intrepid, *all the Twelve Metre boats designed in later years refer back to the ideas and experience of the Lexcen design. This is true not only for the design of Twelve Metre boats;* Australia II *had, and still has, an impact on the designs all of fast sailing boats.*
Victory in the America's Cup was thanks, as always, to a number of contributing factors. In this case it was the good team work of the crew, an experienced skipper and well cut sails. However, undoubtedly a determining factor was "the wing keel". Lexcen aimed to build a hull which displaced as little as possible and had the shortest possible waterline. Taking into account these two factors called for a more linear design with little volume below the waterline, while the shorter waterline length allowed the same sail area to be maintained. Furthermore, a wide stern low in the water would have penalised the tonnage but would have allowed for an increased waterline length when sailing close-hauled.
The problem was to resolve all these points while at the same time maintaining sufficient stability. For the first trials the lead was taken out and hung under the keel like a bulb. This created excessive vortices but tank tests allowed the problem to be resolved by adopting a solution normally used in aeronautics; the well-known Withcomb wing. The subsequent trials were successful and also showed improved performance when the boat was heeled over. It also reduced the problem of a larger area of hull in the water in light winds due to the reduction of the keel and all the weight of the lead being concentrated at the lowest point.
In conclusion, it was a revolutionary hull as can be seen by comparing the data with Liberty *which can be considered an average example in the Twelve Metre class.* Australia II *has about the same overall length and sail area but her waterline is about 51 cm shorter; it is 25 cm wider, its draft is 10 cm less and it has a 6 ton reduction in displacement.*

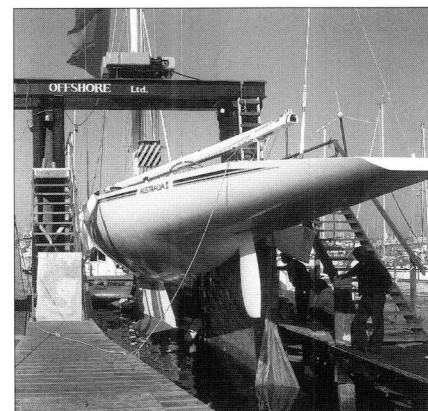

first was designed by Ed Dubois, but did not satisfy de Savary, who ordered the second from Ian Howlett. *Victory '83* was considered the fastest Twelve of her generation, prior to the adoption of keels with lateral fins, and contested the selection as the final challenger against *Australia II*.

The Australians brought three different challengers to the selection races. Alan Bond had ten years experience with Cup challenges which also served to prepare the designer, Ben Lexcen, as well as an excellent crew and an experienced team. As a result, *Australia II* was one of those boats which marked a new era in the history of yachting.

Challenge 12 was a Twelve built for Alan Bond but was replaced by *Australia II* and sold to another syndicate. *Challenge 12* was very similar to *Australia II*, differing in the keel design, with a longer overhang at the stern and a longer waterline; her performance was also similar.

Advance was a design by Alan Payne for a syndicate formed by Syd Fisher and Sir William Pettingall.

The intention was to create a fast hull for light airs and the sea conditions off Newport. No tank tests were made, but Payne built a sailing model of *Freedom* and five others derived from it, all five metres long and radio controlled.

The result, *Advance*, was extreme and ugly and gave poor results; she still survives in the US.

The Americans organised their defence with two syndicates: the first, called the Freedom Campaign, was headed by Ed du Moulin, with Dennis Conner as helmsman. They commissioned a new boat from Johan Valentijn and asked for radical design. The outcome was *Magic*, a short Twelve with very light displacement which was judged a failure. At the same time Bill Langan at Sparkman & Stephens created *Spirit of America* for the same syndicate. She was just the opposite of *Magic*: heavy, hard to steer, with a full underbody and a small keel. Three keel versions were built, but with limited success.

At this point, du Moulin and Conner decided it was better to avoid the extreme solutions and placed a third project with Valentijn to be called *Liberty*. She was furnished with multiple rating certificates, which corresponded to the various keels and rudders which could be changed according to the anticipated conditions of wind and sea.

Chuck Kirsch headed another syndicate which set their new boat *Defender*, designed by David Pedrick, to race against a modified *Courageous* before choosing between them.

Courageous was remodeled in accordance with the new ideas of Bill Langan; the rudder was enlarged, the bottom of the keel flattened and the point at which it met the hull was rounded off. Weight was reduced and new sails made.

The selection of the challenger took place after three Round Robins, and a total of 54 races. The defender's selection was hard fought as well.

The Cup Match was a cliffhanger.

Australia II's victory revived interest in the Cup and, notwithstanding the rising costs, the years between 1984 and 1987 saw the formation of several new challenge syndicates.

The choppy seas and strong steady breezes or at Fremantle replaced the light winds and ocean swells prevalent at Newport, and new designs had to be built accordingly.

In 1986 the 26th America's Cup was the tenth and last to be raced in the Twelve Metre class. Four Australian syndicates presented themselves with six new boats for the defence: *Kookaburra II*, *Kookaburra III*, *Australia III*, *Australia IV*, *Steak 'N Kidney*, and *South Australia*.

There were five American syndicates present with boats like *Stars & Stripes '87*, *USA*, *Eagle*, *America II*, *Heart of America*, and *Courageous*.

They brought along ten other Twelves for training and comparison.

New Zealand brought *New Zealand* (*Kiwi Magic*) and two other Twelves. The three New Zealand boats were the first Twelves built in fibreglass and they were declared eligible to race only after considerable discussion.

France had *French Kiss*, *Challenge France* and two other Twelves.

Italy brought *Italia I* and *Azzurra III* and four other Twelves.

Finally, England and Canada had *White Crusader* and *Canada II* as well as two other boats for tuning and training.

The total was forty-one Twelves for the selection races which lasted three months. The challenger was *Stars & Stripes '87*, and the defender *Kookaburra III*.

Stars & Stripes '87 beat the Australian boat four-nil and brought the Cup back to the United States for the next match to be held in San Diego, California.

Thus ended the involvement of the Twelve Metre Class in competition for the America's Cup.

2. THE 12 METRE REGISTER

12 METRE FIRST RULE - ALPHABETICAL LIST OF NAMES

■ ALACHIE

DESIGNER: *W. Fife III*
BUILDER: *W. Fife & Son - construction no. 556*
YEAR: *1908 late April*
LENGTH OVERALL: *15.70 m.*
LENGTH AT WATERLINE: *11.91 m.*
BEAM: *3.37 m.*
SAIL AREA: *250 sq.m.*
CONSTRUCTION: *wood on steel frames*
FIRST OWNER: *George Coats*
FIRST NAME: *Alachie*
FIRST COUNTRY: *Great Britain*
HOME PORT: *Glasgow*
CONDITION: *broken up*
FURTHER DETAILS AND HISTORY: Built according to the First Int. Rule
Owners and history:

1908 - 1912 George Coats; name: *Alachie*; home port: Glasgow.
Launched in 1908 at the end of April, *Alachie* was the first yacht of the
new class built on the Clyde and was considered as the most advanced
boat built at Fairlie. Like all of the more extreme racers all the sheets were
to be controlled from below so as to obviate the necessity for anyone but
the helmsman to be on deck during a race. She had no bulwarks and the
men were prevented from slipping overboard by an elm toerail fixed along
the deck along the inner edge of the covering board; spars, boom and
bowsprit were hollow. Just after the launch, she was beached for a
complete alteration to her keel, which was recast with eight hundred
weight of lead added as ballast. *Alachie* was one of the leading Twelves in
the 1908, 1909, 1910 and 1911 seasons and out of 137 entries she had
43 firsts and 54 placings. She competed without success at the English
trials for the 1908 Olympic games. In 1912 *Alachie* was not fitted out, her
owner George Coats being busy with the new 15 Metre, *The Lady Anne*.
Racing results: 1909 season: she was third with a total of 29 entries, 7
firsts, 9 seconds and 3 thirds; 1910 season: she was third with 37 entries,
12 firsts, 13 seconds and 4 thirds; 1911 season: she was first with a total
of 41 entries, 13 firsts, 14 seconds and 4 thirds. In 1911 she took part in
the first Europe Week at Cowes together with *Cintra*, *Javotte*, *Ierne* and
Rollo; she was third in the first race and fifth in the second
1914 - 1915 José Antonio Aguirre - home port: Buenos Aires
1916 - 1918 ?
1919 - 1931 Antonio Leon Lanussé. From 1925 registered in Lloyd's
Register as "formerly Int. Rating Class 12 Metre". In a photo dated 1927
Alachie is racing with *Ráfaga* still with gaff rig
From 1932 Disappeared from Lloyd's Register: she is considered as broken up

■ ATALANTA

DESIGNER: *Johan Anker*
BUILDER: *Anker & Jensen*
YEAR: *1917*
LENGTH AT WATERLINE: *13.03 m.*
BEAM: *3.35 m.*
CONSTRUCTION: *wood on steel frames*
FIRST OWNER: *Henrik Ostervold (since 1920)*

FIRST NAME: *Atalanta*
FIRST COUNTRY: *Norway*
HOME PORT: *Bergen*
FIRST SAIL NUMBER: *K5*
CURRENT LOCATION: *unknown*
CONDITION: *broken up?*
FURTHER DETAILS AND HISTORY: Built according to the First Int. Rule
Owners and history:

1917 - 1922 Henrik Ostervold; name: *Atalanta*; home port: Bergen; rig:
bermudan cutter. Winner of the 1920 Olympic games First Int. Rule category
1923 - 1924 Alfred C. Adams and J.R. Piper; home port: Colchester.
In 1923 she entered Burnham Week performing well although outclassed
by *Noreen* and *Vanity*
1925 J.R. Piper (sole owner); home port: London
1926 - 1929 W.F. McAusland
1930 - 1931 C.H. Chapman. Since 1930 registered in Lloyd's Register as
"formerly Int. Rating Class 12 Metre"; engine installed in 1931
1932 Disappeared from Lloyd's Register

■ BRAND IV

DESIGNER: *Johan Anker*
BUILDER: *Anker & Jensen*
YEAR: *1909*
LENGTH OVERALL: *18.67 m.*
LENGTH AT WATERLINE: *11.99 m.*
BEAM: *3.49 m.*
SAIL AREA: *243 sq.m. reduced to 187 sq.m. (1926)*
CONSTRUCTION: *wood*
FIRST OWNER: *Dr. R. Van Rees*
FIRST NAME: *Brand IV*
FIRST COUNTRY: *Netherlands*
HOME PORT: *Amsterdam*
OTHER NAMES: *Isla II (1912) - Dora III (1917) - Brand IV (1921) - Ragna III
(1932) - Elmari (1936) - Solveig I (1953)*
CONDITION: *broken up ?*
FURTHER DETAILS AND HISTORY: Built according to the First Int. Rule
Owners and history:

1909 - 1911 Dr. R. Van Rees; name: *Brand IV*; home port: Amsterdam
She was the first Norwegian Twelve designed and built by Johan Anker and
the one which brought him celebrity. In 1909 *Brand IV* won everywhere –
Copenhagen, Oresund and Kiel. The Kaiser congratulated Anker on *Brand's*
results and the famous Norwegian dramatist Bjornson sent him a telegram:
"My Norwegian heart is bursting with joy, it is still healthy." Thanks to her
winning career, *Brand IV* was called "the flying Norwegian"
1912 - 1916 G.W. Lans Junior; new name: *Isla II*; home port: Rotterdam
1917 - 1919 Burger Lie; new name: *Dora III*; home port: Christiania (Oslo)
1920 - 1925 L. Hannevig; new name: *Brand IV*; home port: Christiania (Oslo).
In 1925 altered to a bermudan cutter with a sail area reduced to 187 sq.m.
1926 - 1929 Ivor Jenkins; home port: Oslo
1930 - 1931 ?
1932 - 1935 Ole Sundö; new name *Ragna III*; home port: Copenhagen;
engine installed in 1934

1936 - 1937 Marius Nielsen; new name: *Elmari II*; home port: Copenhagen
1938 - 1946 ?
1947 H. Kierulff
1948 - 1952 Bôrge Jôrgensen
1953 - 1956 J.C. Petersen; new name *Solveig I*; home port: Aarhus (DK)
1957 Disappeared from Lloyd's Register; probably broken up

■ CINTRA

DESIGNER: *William Fife III*
BUILDER: *W. Fife & Son - design no. 563*
YEAR: *1909 May*
LENGTH OVERALL: *18.82 m.*
LENGTH AT WATERLINE: *11.97 m.*
BEAM: *3.38 m.*
CONSTRUCTION: *wood with steel frames*
FIRST OWNER: *Andrew Coats*
FIRST NAME: *Cintra*
FIRST COUNTRY: *Great Britain*
HOME PORT: *Glasgow*
OTHER NAMES: *Cintro (1947)*
CURRENT LOCATION: *Cala Galera (Italy)*
FURTHER DETAILS AND HISTORY: Built according to the First Int. Rule
Owners and history:

1909 - 1912 Andrew Coats; name: *Cintra;* home port: Glasgow. A. Coats started the 12M class on the Clyde with *Heatherbell. Cintra* was a fast boat in light winds and quite successful in many races against *Alachie* owned by Andrew's brother, George. In 1909 she led the racing season with 33 starts, 13 firsts, 7 seconds and 4 thirds. In 1910 she was again the best with 43 starts, 14 firsts, 12 seconds and 2 thirds; in 1911 she was fourth with 27 starts, 4 firsts, 7 seconds and 5 thirds, while in 1912 she entered 21 starts with 5 firsts and 4 seconds. In 1911 she took part in the first Europe Week in Cowes together with *Alachie, Javotte, Ierne* and *Rollo;* she had a fifth and second placing in the two races
1914 - 1918 F. Smith
1919 - 1930 Axel Wilhelmsen; home port: Christiania (Oslo)
From 1919 in Lloyd's as "formerly Int. Rating Class 12 Metre"
1931 - 1934 ?
1935 - 1937 E. Guyler van Bergh; home port: Copenhagen and Oslo
Altered to a bermudan cutter. Remeasured as 12 Metre I.R.
1938 - 1939 Ernst Schalburg; home port: Sussex and Copenhagen
1946 - 1950 Cecil E. Donne; new name: *Cintro;* home port: London.
RORC R. 1947: 50.53' - 1948: 47.18'
1951 - 1952 Lt.Col. A.E.P. Bridge; new engine installed in 1951
1953 Comdr. H.G. Dobbs
1954 - 1956 A.J. Walter. In 1956 she entered at her last race: the Round the Island Race
1956 W.E. Smith; home port: Southampton
1957 - 1958 L.C. Hardy; home port: London
1959 - 1963 Alwyn Foulkes; home port: London and Bursledon
1964 - 1966 R.D. Attwood; home port: London
1967 - 1972 C. Attwood & R. Attwood; re-engined in 1967. During 1970 *Cintra* was sheltered in a shed
1973 - 1989 ? In 1984 the yacht was transferred to an East Coast yard to be transformed: a large two level cockpit was installed, the stern was shortened and a big engine fitted
1990 - 1999 Alberto Rusconi; name *Cintra;* home port: La Spezia. The yacht was found by Franco Giorgetti and William Collier; she was transported to Italy and refitted as the original at the La Bussola yard in Fiumicino. She entered numerous races in Mediterranean regattas for vintage yachts
1999 Gabriele De Bono; home port: Cala Galera

■ CORONA

DESIGNER: *Anker & Jensen*
BUILDER: *Anker & Jensen*
YEAR: *1913*
LENGTH OVERALL: *18.99 m.*
LENGTH AT WATERLINE: *12.40 m.*
BEAM: *3.60 m.*
DRAFT: *2.50 m.*
SAIL AREA: *242 sq.m. (1920) - 187 sq.m. (1937) - 136 sq.m. (1955)*
CONSTRUCTION: *wood*
FIRST OWNER: *W. Wilhelmsen*
FIRST NAME: *Corona*
FIRST COUNTRY: *Norway*
HOME PORT: *Tornsberg*
OTHER NAMES: *Hawaii VI (1938) - Oslo (1957) - Stormsvala (1961)*
CURRENT LOCATION: *unknown*
FURTHER DETAILS AND HISTORY: Built according to First Int. Rule but never rated as a 12 M. Owners and history:

1913 - 1938 W. Wilhelmsen; name *Corona;* home port: Tonsberg. Rig: yawl; converted in 1920 to a cutter; in 1937 altered to a bermudan cutter
1938 - 1952 Arthur J. Bossum; new name: *Hawaii VI;* home port: Oslo
1948 - 1954 Erna Bossum; according to KNS (Royal Norwegian Sailing Federation) archives she owned the yacht before the year indicated by Lloyd's Register
1955 - 1955 E. Gjölberg; engine installed in 1954
1955 - 1957 Bjørn Ruud-Pedersen
1957 - 1959 Jack Donley; new name: *Oslo;* apparently sold to US in 1959; disappeared off record
1961 - 1963 Henry H. Wolff; new name: *Stormsvala;* home port: Cherbourg and Cannes
1964 - 1969 J.M. Brunet and Jean Rédélé
1970 Disappeared off record

■ CYGNE

DESIGNER: *G. Duperron*
BUILDER: *Ch. G. De Coninck & Co. (Maison Lafitte)*
YEAR: *1907*
LENGTH OVERALL: *12.88 m.*
LENGTH AT WATERLINE: *10.85 m.*
BEAM: *4.08 m.*
SAIL AREA: *93.6 sq.m.*
CONSTRUCTION: *wood*
ENGINE: *petrol, 2 cylinders Mietz G. Weiss*
FIRST OWNER: *G. Lacroix*
FIRST NAME: *Cygne*
FIRST COUNTRY: *France*
HOME PORT: *Meulan*

OTHER NAMES: *Ella (1922) - Maria (1923)*
CONDITION: *broken up*
FURTHER DETAILS AND HISTORY: Built according to the First Int. Rule
Owners and history:
1907 - 1910 G. Lacroix; name: *Cygne;* home port: Meulan and Le Havre.
In 1908 rig was converted to yawl and engine installed; registered as
"auxiliary yawl with engine"
1911 - 1921 A. Chabrier; name *Cygne;* home port: Le Havre. Registered as
"auxiliary yawl". In 1921 registered as "formerly Int. Rating Class 12 Metre"
1922 A. Menchaca; new name: *Ella;* home port: Bilbao
1923 - 1925 F. Sainz & Incháustegui; new name: *Maria;* home port:
Bilbao
1926 - 1932 Vicente Galiana Puchol; home port: Barcelona
1935 - 1937 ?
1937 Disappeared from Lloyd's Register

■ CYRA

DESIGNER: *Alfred Mylne*
BUILDER: *Alexander Robertson & Sons (Sandbank)*
YEAR: *1909 May*
LENGTH OVERALL: *18.47 m.*
LENGTH AT WATERLINE: *12.27 m.*
BEAM: *3.40 m.*
DRAFT: *2.48 m.*
SAIL AREA: *195 sq.m. (1909); 200 sq.m. (1915); 243 sq.m. (1924)*
CONSTRUCTION: *wood on steel frames*
FIRST OWNER: *A. F. Sharman-Crawford*
FIRST NAME: *Cyra*
FIRST COUNTRY: *Great Britain*
HOME PORT: *Greenock*
OTHER NAMES: *Lucella (1926) - Cyra (1927) - Elfe II (1937) - Elsa (1947)*
CURRENT LOCATION: *unknown*
CONDITION: *broken up?*
FURTHER DETAILS AND HISTORY: Built according to the First Int. Rule
Owners and history:
1909 - 1910 A. F. Sharman-Crawford; name: *Cyra;* home port: Greenock
1909 racing season: 32 entries, 6 firsts, 5 seconds and 1 third; 1910
season: 24 entries and just 1 third
1911 - 1922 J.S. Highfield. From 1915 to 1921 registered in Lloyd's
Register as "formerly Int. Rating Class 12 Metre". From 1922 registered as
remeasured as 12 Metre I.R.
1923 J.R. Piper; according to Burnham Yacht Club she "was racing for
the last time in 1923"
1923 - 1924 T.A. Roberts
1925 - 1926 C.E. Nicholson; new name from 1926: *Lucella;* home port
from 1926: Greenock. From 1926 registered as "formerly Int. Rating Class
12 Metre". Altered to bermudian yawl. Sail area: 177.09 sq.m.; engine
installed the same year
1927 - 1932 Col. E.J. Hollway; new name: *Cyra;* re-engined in 1927
1933 - 1934 Frits Johannsen; home port: Copenhagen and Antibes
1935 - 1936 Mrs. R. E. Pascal; home port: Cannes
1937 - 1938 Maurice Harlachol; new name *Elfe II;* home port: Cannes
remeasured as 12 Metre I.R.
1938 - 1946 ?

1947 - 1955 Joseph Regis; new name: *Elsa;* home port: Marseilles
1956 Disappeared from Lloyd's Register

■ DANSEUSE

DESIGNER: *Johan Anker*
BUILDER: *Anker & Jensen*
YEAR: *1911*
LENGTH OVERALL: *18.47 m.*
LENGTH AT WATERLINE: *11.99 m.*
BEAM: *3.38 m.*
SAIL AREA: *246-262 sq.m. (1919); 271 sq.m. (1920)*
CONSTRUCTION: *wood*
FIRST OWNER: *S. Eyde*
FIRST NAME: *Beduin*
FIRST COUNTRY: *Norway*
HOME PORT: *Christiania (Oslo)*
FIRST SAIL NUMBER: *E7*
OTHER NAMES: *Beduin (1911) - Maud III (1914) - Gadie (1919) -
Danseuse III (1929); Danseuse (present)*
CURRENT LOCATION: *Oslo (Norway)*
CONDITION: *good*
FURTHER DETAILS AND HISTORY: Built according to the First Int. Rule
Owners and history:
1911 - 1913 Sam Eyde (vice commodore and then commodore of KNS);
name: *Beduin;* home port: Christiania (Oslo)
1914 - 1915 Finn Bugge; new name: *Maud III:* home port: Tonsberg.
Maud III entered the 1914 Europe Week at Oslo. From 1915 sail area
increased to 262 sq.m.
1916 - 1918 ?
1919 - 1928 H. H. Brock Jr; new name: *Gadie;* home port: Christiania
(Oslo). Since 1926 registered in Lloyd's Register as "formerly Int. Rating
Class 12 Metre"
1929 - 1932 Dagfinn Paust; new name: *Danseuse III;* home port: Oslo
1933 - 1957 Olaf Ellingsen; home port: Bergen. She entered the KNS
Jubilee regatta in 1933 but was not placed
1958 Disappeared from Lloyd's Register
1961 - 1962 Carl Platou Ellingsen; home port: Bergen
1962 - 1969 Mabel Ingalls
1969 - 1976 Carl Platou Ellingsen
1976 - 1980 Lars Chr. and Tor Jorgen Dahl
1980 Jan K. Stang; home port: Oslo. Mrs. Ingvild Thorensen; new name:
Danseuse; home port: Oslo; rated as a 12M I.R. She currently takes part
in vintage yacht events and sails in the Baltic and North Seas

■ DAVO II

DESIGNER: *Max Oertz*
BUILDER: *Max Oertz Yacotwerf (Hamburg)*
YEAR: *1907*
LENGTH AT WATERLINE: *11.28 m.*
BEAM: *3.85 m.*
SAIL AREA: *196 sq.m. (main 98 sq.m.-fore trysail 71.25 sq.m.-topsail 27 sq.m.)*
CONSTRUCTION: *wood*
FIRST OWNER: *C. Vermeer*
FIRST NAME: *Davo II*

FIRST COUNTRY: *Netherlands*
HOME PORT: *Amsterdam*
CONDITION: *broken up*
FURTHER DETAILS AND HISTORY: Built according to the First Int. Rule
Owners and history:
1907 - 1922 C. Vermeer; name: *Davo II*; home port: Amsterdam.
She was probably the first 12 Metre ever built and the only one ever built
with a centreboard. She was said to be a very fast boat: she won the
Zuiderzee Cup twice and also won against *Skeaf II* and *Brand IV*
1923 - 1937 H. Hellebrekers; name: *Davo II*; home port: Rotterdam
1937 Disappeared from Lloyd's Register

■ DAVO III

DESIGNER: *Max Oertz*
BUILDER: *Max Oertz Yachtwerf (Hamburg)*
YEAR: *1911*
LENGTH OVERALL: *18.29 m.*
LENGTH AT WATERLINE: *11.52 m.*
BEAM: *3.47 m.*
DRAFT: *1.98 m.*
SAIL AREA: *135.72 sq. m. (1931)*
CONSTRUCTION: *wood*
ENGINE: *engine installed in 1931*
FIRST OWNER: *C. Vermeer*
FIRST NAME: *Davo III*
FIRST COUNTRY: *Netherlands*
HOME PORT: *Amsterdam*
OTHER NAMES: *Wulp (1931) - Noordster III (1951)*
CONDITION: *broken up?*
FURTHER DETAILS AND HISTORY: Built according to the First Int. Rule
Owners and history:
1911 - 1920 C. Vermeer; name: *Davo III*; home port: Amsterdam. Mr.
Vermeer was formerly the owner of *Davo II*. In 1911 she was entered in
two British races but had no results
1921 - 1930 ?
1931 - 1950 G.H. Brandt; new name: *Wulp;* home port: Middelburg.
Since 1947: Schiedam. In 1931 she was altered to auxiliary bermudan
cutter; engine installed; sail area reduced to 135 sq.m.
1951 - 1970 L.G.A. Stojaczyk; new name: *Noordster III*; home port:
Amsterdam; re-engined in 1960
1971 Disappeared off record

■ DESIREE

DESIGNER: *Anker & Jensen*
BUILDER: *Anker & Jensen*
YEAR: *1913*
LENGTH OVERALL: *19.54 m.*
LENGTH AT WATERLINE: *12.76 m.*
BEAM: *3.35 m.*
DRAFT: *2.40 m.*
DISPLACEMENT: *24 tons*
SAIL AREA: *gaff 261 sq.m.; present 173 sq.m.*
CONSTRUCTION: *wood on steel frames*
ENGINE: *Aifo mod. 8041M - 95 hp*

FIRST OWNER: *Carl D. Danielsson*
FIRST NAME: *Sibyllan*
FIRST COUNTRY: *Sweden*
HOME PORT: *Stockholm*
OTHER NAMES: *Sibyllan (1913) - Sirocco (1919) - Scirocco (1926) - Dux
(1930) - Marisetta (1948) - Valeria (1956)*
CURRENT LOCATION: *Fiumicino (Italy)*
CONDITION: *very good, altered to yawl righ*
FURTHER DETAILS AND HISTORY: Built according the First Int. Rule
Owners and history:
1913 - 1915 Carl D. Danielsson; name: *Sibyllan;* home port: Stockholm.
She entered the 1914 Europe Week at Oslo together with *Symra* (winner),
Erna Signe and *Ierne*
1916 - 1918 ?
1919 - 1922 Chr. Christophersen; new name: *Sirocco;* home port:
Christiania (Oslo)
1923 P. and G. Benson in Lloyd's Register as "formerly Int. Metric Class 12 M"
1924 Camper & Nicholsons Ltd; home port: London; the yacht was for sale
1924 - 1927 Andrea Ossoinack; new name: *Scirocco;* home port: Rijeka
1928 - 1946 Compagnia della Vela; new name: *Dux;* home port: Venezia.
In 1947 new name: *Scirocco.* In July 1928, she entered the Trieste Sailing
Week and won three firsts. Cruises: in 1929 to Barcelona, in 1930 to
Istanbul and in 1933 to Tripoli
1947 - 1955 Francesco Boratto; new name: *Marisetta;* rig altered to
bermudan ketch in 1949; engine installed in 1951
1956 Disappeared from Lloyd's Register
1956 - 1969 Torquato Gennari; new name: *Valeria;* important refit work
with the deckhouse raised
1970 - 1975 Antonio Malipiero, publisher in Bologna (the date of
purchase is doubtful); new name: *Desiree*
1976 - 1984 Antonio, Maurizio and Raffaele Malipiero and then, at
Antonio's death, Maurizio and Raffaele
1984 - 1989 Leonardo Bagni; complete refit at Fratelli Carlini yard; the
yacht was chartered
1990 - 1997 Dr. Romano Calì; home port: Fiumicino
since 1998 Giuseppe Rinaldi; complete refit during 1997 - 1999 at the
Delta yard in Fiumicino. The refit did not conform to the original Twelve
Metre plans but maintains the many changes of the past alterations. The
rig is bermudan ketch and the big doghouse is kept

■ ERNA SIGNE

DESIGNER: *William Fife III; design no. 594*
BUILDER: *Stockholms, Båtbygyeri Aktiebolag (Plym)*
YEAR: *1911 June*
LENGTH OVERALL: *18.90 m.*
LENGTH AT WATERLINE: *11.94 m.*
BEAM: *3.43 m.*
DISPLACEMENT: *28 tons*
SAIL AREA: *166 sq.m. (1948)*
CONSTRUCTION: *wood on steel frames*
FIRST OWNER: *Nils Persson*
FIRST NAME: *Erna Signe*
FIRST COUNTRY: *Sweden*
HOME PORT: *Stockholm*

FIRST SAIL NUMBER: *E8*
OTHER NAMES: *Vogue (1919); Marjorie (1915?)*
CURRENT LOCATION: *Oslo (Norway)*
CONDITION: *refit completed in 2000*
FURTHER DETAILS AND HISTORY: Built according to the First Int. Rule
Owners and history:
1911 - 1915 Nils Persson; name: *Erna Signe*; home port: Stockholm; she
was built to represent Sweden. In the 1912 Stockholm Olympic Games
where she took the silver medal with *Magda IX* winning the gold one.
Later she got her revenge winning Kiel Week that year against *Magda IX*.
She entered in the 1914 Europe Week at Oslo with the other Twelves:
Symra (winner), *Sibyllan* and *Ierne*
1916 - 1918 Name *Marjorie* ?
1919 Dr. G. Jebsen; new name: *Vogue;* home port: Christiania (Oslo)
1920 Sam Bull; new name: *Erna Signe*
1921 - 1953 Ole Schröder, of the famous Norwegian shipping family. She
entered the 1933 Hanko KNS Jubilee regatta where she won the first race.
Gustav Eslander designs are available with alteration of the original interior
and deck layout
1954 - 1997 Disappeared from Lloyd's Register. The new owner left her
to deteriorate with the original interior ripped out
1998 Ole Chr. Schröder; name: *Erna Signe;* home port: Oslo.
The son of the original Schröder owner was made aware that *Erna Signe*
was for sale and bought her back to the family. An extended refit was
done in 2000 by the Walsted yard. The quality is the best, the style has
been respected but not kept to the original design. The rig was changed
to bermudan, the deck is new and on the old, there is an extensive use of
self-tailing steel winches. The interior is completely reshaped

■ HEATHERBELL

DESIGNER: *Thomas C. Glen-Coats*
BUILDER: *Alexander Robertson & Son - no. 51*
YEAR: *1907 July*
LENGTH OVERALL: *18.60 m.*
LENGTH AT WATERLINE: *12.15 m.*
BEAM: *3.45 m.*
SAIL AREA: *231.56 sq.m. (1920)*
CONSTRUCTION: *wood*
FIRST OWNER: *Andrew Coats*
FIRST NAME: *Heatherbell*
FIRST COUNTRY: *Great Britain*
HOME PORT: *Glasgow*
OTHER NAMES: *Teresita (?) - Margit IV (1920) - Yolande (1926) - Sylva (1927)*
CONDITION: *broken up?*
FURTHER DETAILS AND HISTORY: Built according to the First Int. Rule
Owners and history:
1907 - 1908 Major Andrew Coats (uncle of the designer); name:
Heatherbell; home port: Glasgow. She competed without success in the
English trials for the 1908 Olympic games.
1909 - 1915 Ernst Krogius, yacht club deputy commodore; home port:
Helsingfors (Finland), according to Lloyd's Register the yacht was also
named *Teresita*
1916 - 1918 ?
1920 - 1923 Niels M. Magnussen; new name: *Margit IV*; home port:

Christiania. Since 1920 in Lloyd's Register as "formerly Int. Rating Class 12 M"
1924 C. E. Nicholson; home port: Portsmouth
1925 - 1926 P. C. Mérillon; from 1926 new name: *Yolande;* from 1926
home port: Cannes. In 1925 she was altered to auxiliary bermudan cutter
and an engine was installed
1926 - 1949 Comte Jean de Polignac; new name: *Sylva;* home port:
Antibes; rigging altered to yawl; re-engined in 1936
1950 - 1953 Comte Guy de Boisrouvray; home port: Antibes and Golfe Juan
1954 - 1960 André e Georges Auniac
1961 - 1963 André Comette
1964 Disappeared from Lloyd's Register

■ HERA

DESIGNER: *Thomas C. Glen-Coats*
BUILDER: *R. McAlister & Son (Dumbarton)*
YEAR: *1908 May*
LENGTH OVERALL: *15.95 m.*
LENGTH AT WATERLINE: *12.04 m.*
BEAM: *3.35 m.*
DISPLACEMENT: *26 tons*
SAIL AREA: *198.50 sq.m.*
CONSTRUCTION: *wood on steel frames*
FIRST OWNER: *Thomas C. Glen-Coats*
FIRST NAME: *Hera*
FIRST COUNTRY: *Great Britain*
HOME PORT: *Glasgow*
CONDITION: *broken up ?*
FURTHER DETAILS AND HISTORY: Built according to First Int. Rule
Owners and history:
1908 - 1909 Thomas C. Glen-Coats; name: *Hera*; home port: Glasgow; rig:
gaff cutter. She was one of the three Twelves built by McAllister in 1908 (the
other two being *Mouchette* and *Nargie*). She was described as being 26
tons. Between May and July she got three Y.R.A. rating certificates with a
different one from the others for the sail area and a slight reduction in the
freeboard. She competed at the British trials of the 1908 Olympic Games
and she was chosen with *Mouchette* because they held their positions at the
head of the class. *Hera* having ten firsts and *Mouchette* eight. Only these
two 12 M participated (*Hera* with a Scots crew while the crew of *Mouchette*
were from Liverpool); on board *Hera* was Alfred Mylne while T. C. Glen-
Coats was at the tiller). Having an amateur crew on board the two Twelves
kept the interest alive after the first announcement of Olympic racing on the
Clyde was made. The absence of foreign competition was noted with regret.
The 12 M Olympics were raced on a course of two laps of a 13 miles circuit
which, totalled 26 miles. *Hera* got ahead, with *Mouchette* pressing her hard,
and at the end of the first round *Hera* was only seconds in front. Both yachts
then had to make more than 30 short tacks on one leg within a few
minutes. *Hera* won and also won the second race by 62 seconds. Other
good results were achieved in the rest of the 1908 season and in 1909 out
of 34 entries she had 9 firsts, 5 seconds and 4 thirds
1910 - 1915 J. H. Gubbins. In the 1910 season out of 36 entries she won
5 firsts, 5 seconds and 3 thirds. In 1911 out of 23 entries she had 4 firsts,
5 seconds and 1 third. In 1912 she had 19 starts with 3 firsts and 4
seconds. She twice had problems with the mast and gave up the season
after the Royal Victoria Regatta

1916 - 1918 ?

1919 - 1920 Captain P. Clemmatsen; home port: Arendal

1923 - 1924 Nils Brecke; home port: Christiania (Oslo)

1925 Major H.G. Maitland Kersey; home port: London. From 1925 she was registered as "formerly Int. Rating Class 12 Metre"

1926 - 1930 Major H. F. Courage. In 1926 the rig was altered to bermudan cutter

1931 - 1933 George T. Millward

1934 - 1937 Peter Pitt-Millward; home port: London and Capri

1938 Mrs. Odette Langlet; home port: Valenciennes (France)

1939 - 1949 H. Bagnardi; home port: Buenos Aires

1950 Disappeared from Lloyd's Register

■ HETI

DESIGNER: Max Oertz

BUILDER: Max Oertz Yachtwerft

YEAR: 1912

LENGTH OVERALL: 18.63 m.

LENGTH AT WATERLINE: 11.50 m.

BEAM: 3.48 m.

DRAFT: 2.25 m.

SAIL AREA: 263 sq.m.; 134 sq.m. (1930)

CONSTRUCTION: wood on steel and wooden frames

FIRST OWNER: H. Eschenburg

FIRST NAME: Heti

FIRST COUNTRY: Germany

HOME PORT: Travemiinde

FIRST SAIL NUMBER: E 3

OTHER NAMES: Heti (1912) - Traum (1923) - Nathurn (1942); Seeschwalbe (1960) - Moby Dick (1966) - Saturn (1968) - Romeo (1978)

CURRENT LOCATION: Hamburg (Germany)

CONDITION: refit to be started

FURTHER DETAILS AND HISTORY: Built according to First Int. Rule Owners and history:

1912 - 1919 Hermann Eschenburg; name: Heti; home port: Travemunde. She was the first Twelve built by M. Oertz for a German customer. She entered Kiel Week racing against Ierne, Magda IX, Skeaf V and Davo III, winning one of the races. After the Great War she was sold to Berlin, where she sailed in inshore waters only. Due to the Treaty of Versailles, Germany had to deliver all the seagoing yachts to the allied Forces. In order to avoid expropriation, Eschenburg changed the yacht status to an "inshore craft"

1919 - 1922 In 1919 she was altered to a yawl

1923 - 1945 Dr. Max Haners, a coal industrialist and yachtsman, new name Traum; home port: Berlin. Kiel (1930s). From 1928 registered in Lloyd's Register as "cutter & yawl". In 1936 won the Helgoland races. In 1936 she was altered in the Abeking & Rasmussen yard to gaff yawl. During the war the news was confused: according to Haners daughter, Anita von Hochstetter, Traum was hauled up the River Weser. Then, due to the death of her father in 1945, she was confiscated by the allied troops; then she was used as a house boat

1945 - 1949 Heinz Harmssen; new name: Nathurn; home port: Bremen

1950 - 1959 ?

1960 - 1965 Yachtschule Glucksburg; new name: Seeschwalbe; home port: Glucksburg

1966 - August 1968 Karsten Schape; new name: Moby Dick; home port: Flensburg

1967 - September 1977 Peter Himsted and Karl W. Massberg; new name: Saturn. At the Jurgen Heuer yard a general refit was carried out and a new engine installed, the bow section was changed and a new ballast keel added, GRP sheathing; rigged as a very high-masted bermudan cutter. She won the Blue Riband River Elbe races three times

1978 - 1998 Friederich Goebel; new name: Romeo; home port: Imperia (Italy); rigging and interior layout altered. She entered the Mediterranean regattas for vintage yachts. During the 1998 Imperia Festival she had a collision with another Oertz yacht, Aello, just before the start and was dismasted. Due to this accident, Romeo was donated to an unemployment scheme in Hamburg for the education of young craftsmen

Since 1999 Jugend in Arbeit Hamburg e. V; new name: Heti; home port: Hamburg. The programme is to refit Heti according to the original design and rig. In March 2001 the programme is confirmed but has not yet started. Ownership is to be passed to the Hamburg Maritime Foundation in 2001

■ IERNE

DESIGNER: William Fife III; design no. 591

BUILDER: W. Fife & Son

YEAR: 1911 May

LENGTH OVERALL: 18.78 m.

LENGTH AT WATERLINE: 11.96 m.

BEAM: 3.37 m.

DRAFT: 2.31 m.

DISPLACEMENT: 20 tons

SAIL AREA: 248 sq.m; 140 sq.m. (1930)

CONSTRUCTION: wood on steel frames

FIRST OWNER: A. F. Sharman-Crawford

FIRST NAME: Ierne

FIRST COUNTRY: Great Britain

HOME PORT: Glasgow

FIRST SAIL NUMBER: N 5 when in Norway

OTHER NAMES: Natascha (1951)

CURRENT LOCATION: unknown

CONDITION: unknown

FURTHER DETAILS AND HISTORY: Built according to First Int. Rule Owners and history:

1911 - 1912 A. F. Sharman-Crawford; name Ierne; home port: Glasgow. The owner, an Irish yachtsman friend of Sir Thomas Lipton, formerly owned Cyra, sold in 1911, and, once he had sold Ierne in 1914, had an 8m Ierne designed and built by Fife. She was a very fast and successful Twelve. In 1911 on 39 entries she had 13 firsts, 8 seconds and 4 thirds; in 1912 on 30 entries she won 25 times with 2 seconds; she went also racing in Germany sailing from the Clyde via Forth Canal to Cuxhaven in Germany; there she raced against Magda, Skeaf V, Heti and Davo III, on five races she won four times. Together with Alachie, Cintra, Javotte and Rollo in 1911 she took part in the first Europe week in Cowes with a fourth and third placing (in the second race she lost five minutes to help Alachie)

1913 Prof. E. Estlander; home port: Helsingfors

1914 - 1915 Gustaf A. Eslander. She enters at Europe Week 1914 in Norway

1916 - 1918 ?

1919 P.O. Serck; home port: Birmingham and Petrograd

1920 Chas. W. Scappel; home port: Christiania (Oslo)

Since 1920 Registered in the Lloyd's Register as "formerly Int. Rating Class 12 Metres"

1921 - 1928 Olaf Brown; from1924 new name: *Ierne*

1929 - 1936 Willy Wilhelmsen; from 1930 rig altered to bermudan cutter with a sail area of 140 sq. m. She enters at the Jubilee regatta in Hanko with 1 first, 1 second and 2 thirds

1937 Nils Astrup & Ths. Stang

1938 - 1946 ?

1947 - 1950 Ths. Stang; home port: Oslo

1951 - 1957 Egil K. Sundbye; new name *Natascha*; home port: Oslo. According to KNS informations and sail list, the owner between 1954 and 1955 was Melby Fadum and the name *Ierne*

1958 Disappeared from Lloyd's Register

■ IVANOHE

DESIGNER: *G.A. Heal*

BUILDER: *Summers & Payne (Southampton)*

YEAR: *1910 May*

LENGTH OVERALL: *15.24 m.*

LENGTH AT WATERLINE: *12.13 m.*

BEAM: *3.35 m.*

SAIL AREA: *248 sq.m.*

FIRST OWNER: *Alexander Treuberg*

FIRST NAME: *Ivanhoe*

FIRST COUNTRY: *Russia*

HOME PORT: *Petrograd*

CONDITION: *broken up?*

FURTHER DETAILS AND HISTORY: Built according the First Int. Rule Owners and history:

1910 - 1919 Alexander Treuberg; name: *Ivanohe*; home port: Petrograd

Since 1920 Registered in Lloyd's Register as "formerly Int. Rating Class 12 Metres"

1920 ?

1921 - 1923 E. Lorch; home port: Helsingfors

1924 - 1930 J. Dalitz; home port: Riga

1931 Disappeared from Lloyd's Register

■ JAVOTTE

DESIGNER: *Alfred Mylne*

BUILDER: *R. McAlister & Son (Dumbarton)*

YEAR: *1909 April*

LENGTH OVERALL: *18.29 m.*

LENGTH AT WATERLINE: *12.13 m.*

BEAM: *3.38 m.*

SAIL AREA: *245.32 sq.m. (1923)*

CONSTRUCTION: *wood on steel frames*

FIRST OWNER: *Charles MacIver*

FIRST NAME: *Javotte*

FIRST COUNTRY: *Great Britain*

HOME PORT: *Glasgow*

FIRST SAIL NUMBER: *E 5, then in Sweden S 1 (Beduin II)*

OTHER NAMES: *Betty II (1919) - Baccarat (1920) - Javotte (1921) - Beduin II (1922)*

CONDITION: *broken up?*

FURTHER DETAILS AND HISTORY: Built according to the First Int. Rule Owners and history:

1909 - 1913 Charles McIver; name: *Javotte*; home port: Glasgow. Mr. MacIver was the former owner of *Mouchette* and in 1912 took charge of the 15 M *Norada* and sold *Javotte* in France. In the 1909 season *Javotte* was second (*Cintra* first) and out of 33 entries, she had 6 firsts, 11 seconds and 11 thirds. In 1910 she was second again with 47 entries, 12 firsts, 13 seconds and 4 thirds; in 1911 she was third and out of 42 entries, she had 8 firsts, 6 seconds and 3 thirds. She took part in the first Europe Week in 1911 in Cowes together with *Alachie, Cintra, Ierne* and *Rollo.* She had a second and a fourth placing. "Mr. McIver set his teeth in a long cigar, and he had Mylne with him in the cockpit; but neither *Javotte, Alachie,* nor *Ierne* could hold the Norseman (Anker and *Rollo),* with her black hull and red-jerseyed crew." (*Yachting Monthly*, Sept. 1911)

1914 - 1915 Gaston Thubé; home port: Brest. Thubé brothers from Nantes were the 1912 Olympic Games champions in the Six Metre class. In 1913 *Javotte* entered the Le Havre races. Due to the World War it seems that she was sold immediately afterwards

1918 - 1919 Jac. M. H. Lindvig; new name: *Betty II*; home port: Christiania (Oslo)

1920 J. A. Jespersen; new name: *Baccarat;* home port: Tonsberg

Since 1920 registered in Lloyd's Register as "formerly Int. Rating Class 12 Metre", altered to bermudan cutter

1921 Moritz Daumund; new name: *Javotte;* home port: Christiania (Oslo).

1922 - 1950 Oscar Botolfsen; new name: *Beduin II*; home port: Stockholm. In 1938 was altered to yawl.

1951 disappeared from Lloyd's Register

■ LE

DESIGNER: *Christian Jensen*

BUILDER: *Jorgensen & Vik*

YEAR: *1919*

LENGTH OVERALL: *14.65 m.*

LENGTH AT WATERLINE: *12.05 m.*

BEAM: *3.65 m.*

DRAFT: *2.64 m.*

DISPLACEMENT: *24 tons*

CONSTRUCTION: *wood*

FIRST OWNER: *Christensen*

FIRST NAME: *Le*

FIRST COUNTRY: *Norway*

HOME PORT: *Sandefjord*

CURRENT LOCATION: *Norway*

CONDITION: *not at her best, sailing*

FURTHER DETAILS AND HISTORY: Built according to the First int. Rule Owners and history:

1919 - ? Christensen (ship owner); name: *Le;* home port: Sandefjord

Since 1961 Karl H. Hoje. Around 1981 extensive work was done and a big doghouse constructed

■ MAGDA IX

DESIGNER: *Anker & Jensen*
BUILDER: *Anker & Jensen*
YEAR: *1912*
LENGTH OVERALL: *14.78 m.*
LENGTH AT WATERLINE: *11.96 m.*
BEAM: *3.38 m.*
SAIL AREA: *267 sq.m.; 263 sq.m. (1920); 191 sq.m. (1951)*
CONSTRUCTION: *wood on steel frames*
FIRST OWNER: *Alfred W. G. Larsen*
FIRST NAME: *Magda IX*
FIRST COUNTRY: *Norway*
HOME PORT: *Christiania (Oslo)*
OTHER NAMES: *Moyana II (1920) - Liss V (1928) - Moyana (1935) - Moyana II (1951)*
CONDITION: *shipwrecked off the Swedish coast*
FURTHER DETAILS AND HISTORY: Built according to First Int. Rule
Owners and history:
1912 - 1915 Alfred W. G. Larsen; name: *Magda IX;* home port: Christiania (Oslo); *Magda* was Larsen's wife. He was one of the most outstanding Norwegian owners and sailors. He used to have his boats designed by Fife but due to the results of *Rollo* in the 1911 season, he decided to desert Fife and asked Anker to design his Olympic boat. The choice was a winning one as *Magda IX*, having Anker as "sailing master" on board, won the 1912 Stockholm Olympic Games. In the same year she lost against *Erna Signe* at Kiel Week
1916 - 1918 ?
1919 - 1926 Ludwig Wiese; new name: *Moyana II;* home port: Fredrikstad. In 1920 altered to bermudan cutter. Sail area reduced to 263 sq.m. Registered in Lloyd's Register from 1925 as "formerly Int. Rating Class 12 Metre"
1927 - 1933 J. Christensen; from 1928 new name: *Liss V;* home port: Drammen
1934 ?
1935 - 1947 Josef Larsen; new name: *Moyana;* home port: Fredrikstad.
1948 ?
1949 - 1953 Peder Larsen; new name: *Moyana II;* home port: Fredrikstad
1954 disappeared from Lloyd's Register. Shiprecked off the Swedish coast in the summer of 1951

■ MAGNOLIA

DESIGNER: *W. Fife III - design no. 566*
BUILDER: *Anker & Jensen*
YEAR: *1909*
LENGTH OVERALL: *18.80 m.*
LENGTH AT WATERLINE: *11.99 m.*
BEAM: *3.38 m.*
DISPLACEMENT: *26 tons*
SAIL AREA: *249 sq.m. (1923); 151 sq.m. (1947); 161 sq.m. (1953)*
CONSTRUCTION: *wood*
FIRST OWNER: *Alfred W. G. Larsen*
FIRST NAME: *Magda VIII*
FIRST COUNTRY: *Norway*
HOME PORT: *Christiania (Oslo)*

FIRST SAIL NUMBER: *E 4*
OTHER NAMES: *Magda VIII (1909) - Magnolia (1912) - Lucie VIII (1947) - Magnolia (1953)*
CURRENT LOCATION: *Oslo*
CONDITION: *refit finished in 1999, relaunched May 1999*
FURTHER DETAILS AND HISTORY: Built according to the First Int. Rule
Owners and history:
1909 - 1911 Alfred W. G. Larsen; name: *Magda VIII;* home port: Christiania (Oslo). She was the first Larsen 12 Metre and performed well during the first two racing seasons. Larsen sold her when he decided to have a new Twelve designed and built for the 1912 Olympic Games. "The story goes (Nic Compton in *Classic Boat*, Nov. 2000) that while the plans were being delivered in the autumn of 1908, Fife heard that the yard was building another Twelve Metre (*Brand IV?*) to their own design. Anxious in case his plans were copied, Fife had them held back until the Anker & Jensen Twelve was completed"
1912 - 1915 Olaf Bronn; new name: *Magnolia;* home port: Christiania (Oslo)
1916 - 1918 ?
1919 - 1922 Hans M. Vik; home port: Tonsberg
1923 - 1924 Ole Larsen Jr.
1925 - 1936 E. Blikstad; home port: Oslo. In this period *Magnolia* was converted to a cruising yacht and in 1931 was fitted with a bermudan rig
1937 - 1938 Nielsen; home port: Sandefjord
1939 - 1950 C. B. Nielsen, new name: *Lucie VIII;* home port: Skien.
1951 - 1954 Kr. Gjöiberg; from 1954 new name: *Magnolia;* home port: Oslo; in 1953 altered to auxiliary bermudan cutter
1954 Edward Gjölberg
1955 - 1960 Kr. Gjölberg
1960 Disappeared from Lloyd's Register. The yacht was abandoned and she sank in 1970. At the beginning of the Seventies she was taken out of the water and was laid up for nearly a decade until the present owner found her in 1981
1967 - 1968 G.A. Sommerfeldt
1969 - 1974 Ragnar Birkeland (according to KNS); home port: Sarpsborg
1975 - 1976 Edward and Lars Chr. Dahl (according to KNS); home port: Nyren
Since 1982 Trygve Barlag; name: *Magnolia;* home port: Oslo. He bought her in 1982 for £800 not for the vessel itself but "for the boat covers, on principle, as the hull had no value". The refit was run by the owner over a period of 17 years and the relaunch took place in May 1999. The refit does not conform to the original design and *Magnolia* should be considered to be a replica more than the original Twelve. The rig is bermudan, the main cabin hatch is extended to grant more light and headroom in the interior. The planking is replaced by a double one which is cold moulded, the planking is formed by two layers of Norwegian pine followed by two 7mm layers of gaboon mahogany all bonded together with epoxy). The original deck ias overlaid with a layer of Meerbau pine, with mastic in between. The boom and winches are modern. The interior is completely rebuilt in style but not as original although respecting the layout. Her mast is *Iris*'s which was recovered before she was dismantled

■ MARILINE

DESIGNER: *William Fife III; design no. 639*
BUILDER: *Abeking & Rasmussen - no. 380*
YEAR: *1914*

LENGTH OVERALL: *19.90 m. (original); 16.85 m. (present)*
LENGTH AT WATERLINE: *11.80 m. (original); 11.50 m. (present)*
BEAM: *3.30 m.*
DISPLACEMENT: *20.85 tons*
SAIL AREA: *143 sq.m.*
CONSTRUCTION: *wood on steel frames*
FIRST OWNER: *Henry Horn*
FIRST NAME: *Skeaf*
FIRST COUNTRY: *Germany*
HOME PORT: *Scheswig*
OTHER NAMES: *Skeaf (1914) - Treudeutsch (1926)*
CURRENT LOCATION: *Lisbon (Portugal)*
CONDITION: *very bad, to be refitted*
FURTHER DETAILS AND HISTORY: Built according to First Int. Rule. The information collected, also from Lloyd's Register, on the existing *Mariline* says that she was the original *Skeaf*. There were no official documents to confirm this. Owners and history:

1914 - 1915 Consul Henry Horn; name: *Skeaf;* home port: Scheswig. The yacht took part in the 1914 Europe Week at Oslo. With H. Rasmussen at the tiller, she was awarded six prizes. She entered the Oslo-Marstrand race and during the prize giving ceremony notice was given of the outbreak of the first World War. *Skeaf* remained in Sweden and was sold to the Norwegian yachtsman Glad

1916 - 1924 Glad (?)

1925 R.C. Schmidt

1926 - 1928 R.C. Schmidt; new name: *Treudeutsch;* home port: Berlin. In 1928 altered to gaff yawl rig

1929 - 1988 Club Nautico de Portugal; new name: *Mariline;* home port: Lisbon. The yacht was bought to Germany in early 1928 by two important members of the Club Nautico de Portugal to act as a school yacht and remained in commission until the mid-Eighties when due to high costs and the need to operate with smaller and modern units the Lisbon Naval Association (the Club Nautico had closed their doors and all the belongings were bought by the LNA) had to sell her in 1988. During this period she entered every regatta and won trophies. Around 1942-44 the rig was altered to bermudan yawl

1989 - 2000 The yacht was sold to a shipbuilder at a very low price. He had the intention of restoring her but he left her after starting a very bad job. *Mariline* rested in the yard looking for an owner and a refit

2000 Alberto Alfonso. A restoration programme should start in a few months

■ MORNA

DESIGNER: *William Fife III*
BUILDER: *Morrison and Sinclair, Sydney*
YEAR: *1913*
LENGTH OVERALL: *19.81 m.*
LENGTH AT WATERLINE: *13.65 m.*
BEAM: *3.96 m.*
DRAFT: *2.65 m.*
DISPLACEMENT: *55.2 tons*
SAIL AREA: *272 sq.m.*
CONSTRUCTION: *wood*
FIRST OWNER: *Sir Alexander McCornick*
FIRST NAME: *Morna*

FIRST COUNTRY: *Australia*
HOME PORT: *Sydney*
OTHER NAMES: *Kurrewa IV (1954)*
CURRENT LOCATION: *Sydney*
CONDITION: *laid up but not maintained*
FURTHER DETAILS AND HISTORY: Although not rated as a Twelve, she was probably designed according to the First Int. Rule. Owners and history:

1913 - 1929 Sir Alexander MacCormick; name: *Morna;* home port Sydney; rig: auxiliary cutter. Her owner was a distinguished surgeon and she was named after one of his daughters, who later became Lady Anderson, wife of Sir Colin Anderson of the P&O Line. In this period she was used as a daysailer

1929 - 1930 J. March Hardie

1931 - 1935 Robert C. Packer, the newspaper editor

1936 Disappeared off Lloyd's Register

1936 - 1953 Sir Claude Plowman, a radio manufacturer, who raced her in the Sydney to Hobart race in 1946, 1947 and 1948.

1954 - 1977 F and J. Livingston; new name: *Kurrewa IV;* home port: Sydney. From 1954 until 1960 she entered in six Sydney to Hobart races and achieved the fastest time in four of the races. After that she retired from racing and was laid up and not maintained

1977 Till now unknown new owner, waiting for restoration

■ MOUCHETTE

DESIGNER: *Alfred Mylne*
BUILDER: *R. McAlister & Son (Dumbarton)*
YEAR: *1908 June*
LENGTH OVERALL: *15.54 m.*
LENGTH AT WATERLINE: *12.92 m.*
BEAM: *3.27 m.*
DISPLACEMENT: *25 tons*
CONSTRUCTION: *wood on steel frames*
FIRST OWNER: *Charles MacIver*
FIRST NAME: *Mouchette*
FIRST COUNTRY: *Great Britain*
HOME PORT: *Glasgow*
CURRENT LOCATION: *behind Tigre (Buenos Aires) Maritime Museum*
CONDITION: *wreck*
FURTHER DETAILS AND HISTORY: Built according to the First Int. Rule. Owners and history:

1908 - 1909 Charles MacIver; name: *Mouchette;* home port: Glasgow. Built in only six weeks, she was the lightest of the three Twelves built at McAlister (the others being *Hera* and *Nargie*). She won immediately at the Royal Western Club matches due to the absence of both *Alachie* and *Nargie*. Her keel was remodelled and rehung, the mast changed to a lighter one, the mainsail changed. She competed at the British trials of the 1908 Olympic Games and she was chosen with *Hera*. Only these two Twelves participated (*Hera* with a native Scots crew while the crew of *Mouchette* were from Liverpool). The fact that they had an amateur crew on board the two Twelves kept the interest alive after the first announcement of the Olympic racing on the Clyde was made. The absence of foreign competition was noted with regret. The 12 M Olympics were raced on a course of two laps of a 13 miles circuit which totalled 26 miles. *Hera* got ahead, with *Mouchette* pressing her hard, and at the end of the first round *Hera* was only seconds in front. Both yachts then had to make more than

30 short tacks on one leg within a few minutes. *Hera* won, also winning the second race by 62 seconds. Mr. MacIver, as helmsman of *Mouchette*, was awarded with the Olympic silver medal and as the owner with the commemorative Trophy; the Olympic silver medals were also awarded to J. G. Kenion as *Mouchette*'s foreman and to each member of the crew

1910 - 1915 Alberto de Bary (vice commodore of the Yacht Club Argentino); home port: Buenos Aires. *Mouchette* arrived in Argentina at the end of 1909 thanks to Celeste Fernandez Blanco

1916 - 1918 ?

1919 A. J. Séré e Juan J. Séré

1920 - 1921 Ch. Lilloe Fangen and Polaczek; home port: Buenos Aires

1921 - 1923 J. E. Wolden; registered in Lloyd's Register from 1923 as "formerly Int. Rating Class 12 Metre"

1924 - 1931 Haraldo Hauge

1932 - 1935 Carlos Hansen

1936 Disappeared from Lloyd's Register

1954 - 1975 Guillermo P. MacNally. Engine installed in 1954, re-engined in 1957. In 1955 her rig was altered to auxiliary yawl. According to information (German Frers Jr.) the yacht was still visible as a wreck behind the Tigre (Buenos Aires) Maritime Museum

■ NARGIE

DESIGNER: *Alfred Mylne, design no. 148*
BUILDER: *R. McAlister & Son (Dumbarton)*
YEAR: *1908 May*
LENGTH OVERALL: *18.05 m.*
LENGTH AT WATERLINE: *12.04 m.*
BEAM: *3.43 m.*
CONSTRUCTION: *wood on steel frames*
FIRST OWNER: *Jack Little*
FIRST NAME: *Nargie*
FIRST COUNTRY: *Great Britain*
HOME PORT: *Glasgow*
OTHER NAMES: *Malva (1914) - Arrow XVI (1952)*
CURRENT LOCATION: *unknown*
CONDITION: *broken up ?*
FURTHER DETAILS AND HISTORY: Built according to the First Int. Rule
Owners and history:

1908 - 1911 Jack Little; name: *Nargie* home port: Glasgow. She was the first Twelve designed by A. Mylne (design no. 148). The total cost of £1850 representing £1600 for the boat, and £250 for the sails. The fee for the design was 15 guineas. She had main frames of natural oak with two sub-frames between each 2 x 1 3/4 inches main frame, the latter being steam bent. Topside planking: 26 mm. mahogany with 25 mm. pitch pine from one foot below the waterline. The decks were 31 mm yellow pine. The floors were galvanised wrought iron, the sternpost and rudder oak. The keel timber was 19 mm American elm (Freer, Twelve-Metre Yacht). Of the three Twelves built by the McAlister yard in the same year, *Nargie* was the heaviest with a displacement of 27 tons. She competed without success at the English trials for the 1908 Olympic Games. She was not very successful in the regatta. In the 1910 racing season, she had a total of 28 entries and won 3 firsts, 3 seconds and 5 thirds

1912 - 1913 Richard G. Allan; new name: *Malva (1913)*

1914 - 1915 John A. Dunlop

1916 - 1918 ?

1918 - 1923 B. A. Butenschön; home port: Christiania (Oslo)

1924 - 1946 P. H. Matthiessen, in 1931 she disappeared from Lloyd's Register.

1947 - 1952 Sigurd Herlofson

1952 - 1959 A.B. Oweson; new name: *Arrow XVI*

■ RAAK

DESIGNER: *Bjarne Aas*
BUILDER: *Fevigs Batbyggeri (Fevig, Norway)*
YEAR: *1914*
LENGTH OVERALL: *14.17 m.*
LENGTH AT WATERLINE: *12 m.*
BEAM: *3.81 m.*
DRAFT: *2.30 m.*
SAIL AREA: *216 sq.m.; 185 sq.m. (1998)*
CONSTRUCTION: *wood*
FIRST OWNER: *Eilif Von Erpecom*
FIRST NAME: *Raak*
FIRST COUNTRY: *Norway*
HOME PORT: *Bergen*
FIRST SAIL NUMBER: *E 15*
OTHER NAMES: *Ullabrand IV (1921) - Raak (1925) - Vici (1952)*
CURRENT LOCATION: *Krakstad (Norway)*
CONDITION: *good, sailing, gaff rigged*
FURTHER DETAILS AND HISTORY: Built according to the First Int. Rule
Owners and history:

1914 - 1915 Eilif Von Erpecom; name: *Raak;* home port: Bergen. She is a double-ender

1916 - 1919 ?

1920 E. H. Werring; home port: Christiania (Oslo)

1921 - 1924 A. R. Balterszen, new name: *Ullabrand IV*

1925 - 1934 K. W. Johnsen; new name: *Raak*

1935 - 1938 Chr. R. Granoe; home port: Tjone naar Tonsberg

1939 - 1950 Victor Thorn; home port: Oslo

1951 Disappeared from Lloyd's Register

1952 - 1953 Th. Allum; new name: *Vici;* home port: Bryn

1998 Andersen Kjell N.; new name: *Raak;* painstaking restored by the owner a farmer and excellent carpenter. She sailed well in Europe Week 2000

■ RÁFAGA

DESIGNER: *Charles E. Nicholson*
BUILDER: *Camper & Nicholsons Ltd. - no. 180*
YEAR: *1908 January*
LENGTH OVERALL: *15.67 m.*
LENGTH AT WATERLINE: *11.94 m.*
BEAM: *3.45 m.*
SAIL AREA: *224.64 sq.m.*
CONSTRUCTION: *wood on steel frames*
FIRST OWNER: *Pablo Suárez*
FIRST NAME: *Ráfaga*
FIRST COUNTRY: *Argentina*
HOME PORT: *Buenos Aires*
CURRENT LOCATION: *not known*
CONDITION: *broken up wreck*

FURTHER DETAILS AND HISTORY: Built according to the First Int. Rule
Owners and history:

1908 - 1913 Pablo Suárez; name: *Ráfaga;* home port: Buenos Aires.
She was the only Twelve built for an Argentinian owner; *Alachie* and
Mouchette followed and formed an Argentinian Twelve Metre fleet. In
1908 the skipper was F. Stokes

1914 - 1915 Abel Ezeiza

1916 - 1918 ?

1919 Adolfo Williams (Yacht Club Argentino)

1920 - 1923 Dr. José Diego Gornall. Registered in Lloyd's Register from
1920 as "formerly Int. Rating Class 12 Metre".

1924 - 1928 Pedro Yriberry. A 1927 photo published in the
YCA yearbook shows *Ráfaga* racing with *Alachie,* both were
gaff rigged

1929 Disappeared from Lloyd's Register. According to German Frers
information *Ráfaga* was broken up in the late Nineties after having been
altered several times

■ ROLLO

DESIGNER: *Johan Anker*
BUILDER: *Anker & Jensen*
YEAR: *1911*
LENGTH OVERALL: *18.60 m.*
LENGTH AT WATERLINE: *11.99 m.*
BEAM: *3.38 m.*
SAIL AREA: *256 sq.m. (1927)*
CONSTRUCTION: *wood on steel frames*
FIRST OWNER: *Mads Wiel*
FIRST NAME: *Rollo*
FIRST COUNTRY: *Norway*
HOME PORT: *Fredrikshald*
OTHER NAMES: *Caprice (1929)*
CONDITION: *broken up*

FURTHER DETAILS AND HISTORY: Built according to the First Int. Rule
Owners and history:

1911 Mads Wiel; name: *Rollo;* home port: Fredrikshald. In 1911 she
attended Cowes Week winning out of 7 entries, 4 firsts and 1 third.
She also attended the first European Week at Cowes.

"In this class we had the one outstanding victory of the regatta,
Rollo. Mr. Anker's yacht of his own design and building is no slouch.
With a large body and more sail than the others, she is a fine type of
boat, and her designer sailed her with great ability. Mr MacIver set his
teeth in a long cigar, and he had Mylne with him in the cockpit; but
neither *Javotte, Alachie,* nor *Ierne* could hold the Norseman with her
black hull and red-jerseyed crew." (*Yachting Monthly* Sept. 1911).
At the celebration dinner, the President of the Royal Yacht Squadron
greeted Anker and his crew with: "Our Norwegian friends have built
their own boat, have sailed across the North Sea, manned by their
own crew. They arrived here safe and sound and they have now won
nearly all the first prizes in the races. That is what I call sport."

1912 - 1920 P. H. Mathiessen; home port: Christiania (Oslo)

1921 - 1922 Harald Pettersen

1923 - 1927 Ingar Dobloug; in 1927, new name: *Caprice.*

1927 - 1932 Wilhelm Mustad; home port: Oslo.

Registered in Lloyd's Register as "formerly Int. Rating Class
12 Metre"

1933 - 1936 Ludvig Lorentzen; she entered the KNS Jubilee regatta
in Hanko and had one third placing

1937 Magnus Konow

1938 - 1946 ?

1947 - 1952 Sigurd Skaugen

1953 Sold to be broken up. Disappeared from Lloyd's Register

■ SCHWANHILD

DESIGNER: *C. Scharstein*
BUILDER: *C. Scharstein (Kiel)*
YEAR: *1909*
LENGTH OVERALL: *17.07 m.*
LENGTH AT WATERLINE: *12.64 m.*
BEAM: *3.44 m.*
FIRST OWNER: *Dr. Hans Schreiner*
FIRST NAME: *Schwanhild*
FIRST COUNTRY: *Austria*
HOME PORT: *Pola*
CONDITION: *broken up*

FURTHER DETAILS AND HISTORY: Built according to the First Int. Rule
Owners and history:

1909 - 1914 Dr. Hans Schreiner; name: *Schwanhild;* home port: Pola. The
only Twelve built by the small yard of Scharstein.

1919 Disappeared off Lloyd's Register. She was said have been destroyed
during the First World War

■ SKEAF II

DESIGNER: *G. Barg*
BUILDER: *Actien Gesellschaft Neptun (Rostock)*
YEAR: *1908*
LENGTH OVERALL: *16.85 m.*
LENGTH AT WATERLINE: *11.48 m.*
BEAM: *3.51 m.*
DRAFT: *2,30 m.*
SAIL AREA: *186 sq.m. (main sail 107 sq.m.)*
FIRST OWNER: *H. Horn*
FIRST NAME: *Skeaf II*
FIRST COUNTRY: *Germany*
HOME PORT: *Schleswig*
OTHER NAMES: *Mary II (1910)*
CURRENT LOCATION: *unknown*
CONDITION: *broken up?*

FURTHER DETAILS AND HISTORY: Built according to the First Int. Rule
Owners and history:

1908 - 1909 Consul H. Horn; name: *Skeaf II;* home port: Schleswig.
Mr. Horn was an important wood importer and he was owner
of five Twelves. 1908 was a very good year for *Skeaf II* who won
several races including Kiel Week.
In 1909 she lost against *Davo II* and her owner decided to have a new
Twelve built, *Skeaf III*

1910 - 1931 A. Th. Laverge; name: *Mary II;* home port: Rotterdam.

1931 Disappeared from Lloyd's Register

■ SKEAF III

DESIGNER: *G. Barg*
BUILDER: *Actien Gessellschaft Neptun (Rostock)*
YEAR: *1909*
LENGTH OVERALL: *17.9 m.*
LENGTH AT WATERLINE: *12.80 m.*
BEAM: *3.48 m.*
SAIL AREA: *187.67 sq.m.; since 1922: 205.92 sq.m.*
CONSTRUCTION: *wood*
FIRST OWNER: *H. Horn*
FIRST NAME: *Skeaf III*
FIRST COUNTRY: *Germany*
HOME PORT: *Schleswig*
CURRENT LOCATION: *unknown*
CONDITION: *broken up?*
FURTHER DETAILS AND HISTORY: Built according to the First Int. Rule. Owners and history:
1909 - 1913 Consul Henry Horn; name: *Skeaf III*; home port: Schleswig. Mr. Horn was an important importer of wood and he was the owner of five Twelves, all of them named *Skeaf*
1914 - 1931 E. Lorch; name: *Skeaf III;* home port: Riga; from 1923: Helsingfors. Registered in Lloyd's Register from 1930 as "formerly Int. Rating Class 12 Metre".
1934 Disappeared off Lloyd's Register

■ SKEAF IV

DESIGNER: *G. Barg*
BUILDER: *Actien Gessellschaft Neptun (Rostok) - design no. 307*
YEAR: *1910*
LENGTH OVERALL: *18.7 m. (A. G. Neptun records)*
LENGTH AT WATERLINE: *12,99 m. (A. G. Neptun records)*
BEAM: *3,52 m. (A.G. Neptun records)*
DRAFT: *2,20 m. (A.G. Neptun records)*
SAIL AREA: *126.17 sq.m. (1937); 140.40 sq.m. (1947)*
CONSTRUCTION: *wood on steel frames*
FIRST OWNER: *Henry Horn*
FIRST NAME: *Skeaf IV*
FIRST COUNTRY: *Germany*
HOME PORT: *Schleswig*
FIRST SAIL NUMBER: *E 5 about 1928; RORC no. 463 since 1947*
OTHER NAMES: *Sterna (1914) - Freya (1919) - Copeja (1929) - Emmeline (1935) - Maid of Astolat (1947) - Cymbeline (1948) - Gift of the Wind (1966)*
CURRENT LOCATION: *unknown*
FURTHER DETAILS AND HISTORY: Built according to the First Int. Rule. Owners and history:
1910 - 1912 Consul Henry Horn; name: *Skeaf IV*; home port: Schleswig.
1913 - 1915 M.me Van de Poll; new name: *Sterna*; home port: Haarlem (NL)
1916 - 1918 ?
1919 - 1928 C. P. J. Stam Jr; new name: *Freya*; home port: Amsterdam; from 1921: Koog a/d Zan
1928 - 1933 Jan Jacob Van Rietschoten Jr; new name: *Copeja;* home port: Rotterdam
1934 ?
1935 - 1937 Flying Officer G.R. Canavan; new name: *Emmeline;* home port:

Southampton and Portsmouth. Rig altered before 1935 to bermudan cutter
1938 - 1946 Mrs. Elaine Hamer; new name: *Maid of Astolat;* home port: Southampton
1947 - 1954 Dr. J. P. Leckie; new name from 1948: *Cymbeline;* home port: Southampton. RORC rating 1951: 49"26
1955 - 1956 Heirs of the late Dr. Leckie
1957 - 1958 Raymond Richards; engine installed in 1957.
1959 - 1961 Colin A.G. Campbell; home port: Hamble
1962 - 1963 Belsize Boat Yard, Ltd.; home port: Southampton
1963 - 1964 Eric I. H. Ward; home port: Littlehampton; re-engined in 1964
1965 Michael C.G. Ward; sold to Germany
1966 - 1969 Tana Kaleya, Salzburg; new name: *Gift of the Wind.*
1969 - 1970 Tana Kaleya Coty & Co.
1970 - 1972 Tana Kaleya
After 1973 Unknown

■ SKEAF V

DESIGNER: *G. Barg*
BUILDER: *Actien Geselleschaft Neptun*
YEAR: *1912*
LENGTH OVERALL: *18.29 m.*
LENGTH AT WATERLINE: *11.99 m.*
BEAM: *3.35 m.*
DRAFT: *2.18 m.*
SAIL AREA: *131 sq.m. (1938)*
CONSTRUCTION: *wood on steel frames*
FIRST OWNER: *H. Horn*
FIRST NAME: *Skeaf V*
FIRST COUNTRY: *Germany*
HOME PORT: *Schleswig*
FIRST SAIL NUMBER: *RYA no. 20 (c1935) - RORC no. 186 (1951)*
OTHER NAMES: *Istar (1919)*
CURRENT LOCATION: *Langstone Harbour (UK) ?*
CONDITION: *houseboat ?*
FURTHER DETAILS AND HISTORY: Built according to the First Int. Rule Owners and history:
1912 - 1913 Consul Henry Horn; name: *Skeaf V*; home port: Schleswig.
1914 - 1916 Freiherr von Pohl; new name: *Istar;* home port: Hamburg.
1917 - 1922 Max L. Kruger
1923 - 1927 Col. F. H. Cleaver; home port: Colchester and Southampton. Registered in Lloyd's Register from 1923 as "formerly Int. Metric Class 12 Metre". In 1924 rig altered to bermudan cutter. In 1927 rig altered
1928 - 1930 A.R. Luke; home port: Southampton. In 1929 rig altered to bermudan yawl
1931 - 1932 Major Lawrence C. Coates; home port: Southampton. In 1931 altered to bermudan yawl
1933 - 1937 Major W. Bertram Bell; engine installed in 1933
1938 - 1948 Brig. O. L. Prior-Palmer. In 1938 altered to bermudan cutter with a sail area of 131 sq.m.; RORC rating: 50"79 RYA sail number no. 20.
1949 - 1951 Lt.Col. B. C. G. Shore - RORC sail number no. 186
1952 disappeared from Lloyd's Register
1961 - 1964 Martin Brent; home port: Fawley; re-engined before 1961. It was said that she was converted to a houseboat, lying in Langstone Harbour (UK) under the name of *Lofty*

■ SKUM III

DESIGNER: *Charles E. Nicholson - design no. 219*
BUILDER: *J. M. Iversen (Soon, Norway)*
YEAR: *1914*
LENGTH OVERALL: *16.30 m.*
LENGTH AT WATERLINE: *11.58 m.*
BEAM: *3.10 m.*
FIRST OWNER: *Dr. Johan Friele*
FIRST NAME: *Skum III*
FIRST COUNTRY: *Norway*
HOME PORT: *Bergen*
FIRST SAIL NUMBER:
OTHER NAMES: *Alexandra III (1919) - Syrin (1920)*
CURRENT LOCATION: *unknown*
FURTHER DETAILS AND HISTORY: Built according to the First Int. Rule
Owners and history:
1914 - 1915 Dr. Johan Friele (medical surgeon); name: *Skum III*; home port: Bergen
1916 - 1918 ?
1919 Jacob Prebensen; new name: *Alexandra III*; home port: Risør
1920 C. Bjornstadt; new name: *Syrin;* home port: Christiania (Oslo)
1921 G. Simonsen; home port: Oslo and Copenhagen
1922 C. Bjornstadt; home port: Oslo.
1923 - 1930 G. Simonsen; home port: Oslo and Copenhagen. Registered in Lloyd's Register from 1923 as "formerly Int. Rule Class 12 Metre"
1931 Disappeared from Lloyd's Register

■ STORM

DESIGNER: *Anker & Jensen*
BUILDER: *Anker & Jensen*
YEAR: *1913*
LENGTH OVERALL: *15 m.*
LENGTH AT WATERLINE: *12.98 m.*
BEAM: *4.50 m.*
SAIL AREA: *233 sq.m. (1914)*
CONSTRUCTION: *wood*
FIRST OWNER: *Ole Larsen Jr.*
FIRST NAME: *Storm*
FIRST COUNTRY: *Norway*
HOME PORT: *Christiania (Oslo)*
FIRST SAIL NUMBER: *E 31*
CURRENT LOCATION: *Oslo (Norway)*
CONDITION: *sailing*
FURTHER DETAILS AND HISTORY: Built according to the First International Rule
Owners and history:
1914 - ?? Ole Larsen Jr.; name: *Storm*; home port: Christiania (Oslo)
1919 - 1924 Johan K. Haaland; home port: Hangesund
1925 - 1934 A. B. Grondhal; home port: Oslo
1935 - 1957 Anders Jambe; home port: Sandefjord; auxiliary 5 cyl. petrol engine installed. New engine in 1951
1958 Disappeared off Lloyd's Register

■ SYMRA

DESIGNER: *Anker & Jensen*
BUILDER: *Anker & Jensen - no. 148*
YEAR: *1914*
LENGTH OVERALL: *19.38 m.*
LENGTH AT WATERLINE: *11.99 m.*
BEAM: *3.24 m.*
SAIL AREA: *267 sq.m. (1920); 173 sq.m. (1953)*
CONSTRUCTION: *wood*
FIRST OWNER: *Axel Isdahl*
FIRST NAME: *Symra*
FIRST COUNTRY: *Norway*
HOME PORT: *Bergen*
FIRST SAIL NUMBER: *N 2*
CONDITION: *broken up*
FURTHER DETAILS AND HISTORY: Built according the First Int. Rule
Owners and history:
1914 - 1949 Axel Isdahl; name: *Symra*; home port: Bergen. She was said to be the first Twelve Metre in the world to sail with a bermudan rig. Winner of her class at Europe Week in 1914 with Anker on board. She took part in 1933 in KNS Jubilee regatta. Registered in Lloyd's Register from 1936 as "formerly Int. Rating Class 12 Metre"
1950 - 1973 Øivind Lorentzen; home port: Oslo; engine installed in 1952. Broken up by the owner who did not wish to restore her. A 1974 photo shows *Symra* abandoned on a shore in Vollen (Norway)

■ TITANIA

DESIGNER: *Johan Anker*
BUILDER: *Anker & Jensen*
YEAR: *1910*
LENGTH AT WATERLINE: *11.96 m.*
BEAM: *3.48 m.*
CONSTRUCTION: *wood*
FIRST OWNER: *Rolf Nobel*
FIRST NAME: *Titania*
FIRST COUNTRY: *Russia*
HOME PORT: *Petrograd*
CONDITION: *broken up?*
FURTHER DETAILS AND HISTORY: Built according to the First Int. Rule
Owners and history:
1910 - 1919 Rolf Nobel; name: *Titania;* home port: Petrograd
1920 disappeared from Lloyd's Register

■ ULL II

DESIGNER: *Bjorne Aas*
BUILDER: *Damsgaard Båtbiggeri - Damsgaard*
YEAR: *1914*
LENGTH AT WATERLINE: *11.98 m.*
BEAM: *3.81 m.*
SAIL AREA: *216 sq.m.*
CONSTRUCTION: *wood*
FIRST OWNER: *L. P. Johannesen*
FIRST NAME: *Ull II*
FIRST COUNTRY: *Norway*

HOME PORT: *Bergen*
CURRENT LOCATION: *unknown*
CONDITION: *broken up?*
FURTHER DETAILS AND HISTORY: Built according to the First Int. Rule
Owners and history:
1914 - 1915 L. B. Johannesen; name: *Ull II*; home port: Bergen. Double ender and sister ship to *Raak*
1916 - 1918 ?
1919 - 1934 O. Grolle Olsen. Registered in Lloyd's Register from 1928 as "formerly Int. Rating Class 12 Metre"
1935 Disappeared from Lloyd's Register

■ VARUNA

DESIGNER: *A. Richardson*
BUILDER: *Philip & Son Ltd. (Dartmouth)*
YEAR: *1909 July*
LENGTH OVERALL: *18.02 m.*
LENGTH AT WATERLINE: *12.80 m.*
BEAM: *3.48 m.*
DRAFT: *2.28 m.*
SAIL AREA: *189-198 sq.m. (1914); 127 sq.m. (1938)*
CONSTRUCTION: *wood*
FIRST OWNER: *Harter K. Glazebrook*
FIRST NAME: *White Heather*
FIRST COUNTRY: *Great Britain*
HOME PORT: *Dartmouth*
OTHER NAMES: *White Heather (1909)*
CURRENT LOCATION: *Imperia (Italy)*
CONDITION: *under refit at Cantieri di Imperia*
FURTHER DETAILS AND HISTORY: Built according to the First Int. Rule
Owners and history:
1909 - 1928 Harter Kirkland Glazebrook; shipbroker of Liverpool; name: *White Heather*; home port: Dartmouth. Built according to the 12 M Int. Rule but as an auxiliary yacht more than as a racing one - as shown by her lines and her large doghouse. She was said to be a half-scale replica of *Britannia* and she was always known in Cowes as "*Little Britannia*". Constructed with oak main frames and rack elm intermediate frames; beams, deck and planking of teak. In 1914 her sail area was increased from 189.63 sq.m to 198.50 sq.m. Registered in Lloyd's Register from 1914 as "formerly Int. Rating Class 12 Metre". Registered in Lloyd's Register from 1921 as auxiliary bermudan sloop
1928 - 1932 Major William Lidswell. Towers-Clark; new name: *Varuna II*; and the same year *Varuna*; home port: Dartmouth. It seems that in 1928 an engine was installed and the original tiller was changed to a wheel. Rig altered in 1930 to auxiliary bermudan sloop
1933 - 1934 Arthur Henry Ashcroft
1935 - 1946 Robert Charles Vernon, friend of the Towers-Clark. She was widely used for cruising on the West coast of Scotland. In 1936 the mast had twisting problems under pressure and a new one was made. During the war she was laid up on the Clyde at a different place from her gear, which was burnt by an incendiary bomb
1947 - 1953 Major M.S.B. Vernon, Robert Vernon's son; RORC rating: 41'57 feet

1954 - 1966 Col. John S. Ward and Col. Ferris B. St. George. They shared the yacht with Major Vernon, who was building his new boat *Varen*. Re-engined in 1958
1967 - 1977 Mr. and Mrs. G. Earle (Mrs. Earle being Ferris St. George's daughter). Re-engined in 1977; RORC rating: 37'06.
1978 Miss P. G. Richardson Hazard. After 40 years of ownership by the same three families who were all friends, *Varuna* changed owner
1979 - 1983 Neptun Reisen Co. Ltd; *Varuna* was chartered
1983 - 1999 Due to the bankrupcty of the owner, *Varuna* was left at Cantieri di Imperia.
Since 1999 Luigi Donna. *Varuna* is under refit at Cantieri di Imperia. Designer: Franco Giorgetti. The launch planned for 2002. The name *Varuna* will be kept

■ VINETA

DESIGNER: *Johan Anker*
BUILDER: *Anker & Jensen*
YEAR: *1910*
LENGTH OVERALL: *18.67 m.*
LENGTH AT WATERLINE: *11.99 m.*
BEAM: *3.48 m.*
SAIL AREA: *244 sq.m.; 166 sq.m. (1938)*
CONSTRUCTION: *wood*
FIRST OWNER: *Fritz Olsen*
FIRST NAME: *Figaro*
FIRST COUNTRY: *Norway*
HOME PORT: *Christiania (Oslo)*
FIRST SAIL NUMBER: *E 10*
OTHER NAMES: *Bonita (1920) - Vineta (1923)*
CURRENT LOCATION: *Montauban (Brittany, France)*
CONDITION: *wreck*
FURTHER DETAILS AND HISTORY: Built according to the First International Rule
Owners and history:
1910 - 1918 Fritz Olsen; name: *Figaro*; home port: Christiania (Oslo). She was the second *Figaro* built for the owner Olsen, the first one was built by Colin Archer
1919 Fritz and Rudolf Olsen (one of Fred Olsen four sons)
1920 - 1922 Rudolf Olsen; since 1921; new name: *Figaro II*
1922 O. Berresen; new name *Bonita*
1923 - 1935 S. Finne Thiis; new name: *Vineta*. She entered in the July 1933 Jubilee Regatta in Hanko (N), and won a first place in the third race
1936 - 1949 Frank Guillet (owner of the other 12 M *Le Cid*); home port: La Trinité sur Mer. In 1938 the rig was altered from gaff to bermudan. From 1939 to 1945 she was laid up on her cradle and dismasted at the Constantini yard. In 1946, she sailed again. She was sold on July 27
1950 - ?? G. De Surmont; home port: Paimpol. New engine installed in 1950. The yacht was laid up
? - 1953 Mr. and Mrs. Thomas. The yacht was dismantled and her mast broken up. The lead keel was sold
1954 Le Gunehec; in 1955 she disappeared from Lloyd's Register. Laid up as a wreck at Coêt-Castel; maintenance work was done to the hull to preserve it (caulking and treatment with linseed oil); she was transferred to Lézardieux and then to Montauban where she is now located

ANITRA

DESIGNER: *Burgess, Rigg & Morgan Lt.*
BUILDER: *Abeking & Rasmussen - no. 2366*
YEAR: *1928 May*
LENGTH OVERALL: *21.09 m.*
LENGTH AT WATERLINE: *13.03 m.*
BEAM: *3.87 m.*
DRAFT: *2.58 m.*
SAIL AREA: *183 sq.m.*
CONSTRUCTION: *wood on steel frames*
FIRST OWNER: *Charles L. Harding*
FIRST NAME: *Anitra*
FIRST COUNTRY: *United States*
HOME PORT: *Boston*
FIRST SAIL NUMBER: *US5*
CURRENT LOCATION: *Newport (R.I.)*
CONDITION: *restoration to begin in 2002*
PRESENT OWNER: *Yacht Anitra, LLC.*
COUNTRY: *U.S.A.*
FURTHER DETAILS AND HISTORY: Built according to the Second Int. Rule. She was one of the six Twelve Metres designed by Burgess for American owners and built by Abeking & Rasmussen
Owners and history:
1928 - 1942 Charles L. Harding; name: *Anitra;* home port: Boston; rig: bermudan sloop; engine installed in 1934. *Anitra* entered every year in the class races. The best year was 1931 when she was first in class with 3 firsts and 1 third out of 6 starts. In 1934, she was second to *Iris,* the only other competitor
1946 - 1951 Maurice O. Guerin; home port: Boston and Newport, RI; re-engined in 1946. In 1949 she won the King's Cup (New York Yacht Club)
1952 River Mills Corp.; re-engined in 1952
1952 - 1954 Max Meyer; home port: Boston and Tiverton, MA
1955 - 1956 Frank H. Walker; home port: North Weymouth, MA
1957 - 1959 George D Haskell; home port: Marblehead, MA. Rig converted in 1958 to auxiliary yawl. Sail area: 154 sq.m.
1960 - 1963 S. Davis Robins; home port: Oyster Bay, NY; re-engined 1963
1964 - 1965 Joseph S. Montgomery.
1966 - 1967 Baxter R. Still, Jr; home port: Miami, FL.
1968 - 1975 Robert S. Lint; repowered in 1968.
1976 Disappeared off records
1994 - 1995 Rob and Devon Anderson; homeport: Alameda, CA
1995 - 2001 Robert D. Manning; home port: Odessa, Texas
2001 April Yacht Anitra, LLC (McMillen Yachts Inc & Charles Parrish); home port: Newport, RI. Restoration of the yacht to begin in 2002

BARRANQUILLA

DESIGNER: *G. Eslander*
BUILDER: *Stockholm Båtbyggeri Aktiebolag*
YEAR: *1930*
LENGTH OVERALL: *21.95 m.*
LENGTH AT WATERLINE: *13.92 m.*
BEAM: *3.57 m.*
SAIL AREA: *183 sq.m.*
CONSTRUCTION: *wood on steel frames*

FIRST OWNER: *Erik Akerlund*
FIRST NAME: *Princess Svanevit*
FIRST COUNTRY: *Sweden*
HOME PORT: *Stockholm*
FIRST SAIL NUMBER: *S 2 - K 22*
OTHER NAMES: *Irene (1936) - Silvervingen X (1958)*
CURRENT LOCATION: *Hamble*
CONDITION: *beautiful condition*
COUNTRY: *Great Britain*
FURTHER DETAILS AND HISTORY: Built according to the Int. Second Rule. Owners and history
1930 - 1934 Erik Åkerlund; name: *Princess Svanevit;* home port: Stockholm. She was the only Twelve designed by Eslander and one of the last projects before his death, the winter following the launch. She was a heavy and long yacht, very well constructed so as not to cheat the Rule and "her profile and sections are far sweeter throughout than generally seen in yachts to the International Yachts Racing Classes ...; she was completed a few days before the Jubilee Races at Stockholm in 1930, where she came second from the top of a very keen class, for the hundredth birthday party of the Royal Swedish Yacht Club brought together yachts and yachtsmen from almost all over the world, which ensured high-class racing, for only keen and good helmsmen would bring their yachts from America, England and other European countries" (Uffa Fox). She went to Cowes Week in 1933 and "after a marvellous race, the Swedish yacht, cleverly steered by Mr Colin Newman, won by a few seconds beating *Flica* on the finishing line. It was the first visit of her owner Mr. Erik Åkerlund to the Cowes regatta and the victory of his yacht was most popular"
1935 - 1956 E. Lundstrôn; new name since 1936: *Irene;* home port: Malmo
1957 Heirs of the late E. Lundström
1957 - 1959 Nils Gäbel; new name: *Silvervingen X;* home port: Sältsjöbaden; engine installed in 1957
Since 1960 Harry J. Hyams; new name: *Barranquilla;* home port: London, Wiltshire and Southampton. Re-engined in 1961 and 1976. Sail number K 22, probably not officially issued by the YRA

CERIGO

DESIGNER: *W. & R.B. Fife - no.746*
BUILDER: *W. Fife & Son*
YEAR: *1926 August*
LENGTH OVERALL: *20.12 m.*
LENGTH AT WATERLINE: *13.10 m.*
BEAM: *3.70 m.*
DRAFT: *2.59 m.*
SAIL AREA: *143 sq.m.; 164 sq.m.(1965)*
CONSTRUCTION: *wood on steel frames, keel, stem and sternpost in teak*
FIRST OWNER: *Léon Becker*
FIRST NAME: *Cerigo*
FIRST COUNTRY: *Belgium*
HOME PORT: *Antwerp*
FIRST SAIL NUMBER: *K 12 - B 1*
CURRENT LOCATION: *unknown (Virgin Islands ?)*
CONDITION: *unknown*

FURTHER DETAILS AND HISTORY: Built according to the Second Int. Rule
Owners and history:
1926 - 1933 Léon Becker; name: *Cerigo;* home port: Antwerp; rig: bermudan cutter
1934 - 1936 Dr. T.H. Ward; home port: Dartmouth; engine installed in 1935
1937 - 1946 Robert A. O'Brien; rig altered and engine removed in 1946
1947 - 1948 Schalburg & Co.; altered to bermudan sloop
1948 - 1951 Ernst Schalburg
1951 - 1956 Dr. Andrew Tindal; home port: Glasgow and Dartmouth; she was said to be still sailing without an auxiliary engine.
She had to be towed through the Crinan Canal when making a passage to and from the West Coast. May Fife reports that she was frequently sailed by Professor Alexander Thom, a relative of the Tindals, an astronomer, best known for his study of megalithic stone circles. According to his theory, Stone Age people were able to use Pythagorean geometry, and they had devised a unit of measurement which he called 'the Megalithic Yard'. It seems that many of these observations were made when sailing round the islands of the west coast of Scotland. Once he sailed *Cerigo* from Brixham to the Clyde, taking seven days for the passage
1957 Mrs. Alex McGlashan; engine installed in 1957
1958 - 1960 Mr. & Mrs. Alex McGlashan
1961 - 1963 John Maitland; home port: Portsmouth and Dartmouth
1964 - 1970 Mme G. Le Saux Jouany & Julian Dame; home port: La Rochelle; since 1965: Pointe-à-Pitre (Virgin Islands)
1971 - 1972 Registered in Lloyd's Register but with no name given
1973 Disappeared from Lloyd's Register. Reported burned and sunk in Caribbean

■ CLYMENE

DESIGNER: *Charles E. Nicholson*
BUILDER: *Camper & Nicholsons Ltd. - no. 325*
YEAR: *1924 July*
LENGTH OVERALL: *20.47 m.*
LENGTH AT WATERLINE: *13.82 m.*
BEAM: *3.70 m.*
DRAFT: *2.57 m.*
SAIL AREA: *144 sq.m. (1947)*
CONSTRUCTION: *wood*
ENGINE: *petrol engine, 4 cyl. (1929)*
FIRST OWNER: *Philip de G. Benson*
FIRST NAME: *Clymene*
FIRST COUNTRY: *United Kingdom*
HOME PORT: *Portsmouth*
FIRST SAIL NUMBER: *K 10*
OTHER NAMES: *Moyana V (1936) - Alkor II (1948)*
CURRENT LOCATION: *Toulon, France*
CONDITION: *restoration in progress*
PRESENT OWNER: *Clymène Club Association*
FURTHER DETAILS AND HISTORY: Built according to the Second
International Rule
Owners and history:
1924 - 1931 Philip de G. Benson; name: *Clymene;* home port:

Portsmouth and London. In 1924 rig altered from cutter to bermudan sloop. Engine installed in 1928
1932 - 1935 Austin O'Connor; home port: Portsmouth
1936 Wilfred Leuchars; new name: *Moyana V.* Re-engined in 1936
1937 - 1939 Lt. Comdr. Percy T. Dean; new name: *Clymene.* Rig: in 1937, altered to yawl. 1939 Estate of Lt. Comdr. Percy T. Dean, sold to an unknown person in France
1939 - 1947 Marcel Bar; new name: *Alkor II*
1948 - 1950 Louis Canet
1951 - 1952 Georges Villiers
1953 Disappeared from Lloyd's Register
1953 - 1975 ?
1976 Franck Pizzato and Clymène Club Association.
After a period of chartering, *Clymene* was brought ashore at Toulon for a restoration to be completed around 2004. Government funds should cover part of the cost as *Clymene* has been declared a National Monument. *Clymene* has had quite a successful career both as a Twelve and when altered to bermudan cutter and yawl. In 1924 she entered Burnham Week and in other around the coast races. In 1928, altered to bermudan yawl, she beat the ocean racers *Dorade, Mistress, Neptune* and *Lexia.* She was also entered in several handicap races together with *Vanity*

■ CORSARA

DESIGNER: *Vincenzo Vittorio Baglietto*
BUILDER: *Cantieri Baglietto - no. 123*
YEAR: *1929 February 3rd*
LENGTH OVERALL: *21.47 m.*
LENGTH AT WATERLINE: *13.87 m.*
BEAM: *3.90 m.*
DRAFT: *2.62 m.*
DISPLACEMENT: *27 tons*
SAIL AREA: *173 sq.m.; 196 sq.m. (1930)*
CONSTRUCTION: *wood*
FIRST OWNER: *Marchése Franco Spinola*
FIRST NAME: *La Spina*
FIRST COUNTRY: *Italy*
HOME PORT: *Santa Margherita Ligure*
FIRST SAIL NUMBER: *I 1*
OTHER NAMES: *La Vespa (1948)*
CURRENT LOCATION: *Vilanueva i La Geltru (Barcelona, Spain)*
CONDITION: *ashore in a very bad condition*
FURTHER DETAILS AND HISTORY: Built according to the Second Int. Rule
Owners and history:
1929 - 1938 Marchése Franco Spinola; name: *La Spina*; home port: Santa Margherita Ligure; rig: bermudan sloop. The owner's interest was more in seafaring rather than racing and particular care was devoted to the boat's internal accommodation and fittings, with a view to her being used as a habitable cruiser as well as a racer. The accommodation comprised a handsome saloon, an owner's cabin, lavatory and bathroom. The joinery work of mahogany and maple was especially admirable. The crew space comprised a skipper's cabin and berths for four hands. Immediately after launching, the vessel sailed for Genoa, escorted by the 8 Ms *Bamba* and *Vega,* both entrants in the International regatta at Genoa and for the opening of the new head office of the Yacht Club Italiano. The location of

the Baglietto yard on an open beach required the boat to be launched completely equipped and fitted out for sea. One of the most interesting operations was the stepping of the mast. This was done by rigging a pair of shrouds on the roof of the building shed and hauling out the vessel into a suitable position beneath. In 1930 she was altered to a bermudan ketch and the sail area was increased to 196 sq.m., a 35 hp engine was installed, and the hull was sheathed with copper. This decision was taken by Marchése Spinola

1938 - 1956 Marchése Gian Augusto Salina Amorini; new name: *La Vespa*; home port: Santa Margherita Ligure and Venice. The bill of sale was dated April 19th, 1938 and the yacht was registered under no. 321 in the Santa Margherita Ligure Compamare Register; on March 10th, 1939 she was transferred to Compamare Venice with the new number 1098

1956 - 1975 Dr. Alessandro Brunetti; new name: *Corsara;* home port: Portofino. In 1959 disappeared off Lloyd's Register

Since 1976 Dr. Gian Franco Chierici; home port: Savona (transferred from Portofino, 1987). The bill of sale was dated 16th February 1976. *Corsara* was used for personal and charter cruising but for several years she has lain ashore in the south of Spain in a very poor condition

■ Doris

DESIGNER: *Charles E. Nicholson*
BUILDER: *Camper & Nicholsons, Ltd - no. 334*
YEAR: *1925 June*
LENGTH OVERALL: *16.30 m.*
LENGTH AT WATERLINE: *11.99 m.*
BEAM: *3.76 m.*
DRAFT: *2.57 m.*
CONSTRUCTION: *wood on steel frames*
FIRST OWNER: *Frederick Last*
FIRST NAME: *Doris*
FIRST COUNTRY: *United Kingdom*
HOME PORT: *Portsmouth*
FIRST SAIL NUMBER: *K 2 - F 1*
CURRENT LOCATION: *unknown*
CONDITION: *converted to houseboat*
FURTHER DETAILS AND HISTORY: Built according to the Second Int. Rule
Owners and history:
1925 Frederick Last; name: *Doris;* home port: Portsmouth; rig: cutter
1926 - 1928 T.O.M. Sopwith. Rig altered to bermudan cutter
1929 - 1934 Louis Bréguet; home port: Le Havre
1935 - 1949 H. A. Holdsworth; home port: Portsmouth and Southampton; engine installed in 1935
1950 Runnegar Estates Ltd.
1951 Disappeared from Lloyd's Register.
She was said to have been converted to a houseboat. There is little record on *Doris*. It seems that she was not a very successful boat and, although entering in several regattas, her results were only good from time by time. We found her classified under M. Louis Bréguet's ownership. In 1932 she entered in four races with no results; in 1933 she was in Norway for the KNS Jubilee Regatta, with no results and at the end of the same year she was second to last with 13 starts and 1 first

■ Emilia

DESIGNER: *Attilio Costaguta*
BUILDER: *Cantieri Costaguta (Genova Voltri)*
YEAR: *1930 September*
LENGTH OVERALL: *20.93 m.*
LENGTH AT WATERLINE: *14.56 m.*
BEAM: *3.83 m.*
DRAFT: *2.95 m.*
DISPLACEMENT: *28 tons*
SAIL AREA: *203.65 sq.m.*
CONSTRUCTION: *wood*
ENGINE: *Perkins M80T 90 hp*
FIRST OWNER: *Attilio Bruzzone*
FIRST NAME: *Emilia*
FIRST COUNTRY: *Italy*
HOME PORT: *Genoa*
FIRST SAIL NUMBER: *I 1*
CURRENT LOCATION: *St. Jean Cap Ferrat (France)*
CONDITION: *excellent*
COUNTRY: *Italy*
FURTHER DETAILS AND HISTORY: Built according to the Second Int. Rule
Owners and history:
1930 - 1940 Attilio Bruzzone; name: *Emilia;* home port: Genoa; rig: bermudan schooner; engine: Bolinden, 30 hp. Originally she was designed (1929) and built to the Twelve Metre Int. Rule and was the present of Senator Giovanni Agnelli to his son-in-law Carlo Nasi. Due to his unexpected departure to South America, the construction was delayed and she was sold before she was launched to Attilio Bruzzone, a wealthy member of the Royal Yacht Club Italiano. The original rig was altered to a bermudan schooner. The sail number (I 1), already attributed in 1929, was passed to the other Italian Twelve, *La Spina*. The launch took place on Sept. 16th, 1930; *Emilia*, was Bruzzone's wife. During the 1930s, *Emilia* was entered in several regattas held between Genoa and Cannes
1941 - 1975 E. Coppola, a wealthy and well known banker; home port: Genoa, Portofino and Cap Ferrat; *Emilia* stopped racing.
1975 - 1988 Giorgio Trani; home port: Venice
1988 - 1998 Adriana Sterzi; home port: La Spezia. In 1988 she was completely refitted at Beconcini Shipyard in La Spezia. The interior was completely altered to a modern style designed by the well known architect Pinto. She was relaunched on July 28th, 1990
Since 1998 Marco Riccardo Gastaldi; home port: Genoa

■ Figaro III

DESIGNER: *Johan Anker*
BUILDER: *Anker & Jensen*
YEAR: *1918*
LENGTH OVERALL: *19.90 m.*
LENGTH AT WATERLINE: *12.10 m.*
BEAM: *3.50 m.*
SAIL AREA: *215 sq.m.*
FIRST OWNER: *Fred Olsen*
FIRST NAME: *Figaro III*
FIRST COUNTRY: *Norway*
HOME PORT: *Christiania (Oslo)*

FIRST SAIL NUMBER: *N 1*
OTHER NAMES: *Elektra (1925) - Irina III (1926) - Marjana (?)*
CURRENT LOCATION: *unknown*
CONDITION: *broken up?*
FURTHER DETAILS AND HISTORY: Supposed to be built according to "S" Scandinavian Rule and then converted to the 12 M Second Int. Rule
Owners and history:
1918 - 1924 Fred Olsen; name: *Figaro III;* home port: Christiania (Oslo); rig: cutter
1925 Knut T. Strom; new name: *Elektra;* home port: Oslo; rig: altered in 1925 to bermudan sloop
1926 - 1931 Georg von Erpecom; new name: *Irina III;* home port: Bergen.
1931 Sold to an owner in Southern California, USA
1932 Disappeared off Lloyd's Register. According to KNS sail number list; new name: *Marjana*

■ FIGARO IV

DESIGNER: *Johan Anker*
BUILDER: *Anker & Jensen*
YEAR: *1924*
LENGTH OVERALL: *20.88 m.*
LENGTH AT WATERLINE: *12.98 m.*
BEAM: *3.73 m.*
DRAFT: *2.26 m.*
SAIL AREA: *201 sq.m.; 161 sq.m. (1950)*
CONSTRUCTION: *wood*
FIRST OWNER: *Thomas Olsen*
FIRST NAME: *Figaro IV*
FIRST COUNTRY: *Norway*
HOME PORT: *Oslo*
FIRST SAIL NUMBER: *N 6*
OTHER NAMES: *Arrow (1937) - Sylvana (1951) Solveig II (1953)*
CURRENT LOCATION: *unknown*
FURTHER DETAILS AND HISTORY: Built according to the Second International Rule
Owners and history:
1924 - 1936 Thomas Olsen; name: *Figaro IV;* home port: Oslo; rig: bermudan cutter. She was said to be the sister ship of *Noresca*.
In 1933 she entered the KNS Jubilee regatta in Hanko and won one first, two seconds and one third
1937 - 1948 A.B. Owesen; new name: *Arrow;* rig: bermudan sloop
1949 - 1950 ?; rig: converted to auxiliary yawl (1950)
1951 - 1952 Mrs. Elise Blich; new name: *Sylvana*
1953 - 1959 Börge G. Jorgensen; new name: *Solveig II;* home port: Copenhagen
1960 - 1963 Poul Cadovius; home port: Aarhus and Copenhagen
1964 Klaus Baess; home port: Aarhus (Denmark)
1965 Disappeared off Lloyd's Register

■ FLICA

DESIGNER: *Charles E. Nicholson*
BUILDER: *Camper & Nicholsons - no. 367*
YEAR: *1929 May*

LENGTH OVERALL: *20.57 m.*
LENGTH AT WATERLINE: *13.54 m.*
BEAM: *3.65 m.*
DRAFT: *2.62 m.*
CONSTRUCTION: *wood on steel frames*
FIRST OWNER: *C. R. Fairey*
FIRST NAME: *Flica*
FIRST COUNTRY: *United Kingdom*
HOME PORT: *Portsmouth*
FIRST SAIL NUMBER: *K 16*
CURRENT LOCATION: *United Kingdom*
CONDITION: *in need of restoration*
COUNTRY: *England*
FURTHER DETAILS AND HISTORY: Built according to the Second International Rule
Owners and history:
1929 - 1933 C.R. Fairey, the famous aircraft manufacturer; name: *Flica;* home port: Portsmouth; rigging: bermudan cutter.
She was constructed in five months and launched on May 9th 1929. Her lines and construction were perfected with the assistance of the wind-tunnel facilities at Fairey Aviation Ltd. At her debut she was not very successful with a fifth place at the 1929 Cowes Week. She gradually improved in the following seasons and was considered to be the fastest Twelve, mainly in light winds, winning the large majority of races; at the beginning of the 1932 season she was altered in order to increase her speed: "Certainly the feature of the 12 M racing has been the advance of *Flica*. The modifications made to her early this year, coupled with the skill shown by her owner at the helm, have put her right above the rest of the class".
In 1932, out of 39 starts she had 21 firsts, 8 seconds and 6 thirds. In 1933, together with *Morwenna*, she went to Norway for the Norwegian Jubilee Regatta and she took part in the Sweden and Danish events with a total of 8 firsts and 2 seconds.
On the season *Flica* was again first with *Veronica* very close to her: of 45 starts *Flica* had 27 firsts, 10 seconds and 2 thirds
1934 - 1946 Hugh L. Goodson; home port: Brixham.
With her new owner she had a very good season with a second placement overall after the new Third Rule *Westra* but she preceded the other new *Miquette*. She had 33 starts, with 14 firsts and 8 seconds. Again in 1935 she continued her extraordinary long lasting career and at the end of the season she was third behind the new Third Rule *Marina* and *Westra* with 39 starts: 10 firsts, 12 seconds and 4 thirds; in 1936 out of 31 starts she had 6 first and 2 seconds.
In 1939 she was up for sale
1947 - 1949 R.P. Dyer. Engine installed in 1948
1950 Heirs of the late R.P. Dyer
1951 - 1962 Robert A. Hall
1962 Wg. Cdr. R.H.A. Coombs; home port: Brimpton
1963 - 1965 W. W. F. Wyles; home port: Hamble
1966 - 1973 Belsize Boat Yard Ltd.; home port: Southampton
1974 - 1977 R. Thomas; home port: Brixham
1978 Disappeared from Lloyd's Register
1993 - 2001 Richard A. Smith; home port: Epping

■ HEIRA II

DESIGNER: *Johan Anker*
BUILDER: *Anker & Jensen*
YEAR: *1919*
LENGTH OVERALL: *20.12 m.*
LENGTH AT WATERLINE: *12.95 m.*
BEAM: *30.45 m.*
DRAFT: *2.57 m.*
SAIL AREA: *242 sq.m.; 198 sq.m (1926)*
CONSTRUCTION: *wood on steel frames*
FIRST OWNER: *Olaf Orvig*
FIRST NAME: *Heira II*
FIRST COUNTRY: *Norway*
HOME PORT: *Bergen*
OTHER NAMES: *Nanette II (1926) - Mariella (1930) - Tove Lilian (1931) - Barcarolla (1935)*
CURRENT LOCATION: *unknown*
CONDITION: *broken up?*
FURTHER DETAILS AND HISTORY: Built according to the Second International Rule
Owners and history:
1919 - 1923 Olaf Örvig; name: *Heira II*; home port: Bergen; winner of the 1920 Olympic Games in Antwerp in the Second Int. Rule Class, no other entries except *Heira II*
1924 - 1925 W. M. M. Curtis; home port: Dublin. Registered in Lloyd's Register from 1925 as "formerly Int. Rating Class 12 Metre"
1926 - 1928 Percy B. Abrahams; new name: *Nanette II;* home port: London
1929 Lt. Col. Vivian Gabriel
1930 Cyril Wright and Cecil Dormer; new name: *Mariella*. Both were partners in several yachts at different times from the 15 M *The Lady Anne* to several 6 M; Cecil Dormer was named Rhodes after his famous ancestor
1931 - 1934 Consul Hans Borge; new name: *Tove Lilian;* home port: Tonsberg (Norway). In 1933 she took part (with no result) in the KNS Jubilee Regatta in Hanko
1935 - 1949 S. Belaieff; new name: *Barcarolla;* home port: Wiborg (Finland). Engine installed in 1936
1950 Disappeared from Lloyd's Register

■ IRIS

DESIGNER: *Thomas C. Glen-Coats*
BUILDER: *Bute Slip Dock Co, Ltd.*
YEAR: *1926 July*
LENGTH OVERALL: *21.49 m.*
LENGTH AT WATERLINE: *14.69 m.*
BEAM: *3.66 m.*
SAIL AREA: *193 sq.m.*
CONSTRUCTION: *wood on steel frames*
FIRST OWNER: *Sir Thomas Glen-Coats*
FIRST NAME: *Iris*
FIRST COUNTRY: *United Kingdom*
HOME PORT: *Glasgow*
FIRST SAIL NUMBER: *K 6 (as Iris) - N 9 (as Irina V)*

OTHER NAMES: *Irina V (1932)*
CONDITION: *broken up*
FURTHER DETAILS AND HISTORY: Built according to the Second Int. Rule. Owners and history:
1926 - 1928 Sir Thomas C. Glen-Coats; name: *Iris*; home port: Glasgow; rig: bermudan cutter. According to Uffa Fox:
"She was designed and built some twenty years after his first design, *Palace*, and was like her in many ways.
Iris was designed to be twice the length of his 6M *Echo,* which made her longer than any of the then existing 12M yachts, and naturally forced her to carry less sail, but as at that time the height of the sail allowed was in proportion to the length of the waterline, she had the tallest and narrowest rig of the whole lot.
There was no doubt her success was largely due to her length and her tall and narrow rig, for length is speed, and he knew that the taller and narrower the sail area the more efficient it is."
She was the first Twelve with outriggers. Her interior was in pastel colours and had leather seating. In 1927 she raced both in the Solent and on the Clyde: in the Solent she was third with 6 firsts, 5 seconds and 2 thirds; on the Clyde she had 7 firsts and 4 seconds
1929 - 1930 Benjamin S. Guinness. She entered the 1929 Cowes Week where she arrived last but one out of seven competitors
1931 Alexander C. Wilson
1932 - 1937 Georg B. von Erpecom Sr.; new name: *Irina V*; home port: Bergen. Under the ownership of Georg von Erpecom, the famous Norwegian ship owner, she entered in several events, notably in 1932 the Bergen Yacht Club Diamond Jubilee with Crown Prince Olav in the crew and Crown Princess Martha as a guest.
She lost to *Symra*. In 1933 she entered the KNS Jubilee regatta in Hanko with Halfdan Hansen as co-skipper; she won one second place and two thirds. In 1935 she did well in Gothenburg/Mastrand regattas, winning special prizes
1937 - 1950 Ragnar Fredriksen. He took off the keel to keep it from the Germans, but in 1950 he sold it because of the high prices paid for lead. He then used her as a motor boat and added a doghouse.
She was a wreck off Hanko up until 1965, then dismantled, burnt and sunk at Hanko. Her mast was first used on *Mosk 2* and now is on *Magnolia*
1950 Disappeared off Lloyd's Register

■ IRIS

DESIGNER: *Burgess, Rigg & Morgan Ltd.*
BUILDER: *Abeking & Rasmussen - no. 2365*
YEAR: *1928 May*
LENGTH OVERALL: *21.09 m.*
LENGTH AT WATERLINE: *13.03 m.*
BEAM: *3.87 m.*
DRAFT: *2.58 m.*
SAIL AREA: *183 sq.m.*
CONSTRUCTION: *wood on steel frames*
FIRST OWNER: *W .A. W. Stewart*
FIRST NAME: *Iris*
FIRST COUNTRY: *United States*
HOME PORT: *New York*

FIRST SAIL NUMBER: *US 4*

CONDITION: *broken up*

FURTHER DETAILS AND HISTORY: Built according to the Second Int. Rule. She was one of the six Twelve Metres designed by Burgess for American owners and built by Abeking and Rasmussen

Owners and history:

1928 - 1935 W. A. W. Stewart; name: *Iris*; home port: Oyster Bay, NY. Entered the 1928 and 1929 class championship which was won by *Tycoon*; in 1928 out of 13 starts, she had 1 first, 5 seconds and 1 third; in 1929 out off 9 starts she had 1 first, 3 seconds, 2 thirds; in 1930 she had 1 first, 2 seconds and 2 thirds out off 8 entries; similar results are achieved in 1931, 1932, 1933 and 1934; in 1935 she stopped racing

1936 - 1938 Henry L. Maxwell; home port: Greenwich, CT; engine installed

1939 - 1940 Harold W. Brooks; home port: Sag Harbor, NY

1941 - 1948 Harry Fletcher; home port: Alpena, MI

1948 - 1969 Herbert W. Hadcock from September 1948; home port: Detroit & Bay City, MI

1970 - 1972 No name given

1972 Disappeared off Record; believed broken up in Michigan

■ ISOLDE

DESIGNER: *Burgess, Rigg & Morgan Ltd.*

BUILDER: *Abeking & Rasmussen - no. 2363*

YEAR: *1928 May*

LENGTH OVERALL: *21.09 m.*

LENGTH AT WATERLINE: *13.03 m.*

BEAM: *3.87 m.*

DRAFT: *2.58 m.*

SAIL AREA: *183 sq.m.*

CONSTRUCTION: *wood on steel frames*

FIRST OWNER: *Henry L. Maxwell*

FIRST NAME: *Isolde*

FIRST COUNTRY: *United States*

HOME PORT: *Larchmond*

FIRST SAIL NUMBER: *US2*

OTHER NAMES: *Sally Ann (1931) - Ptarmigan (1936) Soliloquy (1937)*

CONDITION: *broken up in 1988*

FURTHER DETAILS AND HISTORY: Built according to the Second Int. Rule She was one of the six Twelve Metres designed by Burgess for American owners and built by Abeking and Rasmussen

Owners and history:

1928 - 1929 Henry L. Maxwell; home port: Larchmont, NY. She entered in the season's races but with poor results: 1 first out of 6 races in 1928 and out of 8 races in 1929

1930 - 1935 Spencer Borden; new name: *Sally Ann*; home port: Larchmont, NY and Fall River, MA

1935 - 1936 Thomas N. Dabney; new name: *Ptarmigan*; home port: Boston, MA

1937 - 1942 Arthur C. Stewart; new name: *Soliloquy*; home port: Los Angeles, CA. Engine installed in 1937, re-engined in 1940

1944/1946 - 1960 Wesley D. Smith; home port: Balboa and Los Angeles, CA

1961 - 1977 Given Machinery Co.; home port: Los Angeles CA

1978 Disappeared off record

c. 1988 Sailed from California to Australia. Reportedly hauled, stripped of keel and broken up

■ IYRUNA

DESIGNER: *Charles E. Nicholson*

BUILDER: *Camper & Nicholsons Ltd. - construction no. 349*

YEAR: *1927 May*

LENGTH OVERALL: *20.49 m.*

LENGTH AT WATERLINE: *12.95 m.*

BEAM: *3.64 m.*

DRAFT: *2.57 m.*

SAIL AREA: *191 sq.m. (1927); 164 sq.m. (1937); 121 sq.m. (1948)*

CONSTRUCTION: *wood on steel frames*

FIRST OWNER: *Sir William P. Burton*

FIRST NAME: *Iyruna*

FIRST COUNTRY: *Great Britain*

HOME PORT: *Portsmouth*

FIRST SAIL NUMBER: *K 11*

CURRENT LOCATION: *unknown*

FURTHER DETAILS AND HISTORY: Built according to the Second International Rule

Owners and history:

1927 - 1930 Sir. William P. Burton; name *Iyruna*; home port: Colchester and Portsmouth; rig: bermudan cutter. Burton, who in that year was president of YRA, named this yacht as an anacronym to commemorate the fact that the North American Yacht Racing Union (NAYRU) had been formed and had finally joined the International Yacht Racing Union (IYRU). Her cost was £4800. She was a boat for light winds. Her hull is painted green. Sir William Burton had already owned *Noresca* and he also owned *Veronica, Marina* and *Jenetta*. In the 1929 Cowes Week she was fourth overall with one first, behind *Mouette, Moyana* and *Rhona*

1931 - 1934 Glynn Terell. In 1932 she was fifth overall out of 26 starts, and 2 firsts, 5 seconds and 1 third. In 1933 she was fourth out of 43 entries, with later had 6 firsts, 9 seconds and 4 thirds. In 1934 she was second on the last race for 12Ms in Burnham-on-Crouch but she was last in the season overall and out of 19 starts had 1 first, 1 second and 1 third

1935 C. E. A. Hartridge. She was last overall in the season with 1 first and 2 thirds

1936 Camper & Nicholsons, Ltd.

1937 - 1947 N. F. Adeney; in 1937 altered to auxiliary bermudan cutter. 4 cyl. petrol engine installed. Sail area reduced

1947 - 1952 F. Clarkson. Re-engined in 1947

1952 Mrs. F. Dobbs; home port: Caernarvon

1953 - 1959 J. Anthony J. Boyden; home port: Portsmouth; RORC rating: 50'76

1959 Belsize Boat Yard, Ltd.

1960 - 1962 Norman H. Woods; home port: Poole

1962 - 1963 G. H. Verner & P. N. Hallowes

1964 - 1965 Thomas C. Bullock; home port: Poole and Hamble

1966 Disappeared off Lloyd's Register

■ LADY EDITH

DESIGNER: *W. & R.B. Fife*
BUILDER: *W. Fife & Son*
YEAR: *1925 June*
LENGTH OVERALL: *18.29 m.*
LENGTH AT WATERLINE: *13.54 m.*
BEAM: *3.92 m.*
DRAFT: *2.77 m.*
SAIL AREA: *128 sq.m. (1954)*
ENGINE: *petrol engine 2 cyl. (1925)*
FIRST OWNER: *Alfred Melson*
FIRST NAME: *Lady Edith*
FIRST COUNTRY: *United Kingdom*
HOME PORT: *Greenock*
OTHER NAMES: *Kailua (1947)*
CURRENT LOCATION: *unknown*
CONDITION: *broken up ?*
FURTHER DETAILS AND HISTORY: Built according to the Second Int. Rule
Owners and history:
1925 - 1926 Alfred Melson; name: *Lady Edith*; home port: Greenock; rig: auxiliary cutter
1927 - 1932 John Good
1933 - 1934 Major B.H. Piercy
1935 - 1937 Sir Robert Burton-Chadwick
1938 Dr. Henri E. Lavielle
1939 E. Sparke-Davies; new name: *Kailua;* home port: Jersey, CI; rig: altered to auxiliary sloop and re-engined in 1939
1947 - 1953 Major C.B. Thorne. In 1947 rig altered to bermudan cutter and re-engined in 1947
1953 - 1964 Lord Avebury. Re-engined in 1953 and 1956; RORC rating: 39'17
1964 - 1969 Sea Hawk Ltd.; home port: London and Jersey, CI
1970 Disappeared from Lloyd's Register

■ LUCILLA

DESIGNER: *Charles E. Nicholson*
BUILDER: *Camper & Nicholsons Ltd - no. 372*
YEAR: *1930*
LENGTH OVERALL: *20.15 m.*
LENGTH AT WATERLINE: *13.68 m.*
BEAM: *3.55 m.*
DRAFT: *2.68 m.*
SAIL AREA: *184 sq.m.*
CONSTRUCTION: *wood on steel frames*
FIRST OWNER: *J. Lauriston Lewis*
FIRST NAME: *Lucilla*
FIRST COUNTRY: *Great Britain*
HOME PORT: *Portsmouth*
CONDITION: *sunk*
FURTHER DETAILS AND HISTORY: Built according to the Second Int. Rule
Owners and history:
1930 J. Lauriston Lewis; name: *Lucilla*; home port: Portsmouth; rig: bermudian sloop. Mr. Lauriston Lewis previously owner of the Twelve Metre *Rhona*. In her first season on the Solent, *Lucilla* sank in August 1930 after a collision with *Lulworth*. Beken of Cowes photographed the incident

■ MAGDA XI

DESIGNER: *Johan Anker*
BUILDER: *Anker & Jensen*
YEAR: *1928*
SAIL AREA: *192 sq.m.*
FIRST OWNER: *Alfred W. G. Larsen*
FIRST NAME: *Magda XI*
FIRST COUNTRY: *Norway*
HOME PORT: *Oslo*
FIRST SAIL NUMBER: *N 7 - US 7*
OTHER NAMES: *Cantitoe*
CONDITION: *wrecked and buried*
FURTHER DETAILS AND HISTORY: Built according to the Int. Second
Rule. Owners and history:
1928 - 1931 Alfred W. G. Larsen; name: *Magda XI;* home port: Oslo; rig: bermudan cutter. In 1930 the owner, with J. Anker as helmsman, represented KNS at the Royal Swedish Yacht Club (KSSS) 100 year jubilee. She was the best 12 Metre there, winning her Class
1929 Disappeared off Lloyd's Register
1931 - 1941 Bayard S. Lichfield; new name: *Cantitoe;* home port: New York, NY. Rig: converted to bermudan sloop; sail number: US 7. In her first season in the U.S.A. she entered 8 races and won 1 first, 2 seconds and 1 third; in 1932 she entered 8 races and won 1 first, 2 seconds and 2 thirds; in 1933, she won the 12M Class at Larchmont Race Week and out of 9 starts she had 5 firsts, 1 second and 2 thirds
1941 - 1942 A. A. Washton; home port: New London, CT
1946 - 1947 Philip J. Corbin; home port: Boston, MA
1948 George D. Chard
1949 Wrecked by a storm, in the summer of 1949. Driven ashore at Ipswich, MA and buried in sand at the Crane Estate

■ MODESTY

DESIGNER: *W. & R.B. Fife*
BUILDER: *W. Fife & Son - construction no. 741*
YEAR: *1926 May*
LENGTH OVERALL: *21.34 m.*
LENGTH AT WATERLINE: *12.80 m.*
BEAM: *3.70 m.*
CONSTRUCTION: *wood on steel frames; stem and keel of teak*
FIRST OWNER: *Sir A. Mortimer Singer*
FIRST NAME: *Modesty*
FIRST COUNTRY: *Great Britain*
HOME PORT: *Greenock*
FIRST SAIL NUMBER: *K 4*
OTHER NAMES: *Roxana (1935) - La Pinta (1955) - Roxana (1967)*
CURRENT LOCATION: *unknown*
CONDITION: *unknown*
FURTHER DETAILS AND HISTORY: Built according to Second Int. Rule
Owners and history:
1926 Sir A. Mortimer Singer and Sir William P. Burton; name: *Modesty;* home port: Greenock. She was the sister boat of *Moyana*. It appears that this yacht was ordered by John M. Robertson and named *Judith*, but before the yacht was completed, Singer and Burton purchased the construction contract and the name was changed to *Modesty*

1927 Sir A. Mortimer Singer
1928 Charles Richard Fairey
1929 - 1932 Lt. Col. Sir John Humphery
1932 - 1950 M. Valery-Ollivier; new name: *Roxana*; home port: Cannes where she was delivered in June 1932; engine installed in 1932
1951 - 1954 ?
1955 - 1965 Albert A. Prouvost; new name: *La Pinta*; home port: Saint-Tropez. She was sold as her owner had bought *Vanity V*, re-named *La Pinta*
1965 - 1971 Jean Berthier; new name: *Roxana*; home port: Toulon.
1972 Disappeared off Lloyd's Register but this yacht was reported to be still in existence in France

■ MOUETTE

DESIGNER: *Charles E. Nicholson*
BUILDER: *Camper & Nicholsons - no. 358*
YEAR: *1928 May*
LENGTH OVERALL: *20.57 m.*
LENGTH AT WATERLINE: *13.48 m.*
BEAM: *3.55 m.*
DRAFT: *2.66 m.*
SAIL AREA: *185 sq.m.*
CONSTRUCTION: *wood on steel frames*
FIRST OWNER: *T.O.M. Sopwith*
FIRST NAME: *Mouette*
FIRST COUNTRY: *Great Britain*
HOME PORT: *Portsmouth*
FIRST SAIL NUMBER: *K 15 - US 8 (in the U.S.A.)*
CONDITION: *sunk*
FURTHER DETAILS AND HISTORY: Built according to Second Int. Rule
Owners and history:
1928 - 1931 T.O.M. Sopwith; name: *Mouette*; home port: Portsmouth. Rig: bermudan cutter; she won the Class championship in 1928 and 1929
1932 - 1940 Horace Havemeyer; home port: New York. Altered by Sparkman & Stephens (plan no. 62)
In the U.S. in the 1932 season she had 32 starts and she won 21 firsts, 4 seconds and 4 thirds.
She raced against *Cantitoe* (formerly *Magda XI*) and two Twelves out of the six designed by S. Burgess.
She won the Long Island Sound Championship in the 12M class in 1932 (4 firsts, 1 second and 3 thirds out of 8 starts) and in 1933 (2 firsts, 2 seconds and 3 thirds out of 9 starts); she won the class in the 1932 Larchmont YC Race Week
1941 - 1942 George Reidy; home port: Glen Cove, NY
1946 - 1947 Frank V. Drake; home port: New York. In 1943 engine installed (Gray 6 cylinders).
1948 - 1949 Ellery C. Midgett; home port: Manteo, NC
1950 - 1955 Gerald W. Ford; home port: Larchmont, NY. Re-engined in 1953
1956 - 1957 Edward T. Rice; home port: Larchmont and Fisher's Island, NY
1958 Mrs. Harriet Church Rice; home port: Fisher's Island, NY and Mystic, CT
1959 - 1970 Robert E. Rohe; Mystic and Norwalk, CT; Plymouth, MA; re-engined in 1959; rig altered in 1960 to auxiliary ketch; sail area reduced to 140 sq.m.

1960 Disappeared off Lloyd's Register
1971 - 1972 No name given; home port: Plymouth, MA
1973 - 1975 E. Bronson Conlin
1976 Fred A. Richards; reported sunk

■ MOYANA

DESIGNER: *W. & R.B. Fife*
BUILDER: *W. Fife & Son - construction no. 742*
YEAR: *1926 May*
BEAM: *3.70 m.*
DRAFT: *198 sq.m.*
CONSTRUCTION: *wood on steel frames; keel, stem and sternpost of teak*
FIRST OWNER: *Wilfred Leuchars*
FIRST NAME: *Moyana*
FIRST COUNTRY: *United Kingdom*
HOME PORT: *Greenock*
FIRST SAIL NUMBER: *K 3 (Moyana) - K 5 (Amity)*
OTHER NAMES: *Amity (1929)*
CONDITION: *disintegrated in Noirmoutier (France)*
FURTHER DETAILS AND HISTORY: Built according to the Second Int. Rule
Owners and history:
1926 - 1928 Wilfred Leuchars; name: *Moyana;* home port: Greenock; rig: bermudan cutter; sister boat to *Modesty*. "*Moyana* was designed and built at Fairlie for Wilfred Leuchars, who lived in Natal, who was a partner in a firm of London solicitors - Hunt, Leuchars and Hepburn. William was asked to go to London to meet Leuchars and discuss requirements for his new boat. Notes of the extras discussed and requested were made on Piccadilly Hotel notepaper. The covering for the cushions had to be 'something like the tapestry in the Piccadilly Hotel'! Mr. Leuchars was obviously a creature of habit. He kept the boat for two years, and then in 1928 he ordered another *Moyana II*" (*Fast and Bonnie*, May Fife Cohn). She was a winner in the first two seasons
1929 - 1930 W. Charles Tozer; new name: *Amity*
1931 H.K. Neale
1932 Lt. Comdr. E.A. Pearce
1932 - 1933 Jean Roubaud; home port: Marseille (France); engine installed in 1932
1935 - 1938 Emile Vidal; home port: Marseille and Cannes
1939 - 1949 Georges Levet; home port: Cannes
1950 Disappeared from Lloyd's Register. "The original *Moyana* ended her sailing days as *Amity* in a mud berth on the Isle of Noirmoutier just off the coast of Southern Brittany. After lying in a mud berth for some years in the 'Cimitière de Bateaux' at Noirmoutier, a Fife enthusiast decided to restore her. Unfortunately it was decided to lift her out of the mud with a crane, and she promptly disintegrated. All that remains is the lead keel and a beam from the boat bearing the Lloyd's specification number" (*Fast and Bonnie*, May Fife Cohn)

■ MOYANA

DESIGNER: *W. & R.B. Fife*
BUILDER: *W. Fife & Son - no. 775*
YEAR: *1929*
LENGTH OVERALL: *21.34 m.*
LENGTH AT WATERLINE: *13.72 m.*

BEAM: *3.79 m.*

DRAFT: *2.66 m.*

FIRST OWNER: *Wilfred Leuchars*

FIRST NAME: *Moyana*

FIRST COUNTRY: *United Kingdom*

HOME PORT: *Greenock*

FIRST SAIL NUMBER: *K 3*

OTHER NAMES: *Morwenna (1932) - Kaylena (1947*

CURRENT LOCATION: *unknown*

CONDITION: *sunk*

FURTHER DETAILS AND HISTORY: Built according to the Second Int. Rule. Owners and history:

1929 - 1931 Wilfried Leuchars, a wealthy South African solicitor; name: *Moyana;* home port: Greenock; rig: bermudan sloop. In the 1929 Cowes Week she scored three firsts with a second overall placement after six races behind *Mouette* but she beat *Rhona, Iyruna, Flica, Iris* and *Doris*

1932 - 1937 Capt. John Bruce Bolitho; new name: *Morwenna.* Under the new name in 1932 she entered 37 races and had 4 firsts, 4 seconds and 5 thirds. In 1933 she was steered by Sir Ralph Gore and she was considered to be at the same level as *Veronica* and *Zoraida, Flica* still being considered as scratch boat; in August together with *Flica* she entered the KNS Jubilee Regatta in Oslo with no placing due to the light wind. She registered the only win on the first day of the regatta at Copenhagen before returning in company with *Vema III, Doris, Flica* and *Princess Svanevit* to be in time for Cowes Week. At the end of the 1933 season out of 31 entries she had 5 firsts, 5 seconds and 8 thirds and was third behind *Flica* and *Veronica.* In 1934 she was raced only occasionally

1938 - 1946 Sir Walter R. Preston

1947 - 1949 Kenneth H. & Bryan W. Preston; new name: *Kaylena;* home port: Jersey

1950 - 1964 Major R.N. MacDonald-Buchanan; home port: Southampton; RORC rating: 56'47, in 1953: 56'47. She was trial horse for *Sceptre* in 1958

1965 - 1968 Dorset Ass. of Boys Clubs; home port: Poole

1969 Sea Cadet Corps; home port: Portsmouth; re-engined in 1969

1970 Disappeared from Lloyd's Register; she was reported sunk

■ MOYANA II

DESIGNER: *Alfred Mylne & Co.*

BUILDER: *Bute Slip Dock Co., Ltd.*

YEAR: *1924 May*

BEAM: *3.77 m.*

CONSTRUCTION: *wood on steel frames*

FIRST OWNER: *Wilfred Leuchars*

FIRST NAME: *Moyana II*

FIRST COUNTRY: *United Kingdom*

HOME PORT: *Greenock*

FIRST SAIL NUMBER: *K8 (Westard Ho) - K14 (Maharana and Estrilda)*

OTHER NAMES: *Westward Ho (1926) - Maharana (1928) - Estrilda (1930) - Sagrace (1947)*

CURRENT LOCATION: *unknown*

CONDITION: *broken up?*

FURTHER DETAILS AND HISTORY: Built according to the Second Int. Rule Owners and history:

1924 - 1925 Wilfred Leuchars, a wealthy South African; name: *Moyana II;*

home port: Greenock

1926 - 1927 B. Meaker; new name: *Westward Ho*

1928 Lt. Col. The Hon. C.H.C. Guest; new name: *Maharana*

1929 - 1938 D. Hanbury; from 1930, new name: *Estrilda;* engine installed in 1932

1939 Mrs. Dorothy Ireland

1940 - 1950 In Lloyd's Register but without the owner's name

1947 - ?? Dr. Roccatagliata; new name: *Sagrace;* home port: Varazze (Italy)

1951 Disappeared from Lloyd's Register.

Very little news on this Twelve. She entered the Royal Burnham Yacht Club Regattas in 1924 and 1925.

In 1947 in very bad condition she was at Cantieri Baglietto (Varazze, Italy), owned by Dr. Roccatagliata, for a complete refit and alteration to an auxiliary yawl. Photos and plans were available but no further news after this date

■ NORESCA

DESIGNER: *Johan Anker*

BUILDER: *Anker & Jensen*

YEAR: *1924*

LENGTH OVERALL: *20.60 m.*

LENGTH AT WATERLINE: *12.67 m.*

BEAM: *3.84 m.*

DRAFT: *1.98 m.*

DISPLACEMENT:

SAIL AREA: *201 sq.m.*

FIRST OWNER: *R. G. Perry*

FIRST NAME: *Noresca*

FIRST COUNTRY: *United Kingdom*

HOME PORT: *Harwich*

FIRST SAIL NUMBER: *K 9 - N 13*

OTHER NAMES: *Dreamchild (1929) - Faraway (1935) - Noresca (1937)*

CURRENT LOCATION: *sunk off Oland Island (Sweden)*

FURTHER DETAILS AND HISTORY: Built according to the Second Int. Rule. Owners and history:

1924 R.G. Perry; name: *Noresca;* home port: Harwich; she was said to be sister ship of *Figaro IV*

1924 Sir William Burton

1925 - 1929 F.G. Mitchell & R. Ellis Brown; in 1925 she had a very good season with capt. Edward Heard as professional skipper (he had a good reputation as a dashing tactician and for taking risks). She had 17 firsts, 3 seconds and 4 thirds

1929 - 1932 J.R. Govett; new name: *Dreamchild* (1929) and *Noresca* (1930)

1933 - 1934 Corbett W. Woodall; home port: London; sail area cut down

1935 - 1936 R.S. Loewenstein; new name: *Faraway;* home port: Brussels

1936 Johan Anker; new name: *Noresca;* home port: Asker (Norway); new sail number: no. 13

1936 - 1953 Th. Johnsen; new name: *Noresca;* home port: Oslo. In the late 1940s, together with *Santa, Diva* and *Norsaga,* she took part in the Twelves regattas organised by KNS

1954 Disappeared from Lloyd's Register

1968 - 1970 Harald Bredo Eriksen; home port: Oslo.

Sold to a Swedish owner and sunk off Oland Island, near Stockholm

◾ ONAWA

DESIGNER: *Burgess, Rigg & Morgan Ltd.*
BUILDER: *Abeking & Rasmussen - no. 2367*
YEAR: *1928 May*
LENGTH OVERALL: *21.09 m.*
LENGTH AT WATERLINE: *13.03 m.*
BEAM: *3.87 m.*
DRAFT: *2.58 m.*
SAIL AREA: *183 sq.m.*
CONSTRUCTION: *wood on steel frames*
FIRST OWNER: *W. Cameron Forbes*
FIRST NAME: *Onawa*
FIRST COUNTRY: *United States*
HOME PORT: *Boston*
FIRST SAIL NUMBER: *US 6*
OTHER NAMES: *Horizons (1953) - Lithuanica - Onawa (1990 ?)*
CURRENT LOCATION: *Newport, RI (U.S.A.)*
CONDITION: *completely rebuilt*
FURTHER DETAILS AND HISTORY: Built according to the Second Int. Rule. She is one of the six Twelve Metres designed by Starling Burgess for American owners and built by Abeking & Rasmussen
Owners and history:
1928 - 1935 W. Cameron Forbes; name: *Onawa*; home port: Boston, MA. Sail area increased to 185 sq.m. (1930). She was very active in the 1928, 1929 and 1930 seasons entering every race but had poor results: 1 first in 1928 out of 10 races and 3 firsts in 1929 out of 12 starts; 1 second in 1930 with 6 starts
1936 - 1942 Horace F. Smith, Jr; home port: Philadelphia, PA
1943 - 1946 disappeared off all records
1946 - 1952 J. Frederic Requardt, Jr; home port: Easton, Oxford and Gibson Is., MD; new lead keel in 1946.
1953 - 1975 Ward H & Virginia E. Bright; new name: *Horizons*; home port: Cape May, NJ and St. Croix, USVI
1976 Disappeared off all records
1976 - 1990 Al Urbelis; new name: *Llithuanica*; home port: New Jersey
1991 - 1994 Daniel Prentiss, Robert H. Tiedemann & Alfred B. Van Liew II; new name: *Onawa*; home port: Newport, RI
1994 - 2000 Daniel Prentiss & Alfred B. Van Liew II
2000 - 2001 Yacht Onawa, LLC (McMillen Yachts Inc., Mgr).
She was completely rebuilt at the American Shipyard Newport, RI, using parts of *Waiandance* (US 1). On March 2001 planking of the hull was finished and she was re-launched on June 9th 2001

◾ RHONA

DESIGNER: *W. & R.B. Fife*
BUILDER: *W. Fife & Son - construction no. 748*
YEAR: *1927 May*
LENGTH OVERALL: *19.86 m.*
LENGTH AT WATERLINE: *12.95 m.*
BEAM: *3.76 m.*
SAIL AREA: *190 sq.m. (1947)*
CONSTRUCTION: *wood on steel frames, keel, sternpost and stem in teak*
FIRST OWNER: *J. Lauriston Lewis*

FIRST NAME: *Rhona*
FIRST COUNTRY: *Great Britain*
HOME PORT: *Greenock*
FIRST SAIL NUMBER: *K 7 - N 10 (1933)*
OTHER NAMES: *Hei II (1933)- Frisco VI (1961)*
CURRENT LOCATION: *unknown*
CONDITION: *broken up?*
FURTHER DETAILS AND HISTORY: Built according to the Int. Second Rule
Owners and history:
1927 - 1929 J. Lauriston Lewis; name *Rhona*; home port: Greenock; rig: bermudan cutter. Mr. Lauriston was also the owner of *Lucilla*. Third overall placement and 1 first in the 1929 Cowes Week
1930 - 1932 Earl of Essex; home port: Greenwich
1933 - 1958 Arnfinn Heje; new name: *Hei II*; home port: Oslo; she entered the KNS Jubilee regatta in Hanko in July 1933 and she was first in one race but was not placed in the other four races
1959 - 1960 Heirs of the late Arnfinn Heje
1961 - 1969 Jan Arthur Iversen; new name: *Frisco VI*; home port: Sarpsborg (Norway). Engine installed in 1960. In 1961 converted to auxiliary yawl
1970 Urban Strom
1971 Disappeared off Lloyd's Register

◾ TATJANA

DESIGNER: *Johan Anker*
BUILDER: *Anker & Jensen*
YEAR: *1917*
LENGTH OVERALL: *19.81 m.*
LENGTH AT WATERLINE: *12.19 m.*
BEAM: *3.38 m.*
SAIL AREA: *224 sq.m. (main 142 sq.m. and headsails 82 sq.m.)*
CONSTRUCTION: *wood on steel frames*
FIRST OWNER: *Emil Glückstadt*
FIRST NAME: *Tatjana*
FIRST COUNTRY: *Denmark*
HOME PORT: *Copenhagen*
FIRST SAIL NUMBER: *K 2*
OTHER NAMES: *Noreen (1921)*
CONDITION: *sunk off Vigo, Portugal*
FURTHER DETAILS AND HISTORY: Built according to the "S" Scandinavian Rule and converted to the Second Int. Rule
Owners and history:
1917 - 1920 Emil Glückstadt; name: *Tatjana*; home port: Copenhagen. Rig: in 1919 she was altered to bermudan cutter. Her owner was an influential Danish banker, owner of the famous *Julnar, Elge* and of several large motoryachts. *Tatjana* was built according to the "S" Scandinavian Rule, an interim rule used for a short period before the revision of the International Rule . According to *Yachting Monthly:* "*Noreen*, a composite-built vessel, shows considerable improvement on Anker's earlier work. The decks of Kauri pine are well laid and the hull planking nicely finished. Everything is sacrificed to speed, so I was not surprised to find the cabin fittings wonderfully light, if comfortable enough. The long tooth-mast is raked and there is no wedging at the deck, the entire thrust being taken on the heel. There are three

crosstrees, one nearer the deck than I have ever seen such a sitting, the other two in normal position. The rigging I thought very light, considering the size of the structure, although with the bermudan rig the heavy thrust of the gaff is absent"

1921 - 1924 Frederick Last; new name: *Noreen*; home port: London. In 1921 she sailed from Denmark to England carrying a spinnaker for three days and two nights. During the season, due to a squall, her mast went overboard. She sailed as a Twelve from 1921 to 1924. Her best season was in 1923: she entered the Burnham on Crouch races and beat *Alachie* and raced against *Vanity*. In the season she had 11 firsts, 11 seconds and 1 third out of 30 starts. In 1924 she won 25 flags but she was dismasted three times

1925 - 1928 Camper & Nicholsons Ltd. She was advertised for sale

1929 - 1939 Hugh M. Crankshaw; home port: London. The owner was a mechanical engineer and an experienced yachtsman interested in experimenting with sail plans and hulls. He altered *Noreen*'s rig to bermudan yawl (1929 - sail area: 225 sq.m.) and the interior with the owner's cabins forward of the saloon. The saloon itself had accomodation for three people. The owner aimed to live on board during the summer and compete in the handicap class. In 1932, after three years of successful cruising and handicap racing, he asked C. E. Nicholson to design a new rig: the first proposal was for a schooner rig but it was never fitted; the approved one was a bermudan cutter with staysail, jib and jib topsail and the mast left in its original position. The boom was shortened (total sail area: 156 sq.m.). She entered the Solent Races for Twelve Metres without a big success: at the end of the season out of three entries she had one third placing. In 1933, Crankshaw modified the rigging once more. This change was watched with great interest as the mast was moved ten feet aft, almost amidship. Due to the re-rigging of *Britannia* from gaff to bermudan cutter and the consequent acquisition by the owner of a topmast and a jackyard, the mast was made of the two pieces scarphed together to make a new lighter unit. The yacht was also deepened in the keel by 30 cm. In 1934 she got better results racing in the other 40ft handicap races and she continued to sail in this class in the following years with some exceptional results such as the one achieved in the 1938 Weymouth R. Thames Y.C. race, when she finished 1 min. 19 sec. ahead of the winning Twelve *Evaine* although she started 15 min. after the 12 Metre Class. In the season she won 9 flags in 10 starts: 5 firsts, 3 seconds and 1 third. In 1938-39, the last racing under his flag, Crankshaw again made alteration reducing the headsails to two instead of three, with the staysail set on a boom and with solid steel tube spreaders. In 1938 she entered 21 races with 7 firsts, 3 seconds and 5 thirds

1940 - 1946 G. L. Welstead; home port: Poole; engine installed in 1946

1947 Registered in Lloyd's Register but without the owner's name

1948 Harold F. Smith; home port: London. In June 1948, she sailed to her new port of Barcelona in Spain; the boat was in a bad condition: rigging was not reliable and the deck and hull leaked; on June 30th, during a storm, towed by a French tanker towards Vigo, *Noreen* sank

1949 Disappeared off Lloyd's Register

■ THEA

DESIGNER: *Johan Anker*
BUILDER: *Anker & Jensen*
YEAR: *1918 May*

LENGTH OVERALL: *20.07 m. (present)*
LENGTH AT WATERLINE: *13.48 m. (original)*
BEAM: *3.48 m. (present)*
DRAFT: *2.62 m.*
DISPLACEMENT: *26 tons*
SAIL AREA: *253 sq.m.; 223 sq.m. (1937); 147 sq.m. (present)*
CONSTRUCTION: *wood (mahogany on oak)*
ENGINE: *Perkins 465 hp (2001)*
FIRST OWNER: *Jacob B. Stolt Nielsen*
FIRST NAME: *Santa*
FIRST COUNTRY: *Norway*
HOME PORT: *Haugesund*
FIRST SAIL NUMBER: *N4 - D1*
OTHER NAMES: *Santa (1918) - Tenderen III (1922) - Gavotte II (1936) - Santa (1937) - Nina (1972)*
CURRENT LOCATION: *Copenhagen, Denmark*
CONDITION: *excellent, sailing*
PRESENT OWNER: *Hans Michael Jabsen*
FURTHER DETAILS AND HISTORY: Built according to the "S" Scandinavian Rule and converted to the Second Int. Rule
Owners and history:

1918 - 1921 Jacob. B. Stolt-Nielsen; name: *Santa*; home port: Haugesund; rig: bermudan cutter. She was commissioned by the grandfather of the present Jacob Stolt Nielsen, the owner of the big shipping company with the same name. Originally built according to the "S" formula proposed by J. Anker in Scandinavia during the First Rule renegotiation, which changed in 1919 to the second version of the formula. Since then *Santa* was rated as a 12 M S.I. The building started on Dec. 5th, 1917

1922 - 1932 And. F. Kiaer; new name: *Tenderen III;* home port: Fredrikstadt (Norway)

1933 - 1936 L. Rolfsen; new name: *Gavotte III*. She entered the KNS Jubilee Regatta in July 1933 in the class of the Twelves without an R rating and she was awarded one first and two seconds

1937 - 1969 Leif Hôegh; new name: *Santa*; home port: Oslo; engine installed in 1959, re-engined in 1964

1970 - 1998 Baron Ebbe Wedell-Wedellsborg; new name: *Nina*; home port: Rungsted. In 1993 she underwent major maintenance work. In 1998 she was for sale at the price of $340.000. From 1972 she spent every winter at the Walsted yard and has had continuous maintenance. Most of the hull timber is still original.

Since Aug. 1998 Hans Michael Jebsen; new name: *Thea*; home port: Copenhagen. Since then she has had a major restoration, including new spruce spars, a new engine; and the interior has been brought back very close to the original. She is a very active racer both in the classic circuit in Scandinavia and in Danish races where she sails under the DH Danish handicap system

■ TYCOON

DESIGNER: *Burgess, Rigg & Morgan Ltd.*
BUILDER: *Abeking & Rasmussen - no. 2364*
YEAR: *1928 May*
LENGTH OVERALL: *21.09 m.*
LENGTH AT WATERLINE: *13.03 m.*

BEAM: *3.87 m.*
DRAFT: *2.58 m.*
SAIL AREA: *183 sq.m.*
CONSTRUCTION: *wood on steel frames*
FIRST OWNER: *Clifford D. Mallory*
FIRST NAME: *Tycoon*
FIRST COUNTRY: *United States*
HOME PORT: *Greenwich, Connecticut*
FIRST SAIL NUMBER: *US 3*
OTHER NAMES: *Zio (1936) - Arundel (1940) - Trull (1954);*
CONDITION: *destroyed*
FURTHER DETAILS AND HISTORY: Built according to the Second Int. Rule. She was one of the Twelve Metres designed by Starling Burgess for American owners and built by Abeking & Rasmussen
1928 - 1935 Clifford D. Mallory; name: *Tycoon*; home port: Greenwich; rig: bermudan cutter; altered to sloop in 1931. Mr. Mallory was one of the founders of the North American Yacht Racing Union (now US Sailing). In honour of Mr. Mallory, the cover of the annual book published by NAYRU was embossed with a gold seal showing the profile of *Tycoon* and her sail number 3. She was the best of the six Abeking & Rasmussen Twelves and she won the 12 Metre Long Island Sound Championship in 1928 and 1929 and the 12 Metre Class at Larchmont Race Week in 1928, 1929 and 1930. In 1928: she had 8 firsts and 3 seconds out of 14 starts. In 1929, 3 firsts and 1 second out of 6 starts and in 1930, 5 firsts and 1 third out of 7 starts
1936 - 1939 Herbert T. von Frankenberg; new name: *Zio*; home port: Larchmont, NY; engine installed in 1936
1940 - 1953 A. Atwater Kent, Jr; new name: *Arundel*; home port: Philadelphia, PA and Bar Harbor, ME; re-engined in 1950
1954 Photoswitch Marine Div. Inc (Arthur G.B. Metcalfe, Pres.); new name: *Trull*; home port: Marblehead, MA. In 1954 she was destroyed in the harbour at Marblehead by Hurricane Carol. *The Boston Globe* published in 1954 a spectacular photo showing *Trull* on fire during the hurricane

■ VANITY

DESIGNER: *W. & R.B. Fife - design no. 709*
BUILDER: *W. Fife & Son*
YEAR: *1923 July*
LENGTH OVERALL: *19.81 m.*
LENGTH AT WATERLINE: *13.41 m.*
BEAM: *3.73 m.*
DRAFT: *2.74 m.*
SAIL AREA: *182 sq.m.; 161 sq.m (1963)*
CONSTRUCTION: *wood on steel frames; oak keel*
FIRST OWNER: *J. R. Payne*
FIRST NAME: *Vanity*
FIRST COUNTRY: *England*
HOME PORT: *Greenock*
FIRST SAIL NUMBER: *K 1*
CONDITION: *sunk in the Caribbean*
FURTHER DETAILS AND HISTORY: Built according to the Second Int. Rule Owners and history:
1923 - 1932 J.R. Payne; name: *Vanity*; home porto: Greenock; *Vanity* was the most successful Twelve of the 1920s with entries in most of the important races around the coast and across the Channel (Le Havre,

etc.). Mr. Payne was famous as perhaps the best helmsman in the 15 and 12 Metre and 52-footers since about 1905. He used to live aboard *Vanity* and sail round the coast for much of the season. He was an accomplished violinist and known as "Fiddler" Payne. In 1929 the rig was altered to a bermudan cutter. Beken of Cowes has photos of *Vanity* racing with the two rigs. In 1923 she entered in the class regatta in Burnham Week where she was the scratch yacht. In 1924 she did well until she broke her boom. In 1925 she had three firsts racing against *Noresca, Moyana II, Clymene* and *Doris*. Then the interest in Twelves at the Crouch races waned although *Vanity* continued to enter. In 1930 she entered the Town Cup at Burnham on Crouch in the cruiser class. In 1932 and 1933 the 12 class was arranged again and *Vanity* took part, together with other four Twelves. She entered in the other races round the coast (Harwich, Cowes, etc.) and it was said "the old *Vanity* is still able to hold her own with the newer boats under conditions that suit her". In 1932 she entered seven races and had 2 firsts and 1 third. In 1930 she was altered to bermudan cutter
1933 - 1934 F.E.S. Bowlby; *Vanity* was used as a cruiser and she entered from time to time in handicap races, against other ex Twelves. The first one was in 1933 at Ramsgate where a new handicap system was tested. In August she won at Cowes Week in the under 35 tons handicap race
1935 John R. Payne
1936 Walter R. Westhead. In 1936 she entered in 8 races and had 1 first and 1 second. Rig: altered to bermudan sloop
1937 - 1946 David Anderson
1947 - 1948 W. Stannard; RORC rating: 53' 29
1949 - 1950 Lt. Col. D.A.G. Dallas
1950 Mrs. Katherine MacDonnell; home port: Guernsey, CI.
1951 - 1955 Lt. Comdr. P.S. Boyle; home port: Greenock; engine installed in 1951; RORC rating: 1951: 49'48; 1955: 47'73.
1956 - 1962 M.P.R. Boyle; re-engined in 1955, removed in 1958 and she was modernised with the rigging and deck layout designed by David Cheverton in order to be used as a trial horse for *Sceptre's* America's Cup English challenge
1963 - 1972 Martin Sharp. In 1963 re-engined and altered to auxiliary yawl with a RORC rating: 42'37
1973 - 1980 G. Hommel; home port: Cowes, Nyon and Geneva;
1974 Hamburg; re-engined in 1974
1992 Sunk by Hurrican Hugo in Caribbean

■ VERONICA

DESIGNER: *Alfred Mylne & Co.*
BUILDER: *Bute Slip Dock Co, Ltd.*
YEAR: *1931 May*
LENGTH AT WATERLINE: *13.41 m.*
BEAM: *3.50 m.*
DRAFT: *2.71 m.*
SAIL AREA: *170 sq.m.; 141 sq.m. (1935)*
CONSTRUCTION: *wood*
FIRST OWNER: *Sir William P. Burton*
FIRST NAME: *Veronica*
FIRST COUNTRY: *Great Britain*
HOME PORT: *Ipswich*
FIRST SAIL NUMBER: *K 10*

CURRENT LOCATION: *unknown*

CONDITION: *broken up?*

FURTHER DETAILS AND HISTORY: Built according to the Second International Rule

Owners and history:

1931 - 1934 Sir. William P. Burton; name: *Veronica*; home port: Ipswich; rig: bermudan sloop. *Veronica* was the third Twelve built for the owner, former owner of *Noresca* and *Iyruna* and the future owner of *Marina* and *Jenetta*. In 1932 she was second to *Flica* starting in every race. Out of 41 entries, she won 6 firsts, 12 seconds and 8 thirds.

The 1933 season was a very good one for *Veronica*: "The Mylne boat, *Veronica*, has had her mast moved a lot farther aft than it was last season. In my opinion this has not only much improved her appearance but it seems to have made her much more lively. She was rather dull and sluggish in light winds last year, but at Burnham no vessel was more slippery when the wind was soft" (Heckstall-Smith in *Yachting World,* May 26th, 1933). She won at Burnham, Southend and when *Flica* and *Morwenna* moved to Norway, she moved to the Clyde to race against *Iyruna* and the new boat *Zelita*. She performed well in Cowes, although she was second to *Flica*. At the end of the season: "Sir William Burton so cleverly altered *Veronica* that she won 22 first prizes in fifty starts in 1933". She was second to *Flica* with 50 starts, 22 firsts, 13 seconds and 7 thirds. In 1934, the first year of the Third Rule, she was fourth in the season behind *Westra*, *Flica* and *Miquette* and out of 40 entries, she had 5 firsts, 6 seconds and 6 thirds. She entered and was dismasted in the last race for the 12 Metre class given by Royal Burnham YC

1935 - 1947 Robt. J. Dunlop; in 1935 she was converted by Mylne himself to bermudan yawl. She was completely rearranged below and re-rigged. A Kelvin 15 hp engine was installed. The work was done by the Aldous shipyard in Brightlingsea. 1947: RORC rating: 55'27

1948 - 1954 Lieut. E. S. Chance

1955 Disappeared off Lloyd's Register

■ WAIANDANCE

DESIGNER: *Burgess, Rigg & Morgan Ltd.*

BUILDER: *Abeking & Rasmussen - no. 2362*

YEAR: *1928 May*

LENGTH OVERALL: *21.09 m.*

LENGTH AT WATERLINE: *13.03 m.*

BEAM: *3.87 m.*

DRAFT: *2.58 m.*

SAIL AREA: *183 sq.m.*

CONSTRUCTION: *wood on steel frames*

FIRST OWNER: *F. Spencer Goodwin*

FIRST NAME: *Waiandance*

FIRST COUNTRY: *United States*

HOME PORT: *New York*

FIRST SAIL NUMBER: *US 1*

OTHER NAMES: *Clytie (1932) - Night Wind (1936) - Cotton Blossom III (1941)*

CONDITION: *scrapped by owner*

FURTHER DETAILS AND HISTORY: Built according to the Second Int. Rule. She was one of the Twelve Metres designed by Starling Burgess for

American owners and built by Abeking & Rasmussen

1928 - 1930 F. Spencer Goodwin; name: *Waiandance*; home port: New London, CT

1931 - 1935 Henry B. Plant; new name: *Clytie*; she won the 12 Metre Class Long Island Sound Championship in 1931 and won the 12 M Class at Larchmont Race Week in 1931

1936 - 1940 W. Roy Manny; new name: *Night Wind*; home port: Larchmont, NY

1941 - 1951 Walter B. Wheeler, Jr. New name: *Cotton Blossom III*; home port: Stamford and Norton, CT. Rig altered to yawl in 1942; engine installed in 1946

1952 Scrapped by owner at Schofield Shipyard, Stamford, CT after a fire while hauled out. Parts of this yacht were used in the reconstruction of *Onawa* (US 6) in 2000

■ ZINITA

DESIGNER: *W. & R.B. Fife*

BUILDER: *W. Fife & Son no. 749*

YEAR: *1927 May*

LENGTH OVERALL: *19.96 m.*

LENGTH AT WATERLINE: *11.96 m.*

BEAM: *3.76 m.*

DRAFT: *2.57 m.*

SAIL AREA: *147 sq.m.*

CONSTRUCTION: *wood on steel frames, keel and sternpost in teak*

FIRST OWNER: *Arthur C. Connell*

FIRST NAME: *Zinita*

FIRST COUNTRY: *Great Britain*

HOME PORT: *Greenock*

FIRST SAIL NUMBER: *K 8 - N 8 (1931 in Norway))*

OTHER NAMES: *Zinita of Chichester (1971)*

CURRENT LOCATION: *Amsterdam (Netherlands)*

CONDITION: *refit completed in 2000*

FURTHER DETAILS AND HISTORY: Built according to the Second International Rule

Owners and history:

1927 - 1930 Arthur C. Connell; name: *Zinita*; home port: Greenock; rig: bermudan cutter. Mr. Connell, partner of an old established Clyde shipbuilding company, was a faithful customer of the Fife yard and his family had already built three other *Zinitas*: a 20-Linear Rater, the second was a 30-Linear Rater and the third a 65-Linear Rater. He was also quite fussy on the details but was a very experienced sailing man. She was re-rigged in 1929

1931 - 1936 Frithjof Larsen; home port: Oslo; converted to a cruising yacht with a shortened rig but still using the same 1929 mast

1937 - 1968 Knut Aspelin; engine (Gray, 4 cyl.) installed in 1948; re-engined in 1961

1969 - 1970 Ulf Rogeberg

1971 Clive D. Bourchier; new name: *Zinita of Chichester*; home port: Chichester; re-engined in 1971

1973 Disappeared off Lloyd's Register

1995 Sea-Bird Sailing BV; new name: *Zinita*; home port: Amsterdam. She was chartered but she was not in perfect condition. She was up for sale for 230.000 Dutch florins. Restoration budget (signed by Gerard Dijkstra) for

Dutch florins 975.000 in search of a syndicate
Since 1995 Leo Arends. During 2000 *Zinita* was re-launched after a long refit; the hull was sheathed in an epoxy layer and the caulking substituted with splines

■ ZORAIDA

DESIGNER: *W. & R.B. Fife*
BUILDER: *William Fife and Son - no. 792*
YEAR: *1931 May*
BEAM: *3.53 m.*
CONSTRUCTION: *wood on steel frames; keel, stem, sternpost, rudder of teak*
FIRST OWNER: *Arthur C. Connell*
FIRST NAME: *Zoraida*
FIRST COUNTRY: *Great Britain*
HOME PORT: *Greenock*
FIRST SAIL NUMBER: *K 8*
CONDITION: *broken up?*
FURTHER DETAILS AND HISTORY: Built according to the Second Int. Rule

Owners and history:
1931 - 1932 Arthur C. Connell (partner of an old established Clyde shipbuilding company); name: *Zoraida*; home port: Greenock. The owner wanted to keep the same sail number (K 8) formerly attributed to his previous Twelve *Zinita*. Mr. Connell was a well-known "Twelves owner" having already owned other Fife yachts and later owned of *Westra* and *Ornsay*. Built at the same time as *Altair*, *Zoraida* did not perform as well as her predecessors. She was considered a slow boat and Fife received quite a number of complaints. Sherman Hoyt, the well known 6 M helmsman, confirmed *Zoraida* as a slow boat after having sailed her in Weymouth. In fact, in 1932 on 31 entries she had only 6 firsts, 9 seconds and 2 thirds. At the end of the season Connell decide to sell
1933 - 1934 John R. Payne; after selling *Vanity,* Payne looked for a more modern boat and he bought *Zoraida* with whom he has nothing but disappointment. In 1933, she was last with 10 entries, with 3 seconds and 3 thirds. In 1934 she was last but one (*Iyruna*) with only 5 entries, 1 first, 1 second and 2 thirds.
1935 - 1939 Lorenzo Ferranti; home port: Venice
1940 - 1946 ?
1947 Disappeared off Lloyd's Register

ANITA

DESIGNER: *Henry Rasmussen*
BUILDER: *Abeking & Rasmussen - construction no. 3241*
YEAR: *1938*
LENGTH OVERALL: *21.50 m.*
LENGTH AT WATERLINE: *13.95 m.*
BEAM: *3.55 m.*
DRAFT: *2.74 m.*
DISPLACEMENT: *26 tons*
SAIL AREA: *197 sq.m.*
CONSTRUCTION: *wood on steel frames*
FIRST OWNER: *Walter Rau*
FIRST NAME: *Anita*
FIRST COUNTRY: *Germany*
HOME PORT: *Warnemünde*
FIRST SAIL NUMBER: *G 2*
CURRENT LOCATION: *Gluckstadt (Elbe, Germany)*
CONDITION: *good*
FURTHER DETAILS AND HISTORY: Built according to the Third Int. Rule
Owners and history: **1938 - 1947** Walter Rau; name: *Anita;* home port:
Mecklenburg and Warnemünde. Built for the margarine manufacturer Mr.
Rau under Abeking&Rasmussen construction number 3241. After the war
her interiors were completely rebuilt by Abeking&Rasmussen
1951 - 1953 Mr. Paulsen (relative of the Rau family); rig - altered to yawl
1961 - 1964 Jellrich Rassau (Commodore of the SKO), Alois Kranz and
August Schulte
Since 1965 Segelkameradschaft Ostsee (Yachting Camaraderie Ostsee);
home port: Wiesbaden. The members of the club sail the yacht and
crossed the Atlantic in 1992

ASCHANTI III

DESIGNER: *Henri Gruber*
BUILDER: *Burmester Yacht-und Bootswerft*
YEAR: *1939*
LENGTH OVERALL: *20.79 m.*
LENGTH AT WATERLINE: *13.72 m.*
BEAM: *3.64 m.*
DRAFT: *2.68 m.*
DISPLACEMENT: *27 tons*
SAIL AREA: *176 sq.m.*
CONSTRUCTION: *wood on steel frames*
FIRST OWNER: *Ernst Burmester*
FIRST NAME: *Aschanti III*
FIRST COUNTRY: *Germany*
HOME PORT: *Bremen*
FIRST SAIL NUMBER: *G 3*
CONDITION: *broken up*
FURTHER DETAILS AND HISTORY: Built according to the Third Int. Rule
Owners and history: **1939 - 1953** Ernst Burmester; name: *Aschanti III;* home
port: Vegesack; rig: bermudan sloop. E. Burmester built *Aschanti III* to race
against the A&R Twelves. The design is by Henri Gruber, a great German
naval architect, assistant to Starling Burgess in the design of *Enterprise* and
Nina. According to Uffa Fox, *Aschanti* has "a very pleasing set of sections, a
long easy rise to the floor and the turn of the bilge is not reached until just

above the waterline, all of which makes an easily driven yet powerful boat,
able to carry her spars and sails to windward in a breeze of wind". She
entered the 1939 Kiel Week but soon after her racing career was stopped by
the war. In 1953 she crossed the Atlantic ocean on board a ship to enter the
Larchmont Week. She got a warm welcome from the Americans as if the war
had not taken place. The first races were disappointing and Burmester
decided to change the mast with an aluminum one and to have a set of
Dacron sails. She won four out of five races!
1954 Fritz von Opel; rig altered to yawl; engine installed after a very short
period. *Aschanti III* was sold back to Burmester
1954 - 1962 Ernst Burmester; rig: brought back to the original one. In 1962,
while at the Burmester yard, after an explosion on board, she was broken up

BLUE MARLIN

DESIGNER: *Charles E. Nicholson*
BUILDER: *Camper & Nicholsons, Ltd. - constuction no. 454*
YEAR: *1937*
LENGTH OVERALL: *21.30 m.*
LENGTH AT WATERLINE: *13.76 m.*
BEAM: *3.55 m.*
DRAFT: *2.71 m.*
SAIL AREA: *183 sq.m.*
CONSTRUCTION: *wood on steel frames*
FIRST OWNER: *Miss Marion B Carstairs*
FIRST NAME: *Hurricane*
FIRST COUNTRY: *United Kingdom*
HOME PORT: *Portsmouth*
FIRST SAIL NUMBER: *K 10 (Alanna) - K2 (Alanna) - K 17 (Blue Marlin)*
OTHER NAMES: *Alanna (1937) - Blue Marlin (1938)*
CURRENT LOCATION: *Marina di Isola (Slovenia)*
CONDITION: *good*
FURTHER DETAILS AND HISTORY: Built according to the Third Int. Rule
Owners and history: **1936** Miss Marion B. Carstairs; name *Hurricane;*
home port: Portsmouth. The owner was an American heiress who lived in
the Bahamas. She was quite active in powerboat racing and tried to win
the Harmsworth Trophy. The yacht was built but not launched in 1936.
Sold to the new owner and commissioned as *Alanna*
1937 C.E.A. Hartridge; new name: *Alanna;* home port: Portsmouth
1938 T.O.M. Sopwith; new name: *Blue Marlin.* She was not a very
successful Twelve, although owned by Mr. Sopwith. In 1938 out of 31 starts,
she had 0 firsts, 2 seconds and 9 thirds racing against *Trivia, Marina, Evaine,
Little Astra* and *Flica.* At the beginning of the new season *Blue Marlin* was
sold to a new owner. Mr. Sopwith started racing with his new *Tomahawk*
1939 - 1945 W.R. Westhead in the 1939 season, *Blue Marlin* performed
better. Although dismasted at the beginning of the season, she was third in
overall after *Vim* and *Tomahawk* with 6 firsts, 2 seconds and 3 thirds. She
was considered to be a fast boat; she was the only British Twelve to have
beaten *Vim* in a real race by 13 seconds (Royal Albert Y.C. regatta at
Southsea-August 9). At the end of the season, Major Heckstall-Smith wrote
(*YW* Sept. 8,39): "...Now none had a career so interesting as that of *Blue
Marlin.* Mr. Sopwith never did any good with her in 1938. Mr. Westhead
brought her out late in the season which she began by losing her mast and it
was some time before there was any indication of her being any better than
before. Mr. Colin Newman steered her with considerable skill and as time

went on *Blue Marlin* became a very formidable member of the Class. In very light airs, in particular, she was good. She was a very fast drifter. There were races when she beat *Trivia* to windward in the latter's weather, but I think *Trivia* was a little faster running"

1946 Geoffrey and Ralph Hawkes
1947 Mrs. J.W. Boumphrey; engine installed in 1947
1948 - 1950 C.E.A. Hartridge
1951 John G. Fairweather
1951 - 1956 Ippolito Berrone; home port: Genova (Italy). Disappeared from Lloyd's Register
1956 Alessandro Colussi; home port: Marina di Isola (Slovenia). Two engines installed (Ford 68 hp). She entered in several races in Italian and Dalmatian waters and won several firsts. Still sailing in 2001

■ CALEDONIA
DESIGNER: *David Boyd*
BUILDER: *not built*
YEAR: *1938*
LENGTH OVERALL: *22.10 m.*
LENGTH AT WATERLINE: *14.02 m.*
BEAM: *30.60 m.*
DRAFT: *2.43 m.*
DISPLACEMENT: *25.25 tons*
SAIL AREA: *167 sq.m.*
FURTHER DETAILS AND HISTORY: Project, not built

■ DEVONIA
DESIGNER: *Morgan Giles*
BUILDER: *not built*
YEAR: *1932*
LENGTH OVERALL: *22.03 m.*
LENGTH AT WATERLINE: *13.47 m.*
BEAM: *3.63 m.*
DRAFT: *2.70 m.*
DISPLACEMENT: *23.5 tons*
SAIL AREA: *170 sq.m.*
FURTHER DETAILS AND HISTORY: This Twelve was designed by Morgan Giles but due to the illness of the owner, never built

■ EVAINE
DESIGNER: *Charles E. Nicholson*
BUILDER: *Camper & Nicholsons Ltd. - construction no. 435*
YEAR: *1936 June*
LENGTH OVERALL: *21.33 m.*
LENGTH AT WATERLINE: *13.93 m.*
BEAM: *3.55 m.*
DRAFT: *2.67 m.*
SAIL AREA: *177.84 sq.m.; 189.07 sq.m (1969)*
CONSTRUCTION: *wood on steel frames*
FIRST OWNER: *C. R. Fairey*
FIRST NAME: *Evaine*
FIRST COUNTRY: *Great Britain*
HOME PORT: *Portsmouth*
FIRST SAIL NUMBER: *K 2 later used K 12*

OTHER NAMES: *Alanna (1935)*
CURRENT LOCATION: *Great Britain*
CONDITION: *restoration completed in 2001*
FURTHER DETAILS AND HISTORY: Built according to the Third Int. Rule
Owners and history: **1935** C.E.A. Hartridge; name: *Alanna*; originally ordered by Mr. Hartridge, but sold for "family reasons" before completion. He purchased another yacht from Nicholsons the following year and named her *Alanna*
1936 - 1956 Sir Richard C. Fairey (President of Fairey Aviation); name: *Evaine*; home port: Portsmouth. This was the second Twelve built for Sir Fairey after *Flica* and although not so successful as *Flica*, she was one of the outstanding designs of Nicholson. In her first season she was third after *Marina* and *Westra* out of 31 entries with 7 firsts, 10 seconds and 1 third. The 1937 and 1938 seasons were marked by the duels between *Evaine* and *Trivia* "which have added to the English yacht racing a new chapter even comparable with those of past history". In 1937 she was second behind *Trivia* with 44 entries, 11 firsts, 10 seconds and 10 thirds. The 1938 season was very competitive and at the end *Trivia* and *Evaine* had 40 entries with *Trivia* again first with 20 firsts while *Evaine* had 19 firsts, 13 seconds and 4 thirds. The 1939 scene was dominated by *Vim* and the new British Twelves: *Jenetta*, *Ornsay* and *Tomahawk*. At the end of the season, she was fifth with 2 firsts, 4 seconds and 5 thirds, out of 31 entries. During the Second World War she was laid up in a shed
1957 Estate of the late Sir Richard C. Fairey
1957 - 1959 Owen Arthur Aisher. On the occasion of the 1958 America's Cup, she underwent important work including a new aluminium mast. She was selected to be a trial horse against *Sceptre*. While waiting for *Sceptre*, together with *Flica II* and *Kaylena*, she was used for the selection and the training of the crew. After the launch of *Sceptre* she raced against the challenger and at the beginning she was much faster; only after a long and exhaustive setting up *Sceptre* began to win and *Evaine* was beaten, winning only four out of the Twelve's final races; forty three days of trials passed and *Sceptre* gained thirty three seconds per mile on *Evaine*. Very large spinnakers, manufactured by Herbulot, were used by both Twelves. These results explained why no one was surprised when *Sceptre* did not win the Cup, having been already beaten by a twenty-year-old design, albeit a good one and moreover always beaten by *Vim*
1959 - 1964 Guy G. Lawrence. Engine installed in 1959. She got a RORC certificate with a rating of 51'21. She entered the races for the 1964 America' Cup British selections
1965 - 1967 H. Porteu de la Marandière
1968 Evaine Ltd.
1969 - 1975 Graham Godfrey; home port: Jersey and Barry (from 1974). Engine removed in 1968. She was said to have sailed the Atlantic twice from Britain to the U.S. Due to unfortunate circumstances, in 1972 she fell over in a harbour on Jersey. In 1974 she was taken to Barry in South Wales where she lay until 1983
1976 John Johnson
1977 - 1980 G. Gough
1983 - 1995 Ian Smith; home port: Fochabera and Inverness. He did enough remedial work to enable *Evaine* to be sailed to Inverness (Scotland) and they stripped her out entirely, repaired the hull structure as necessary and rebuilt the accommodation throughout. She was used for charter
Since 1996 Andreas Wehner; *Evaine* underwent extensive work at the New Century yard (former McGruer)

■ FIGARO VI

DESIGNER: *Johan Anker*
BUILDER: *Anker & Jensen*
YEAR: *1936*
LENGTH OVERALL: *21.49 m.*
LENGTH AT WATERLINE: *13.93 m.*
BEAM: *3.73 m.*
SAIL AREA: *183 sq.m.*
ENGINE: *engine installed in 1962*
FIRST OWNER: *Thomas Olsen*
FIRST NAME: *Figaro VI*
FIRST COUNTRY: *Norway*
HOME PORT: *Oslo*
FIRST SAIL NUMBER: *N 12*
OTHER NAMES: *Silvervingen XI (1961)*
CONDITION: *sunk*
FURTHER DETAILS AND HISTORY: Built according to the Int. Third Rule. Owners and history: **1936 - 1960** Thomas Olsen; name: *Figaro VI*; home port: Oslo.
1961 - 1962 Nils Gäbel; new name: *Silvervingen XI*; home port: Saltsjö-Duvnäs (Sweden)
1963 - 1965 Nils Gabel; new name: *Figaro VI*
1966 Armand Goldmuntz; home port: Brussels
1967 Disappeared off Lloyd's Register; sunk

■ FLICA II

DESIGNER: *Laurent Giles & Partners*
BUILDER: *W. Fife & Son - construction no. 829*
YEAR: *1939 June*
LENGTH OVERALL: *20.45 m.*
LENGTH AT WATERLINE: *14.15 m.*
BEAM: *3.58 m.*
DRAFT: *2.77 m.*
SAIL AREA: *143 sq.m.*
CONSTRUCTION: *wood on steel frames*
FIRST OWNER: *Hugh Goodson*
FIRST NAME: *Flica II*
FIRST COUNTRY: *Great Britain*
HOME PORT: *Dartmouth*
FIRST SAIL NUMBER: *K14*
CURRENT LOCATION: *Hamburg (Germany)*
CONDITION: *at her best*
FURTHER DETAILS AND HISTORY: Built according to the Third Int. Rule Owners and history: **1939 - 1946** Hugh L. Goodson; name: *Flica II;* home port: Dartmouth; rig: bermudan sloop. *Flica II* was the last boat to be given a yard number at W. Fife & Son, which closed the same year after 140 years of activity. There was great attention drawn to the performance of the new yacht, her owner being an experienced yachtsman had had many good results with *Flica*. She was the first and only Twelve designed by J. Laurent Giles and it was said that her lines were the result of the tests of five models in the experimental tank. She was one of the largest Twelves ever built. Particularly noteworthy: the deck gear with a coffee grinder, the stainless steel bar shrouds of flat section, the aluminium alloy fittings, and the light interior thanks to plywood with a balsa core. After the first races

Flica II provided the greatest disappointment in the class: the hull form seemed capable of speed equal to other Twelves but the rigging seemed to be creating problems. In the second part of the season no better results were achieved: she seemed to be too long, too narrow and too heavy. In fact, at the end of the season, she won just 1 first, 1 second and 5 thirds out of 24 starts; what a disaipointment for her owner!
1946 - 1948 Charles E. Gardner
1948 E. Salem & Co. Ltd.
1949 - 1954 Jack Salem
1954 - 1959 H. R. Attwood; engine installed in 1955. *Flica II* model was used as point of reference for the eight models created by David Boyd of the British America's Cup 1958 challenge. Under the supervision of J. Illingworth, *Flica II* was tuned up in order to train the challenger crew and to serve as a trial horse for *Sceptre*. She won the 12-Metre Class in the 1958 Cowes Week
1959 - 1964 J. Anthony J. Boyden; home port: Hamble; engine removed. She entered in several races and she won the 1961 Royal Thames Yacht Club Queen's Cup. She was trial horse to *Sovereign* and *Kurrewa V* for the 1964 America's Cup British challenge
1964 - 1974 John G. Clegg; home port: Hamble & Dartmouth; engine re-installed in 1964 and rig altered. In 1964 to auxiliary yawl and in 1967 altered to auxiliary ketch. Portholes were put in and a doghouse
1974 - 1977 T.D. McComb; home port: Dartmouth and Grenada, WI
1978 Disappeared off Lloyd's Register
1977 - 1989 Hans Zimmer; home port: Westbrook, CT (USA); she was found abandoned on a shore in the Caribbean
1989 - 1990 Robert Tiedemann; home port: Newport, RI
1990, May - 1992 Bruno Pozzi; home port: Santa Margherita Ligure (Italy). She underwent a complete restoration at Camper & Nicholsons under the supervision of Giorgetti & Magrini. Only the lead keel, the rudder and a part of the planking remained of the original construction
1993 - 1999 Stefano and Francesca Tanzi; she entered successfully in the Mediterranean races for Twelve Metres; in 1995 she won the Coppa Europa reserved for the Twelve Metre
Since 2000 Alexander Falk; home port: Hamburg

■ FRATERNITAS

DESIGNER: *Henrik Robert*
BUILDER: *Holmens Yachtwerft A.S. - Asker*
YEAR: *1937*
LENGTH OVERALL: *18.40 m.*
LENGTH AT WATERLINE: *12.13 m.*
BEAM: *3.32 m.*
DRAFT: *2.38 m.*
SAIL AREA: *180 sq.m.*
CONSTRUCTION: *wood*
ENGINE: *petrol Universal*
FIRST OWNER: *H. A. Hartner*
FIRST NAME: *Vivo VIII*
FIRST COUNTRY: *Norway*
HOME PORT: *Oslo*
FIRST SAIL NUMBER: *E 20*
CURRENT LOCATION: *Arendal (Norway)*
CONDITION: *under refit*
FURTHER DETAILS AND HISTORY: Built according to the Third Int. Rule

Owners and history: **1937 - 1954** H.A. Hartner; name: *Vivo VIII*; home port: Oslo; rig: auxiliary bermudan sloop
1955 Disappeared off Lloyd's Register
1994 Trond B. Frigstad; name: *Fraternitas*; home port: Arendal. In the year 2001 she was said to be under refit which was supposed to be finished for the 2001 season

■ **GLEAM**
DESIGNER: *Clinton H. Crane*
BUILDER: *Henry B. Nevins Inc - construction no. 423*
YEAR: *1937 May*
LENGTH OVERALL: *20.65 m.*
LENGTH AT WATERLINE: *13.54 m.*
BEAM: *3.66 m.*
DRAFT: *2.64 m.*
SAIL AREA: *181 sq.m.*
CONSTRUCTION: *double-planked (mahogany on cedar) on oak frames*
FIRST NAME: *Gleam*
FIRST COUNTRY: *United States*
HOME PORT: *New York*
FIRST SAIL NUMBER: *US 11*
OTHER NAMES: *Charlotte II (1950)*
CURRENT LOCATION: *Newport (U.S.)*
FURTHER DETAILS AND HISTORY: Built according to the Third Int. Rule Owners and history: **1937 - 1942** Clinton H. Crane; name: *Gleam*; home port: New York, NY; rig: bermudan sloop. New lead keel in 1939; dismasted in 1939; mast replaced with wooden mast made for *Vim* in 1939. *Gleam* was designed by Crane for his own use using an innovative concept of tank testing as she was tested against a model of *Seven Seas*. Crane made available his studies to both Olin Stephens and Francis Herreshoff but only the first accepted. With the exception of her first season in 1937 (*Gleam* was first beating *Seven Seas* with 3 firsts and 2 seconds out of 5 races and was also very successful in the Astor Cup when she beat the "J"-Class boats on corrected time) her racing results before and after the war were not brilliant
5/1946 - 1949 B. Devereux Barker & B. Devereux Barker Jr.; home port: Marblehead, MA; engine installed in 1940
1950 - 1952 John N. Potter; new name: *Charlotte II;* home port: Darien, CT; re-engined in 1950
1953 - 1968 W. Mahlon Dickerson; new name: *Gleam*; home port: Oyster Bay, NY: re-engined in 1958. Mast broken again in 1967, replaced with a copy of *Vim*'s mast. She was the trial horse for *Vim* and *Sceptre* in the 1958 America's Cup and again of *Gretel* in the 1962 Cup
1969 - 1976 C.W. Ufford; re-engined in 1970
Since 1977 Gleam Charters, Inc (Robert H. Tiedemann); home port: New York, NY, Greenwich, CT and Newport, RI; re-engined

■ **GURI**
DESIGNER: *Skalurens Skybsbygg*
BUILDER: *Skalurens Skybsbygg*
YEAR: *1938*
LENGTH OVERALL: *17.00 m.*
LENGTH AT WATERLINE: *12.19 m.*
BEAM: *3.84 m.*
DRAFT: *2.44 m.*

SAIL AREA: *127 sq.m.*
CONSTRUCTION: *wood*
FIRST OWNER: *C. K. Wiese*
FIRST NAME: *Guri*
FIRST COUNTRY: *Norway*
HOME PORT: *Bergen*
FIRST SAIL NUMBER: *N 2*
CURRENT LOCATION: *Oslo (Norway)*
CONDITION: *sailing*
FURTHER DETAILS AND HISTORY:
Built according to the 12 M Int. Rule. Her dimensions do not correspond with the Third Int. Rule. Despite this she was classified as a Third Rule Twelve having being built during the Third Rule validity period. Owners and history:
1938 - 1950 C.K. Wiese; name: *Guri*; home port: Bergen; rig: bermudan yawl
1951 - 1960 Odd Nielsen; home port: Oslo; in 1952 petrol 4 cyl. Morris engine was installed; RORC rating: 35'55ft (1952), 32"73ft (1954)
1961 ? Sten Tornquist
1963 Disappeared off Lloyd's Register
2001 Hegnar Trygve

■ **JENETTA**
DESIGNER: *A. Mylne & Co.*
BUILDER: *Bute Slip Dock Co., Ltd - construction no. 395*
YEAR: *1939 May*
LENGTH OVERALL: *21.70 m.*
LENGTH AT WATERLINE: *14.17 m.*
BEAM: *3.66 m.*
DRAFT: *2.74 m.*
SAIL AREA: *159 sq.m.*
CONSTRUCTION: *wood on steel frames*
FIRST OWNER: *Sir William P. Burton*
FIRST NAME: *Jenetta*
FIRST COUNTRY: *Great Britain*
HOME PORT: *Ipswich*
FIRST SAIL NUMBER: *K 1 - KC 1 (probably not official)*
CONDITION: *destroyed in Canada*
FURTHER DETAILS AND HISTORY: Built according to the Third Int. Rule Owners and history: **1939 - ?** Sir William P. Burton; name: *Jenetta*; home port: Ipswich; rig: bermudan sloop. She was the fourth and last Twelve to be owned by Sir William Burton after *Noresca*, *Veronica* and *Marina*. 1939 was *Vim*'s season and it is difficult to say how *Jenetta* was performing. Around mid season she was considered, together with *Tomahawk* to be part of the best English pair. In that season she entered 38 races and won 1 first, 9 seconds and 10 thirds
1946 - 1947 L.J. Clements; converted to auxiliary bermudian sloop as engine installed in 1947
1948 - 1952 A.W. Steven. She entered the handicap races successfully. Her owner was more than 80 years old
1953 Estate of the late A.W. Steven
1953 - 1958 F.W., D.P. Mrs. & V.M. Urry; home port: Vancouver, BC. In 1957 rig altered to auxiliary ketch, sail area 159 sq.m.; re-engined in 1959. Yacht may have used Sail number KC 1 (probably, although not officially issued)
1959 - 1962 F. W. Urry
1963 - 1971 F. W. Urry & V. M. (Mrs) Urry

1972 - 1975 Mrs. V. W. M. Urry
1976 Disappeared off Lloyd's Register
1993 - 1994 Tom Holmes; home port South Burnaby, BC. In the 1990's it was reported that *Jenetta* had been destroyed at Ohman Marina in British Columbia (Canada)

■ **LITTLE ASTRA**
DESIGNER: *Charles E. Nicholson*
BUILDER: *Camper & Nicholsons - construction no. 452*
YEAR: *1937 May*
LENGTH OVERALL: *21.34 m.*
LENGTH AT WATERLINE: *13.84 m.*
BEAM: *3.55 m.*
DRAFT: *2.71 m.*
SAIL AREA: *180 sq.m.*
CONSTRUCTION: *wood on steel frames*
FIRST OWNER: *Hugh F. Paul*
FIRST NAME: *Little Astra*
FIRST COUNTRY: *Great Britain*
HOME PORT: *Portsmouth*
FIRST SAIL NUMBER: *K 18*
CONDITION: *burnt and broken up*
FURTHER DETAILS AND HISTORY: Built according to the Third Int. Rule Owners and history: **1937 - 1947** Hugh F. Paul; name: *Little Astra*; home port: Portsmouth; rig: bermudan sloop. *Little Astra* was the "little sister" of the 23 Metre *Astra*, also owned by Mr. Paul, which became a houseboat and tender to the Twelve. She was not very successful despite being an active participant in to the seasonal races; in 1937 she was fifth and out of 41 entries she had 3 firsts, 1 second and 9 thirds; in 1938 she was fourth and out of 38 entries she had 2 firsts, 8 seconds and 5 thirds
1947 Estate of Hugh F. Paul
1948 P. Hursell
1949 - 1951 C.E. Gardner & P. Mursell
1952 C.E. Gardner
1952 - 1965 O.M.S.A. - Officine Meccaniche S.A.; home port: Genova (Italy); engine installed in 1952
1966 Disappeared off Lloyd's Register
1970 She was laid upon behalf of Cantiere Valdettaro at Cantieri Ricciotti in Fezzano (La Spezia, Italy), broken up and burnt

■ **MARINA**
DESIGNER: *Alfred Mylne & Co. - design no. 368*
BUILDER: *Bute Slip Dock Co. Ltd.*
YEAR: *1935*
LENGTH OVERALL: *20.12 m.*
LENGTH AT WATERLINE: *13.41 m.*
BEAM: *3.70 m.*
CONSTRUCTION: *wood on steel frames*
FIRST OWNER: *Sir. William P. Burton*
FIRST NAME: *Marina*
FIRST COUNTRY: *Great Britain*
HOME PORT: *Ipswich*
FIRST SAIL NUMBER: *K 6*
CURRENT LOCATION: *unknown*

FURTHER DETAILS AND HISTORY: Built according to the Third Int. Rule Owners and history: **1935 - 1938** Sir William P. Burton; name: *Marina*; home port: Ipswich. The owner was a great personality of British yachting: he represented Great Britain in the 1906 London Conference, he was President of Y.R.A. and the former owner of the Twelves *Noresca*, *Iyruna* and *Veronica* and later owned *Jenetta*. He was considered to be a very valuable helmsman and according to *The Yachtsman*, the only Corinthian to handle a yacht with the skill of a professional. He was the helmsman of *Shamrock IV* in the 1920 America's Cup. *Marina* was the top boat of the 1935 year in with a very advanced rig - the first to use jumper struts, consequently avoiding the need to have the topmast stay attached to the stemhead. Mylne designed this new rig for two reasons: the jib would stand much better on the wind and the spinnaker could be handled more easily and would set much more easily when running. Special attention was also devoted to the mast, which was higher than usual (83 feet compared to the standard 82) and built with special care conforming to Mylne's new plan. She was a light boat too. Although designed for light winds, she proved to be a safe and seaworthy Twelve as she did very well in her passage from the Clyde to the South when she was caught out in a gale. In the 1935 season she was first over *Westra*, *Flica*, *Miquette*, *Zelita*, *Vanity* and *Iyruna* with 39 starts, 14 firsts, 10 seconds and 5 thirds. In 1936 her ballast was modified and her sail area was reduced by a reef. In the season she led again over *Westra*, *Evaine*, *Flica*, *Vanity* and *Vanity V* with 40 starts, 13 firsts, 11 seconds. In 1937, she was third, behind *Trivia* and *Evaine* with 44 entries and 9 firsts, 11 seconds and 11 thirds. She was dismasted twice. In 1938, she was again third behind the same two Twelves with 41 starts, 4 firsts, 7 seconds and 7 thirds
1947 Disappeared off Lloyd's Register

■ **MIQUETTE**
DESIGNER: *W. & R.B. Fife*
BUILDER: *W. Fife & Son - construction no. 808*
YEAR: *1934 April*
LENGTH OVERALL: *21.00 m.*
LENGTH AT WATERLINE: *13.54 m.*
BEAM: *3.53 m.*
DRAFT: *2.67 m.*
SAIL AREA: *152 sq.m.*
CONSTRUCTION: *wood on steel frames, rudder, keel, sternpost of teak*
FIRST OWNER: *H. L. Wessel*
FIRST NAME: *Miquette*
FIRST COUNTRY: *Chile*
HOME PORT: *Valparaiso*
FIRST SAIL NUMBER: *K14 - X1*
CURRENT LOCATION: *Hamble (Great Britain)*
CONDITION: *in need of refit*
PRESENT OWNER: *Fairlie Restorations Ltd.*
FURTHER DETAILS AND HISTORY: Built according to the Third Int. Rule Owners and history: **1934** R. S. Grigg; name *Miquette*; home port: Greenock; rig: bermudan sloop. She was the last but one Twelve designed by W. Fife III (the last one being *Vanity V*) in a period of lack of orders for the yard; the owner was the brother-in-law of Sir Ralph Gore, who was to be the skipper of the new Fife Twelve. At the opening of the 1934 seasonattracted great great attention the new boats as the results of the last Twelves from the yard were disappointing. Her debut at the Burnham-on-Crouch races was

a winning one against *Veronica*. In the season's overall results, she was third after *Westra* and *Flica* with 37 starts and 10 firsts, 9 seconds and 8 thirds

1935 - 1937 H. L. Wessel; home port: Copenhagen and Valparaiso. In the 1935 season she was fourth out of 29 starts with 3 firsts, 3 seconds and 5 thirds

1938 - 1939 Austin H. O'Connor; home port: London; engine installed in 1939

1947 - 1951 H.S. Broom; home port: Colchester

1952 - 1954 Sir Rowland Smith

1955 - 1957 Comdr. Hector G. Dobbs

1957 - 1967 G.J Robinson; home port: Hamble and Ibiza; re-engined in 1957

1968 - 1969 Paul Maitland-Smith; home port: Ibiza.

1970 - 1972 Paul Maitland-Smith, G. R. C. Shaw, A. J. Kay & L. B. Blair; re-engined in 1971

1973 Paul Maitland-Smith and G.R.C Shaw

1974 S. Chaplin

1974 - 1975 N.S.M. Yeats; home port: Ibiza and Leshoto (South Africa)

1976 Disappeared off Lloyd's Register; sold to an owner in U.S.A., reported to have been in Florida

1976 Ashley James. During these years she was said to have been in Canada and her port of registry in Sidney, BC

1993-1994 Albert Obrist

Since 1999 Currently at Fairlie Restorations; home port: Hamble, Hants (U.K.). Awaiting owner who will restore her

■ MITENA

DESIGNER: *L. Francis Herreshoff*
BUILDER: *Herreshoff Manufacturing Co. - construction no. 1275*
YEAR: *1935 June*
LENGTH OVERALL: *21.95 m.*
LENGTH AT WATERLINE: *13.41 m.*
BEAM: *3.40 m.*
DRAFT: *2.65 m.*
SAIL AREA: *164 sq.m.*
CONSTRUCTION: *composite*
FIRST OWNER: *William J. Strawbridge*
FIRST NAME: *Mitena*
FIRST COUNTRY: *United States*
HOME PORT: *New York*
FIRST SAIL NUMBER: *US 10*
CURRENT LOCATION: *Dearborn, MI (USA)*
CONDITION: *good*
FURTHER DETAILS AND HISTORY: Built according to the Third Int. Rule Owners and history: **1935 - 1939** William J. Strawbridge; name: *Mitena*; home port: Glen Cove, NY; rig: sloop. She was the first Twelve launched in the USA according to the Third Rule. She was a very long Twelve and had a canoe stern, and had a reduced sail area. Although unable to win, she entered the Long Island Sound regattas in 1939. Her owner was later the head of the Intrepid Syndicate in 1967

1939 - 1940 Aemilius Jarvis and George E. Ratsey; home port: City Island; NY

1940 - 1961 John Van Voorhis; home port: Rochester, NY; engine installed in 1958

1961 Yale University; home port: New Haven, CT

1962 - 1963 Charles S. Withey; home port: Macatawa Bay, MI

1964 - 1966 Paul Brown

1967 - 1969 Mitena, Inc.

1970 - 1975 R.F. Smith

1976 Disappeared off record

1994-2001 Jim Henley; home port: Dearbon, MI. The current mast may be the original spar from *Nyala*

■ NORTHERN LIGHT

DESIGNER: *Olin Stephens; design no. 239*
BUILDER: *Henry B. Nevins Inc. - construction no. 435*
YEAR: *1938*
LENGTH OVERALL: *21.33 m.*
LENGTH AT WATERLINE: *13.72 m.*
BEAM: *3.65 m.*
DRAFT: *2.67 m.*
SAIL AREA: *179 sq.m.*
CONSTRUCTION: *wood double planked (mahogany over cedar)*
FIRST OWNER: *Alfred L. Loomis Jr.*
FIRST NAME: *Northern Light*
FIRST COUNTRY: *United States*
HOME PORT: *New York*
FIRST SAIL NUMBER: *US 14*
OTHER NAMES: *Nereus (1941)*
CURRENT LOCATION: *Newport (United States)*
FURTHER DETAILS AND HISTORY: Built according to the Int. Third Rule Owners and history: **1938 - 1939** Alfred L. Loomis Jr; name: *Northern Light*; home port: New York, NY. She was the second Twelve designed by Olin Stephens and launched just a few weeks after *Nyala*. The two boats have the same dimensions and above waterline shape but *Northern Light* has a higher prismatic by a small margin and she was faster on a reach while *Nyala* was marginally better in light winds, especially upwind. In 1938 she won one race out of six with 3 seconds, in 1940 out of 9 starts she had 1 first and 4 seconds and 4 thirds

1940 - 1941 Van S. Merle-Smith; home port: Oyster Bay, NY

1941 - 1952 Starling, Inc.; new name: *Nereus*; home port: New York, NY; engine installed in 1941. She raced from 1947 to 1953 in the NYYC season and had the best year in 1947 with 6 firsts and 2 seconds out of 9 starts

1952 - 1955 North American Shipping & Trading Co., Inc (F.M. Ferris, President); home port: Greenwich, CT

1958 - 1961 Imperial Shipping Investment Co., Ltd. (Stavros Niarchos); home port: Hamilton (Bermuda). She was the trial horse for *Columbia* in the 1958 America's Cup defender trials

1962 - 1971 Wilbur E. Dow, Jr; home port: Oyster Bay, NY; engine removed in 1964. She was the trial horse for *Constellation* in the 1964 America's Cup defender trials

1971 - 1976 John B. Andreae & Buck L. Neesley; new name: *Northern Light*; home port: Detroit, MI

1978 - 1984 David G. Andrea; home port: Pentwater, MI; re-engined and interior rebuilt by Palmer-Johnson in 1976. Inadvertently sunk alongside a dock on Lake Michigan

Since 1984 Northern Light Charters (Robert H. Tiedemann); home port: Newport, RI; *Northern Light* was bought in too far gone a condition and she had to undergo an extensive restoration which took two years to complete. She was reframed and a third of her planking replaced, a new mast was stepped and the interior replaced

NYALA

DESIGNER: *Olin J. Stephens - plan no. 214*
BUILDER: *Henry B. Nevins, Inc. - construction no. 434*
YEAR: *1938 May*
LENGTH OVERALL: *21.35 m.*
LENGTH AT WATERLINE: *13.72 m.*
BEAM: *3.60 m.*
DRAFT: *2.67 m.*
DISPLACEMENT: *24.5 tons*
SAIL AREA: *179 sq.m.*
CONSTRUCTION: *wood, double planked*
FIRST OWNER: *Frederick T. Bedford*
FIRST NAME: *Nyala*
FIRST COUNTRY: *United States*
HOME PORT: *Southport*
FIRST SAIL NUMBER: *US 12*
CURRENT LOCATION: *Porto Santo Stefano (Italy)*
CONDITION: *at the best*
FURTHER DETAILS AND HISTORY: Built according to the Third Int. Rule. Owners and history: **1938 - 1942** Frederick T. Bedford; name: *Nyala*; home port: Southport, CT. *Nyala* was ordered by Frederick T. Bedford, president of Standard Oil Corporation and a well-known yachtsman, as a present to his daughter Lucie on the occasion of her wedding to Briggs Cunningham, who was a valuable skipper who became known for inventing the Cunningham hole and for skippering the 1958 America's Cup winner *Columbia*. She was the first Twelve designed by Olin Stephens, launched just a few weeks before *Northern Light*. The two boats had the same dimensions and above waterline shape but *Northern Light* has a higher prismatic by a small margin and she was faster on a reach while *Nyala* was marginally better in light airs, especially upwind. She was a very fast boat and in the 1938 season she won two out of 6 races with 2 seconds and 3 thirds. In 1939 she had a record of 10 firsts (first in the NYYC King's Cup) out of 14 races with 3 seconds and 1 third; in 1940, out of 8 races, she won 1 first, 3 seconds and 4 thirds; she won again in the 1940 season against *Vim*, although *Vim* won the Larchmont Race Week and the King's and Astor Cup
1942 - 1946 Bob Shelman; home port: Detroit, MI
1947 - 1948 South Bend Tool & Die Co.; engine installed in 1947. In 1947 due to a sudden storm while racing in the Mackinac Race she was dismasted and her aluminium mast replaced by the wooden one of *Mouette*
1949 - 1950 Streameze, Inc. (R.W. Schleman, Pres.)
1951 - 1980 Gerald W. Ford; home port: Larchmont, NY; engine removed in 1953 and re-installed in 1956 and again several times in the years 1959/1960/1961 and 1970 (installed). She entered several races; in 1960, during hurricane *Donna*, she was wrecked on the rocks at City Island. Several structural changes were introduced during the restoration: the stern was changed, the mast was moved back about one metre. *Nyala* was the trial horse for *Vim* in 1957 for the 1958 America's Cup
1983 - 1988 Dale Crabtree; home port: Newport, RI. She was used for three years and underwent several restoration works. She was then abandoned in a shed
1988 Thorpe Leeson; Nyala Holding, Inc.; home port: Dover, DE
1994 Ugo Baravalle
Since 1995 Patrizio Bertelli; name: *Nyala*; home port: Porto Santo Stefano (Italy). Shipped to Cantieri dell'Argentario (Porto Santo Stefano) she was completely rebuilt according to the original plans - the only difference being in the mast and the rudder which was made of carbon fibre. Due to the disqualification in the 1997 12m Europe Cup these were replaced with a wooden rudder and an aluminium mast

ORNSAY

DESIGNER: *Charles E. Nicholson*
BUILDER: *Camper & Nicholsons Ltd. - construction no. 469*
YEAR: *1939*
LENGTH OVERALL: *21.18 m.*
BEAM: *3.63 m.*
FIRST OWNER: *Arthur C. Connell*
FIRST NAME: *Ornsay*
FIRST COUNTRY: *Great Britain*
HOME PORT: *Portsmouth*
CONDITION: *broken up in 1941*
FURTHER DETAILS AND HISTORY: Built according to the Third Int. Rule. Owners and history: **1939** Arthur C. Connell; name: *Ornsay*; home port: Portsmouth. Mr. Connell was already the owner of *Zinita*, *Zoraida*, *Zelita* and *Westra*. *Ornsay* was his second Twelve built by C&N, a sister ship to *Tomahawk*. Her racing career was not very encouraging with no firsts, 1 second and 5 thirds out of 17 starts
Dec. 1942 Destroyed together with *Westra* in an air-raid while stored at the Camper & Nicholsons yard in Gosport

OSTWIND

DESIGNER: *Henry Rasmussen*
BUILDER: *Abeking & Rasmussen - constuction no. 3312*
YEAR: *1939*
LENGTH OVERALL: *21.38 m.*
LENGTH AT WATERLINE: *13.90 m.*
BEAM: *3.96 m.*
DRAFT: *2.82 m.*
DISPLACEMENT: *27 tons*
SAIL AREA: *191 sq.m.*
CONSTRUCTION: *wood on steel frames*
FIRST OWNER: *Norddeutscher Regatta-Verein*
FIRST NAME: *Sphinx*
FIRST COUNTRY: *Germany*
HOME PORT: *Hamburg*
FIRST SAIL NUMBER: *G 4*
OTHER NAMES: *Lobito (1956) - Ostwind (1960)*
CURRENT LOCATION: *Flensburg (Germany)*
CONDITION: *good*
FURTHER DETAILS AND HISTORY: Built according to the Third International Rule. Owners and history: **1939 - 1955** Norddeutscher Regatta-Verein-NRV (North German Racing Club). Name: *Sphinx*; home port: Hamburg. After the war *Sphinx* was bartered by the club to Abeking & Rasmussen for different sailing boats to be used by the club's youth section
1956 - 1960 H. Freudenberg; new name: *Lobito*
Since 1961 German Federal Navy; new name: *Ostwind*; home port: Flensburg

SEVEN SEAS OF PORTO

DESIGNER: *Clinton H. Crane*

BUILDER: *Henry B. Nevins Inc.*
YEAR: *1935 July*
LENGTH OVERALL: *20.79 m.*
LENGTH AT WATERLINE: *13.84 m.*
BEAM: *3.66 m.*
DRAFT: *2.71 m.*
SAIL AREA: *181 sq.m.*
CONSTRUCTION: *wood*
FIRST OWNER: *Van S. Merle-Smith*
FIRST NAME: *Seven Seas*
FIRST COUNTRY: *United States*
HOME PORT: *New York*
FIRST SAIL NUMBER: *US 9 - P1 - K 26*
OTHER NAMES: *Sunday (1946) - Seven Seas of Porto (1993)*
CONDITION: *at her best*
FURTHER DETAILS AND HISTORY: Built according the Third Int. Rule Owners and history: **1935 - 1942** Van Santford Merle-Smith; name: *Seven Seas*; home port: Oyster Bay, NY; rig: bermudan cutter. In May 1939 the lead keel was modified to a Sparkman & Stephens (design no. 293). *Seven Seas* was the first Twelve designed by Crane, who had already worked on the Int. Rule 8 and 6-Metre. She represented an improvement in the American Twelves design. She was placed second behind *Cantitoe* in Larchmont Race Week in 1935 and she topped the class in 1936 (5 firsts out of 6 races) and she is second in 1937 behind *Gleam* (3 seconds and 1 third) and 1938 (1 first, 2 seconds and 1 third) behind *Nyala*

1943 - 1985 José Goncalves; new name: *Sunday*; home port: Lisbon; she raced hard until the late Sixties in handicap regattas, winning on real time but losing on corrected. In that period she had the sail number P1. In the following years the interior was modified by Colin Mudie and she was used for cruising occasionally

1951 Disappeared off Lloyd's Register

1985 she was sold to Spain and in 1990 she was at Astilleros Lagos in Vigo for a partial refit

Since 1993 Rui Macedo Silva; new name *Seven Seas of Porto*; home port: Porto (Portugal); new sail number: K 26. New rating certificate issued in July 1993. During the latter part of 1992 and the first part of 1993, the yacht hull was rebuilt by Astilleros Lagos and was substantially restored with the planking replaced and a portion of lead ballast removed from the keel. The bare hull was then moved to Southampton Yacht Services where, under Lloyd's supervision, a new deck was fitted, all spars and rigging were replaced and the interior was completely refitted. The restoration was carried out to the same design as original although some modern practicalities were added

■ TOMAHAWK

DESIGNER: *Charles E. Nicholson*
BUILDER: *Camper & Nicholsons Ltd. - construction no. 478*
YEAR: *1939 June*
LENGTH OVERALL: *21.11 m.*
LENGTH AT WATERLINE: *13.90 m.*
BEAM: *3.56 m.*
DRAFT: *2.71 m.*
DISPLACEMENT: *24.15 tons*
SAIL AREA: *189 sq.m.*
CONSTRUCTION: *wood on steel frames*

FIRST OWNER: *Thomas O. Murdoch Sopwith*
FIRST NAME: *Tomahawk*
FIRST COUNTRY: *Great Britain*
HOME PORT: *Portsmouth*
FIRST SAIL NUMBER: *K 13*
CURRENT LOCATION: *La Spezia (Italy)*
CONDITION: *at her best*
FURTHER DETAILS AND HISTORY: Built according to the Third Int. Rule Owners and history: **1939 - 1947** Thomas O. Murdoch Sopwith; name: *Tomahawk*; home port: Portsmouth; rig: bermudan sloop. With *Jenetta*, *Ornsay* and *Flica II*, *Tomahawk* was one of the large Twelves built just before the war; Sopwith wanted a very competitive yacht to race against his friend and America's Cup (*Endeavour II* and *Ranger*) rival Harold Vanderbilt who was building *Vim* with the aim of coming to Britain for the famous Twelve Metre races. *Tomahawk* turned out to be a very fast boat, with *Jenetta*. The best British Twelve of the season. Her design was an evolution of the past Twelves with some new ideas such as one coffee grinder and stainless steel shrouds; *Vim* was a total revolution in terms of the hull design, in the deck and interior layout, in the rigging, in the sails and in the fittings. *Vim* was successful in every race and the only consolation for Sopwith was to have the best Twelve of the season: out of 41 starts, she had 11 firsts, 11 seconds and 5 thirds with a second placement overall to *Vim*. While racing, *Tomahawk* had a very special crew: T. Sopwith at the tiller, Lady Sopwith was sail trimmer, Ernst Scarlet the tactician, and Franck Murdoch, Tony Thorneycroft and Charles E. Nicholson

1947 - 1955 Lt. Col. Sir Ralph Gore, president of Y.R.A.

1956 - 1962 Giovanni Agnelli; home port: Savona (Italy); engine installed in 1962

1963 - 1965 Susanna Agnelli Rattazzi; home port: Savona and Viareggio (Italy)

1966 - 1979 Circolo del Remo e della vela "Italia"; home port: Napoli

1980 M. Bandazzo

1982 - 1986 Kari Blaudet; home port: Finale Ligure. She was used for charter. In 1983 she won the Veteran Boat Rally at Porto Cervo

Since 1987 Alberto Rusconi; home port: La Spezia. *Tomahawk* was the first Twelve to be restored for the new summer of the Twelves in the Mediterranean. The restoration took place at the Beconcini Shipyard under the supervision of Giorgetti & Magrini. It did not strictly conform to the original designs as she was directed more towards a luxury cruising yacht than to a racing Twelve and one day *Tomahawk* will undergo restoration which will bring her back to the original plan. She entered in the vintage regattas in the Mediterranean and with her lines and results attracted the interest of other owners of the old Twelves: a new renaissance started again for these yachts

■ TRIVIA

DESIGNER: *Charles E. Nicholson*
BUILDER: *Camper & Nicholsons - construction no. 440*
YEAR: *1937*
LENGTH OVERALL: *21.37 m.*
LENGTH AT WATERLINE: *13.94 m.*
BEAM: *3.55 m.*
DRAFT: *2.71 m.*
DISPLACEMENT: *27 tons*
SAIL AREA: *178 sq.m.*
CONSTRUCTION: *wood on steel frames*
FIRST OWNER: *V. W. Mac Andrew*

FIRST NAME: *Trivia*
FIRST COUNTRY: *Great Britain*
HOME PORT: *Dartmouth*
FIRST SAIL NUMBER: *K10 - N16 - US 16*
OTHER NAMES: *Norsaga (1949) - Phoenix (1972) - Trivia of Gosport (1993)*
CURRENT LOCATION: *Hamburg (Germany)*
CONDITION: *at her best*
PRESENT OWNER: *Alfred Beeck*
FURTHER DETAILS AND HISTORY: Built according the Third Int. Rule
Owners and history: **1937 - 1939** V. W. MacAndrew; name: *Trivia*; home
port: Dartmouth; rig: bermudan sloop. She was a very successful Twelve,
her traditional adversary being *Evaine*. In 1937 she was first in the season
with 13 firsts, 11 seconds and 6 thirds out of 41 starts and again she was
first in the 1938 season: out of 48 starts, she had 20 firsts, 15 seconds
and 4 thirds. *Evaine* was again a very close second and Heckstall-Smith
claimed that the fight between the two yachts: "Have added to the
English yacht racing a new chapter even comparable with those of past
history." In 1939, the presence of the new Twelves: *Tomahawk*, *Ornsay*,
Jenetta and *Vim* did not allow *Trivia* to have similar positive results. Out
of 32 starts, she had 3 firsts, 9 seconds and 6 thirds
1945 Charles E. Gardner
1947 - 1948 J. Howden Hume; engine installed in 1948
1948 - 1956 Charles Ulrick Bay; new name: *Norsaga*; home port: Oslo and
New York; engine removed in 1952; rating RORC: 54'84 with the new name
of *Norsaga* she entered in several races with positive results particularly the
victory in the three races of the Milkweek 12 Metre Series in the U.S.A.
1956 - 1957 Estate of Charles Ulrick Bay; home port: Oslo
1957 - 1959 Mrs. Charles Ulrick Bay; engine installed 1958
1959 Josephine Bay Paul (Mrs. C. Michael Paul)
1960 - 1967 Lord Craigmyle; home port: Cowes; engine removed in 1959;
Lord Craigmyle was the chairman of the Red Duster Syndicate and *Norsaga*
was modified by John Arthur Robb in order to act in 1963 and 1964 as the
trial horse for *Sovereign* and *Kurrewa V* in the 1964 America's Cup
selections for the challenger. During the 1963 Cowes Week she beat
Sovereign in a series of unimpressive and inconclusive results for the British
challenger. In May and June 1964 she entered the trials organised in Britain
with nineteen runs between *Sovereign*, *Kurrewa V*, *Sceptre*, *Flica II* and
Norsaga. She was then transported to the U.S. to continue her training of
Sovereign with the selection trials organised to appoint the challenger
between *Sovereign* and *Kurrewa V*. She was then sold in the U.S.A.
1967 - 1972 Harry J. Ziemann; new name: *Phoenix* (from 1972); home
port: Milwaukee, WI; re-engined in 1967
1973 - 1979 Charles B. Coyer; home port: Washington, DC
?? home port: Port Washington, NY
1993 - 2000 Renato della Valle; new name: *Trivia of Gosport*; home port:
Monaco. She was restored by Giorgetti & Magrini at the Camper &
Nicholsons yard with a new mast and rigging by Harry Spencer. She entered
the Mediterranean programme of races for the Twelves. She is an example
of restoration which strictly conforms to the original design and construction
Since 2000 Wilfred Beeck; new name: *Trivia*; home port: Hamburg

■ VANITY V

DESIGNER: *W. & R.B. Fife design no. 816*
BUILDER: *W. Fife & Sons*

YEAR: *1936 March*
LENGTH OVERALL: *21.58 m.*
LENGTH AT WATERLINE: *13.54 m.*
BEAM: *3.72 m.*
DRAFT: *2.65 m.*
CONSTRUCTION: *wood on steel frames, rudder & keel of teak*
ENGINE: *engine installed in 1953; removed in 1960*
FIRST OWNER: *J.R. Payne*
FIRST NAME: *Vanity V*
FIRST COUNTRY: *England*
HOME PORT: *London*
FIRST SAIL NUMBER: *K 5*
OTHER NAMES: *La Pinta (1965)*
CURRENT LOCATION: *Copenhagen (Denmark)*
CONDITION: *very good, just refitted*
FURTHER DETAILS AND HISTORY: Built according to the Third Int. Rule
Owners and history: **1936 - 1946** J.R. Payne; name: *Vanity V*; home port:
London and Greenock. *Vanity V* cost of £3572 (labour £1800, wood £441,
other materials £951, sails £380). Fife was aged 79 when he designed
Vanity V. Mr. Payne was famous for being one of the best helmsman in the
52 footers, 15M and 12M classes since 1905. He had been the owner of
Vanity one of the most successful Twelves of the Twenties. He was also an
accomplished violinist known as the Fiddler Payne. As for the previous
Vanity, her owner wanted to live on board and to use her for cruising and
racing. An exchange of letters between Payne and Fife told us about Payne's
disappointment as he did not like the accommodation typical on a racing 12
Metre. After he complained about her racing performance Fife replied that
this was caused by too much weight on board. There were also complaints
about the mast which showed a bad bend between the lower crosstrees
and the deck when on port tack in a fresh breeze. In fact, just a few weeks
after her launch, *Vanity V* lost her mast. During the 1936 season she entered
11 races and won 2 firsts, 1 second and 1 third. In the 1937 season *Vanity V*
entered the handicap class where she won by outclassing her competitors
and, by performing better than some of the competing Twelves. The 1938
season was one of the greatest for the Twelves. "*Vanity V*, the only Fife boat
in the class, started ten times. Owing to Mr. Payne's bad health, he was not
able to undergo the strain of continuous racing. In light to medium winds
the yacht was in her first flight, especially to windward and there were
several occasions when it was a treat to see how the veteran helmsman
steered to windward, leading the whole fleet." At the end of the season,
she had ten starts with one first, one second and three thirds for a total of
five flags. *Trivia*, the leader that year, totalled 48 starts with 39 flags. She
was again on the race course in 1939 in the handicap class for yachts over
20 tons where she raced against *Noreen*
1947 - 1960 Sir Hartley Shawcross, (U.K. Attorney General); home port:
Falmouth. Engine installed in 1953
1961 - 1964 Capt. Michael P.R. Boyle; home port: Cowes; engine
removed in 1960. In 1963 she was altered to yawl rig and modernised for
cruising at the Groves and Guttbridge yard
1965 - 1996 Albert A. Prouvost; new name: *La Pinta*; home port: Toulon.
In 1981 she disappeared from Lloyd's Register. Extensive cruising along the
Portuguese coast and in the Mediterranean. In the early 90's she entered
La Nioulargue. She was then transported to the Labbé yard at St. Malo to
be refitted but she was left for several years

1997 - 2000 Robert Daral and Jean-Paul Guillet; new name: *Vanity V*. Relaunched in Brest on the 14th June 2000. The yacht was completely rebuilt sticking close to the original design (but for a part of the interior and deck layouts, a new mast, the stainless steel rigging and the winches) by naval architect Guy Ribadeau Dumas at Chantier du Guip in Brest
Since 2001 Klaus Helmersen; home port: Copenhagen

■ VEMA III

DESIGNER: *Johan Anker*
BUILDER: *Anker & Jensen*
YEAR: *1933*
LENGTH OVERALL: *21.20 m.*
LENGTH AT WATERLINE: *13.87 m.*
BEAM: *3.53 m.*
DRAFT: *2.74 m.*
DISPLACEMENT: *27 tons*
SAIL AREA: *185 sq.m.*
CONSTRUCTION: *wood on steel frames*
FIRST OWNER: *G. Unger Vetlesen*
FIRST NAME: *Vema III*
FIRST COUNTRY: *Norway*
HOME PORT: *Oslo (Norway)*
FIRST SAIL NUMBER: *N 11*
OTHER NAMES: *Varg VI (1947) - Diva III (1949) Lakme VI (1956) - Vema III (1980)*
CURRENT LOCATION: *Oslo*
CONDITION: *refit completed in 2000*
FURTHER DETAILS AND HISTORY: Built according to the Third Int. Rule Owners and history: **1933 - 1936** George Unger Vetlesen; name: *Vema III*; home port: Oslo; rig: bermudan cutter. The owner was a wealthy Norwegian living in the U.S.A. and owner of *Vema*, a 300-ton schooner and *Vema II*, a 14ft dinghy. The name *Vema* came from the first two letters of the owner's name and his American wife's surname Maud. In summer Vetlesen crossed the Atlantic with his schooner to Norway. He ordered from Anker a Twelve Metre to attend the Hanko regattas. The name *Little Vema* comes from the fact that his wife found the yacht too small and refused to go on board. Uffa Fox wrote that he admired *Vema*'s lines and construction; he said that: "*Vema III* proves that the present International Rule has succedeed in developing a cruiser for racing purposes, or, put the other way round, a racer that is a fine cruiser. *Vema III* has raced with a fair amount of success in Norwegian and European waters and while in British waters won a reputation for her light weather ability. Even now, some years after her visit, 12 Metre people still have vivid recollections of this, while her long waterline length enables her to travel fast in a breeze. In *Vema III*, then, we have a racer fast in light or hard weather that is also a comfortable cruiser, the type of vessel those responsible for the International Rule should be proud of. For when designers such as Anker, who understand the Rule and all its ways, produce such a vessel to race and when she wins races in the largest class on the International Rule, there can evidently be very little indeed wrong with it." In 1933 she entered the KNS Jubilee Regatta where she was disqualified twice and she won 1 first and 2 thirds. In the 1933 season in British waters, she had 17 starts with 2 firsts, 1 second and 3 thirds
1937 T. Larsen
1938 - 1948 Frithjof Larsen; new name: *Varg III*. With her new owner she

entered in several races.
1949 - 1955 Johan "Teddy" Sommerschield; new name: *Diva III*. She entered the races on the Oslo Fjord together with *Blue Marlin, Santa, Figaro VI* and *Norsaga* (formerly *Trivia*), owned by the American ambassador in Norway, Charles "Rick" Bay, who was one of the regatta promoters
1956 - 1979 Sam Ugelstad; new name: *Lakme VI*; engine installed in 1973. In 1956, due to Bay's death, the races lost their importance and the Twelve fleet was lost. *Lakmé VI* was the only Twelve still active
1980 - 1999 Chr. Lars & Tor J. Dahl; new name: *Vema III*. She was used for charter
1999 Einar Nagell Ericksen and Tor-Jorgen Dahl. Total refit at Walsteds yard in Denmark with a new deck, partial replanking, oak keel and bolt replacement. The interior was partially kept as original (a new cabin was included to starboard thanks to the rearrangement of the galley; new hydraulic self-tailing winches were installed. New sails with modern cuts

■ VICTORIA

DESIGNER: *Uffa Fox*
BUILDER: *not built*
YEAR: *design 1932 ?*
LENGTH OVERALL: *22.25 m.*
BEAM: *3.73 m.*
DRAFT: *2.70 m.*
FURTHER DETAILS AND HISTORY: Project - not built

■ VIM

DESIGNER: *Olin J. Stephens - design no. 279*
BUILDER: *Henry B. Nevins, Inc.*
YEAR: *1939 May*
LENGTH OVERALL: *21.18 m.*
LENGTH AT WATERLINE: *13.71 m.*
BEAM: *3.66 m.*
DRAFT: *2.67 m.*
DISPLACEMENT: *28.44 tons*
SAIL AREA: *179 sq.m.*
CONSTRUCTION: *wood, double planking*
FIRST OWNER: *Harold S. Vanderbilt*
FIRST NAME: *Vim*
FIRST COUNTRY: *United States*
HOME PORT: *Newport*
FIRST SAIL NUMBER: *US 15*
CURRENT LOCATION: *Genoa (Italy)*
CONDITION: *perfect, refit completed in May 2001*
FURTHER DETAILS AND HISTORY: Built according to the Third Int. Rule Owners and history: **1939 - 1951** Harold S. Vanderbilt; name: *Vim*; home port: Newport. *Vim*'s lead keel was laid on January 20th, 1939 and she was launched at Henry B. Nevins boatyard in New York on April 29th. Specially ordered by H Vanderbilt to enter the famous 12 Metre races organised in British waters, *Vim* was Olin Stephens design no. 279, and very advanced for the period, based on the results of extensive tank tests and inspired by the previous design of the 6 Metre *Goose*. Olin Stephens said "that she was a real refinement on what I had done before". She was an "outsize", Twelve as the latest British ones (*Trivia, Evaine* and the 1939 - built *Tomahawk, Flica II, Ornsay* and *Jenetta*) but with a more aggressive keel and

fuller shape in the bow. Although she respected the minimum weight allowed by the class Rule, her mast was of duralumin in order to be stronger and stiffer than a mast of similar weight in other materials. She had the first two speed coffee grinders to be mounted on a Twelve. The cockpit was smaller than usual and watertight. She also had one of the first, or the first, trim tab described as "a special device on her rudder; a special adaptation from aeroplane practice; by means of which the after edge of the rudder can be controlled from the cockpit independently of the rudder itself". This device was controlled by a hand wheel and internal worm gear which was located at the rudder head. This gear rotated a shaft inside the hollow rudder stock which in turn moved a small tiller arm and ultimately the tab itself. Travel was fourteen degrees to port and the same to starboard. Below deck, she was very simple with one small cabin with two full berths and two berths which ran partly under the quarters. Forward of that a large space was arranged for sail stowage and handling; this kept weight amidships and did not interfere with the galley and fo'c's'le right forward. There was a warm welcome and great attention paid to Mr. Vanderbilt and *Vim*'s arrival in the UK just after her launch in New York. Success came immediately: "In the first two races, to put matters quite bluntly, *Vim* has practically left her rivals standing" and again (Heckstall-Smith in *Yachting World* June 23rd, 1939) "The advantages of improved design through the tank tests, of improved rig through her metal mast and lesser windage of gear aloft, of greater power in her deck winches, of superior cut of canvas, particularly her jib and spinnaker - all these details tell in *Vim*'s favour. But added to these factors contributing to her success for which her designer, Olin Stephens, deserves the credit. I, myself have seen and admired the skill of her owner, Mr. Vanderbilt, at his wheel and the excellence of *Vim*'s crew, the trimming of her sheets, the accuracy of her manoeuvres, together with steering the courses and coping with strong tides without the help of any local pilot. The combination of all these details has contributed to the victories of *Vim*, although possibly in any single one of them the superiority may amount to nothing of very marked importance." At the end of the season *Vim* won 19 races out of 28. She sailed seven races in the shallow East Coast tidal waters and won five. She then proceeded to the deep waters "down west where she again sailed seven races and won six; then she came to the tidal waters of the Solent, where she sailed fourteen races and won eight. Her success was phenomenal and the popularity of her owner and his crew added to the enjoyment of the season at all ports." In 1940 and 1949 she won the King's Cup (New York Yacht Club) and in 1940 the Astor Cup and Larchmont Race Week

1951 - 1964 John N. Matthews; home port: Oyster Bay (N.Y.); altered to auxiliary yacht. The owner entered the selection races for the 1958 America's Cup and in 1957 Olin Stephens was required to return *Vim* to the original version. The engine was removed together with some other heavy fittings; the hull was re-planked; new sails in Dacron and a new rig was tuned up. *Vim*'s photo was on the cover of the August 4, 1958 *Life* magazine which was devoted to the America's Cup. Her design was also used as the basis for the new S&S Twelve, *Columbia*. She had a great crew, headed by Bus Mosbacher and Dick Matthews (son of the owner) as co-helmsman. The other son, Donald, Brad Noyes, Dick Bertram and Ted Hood, who was in charge of experimenting with new sail fabrics, were crew members. *Vim* was very successful and, at the end of the trial races, she was the best of all the other contenders apart from *Columbia* who was slightly faster to windward in fresh winds. The final series was yacht racing at its

closest with *Vim* probably being better sailed. *Columbia* won the fifth race by twelve seconds and was chosen as the defender of the 1958 Cup. In 1952 she won the Astor Cup (NYYC) and in 1955 the Queen's Cup (1955). In 1959, she was given to a Roman Catholic charity and chartered for four years by Sir Frank Packer's Australian syndicate. *Gretel*, the 1962 America's Cup Australian challenger, was inspired by *Vim*'s design and performance and *Vim* was used as Packer's trial horse for the tuning up of *Gretel*

1965 - 1972 Sir Frank Packer; home port: Sydney (Australia; *Vim* was trial horse for *Dame Pattie* in 1967 and for *Gretel II* in 1970

1973 Yanchep Estates Pty Ltd.

1973 - 1976 Dr. Tony Fisher; home port: Tarent Point (NSW, Australia)

1977 Disappeared off Lloyd's Register; *Vim* remained in Australia

1980 - 1985 Leo Berliner; the transom was removed

1985 - 1990 Paul and Yvonne Maule. *Vim* was rebuilt at Ken Beashel's boat yard and the original stem was found and replaced as were several other parts of the original fittings such as the coffee grinders. The original rigging was also reinstated with running backstays. After two years of work, *Vim* was relaunched and used for charter

Since 1990 Alberto Rusconi; home port: La Spezia and Genova. *Vim* underwent a first partial refit. She entered the class races in the Mediterranean but, mainly due to not having a valid crew, she did not achieve good results. She competed again against *Tomahawk*, owned by Mr. Rusconi. In 1999 an important refit was carried on with a new deck, partial replanking and a new engine

■ WESTRA

DESIGNER: *Charles E. Nicholson*
BUILDER: *Camper & Nicholsons - construction no. 414*
YEAR: *1934 May*
LENGTH OVERALL: *21.13 m.*
LENGTH AT WATERLINE: *13.49 m.*
BEAM: *3.73 m.*
DRAFT: *2.67 m.*
CONSTRUCTION: *wood on steel frames*
FIRST OWNER: *Arthur C. Connell*
FIRST NAME: *Westra*
FIRST COUNTRY: *Great Britain*
HOME PORT: *Portsmouth*
FIRST SAIL NUMBER: *K 4*
CONDITION: *damaged by an air raid and broken up*
FURTHER DETAILS AND HISTORY: Built according to the Third Int. Rule Owners and history: **1934 - 1939** Arthur C. Connell; name: *Westra*; home port: Portsmouth. Mr. Connell, partner of an old established Clyde shipbuilding company, was a very experienced sailing man and a well known "Twelves owner" having already owned *Zinita* and *Zoraida*. He was also the future owner of *Ornsay*. "*Westra* was a powerful-looking boat. Her bow was quite round on the waterline, so that the actual stem piece was like the letter U. Her sail area seemed small. She looked like a more chubby and less elongated boat than *Flica*." (*YW*, July 20,1934)

■ WESTWIND

DESIGNER: *Henry Rasmussen*
BUILDER: *Abeking & Rasmussen - construction no. 3242*
YEAR: *1938*

LENGTH OVERALL: *21.50 m.*
LENGTH AT WATERLINE: *14.98 m.*
BEAM: *3.45 m.*
DRAFT: *2.74 m.*
DISPLACEMENT: *26 tons*
SAIL AREA: *197 sq.m.*
CONSTRUCTION: *wood on steel frames*
FIRST OWNER: *John T. Essberger*
FIRST NAME: *Inga*
FIRST COUNTRY: *Germany*
HOME PORT: *Hamburg*
FIRST SAIL NUMBER: *G 1*
OTHER NAMES: *Inga*
CURRENT LOCATION: *Flensburg (Germany)*
CONDITION: *good*
PRESENT OWNER: *Flotillen Admiral Von Puttkamer*
FURTHER DETAILS AND HISTORY: Built according to the Int. Third Rule Owners and history: **1938 - 1958** Staatsrat John T. Essberger; name *Inga*; home port: Hamburg. *Inga*, sister ship of the other Twelve *Anita*, was built for the shipowner Essberger, founder of the tanker line bearing the same name and owner at the same time of other well-known yachts. She entered Kiel Week with the other German Twelves in 1938 and 1939. During the war she was laid up in a shed in Rendsburg
1947 - 1948 David Ryder-Turner (the Scottish naval architect) and friends (UK forces, Eckernforde). They discovered *Inga* in the summer of 1947 and became interim owners. They used the original sails from *Ornsay* (destroyed during the war) found at Ratsey and Lapthorn's
1948 - 1958 John T. Essberger. She was given back to John T. Essberger. From 1953 to 1958 she was laid up in a shed. In 1958 she was sold for the symbolic amount of DM25.000 to the German Federal Navy for the training of young officers
Since 1958 Kommandrur Marineschule Murwick; new name: *Westwind*; home port: Flensburg

■ WINGS
DESIGNER: *Charles E. Nicholson*
BUILDER: *Camper & Nicholsons - construction no. 451*
YEAR: *1937*
LENGTH OVERALL: *21.36 m.*
LENGTH AT WATERLINE: *13.93 m.*
BEAM: *3.55 m.*
DRAFT: *2.71 m.*
SAIL AREA: *179 sq.m.; 176 sq.m. (1969)*
CONSTRUCTION: *wood on steel frames*
FIRST OWNER: *Maurice Solvay*
FIRST NAME: *Wings*
FIRST COUNTRY: *Belgium*
FIRST SAIL NUMBER: *K 15*
OTHER NAMES: *Mohita II (1971)*
CURRENT LOCATION: *Tetbury (Gloucestershire, Great Britain)*
CONDITION: *very good*
FURTHER DETAILS AND HISTORY: Built according to the Third Int. Rule Owners and history: **1937 - 1960** Mauirice Solvay; name: *Wings*; rig: auxiliary bermudan sloop. Every year after 1951 maintenance work was

carried by Cantieri Baglietto, Varazze (Italy)
1960 - 1961 Estate of Maurice Solvay
1961 - 1962 T. W. Duprée
1962 Duke Edouardo Visconti; home port: Cannes
1962 - 1964 Millstone Cruising Co. Ltd.; home port: Cannes
1965 - 1970 Georges Teychené; home port: Bandol and Marseille; rig: altered to auxiliary yawl in 1969. Re-engined in 1969
1970 - 1979 Jean Goutail; new name *Mohita II*; home port: Marseille
1980 - 2000 Mr. Turlan; new name: *Aile* (some time around 1994); rig altered to auxiliary ketch
2001 John Lister; home port: Tetbury (Gloucestershire, UK); refit programme to be defined

■ YATSET
DESIGNER: *J. Burell*
BUILDER: *P. Arasa (Barcelona)*
YEAR: *1933*
LENGTH AT WATERLINE: *13.45 m.*
BEAM: *3.96 m.*
DRAFT: *2.17 m.*
SAIL AREA: *159 sq.m.*
CONSTRUCTION: *wood*
ENGINE: *petrol engine "CIM"*
FIRST OWNER: *Fernando Fuster Fabra*
FIRST NAME: *Yatset*
FIRST COUNTRY: *Spain*
HOME PORT: *Barcelona*
CURRENT LOCATION: *unknown*
FURTHER DETAILS AND HISTORY: Built according to the Third Int. Rule Owners and history:
1933 - 1936 Fernando Fuster Fabra; name: *Yatset*; home port: Barcelona
1937 - 1948 Syndicato Unico Maritimo
1949 Disappeared off Lloyd's Register

■ ZELITA
DESIGNER: *W. & R.B. Fife*
BUILDER: *W. Fife & Son - construction no. 800*
YEAR: *1933 April*
LENGTH OVERALL: *20.42 m.*
LENGTH AT WATERLINE: *14.02 m.*
BEAM: *3.53 m.*
DRAFT: *2.74 m.*
SAIL AREA: *187 sq.m.*
CONSTRUCTION: *wood with teak keel, rudder, stem and sternpost*
FIRST OWNER: *G.F. Carrington*
FIRST NAME: *Zelita*
FIRST COUNTRY: *Great Britain*
HOME PORT: *Greenock*
FIRST SAIL NUMBER: *K 9*
CURRENT LOCATION: *unknown*
CONDITION: *broken up?*
FURTHER DETAILS AND HISTORY: Built according to the Int. Third Rule Owners and history:
1933 Arthur C. Connell; name: *Zelita*; home port: Greenock; rig:

bermudan sloop. Mr. Connell (partner of an old established Clyde shipbuilding company) had already owned *Zinita* and *Zoraida* and later owned *Westra* and *Ornsay*. The 1933 season started up on the Clyde and *Zelita*'s debut was discouraging as she was always behind *Veronica* and *Iyruna*. She was dismasted during the last race. At the end of the season, she was fifth with 29 starts and 3 firsts, 8 seconds and 6 thirds
1934 - 1939 G.F. Carrington. In 1934, *Zelita* did not perform better with a fifth placement. Out of 27 starts she had 1 first, 4 seconds and 3 thirds.

No better results in 1935
1946 - 1955 G.S. Payne; engine installed in 1949; RORC rating: 50'89
1956 - 1960 No name or port given
1961 - 1964 Lemar S.A.; home port: Barcelona (Spain) and Panama; re-engined. In 1961, according to Real Club Nautico de Barcelona, the yacht was owned by Miguel Hostench and a photo in the 125th year book of the club shows *Zelita* sailing in the Mediterranean
1965 Disappeared off Lloyd's Register

12 METRE THIRD RULE CRUISING - ALPHABETICAL LIST OF NAMES

■ BLOODHOUND
DESIGNER: *Charles E. Nicholson & Olin J. Stephens*
BUILDER: *Camper & Nicholson - construction no. 438*
YEAR: *1936 June*
LENGTH OVERALL: *19.30 m.*
LENGTH AT WATERLINE: *13.71 m.*
BEAM: *3.78 m.*
DRAFT: *2.77 m.*
SAIL AREA: *149 sq.m.; 146 sq.m. (1963)*
CONSTRUCTION: *wood with every third frame in steel*
FIRST OWNER: *Isaac Bell*
FIRST NAME: *Bloodhound*
FIRST COUNTRY: *Great Britain*
HOME PORT: *Poole*
FIRST SAIL NUMBER: *K 101 (RORC Sail Number)*
CURRENT LOCATION: *Cannes - Southampton*
CONDITION: *good*
FURTHER DETAILS AND HISTORY: One of the Nicholson ocean racers built to 12M Third Rule but never classed, measured or raced as a 12 Owners and history:
1936 - 1939 Isaac Bell; name: *Bloodhound*; home port: Poole. rig: Bermudan yawl. She was the second of the three ocean racers (the others being Foxhound and Stiarna) designed by Nicholson to conform to the ocean racing rule and to the Twelve Metre Class of the International Rule. They were built from the same hull design. The owner was a wealthy american citizen living in Great Britain, already owner of *Foxhound*. Just after her sale, Bell commissioned a new boat from Nicholson of the same design although with some slight differences in the deck and interior layout.
The yawl rig was designed by Olin Stephens in an unique collaboration with Nicholson, which was largely unacknowledged. In the 1936 season she won the Morgan Cup, the Channel Race and she was second in the Benodet Race. In 1939 she won the Fastnet
1946-1947 Patrick G. Egan & Lt. Cdr. G.C. Hans Hamilton; home port: Southampton; RORC rating (1937): 43'92
1948 - 1962 M.D.N. Wyatt. Engine installed in 1956. She was second in the 1952 Bermuda Race
1962 - 1969 HM The Queen and HRH Prince Philip, Duke of Edinburgh; home port: Cowes. RORC rating: 40'79. Re-engined in 1962 and 1968. Rig and interior layout plans were modified by Illingworth & Primrose
1970 - 1977 R. Coureau
1978 Disappeared off Lloyd's Register
Since 1978 Robert Cook; home port: Southampton and Cannes

■ EILEEN
DESIGNER: *Christian Jensen*
BUILDER: *Soon Slip og Baat A/S*
YEAR: *1938*
LENGTH OVERALL: *18.26 m.*
LENGTH AT WATERLINE: *12.72 m.*
BEAM: *3.63 m.*
DISPLACEMENT: *24 tons*
SAIL AREA: *159 sq.m.*
CONSTRUCTION: *wood on steel frames*
ENGINE: *Yanmar 4JH/D*
FIRST OWNER: *Einmar Stange*
FIRST NAME: *Eileen II*
FIRST COUNTRY: *Norway*
HOME PORT: *Oslo*
FIRST SAIL NUMBER: *E 21*
CURRENT LOCATION: *St.-Tropez (France)*
CONDITION: *at the best*
FURTHER DETAILS AND HISTORY: Built according to the 12m Third Int. Rule Cruising. Owners and history: **1938 - 1948** Einmar Stange; name: *Eileen II*; home port: Oslo. Built as a C/R Twelve according to the Scandinavian tradition to assign to this class the yachts built in conformity to the International Rule but not for racing. The Twelve yachts were provided with an "E" identification letter *Eileen* is known as *Eileen II* because there was a much older *Eileen* (1907)
1949 - 1958 Niels Onstad
1958 - 1969 She was said being owned by Sonia Henie, the famous skating olympic athlete and actress
1970 - 1985 Unknown owners. On Sonia Henie's death the yacht was sold in Sweden and altered to ketch
1985 - 1993 Erling Storm; home port: Oslo. She was used for charter after a restoration work
1993 - 1999 Paul van der Bijl; home port: Cogolin (France). *Eileen* underwent restoration under the supervision of architecte Cees van Tongeren of the Van de Stadt firm. She was brought back to the original design of a C/R Twelve with some innovations in the interior and in the rigging
Since 2000 Rick Langlaan; home port: St. Tropez

■ FOXHOUND
DESIGNER: *Charles E. Nicholson*
BUILDER: *Camper & Nicholsons - construction no. 424*
YEAR: *1935 June*
LENGTH OVERALL: *19.26 m.*

LENGTH AT WATERLINE: *13.71 m.*
BEAM: *3.78 m.*
DRAFT: *2.77 m.*
SAIL AREA: *154 sq.m.*
CONSTRUCTION: *wood with every third frame in steel*
FIRST OWNER: *Isaac Bell*
FIRST NAME: *Foxhound*
FIRST COUNTRY: *Great Britain*
HOME PORT: *Poole*
FIRST SAIL NUMBER: *K 126 (RORC Sail number)*
OTHER NAMES: *Foxhound of Lepe (1952)*
CURRENT LOCATION: *unknown*
CONDITION: *broken up?*
FURTHER DETAILS AND HISTORY: One of the Nicholson ocean racers built to 12m Third Rule but never classed, measured or raced as a 12
Owners and history:
1935 Isaac Bell; name: Foxhound; home port: Poole and Southampton; rig: bermudan cutter. Foxhound is the first of the three ocean racers (the others being *Bloodhound* and *Stiarna*) designed by Nicholson to conform to the ocean racing rule and to the Twelve Metre Class of the International Rule. The three are built from the same hull design.
In fact, Foxhound is a losing yacht in light airs compared to a Twelve but is a winning yacht in blue water sailing.
Her first season confirmed this success (first in the Morgan Cup Race to Cherbourg and back, second in the Bell Isle Race, third in the Dinard Race and fourth in the Fastnet) and the owner, a wealthy american citizen leaving in England, could not refuse the offer received from Compte de Gasquet
1936 - 1949 Comte Georges de Gasque-James; home port: Dinard and Nantes
1950 - 1951 D.H.E. McCowen; home port: Southampton
1951 - 1957 Mrs. Rachel Pitt-Rivers; new name (1952): *Foxhound of Lepe*; home port: Cowes and Southampton. Engine installed in 1951. RORC rating: 42'18
1958 - 1969 Ernesto Vieira de Mendonça; home port: Lisbon. Re-powered in 1967
1970 Disappeared off Lloyd's Register

■ KAHURANGI

DESIGNER: *Arthur C. Robb*
BUILDER: *P. Vos Ltd. (Auckland, New Zealand)*
YEAR: *1952*
LENGTH OVERALL: *18.90 m.*
LENGTH AT WATERLINE: *12.68 m.*
BEAM: *3.78 m.*
DRAFT: *2.50 m.*
SAIL AREA: *135 sq.m.*
CONSTRUCTION: *triple planked Kauri*
ENGINE: *Perkins 4-236 85 HP*
FIRST OWNER: *Lawrence D. Nathan*
FIRST NAME: *Kahurangi*
FIRST COUNTRY: *New Zealand*
HOME PORT: *Auckland*
CURRENT LOCATION: *chartering in Turkey*
CONDITION: *sailing, good*
FURTHER DETAILS AND HISTORY: Built according to the Third Int. Rule Cruising. Owners and history:
1952 - 1962 Lawrence D. Nathan; name *Kahurangi*; home port: Auckland
1963 - 1966 Lawrence D. Nathan, W.D. Bremner and L. Scott Colville
1966 Disappeared off Lloyd's Register

■ NAAGH

DESIGNER: *André Mauric*
BUILDER: *Chantier Navale l'Esterel*
YEAR: *1951*
LENGTH OVERALL: *20.42 m.*
LENGTH AT WATERLINE: *14.96 m.*
BEAM: *4.20 m.*
DRAFT: *2.59 m.*
SAIL AREA: *166 sq.m.*
FIRST OWNER: *René Combastet*
FIRST NAME: *Naagh*
FIRST COUNTRY: *France*
HOME PORT: *St.-Tropez and Cannes*
CURRENT LOCATION: *unknown*
FURTHER DETAILS AND HISTORY: Built according to Third International Rule Cruising but never classed. Owners and history: **1951 - 1961** René Combastet; name: *Naagh*; home port: St.-Tropez and Cannes
1962 - 1963 Henri Villand; home port: Toulon
1964 - 1968 Marcel Mongin; home port: Toulon
1969 Disappeared off Record

■ STIARNA

DESIGNER: *Charles E. Nicholson*
BUILDER: *Camper & Nicholsons - construction no. 445*
YEAR: *1937*
LENGTH OVERALL: *19.30 m.*
LENGTH AT WATERLINE: *13.51 m.*
BEAM: *3.78 m.*
DRAFT: *2.77 m.*
DISPLACEMENT:
SAIL AREA: *156 sq.m.; 151 sq.m. (1958)*
CONSTRUCTION: *wood with every third frame in steel*
FIRST OWNER: *Liet. J.F.B. Gage*
FIRST NAME: *Stiarna*
FIRST COUNTRY: *Great Britain*
HOME PORT: *Portsmouth*
FIRST SAIL NUMBER: *K 218 (RORC Sail Number)*
CONDITION: *sunk*
FURTHER DETAILS AND HISTORY: One of the Nicholson ocean racers built to 12m Third Rule but never classed, measured or raced as a 12
Owners and history: **1937 - 1947** J.F.B. Gage; name: *Stiarna*; home port: Portsmouth. Rig: bermudan cutter. Rating RORC: 45'28. She was the third of the three ocean racers (the others being *Foxhound* and *Bloodhound*) designed by Nicholson to conform to the ocean racing rule and to the Twelve Metre Class of the International Rule. They were built from the same hull design although with some slight differences in the deck and interior plans. *Stiarna* was the only one with an auxiliary engine installed at the beginning. *Stiarna* was built by C&N without a commission, but was bought by Mr Cage before her launch. Although she was never campaigned to the same extent as her two predecessor, she was second in the 1937 Fastnet. In 1938 she was not sailed in UK but she won the second place in the Dover-Christiansand Race
1948 - 1950 Cecil E. Donne
1951 - 1957 C. Peto Bennett; rating RORC: 42'17
1958 - 1960 E. Vintiadis; home port: Pireo and Genoa; rating RORC: 40'34. Re-engined in 1958
1961 - 1963 Lord Shawcross; home port: Falmouth. Rating RORC: 41'09
1963 - 1976 A.H. David Rowse; home port: Hamble. Re-engined in 1964
1977 - 1980 Broadsword Ltd.; home port: Palma de Mallorca
1998 A. Hanover; home port: Boston, MA. Sunk due to fire while being towed from Trinidad to Grenada, destination New England for extensive refit work

■ AMERICA II (LEGO)

DESIGNER: *M. William Langan - Sparkman & Stephens*
BUILDER: *Williams & Manchester Shipyard*
YEAR: *1984*
LENGTH OVERALL: *20.75 m.*
BEAM: *3.65 m.*
DRAFT: *2.44 m.*
CONSTRUCTION: *aluminium alloy*
FIRST OWNER: *America II Syndicate*
FIRST NAME: *America II*
FIRST COUNTRY: *U.S.A.*
HOME PORT: *Kings Point, NY*
FIRST SAIL NUMBER: *US 42*
CURRENT LOCATION: *San Diego (U.S.A.)*
FURTHER DETAILS AND HISTORY: Built according to the Third Int. Rule America's Cup. Owners and history:
1984 - 1989 America II Syndicate, USMMA Foundation; name: *America II;* home port: Kings Point, NY. Sold on April 12th 1989; the nickname *"Lego"* came about because the yacht (keels, rigs, rudder, etc.) could be set up in different configurations as a 12 Metre. The yacht was used in the making of the film *Wind*
Since 1989 Philip Charles Freedman; home port: San Diego, CA

■ AMERICA II - US 44

DESIGNER: *M. William Langan - Sparkman & Stephens*
BUILDER: *Williams & Manchester Shipyard*
YEAR: *1985*
LENGTH OVERALL: *17.70 m.*
BEAM: *3.68 m.*
DRAFT: *2.74 m.*
CONSTRUCTION: *aluminium alloy*
FIRST OWNER: *America II Syndicate*
FIRST NAME: *America II*
FIRST COUNTRY: *U.S.A.*
HOME PORT: *Kings Point, NY*
FIRST SAIL NUMBER: *US 44*
FURTHER DETAILS AND HISTORY: Built according to the Third Int Rule America's Cup. Owners and history:
1985 - 1988 America II Syndicate, USMMA Foundation; name: *America II;* home port: Kings Point, NY. Sold November 4th 1988
Since 1988 American Challenge Sailing Inc. (Richard Elder); home port: Seattle, WA and Honolulu, HI

■ AMERICA II - US 46

DESIGNER: *M. William Langan-Sparkman & Stephens*
BUILDER: *Williams & Manchester Shipyard*
YEAR: *May 16 1986*
LENGTH OVERALL: *20.14 m.*
BEAM: *3.70 m.*
DRAFT: *2.74 m.*
CONSTRUCTION: *aluminium alloy*
FIRST OWNER: *The America II Syndicate*
FIRST NAME: *America II*
FIRST COUNTRY: *U.S.A.*

HOME PORT: *Kings Point, NY*
FIRST SAIL NUMBER: *US 46*
OTHER NAMES: *Fiddler (1993)*
CURRENT LOCATION: *Middletown (U.S.A.)*
CONDITION: *at her best*
FURTHER DETAILS AND HISTORY: Built according to Third Int. Rule America's Cup. Owners and history:
1986 - 1989 America II Syndicate, USMMA Foundation; name: *America II;* home port: Kings Point, NY. S&S design no 2500. Built as a challenger for the 1987 America's Cup in Fremantle, skipper John Kolius. Sold September 25th 1989
1989 - ? Lennard A. Gulson; home port: San Diego, CA and Nadi, Fiji
Since 1993 US 46 LLC (Alfred B. Van Liew, II); new name: *Fiddler;* home port: Middletown, RI; engine installed in 1994. Winner of the Chandler Hovey Gold Bowl (NYYC) 1994 and 1997. Winner of the Caritas Cup (NYYC) 1997. Sailing and raced with success in the 12 Metre regattas

■ AMERICA EAGLE

DESIGNER: *A.E. Luders, Jr.*
BUILDER: *Luders Marine Construction Co. - no 1043*
YEAR: *1964*
LENGTH OVERALL: *20.32 m; 20.52 m. (1975)*
LENGTH AT WATERLINE: *14.02 m.*
BEAM: *3.81 m.*
DRAFT: *m. 2.74*
DISPLACEMENT: *27.35 tons*
SAIL AREA: *178 sq.m.*
CONSTRUCTION: *double-planked mahogany, white oak frames*
FIRST OWNER: *Aurora Syndicate*
FIRST NAME: *America Eagle*
FIRST COUNTRY: *U.S.A.*
HOME PORT: *New York, NY (U.S.A.)*
FIRST SAIL NUMBER: *US 21*
OTHER NAMES: *Golden Eagle (1968) - War Baby (1975)*
CURRENT LOCATION: *Newport (U.S.A.)*
CONDITION: *at her best*
FURTHER DETAILS AND HISTORY: Built according to the Third Int. Rule America's Cup. Owners and history:
1964 - 1968 Aurora Syndicate (Pierre S. Dupont III); name: *American Eagle;* home port: New York. The name was that of the sailing ship on which the first Dupont arrived in the U.S. Built for the 1964 America's Cup campaign, her keel was quite innovative compared with conventional Twelve lines and her mast passed through a raised section in the deck (known as "Mount Luders") gaining an extra few inches in height. She ran off a 20-1 record in the June-July trials, only to be overtaken by *Constellation* in the selection series. Still renowned for a 42-tack duel on the final windward leg of the second race. In 1964 she won the Lipton Memorial Trophy (NYYC)
1968 Firwood Investment, Ltd. (Herbert P. Wahl); new name: *Golden Eagle.* The new Canadian owner commissioned Luders to design a new interior and deck layout. But when he wanted to bring the boat home, the Canadian customs taxed her for her replacement value, not for the market value this added a $155.000 duty, forcing the owner to sell her to Ted Turner

1968 - 1973 Robert E. "Ted" Turner, III; new name: *American Eagle*. Trial horse for *Gretel II* for the 1970 America's Cup. Converted to IOR, engine installed in 1968. She entered the most challenging races in the world, winning the Southern Ocean Racing Circuit, the Annapolis-Newport Race and the Fastnet
1974 - 1983 Warren A. Brown; new name: *War Baby*; home port: Hamilton, Bermuda
1983 - 1987 American Eagle Syndicate; home port: Annapolis, MD
Since 1987 American Eagle, Inc. (W. Herbert Marshall, II); home port: Barnstable, MA, and Newport, RI

■ AUSTRALIA

DESIGNER: *Miller & Valentijn*
BUILDER: *Steve E. Ward & Brian Raley*
YEAR: *1977*
LENGTH OVERALL: *19.81 m.*
LENGTH AT WATERLINE: *13.71 m.*
BEAM: *3.71 m.*
DRAFT: *2.74 m.*
DISPLACEMENT: *24.85 tons*
SAIL AREA: *168 sq.m.*
CONSTRUCTION: *aluminium alloy*
FIRST OWNER: *America's Cup Challenge 77 Ltd.*
FIRST NAME: *Australia*
FIRST COUNTRY: *Australia*
HOME PORT: *Yanchep*
FIRST SAIL NUMBER: *KA 5*
OTHER NAMES: *Temeraire (1980)*
CURRENT LOCATION: *Sydney (Australia)*
CONDITION: *good*
FURTHER DETAILS AND HISTORY: Built according to the Third Int. Rule America's Cup. Owners and history:
1977 - 1979 America's Cup Challenge '77 Ltd.; name: *Australia*; home port: Yanchep, WA. Challenger for the 23rd America's Cup in 1977. Her design is an evolution of *Southern Cross* and the yacht was built after exhaustive tests with five models in the test tank of the Dutch University of Delf. She has V-shaped midship sections, low freeboard and a large bustle. The ballast was placed very low and she dominated her trial horse *Southern Cross* in all trims. She defeated *Gretel II* (KA3), *France* I (F I) and *Sverige* (S 3) in the challenge trials but she lost in the Match to *Courageous* (US26) skippered by R.E. "Ted" Turner by a score of 4-0
1979 - 1980 West Australian Syndicate '80, Ltd.; home port: Perth, WA. Altered by Ben Lexcen 1979/80 with new redesigned rigging, new sails, new rudder, new mast and modifications to the bustle and the bottom of the keel
1980 America's Cup Challenge 80 Ltd.; home port; Yanchep, WA. Challenger for the 24th match in 1980. She defeated in the challenge trials *Sverige*, *Lionheart* and *France III*, but in the match was defeated by *Freedom* (US 30), skippered by Dennis Conner, by a score of 4-1
1980 - 1983 Victory Syndicate; new name *Temeraire*. Trial horse *Victory* '82 and '83
1985 Eastern Australia America's Cup defence (Syd Fisher); new name: *Australia*; home port: Sydney, NSW. Trial horse for *Steak 'n' Kidney*
Since Jan. 1993 Syd Fischer; home port: Sydney, NSW

■ AUSTRALIA IV

DESIGNER: *Ben Lexcen*
BUILDER: *Steve E. Ward & Co.*
YEAR: *1986 August*
CONSTRUCTION: *aluminium alloy*
FIRST OWNER: *America's Cup Defence '87, Ltd.*
FIRST NAME: *Australia IV*
FIRST COUNTRY: *Australia*
HOME PORT: *Perth*
FIRST SAIL NUMBER: *KA 16*
CURRENT LOCATION: *Japan*
FURTHER DETAILS AND HISTORY: Built according to the Third Int. Rule America's Cup version
Owners and history:
1986 - 1987 America's Cup Defence '87, Ltd. (Alan Bond); name: *Australia IV*; home port: Perth, WA. She was the second boat designed by Ben Lexcen for Alan Bond for the 26th America's Cup. She entered the finals for the defender trials and she lost against *Kookaburra III* who defended, losing the cup against *Stars & Stripes*
Since 1993 Bengal Bay Club Challenge; home port: Japan

■ AUSTRALIA II

DESIGNER: *Ben Lexcen*
BUILDER: *Steve E. Ward & Co.*
YEAR: *1982 June*
LENGTH OVERALL: *19.22 m.*
LENGTH AT WATERLINE: *13.10 m.*
BEAM: *3.65 m.*
DRAFT: *2.59 m.*
DISPLACEMENT: *21.8 tons*
SAIL AREA: *171 sq.m.*
CONSTRUCTION: *aluminium alloy*
FIRST OWNER: *America's Cup Challenge '87 Ltd.*
FIRST NAME: *Australia II*
FIRST COUNTRY: *Australia*
HOME PORT: *Perth*
FIRST SAIL NUMBER: *KA 6*
CURRENT LOCATION: *Perth, Australia*
PRESENT OWNER: *National Museum of Australia*
FURTHER DETAILS AND HISTORY: Built according to the Third Int. Rule America's Cup. Owners and history:
1982 - 1983 America's Cup Challenge '87 Ltd. (Alan Bond); name: *Australia II*; home port: Perth, WA. She was the challenger for the 25th America's Cup in 1983. Skippered by John Bertrand. Innovative wing keel design led to the first defeat of the New York Yacht Club in an America's Cup match. In the longest match to date, *Australia II* defeated *Liberty* (US 40), skippered by Dennis Conner, by a score of 4-3. Lexcen's aim was to design an innovative Twelve with reduced displacement and waterline length. With a reduced waterline the sail area could be mantained at the maximum. He also accepted a small penalty to have a beamy stern, close to the water, granting a long waterline when the yacht was heeled. All this found a limitation in the lack of stability. Thanks to long tank tests, the solution was found by taking the lead from the inside of the hull and attaching it to the bottom as a bulb. The related vortex problems were

solved by adopting Withcomb winglets from the aeronautical industry: the lead ballast wings took shape as a new idea in hull design. This solution enabled the keel to be cut away at the hull, therefore reducing the wetted surface, and to add more lead to the bottom. The final result was a Twelve which had a traditional design but a waterline length reduced by 51 cm., a greater beam of 25 cm., a reduced draft of 10 cm. and a lower displacement of six tons

1984 - 1987 America's Cup Defence '87 Ltd (Alan Bond). Trial-horse to *Australia III* and *IV* in 1986. She participated in the Twelve Metre World Championship in Fremantle in 1986 where she was second behind *Australia III*

1993-1995 National Museum of Australia, Canberra ACT
Since 1997 National Museum of Australia exhibit in Perth, WA

■ AUSTRALIA III

DESIGNER: *Ben Lexcen*
BUILDER: *Steve E. Ward & Co.*
YEAR: *1985*
CONSTRUCTION: *aluminium alloy*
FIRST OWNER: *America's Cup Defence '87, Ltd.*
FIRST NAME: *Australia III*
FIRST COUNTRY: *Australia*
HOME PORT: *Perth*
FIRST SAIL NUMBER: *KA 9*
CURRENT LOCATION: *Japan*
FURTHER DETAILS AND HISTORY: Built according to the Third Int. Rule America's Cup. Owners and history:

1985 - 1987 America's Cup Defence '87, Ltd. (Alan Bond); name: *Australia III*; home port: Perth. She was the first of two boats designed by Ben Lexcen for the 26th America's Cup. She was sistership to *South Australia* as Bond and Sir James Hardy had decided to work together for the Cup defence. She had more freeboard and more volume in her ends than *Australia II* which was designed specifically for light airs and the relatively smooth seas off Newport. In fact, she was a powerful boat and she won (skipper Colin Beashel) the 1986 World Championship held in Fremantle. She was then outperformed by *Australia IV*, a very different boat and much faster thanks to the experience acquired in the trials with *Australia II*
Since 1993 Bengal Bay Club Challenge

■ AZZURRA

DESIGNER: *Andrea Vallicelli & Co.*
BUILDER: *Off. Meccaniche Ing. Mario Cobau*
YEAR: *1982*
LENGTH OVERALL: *19.98 m.*
LENGTH AT WATERLINE: *13.87 m.*
BEAM: *3.81 m.*
DRAFT: *2.72 m.*
DISPLACEMENT: *24 tons*
SAIL AREA: *164 sq.m.*
CONSTRUCTION: *aluminium alloy*
ENGINE: *no*
FIRST OWNER: *Consorzio Sfida Italiana America's Cup '83*
FIRST NAME: *Azzurra*

FIRST COUNTRY: *Italy*
HOME PORT: *Porto Cervo (Italy)*
FIRST SAIL NUMBER: *I 4*
CURRENT LOCATION: *Porto Cervo*
CONDITION: *laid up*
PRESENT OWNER: *Yacht Club Costa Smeralda*
FURTHER DETAILS AND HISTORY: Built according to the Third Int. Rule America's Cup. Owners and history

Since 1982 Consorzio Sfida Italiana America's Cup '83 (Gianni Agnelli, Karim Aga Khan); name *Azzurra*; home port: Porto Cervo. In the early Sixties Gianni Agnelli and Beppe Croce had a first informal attempt at an Italian challenge for the America's Cup but their application was not accepted by the NYYC. *Azzurra* was the first Italian Twelve built for the Cup (two other Twelves had been built before the war: *La Spina* and *Emilia*) and she was both important for her good results in the challenger trials and for success in Italy. Agnelli and Aga Khan were joined by other Italian industries to cover the coss which was about 6 billion Italian Lire. *Enterprise* had been bought by the Consorzio and Studio Vallicelli (Vallicelli himself, Mariani and Sironi) and the first model for *Azzurra*, which was based on her lines, was tested in the Italian Navy test tank. Thanks to a good organisation and special harmony between the crew and Italian team, *Azzurra* was third in the semi-finals with *Australia II*, *Victory '83* and *Canada I*. She was second in the Porto Cervo 1984 World Championship behind *Victory '83* and she was the trial horse for *Azzurra II* and *Azzurra III* for the 1987 America's Cup. Since then she has been laid up in a shed

■ AZZURRA II

DESIGNER: *Studio Andrea Vallicelli*
BUILDER: *Industrie Meccaniche Scardellato*
YEAR: *1985*
CONSTRUCTION: *aluminium alloy*
FIRST OWNER: *Consorzio Azzurra Sfida America's Cup '87*
FIRST NAME: *Azzurra II*
FIRST COUNTRY: *Italy*
HOME PORT: *Porto Cervo*
FIRST SAIL NUMBER: *I 8*
OTHER NAMES: *Fritzz (1990?)*
CURRENT LOCATION: *Venice (Italy)*
CONDITION: *sailing*
FURTHER DETAILS AND HISTORY: Built according to the Third Int. Rule America's Cup
Owners and history:

1985 - 1987 Consorzio Azzurra Sfida America's Cup '87; name: *Azzurra II*; home port: Porto Cervo. She was the first of three built for the 26th America's Cup in Fremantle. Based on the lines of the first successful *Azzurra*, she never achieved good results possibily due to problems related to organisation and crew.
She was fifth in the third World Championship in Fremantle
1987 - 1996 G. Clausen; new name: *Fritzz*; home port: Hamburg

Since 1996 Michael Kiersgaard; new name *Azzurra II*; home port: Venice (Italy)

■ Azzurra III

Designer: *Studio Andrea Vallicelli*
Builder: *SAI Ambrosini*
Year: *1986 July 23*
Construction: *aluminium alloy*
First owner: *Consorzio Azzurra Sfida America's Cup '87*
First name: *Azzurra III*
First country: *Italy*
Home port: *Porto Cervo*
First sail number: *I 10*
Other names: *Fratzz (1993)*
Current location: *Hamburg (Germany)*
Further details and history: Built according to the Third Int. Rule America's Cup
Owners and history:
1986 - 1987 Consorzio Azzurra Sfida America's Cup '87; name: *Azzurra III*; home port: Porto Cervo. She was one of three boats built for the 26th America's Cup. She had very poor results with only four wins
1987 - 1994 G. Clausen; new name: *Fratzz*; home port: Hamburg
Since 1994 Jurgen Rohel; new name: *Azzurra III*; home port: Hamburg

■ Azzurra IV

Designer: *Studio Sciomachen & Carlo Bertorello*
Builder: *S.A.I. Ambrosini*
Year: *1986*
Construction: *aluminium alloy*
First owner: *Consorzio Azzurra Sfida Italiana America's Cup*
First name: *Azzurra IV*
First country: *Italy*
Home port: *Porto Cervo*
First sail number: *I 11*
Current location: *Olbia (Italy)*
Condition: *laid up*
Further details and history: Built according to the Third Int. Rule America's Cup
Owners and history:
1986 - 1987 Consorzio Azzurra Sfida Italiana America's Cup '87; name: *Azzurra*; home port: Porto Cervo.
She was one of the three boats built for Consorzio Azzurra for the 26th America's Cup
Since 1988 Lorenzo Orrù; home port: Olbia. She is laid up in a shed

■ Canada I

Designer: *Bruce Kirby*
Builder: *Fred McConnell Marine, Ltd.*
Year: *1982*
Length overall: *19.00 m.*
Length at waterline: *13.78 m.*
Beam: *3.84 m.*
Draft: *2.72 m.*
Displacement: *25.2 tons*
Sail area: *168 sq.m.*
Construction: *aluminium alloy*

First owner: *Secret Cove Yacht Club Challenge*
First name: *Canada I*
First country: *Canada*
Home port: *Half Moon Bay, BC*
First sail number: *KC 1*
Condition: *re-built as Canada II*
Further details and history: Built according to the Third Int. Rule America's Cup. Owners and history:
1982 - 1985 Secret Cove Yacht Club Challenge (Marvin McDill); name: *Canada I*; home port: Half Moon Bay, BC.
She competed in the challenge trials in Newport in 1983 for the Louis Vuitton Cup: she was fourth in the semi-finals behind *Australia II*, *Victory '83* and *Azzurra*. She was subsequently redesigned and considerably re-built as *Canada II*

■ Canada II

Designer: *Bruce Kirby*
Builder: *Fred McConnell Marine, Ltd.*
Year: *1985*
Length overall: *20.11 m.*
Length at waterline: *13.87 m.*
Beam: *3.65 m.*
Draft: *2.72 m.*
Sail area: *166 sq.m.*
Construction: *aluminium alloy*
First owner: *Secret Cove Yacht Club*
First name: *Canada II*
First country: *Canada*
Home port: *Half Moon Bay, BC*
First sail number: *KC 2*
Current location: *St. Maarten (Caribbean)*
Condition: *modified for charter*
Further details and history: Built according to Third Int. Rule America's Cup
Owners and history:
1985 - 1986 Secret Cove Yacht Club; name: *Canada II*; home port: Half Moon Bay, BC. *Canada II* is *Canada I* redesigned and considerably re-built
1986 - 1987 Canada's Challenge '87 for the America's Cup. This was the amalgamation of two separate challenges issued from the Secret Cove Yacht Club (*Canada II*) and the Royal Nova Scotia Yacht Squadron (*True North*). She was a competitor in the 1986 Louis Vuitton Cup challenger trials in Fremantle (Australia)
Since 1993 Colin Percy; home port: St. Martin (Netherland Antilles). She is currently modified for use in the day charter business together with other Twelves

■ Challenge France

Designer: *Daniel Andrieu*
Builder: *Alsthom Chantier Atlantique*
Year: *1986*
Length overall: *19.68 m.*
Length at waterline: *13.58 m.*
Beam: *3.73 m.*
Draft: *2.67 m.*

DISPLACEMENT: *24 tons*
SAIL AREA: *164 sq.m.*
CONSTRUCTION: *aluminium alloy*
FIRST OWNER: *Challenge Fançaise pour la Coupe de l'Amérique*
FIRST NAME: *Challenge France*
FIRST COUNTRY: *France*
HOME PORT: *Marseilles*
FIRST SAIL NUMBER: *F 8*
CURRENT LOCATION: *St. Tropez (France)*
CONDITION: *good sailing*
FURTHER DETAILS AND HISTORY: Built according to the Third Int. Rule America's Cup. Owners and history:

1986 - 1987 Challenge Française pour la Coupe de l'Amérique; name: *Challenge France*; home port: Marseilles. Built for the 26th in 1987 America's Cup in Fremantle on behalf of Société Nautique de Marseilles (Yves Pajot) who had bought *Challenge 12* as a trial horse and reference for the design. Andrieu developed his design using the Paris test tank where he tested several models against one of *Challenge 12* with a simulation of the Fremantle swell. He was also assisted by computer simulation from aeronautical industry computer centres. There were many financial difficulties and *Challenge France* was shipped to Australia at the very last minute. She was never able to develop her potential and dropped out of the series during the round robins where her mast broke
Since 1994 Codara S.A. (Albert Khodara); home port: St. Tropez

■ CHALLENGE 12

DESIGNER: *Ben Lexcen*
BUILDER: *Steve E. Ward & Co.*
YEAR: *1982*
LENGTH OVERALL: *19.25 m.*
LENGTH AT WATERLINE: *13.43 m.*
BEAM: *3.65 m.*
DRAFT: *2.66 m.*
DISPLACEMENT: *23.8 tons*
SAIL AREA: *167 sq.m.*
CONSTRUCTION: *aluminium alloy*
FIRST OWNER: *Alan Bond*
FIRST NAME: *Challenge 12*
FIRST COUNTRY: *Australia*
HOME PORT: *Perth*
FIRST SAIL NUMBER: *KA 10 - F 5*
CURRENT LOCATION: *Antibes (France)*
CONDITION: *refit completed*
FURTHER DETAILS AND HISTORY: Built according to the Third Int. Rule America's Cup. Owners and history:
1982 Alan Bond; name: *Challenge 12*; home port: Perth. She represented the first result of Ben Lexcen cooperation with Peter Van Oosanen of the Netherlands Ship Model Basin of Wageningen. Requested by Alan Bond to design a challenger for the 1983 America's Cup, *Challenge 12* was the first attempt at a new design and represented a point of reference for *Australia II*. Although traditional in her lines, she was unusual for having midship sections narrower than usual, a small bulge below the waterline artificially reducing. She was very fast in light airs and competed successfully against *Australia II*

1983 Royal Yacht Club of Victoria (Richard Pratt); home port: Melbourne. Just two months after her launch, *Challenge 12* was sold to a new owner and she participated in the challenger trials in Newport for the 1983 America's Cup
1985 Fabio Perini; home port: Marina di Carrara. She was bought on behalf of the Club Nautico Marina di Carrara Consorzio Futura for one of the Italian challenges for the 1987 America's Cup. Due to financial problems the challenge did not take place
1996 - 1995 Challenge Française pour la Coupe de l'Amérique; home port: Sète. She was the trial horse for *Challenge France*. Due to financial problems she was seized in the port of Sète.
Since 1996 Chantier Naval Tréhard; home port: Antibes. She underwent a three-year refit and was back on the race course in 1999 when she entered the St. Tropez Rolex Cup

■ CLIPPER

DESIGNER: *David R. Pedrick; design no 12*
BUILDER: *Newport Offshore, Ltd.*
YEAR: *1980*
LENGTH OVERALL: *19.48 m.*
LENGTH AT WATERLINE: *13.74 m.*
BEAM: *3.76 m.*
DRAFT: *2.69 m.*
DISPLACEMENT: *24.85 m.*
SAIL AREA: *164 sq.m.*
CONSTRUCTION: *aluminium alloy*
FIRST OWNER: *People to People Sports Committee*
FIRST NAME: *Clipper*
FIRST COUNTRY: *U.S.A.*
HOME PORT: *Newport, RI*
FIRST SAIL NUMBER: *US 32*
CURRENT LOCATION: *Sweden*
CONDITION: *sailing*
FURTHER DETAILS AND HISTORY: Built according to the Third Int. Rule America's Cup
Owners and history:
1980 People to People Sports Committee; name: *Clipper*; home port: Newport, RI. *Clipper* was the old *Independence* redesigned and rebuilt by David Pedrick for the Huey Long syndicate for the 1980 America's Cup; skipper was Russell, Huey's son. *Clipper* was a good Twelve but suffered from the inexperience of her crew and she only had positive results when Tom Blackaller became her helmsman. Winner of the 1980 Lipton Memorial Trophy
1982 Secret Cove Y.C.; home port: Half Moon Bay, BC (Canada). Trial horse for *Canada* in 1981 and 1982
1986 *Heart of America* challenge. Trial horse for *Heart of America* in 1986
1995 - 2000 Peter Rubenstein; home port; Lidkoping (Sweden)

■ COLUMBIA

DESIGNER: *Olin J. Stephens; design 1343*
BUILDER: *Nevins Yacht Yard Inc.*
YEAR: *1958*
LENGTH OVERALL: *21.15 m.*
LENGTH AT WATERLINE: *13.93 m.*
BEAM: *3.55 m.*

DRAFT: *2.73 m.*
DISPLACEMENT: *28.35 tons*
SAIL AREA: *173 sq.m.*
CONSTRUCTION: *double-planked mahogany on oak frames*
FIRST OWNER: *Sears-Cunningham Syndicate*
FIRST NAME: *Columbia*
FIRST COUNTRY: *U.S.A.*
HOME PORT: *New York*
FIRST SAIL NUMBER: *US 16*
CURRENT LOCATION: *Newport (U.S.A.)*
CONDITION: *rebuilt in 2000*
FURTHER DETAILS AND HISTORY: Built according to Third Int. Rule
Owners and history:
1958 - 1961 Sears-Cunningham Syndicate; name: *Columbia*; home port:
New York, NY. She was built for the 17th America's Cup, the first to be
raced with a Twelve Metre. Her design was a development of *Vim* and
Stephens, after numerous comparison tests of six models in the Hoboken
tank, considered *Columbia* to be slightly superior to *Vim*. Compared to
Vim, she was longer on the waterline but had a reduced beam and a
slightly reduced sail area. This was compensated by the increased
efficiency of new sails and later on by the Dacron ones supplied by Hood
after the selection was made. The thickness of the keel was also reduced
in order to reduce resistance. Special attention was given to the point
where the keel meets the body by making it as thin as possible at its point
of entry. The cost of *Columbia* was estimated to be in the range of
$300.000. *Columbia* (skippered by Briggs Cunningham) won the defender
trials against *Weatherly*, *Easterner* and *Vim* after three series of races. Only
the races with *Vim* (skipper Bus Mosbacher) were closely fought and the
result came only at the end of a supplementary race which *Columbia* won
by thirteen seconds. The match race saw *Columbia* dominating *Sceptre* by
4-0. In 1958 she won also the Caritas Cup (NYYC)
1960 - 1963 Paul Shields. The keel was altered and *Columbia* participated
in the defender trials for the 1962 America's Cup
1963 - 1964 Estate of Paul V. Shields
1964 - 1975 Thomas Patrick Dougan; home port: Southampton, NY and
Newport Beach, CA. Dougan, a west coaster, was the defender in both
the 1964 and 1966 America's Cup races. In 1966 the hull was altered by
Olin Stephens at Driscoll Custom Yachts in San Diego: the hull was
shortened and completely redesigned with a relatively pronounced bustle
which extended the aft section of the hull beyond the keel and the rudder.
This was an extension of the keel and not a separate appendage as on
Intrepid. *Columbia* performed well in the trials dominated by *Intrepid*,
marking the first time with West Coast participation and a West Coast
crew. In 1967 she won the Lipton Memorial Trophy and the Caritas Cup
1975 In summer 1975 she was bought by the Swedish Syndicate for the
America's Cup as a trial horse for the Swedish challenge
1976 Handelsbolaget Modern Boating; home port: Gothenbourg.
Trial horse to *Sverige*
1976 - 1978 Pelle Petterson, Lars Wiglund & Stellan Westerdhal.
She was modified
1978 - 1980 Xavier Rouget-Luchaire (Société des Régates Rochelaises);
home port: La Rochelle (France). *Columbia* was the trial horse to *Lionheart*
in 1979
1985 - 1997 Bernard Pollet; home port: Cannes (France)

1997 - 4/2000 Paul Gardener and Bill Collins; home port: Newport, RI
Since 6/2000 12 Metre Yacht. Charters LLC (Alain J. Hanover); home port:
Boston, MA. Rebuilt at New England Boat Works (Portsmouth, RI) with a
new keel designed by David Pedrick

■ CONSTELLATION
DESIGNER: *Olin J. Stephens; design no 1733*
BUILDER: *Minneford Yacht Yard Inc.*
YEAR: *1964*
LENGTH OVERALL: *20.83 m.*
LENGTH AT WATERLINE: *14.02 m.*
BEAM: *3.66 m.*
DRAFT: *2.66 m.*
DISPLACEMENT: *27.2 tons*
SAIL AREA: *170 sq.m.*
CONSTRUCTION: *double-planked mahogany on oak frames*
FIRST OWNER: *The Constellation Syndicate*
FIRST NAME: *Constellation*
FIRST COUNTRY: *United States*
HOME PORT: *Oyster Bay, NY*
FIRST SAIL NUMBER: *US 20 - UK 20*
CURRENT LOCATION: *sunk*
FURTHER DETAILS AND HISTORY: Built according to the Third Int. Rule
America's Cup. Owners and history:
1964 - 1965 The Constellation Syndicate (Walter S. Gubelmann); name:
Constellation (*Connie*); home port: Oyster Bay, NY. Built for the 19th
America's Cup in 1964. The aim of Olin Stephens was to have
Constellation as an improved version of *Columbia* with a further
refinement of the keel area and an improvement of the equipment as
lightweight as was permitted by the rule. She had the boom, the mast tip
and the winch drums in titanium. Strain gauges were placed over the
entire boat in order to measure the dynamic loading under sail. Mast and
boom bent more than those of her competitors thus allowing a greater
control of sails according to wind conditions. The first results of the defender
trials were rather disappointing with *American Eagle* dominating the other
competitors in the first half of the trials. The results were thanks to the
involvement of the Stephens brothers and the change of the skipper from
Eric Ridder to Bob Bavier. In the second part *Constellation* faced up and
dominated *American Eagle* and easily defeated by 4-0, the British challenger
Sovereign. In the same year she won the Caritas Cup and the Chandler
Hovey Gold Boal (NYYC)
1966 - 1978 Pierre E. Goemans; home port: Montecarlo, Monaco. The
owner acted on behalf of Baron Bich who organised the French challenge
(Association Française pour la Coupe de l'Amérique - AFCA). In 1967
Constellation was chartered to the McCullough Syndicate at first as a trial
horse for the future *Intrepid* and then as one of the Twelves competing for
the defender trials. In 1970 and 1974 she was trial horse for France and
she was altered in 1971 by Paul Elvstrom, at the time requested by Baron
Bich to follow the French challenge
1979 AFCA
1980 Security Change Ltd.; home port: Hamble
1980 British Industry 1500 Syndicate (J. Anthony J. Boyden); home port:
London; a trial horse for *Lionheart*
Curent location Sunk while being towed off Turkey

▪ COURAGEOUS

DESIGNER: *Olin J. Stephens; design no. 2085*
BUILDER: *Minneford Yacht Yard Inc.*
YEAR: *1974*
LENGTH OVERALL: *19.94 m.*
LENGTH AT WATERLINE: *13.71 m.*
BEAM: *3.73 m.*
DRAFT: *2.64 m.*
DISPLACEMENT: *24.6 tons*
SAIL AREA: *166 sq.m.*
CONSTRUCTION: *aluminium alloy*
FIRST OWNER: *Courageous Syndicate*
FIRST NAME: *Courageous*
FIRST COUNTRY: *U.S.A.*
HOME PORT: *New York*
FIRST SAIL NUMBER: *US 26*
OTHER NAMES: *Courageous I I (1979); Courageous III (1984); Courageous IV (1986)*
CURRENT LOCATION: *Newport (U.S.A.)*
CONDITION: *sailing, good*
FURTHER DETAILS AND HISTORY: Built according to Third Int. Rule America's Cup. Owners and history:

1974 - 1976 Courageous Syndicate; name: *Courageous*; home port: New York. David Pedrick assisted Olin Stephens in the design of *Courageous* for the 22nd America's Cup in 1974. She was another landmark in the design of Twelves being the first 12M to be built in aluminium alloy according to Lloyd's scantling rules - new standards authorising this material to be used in the building of Twelves. This meant an advantage of about two tons in the weight of the hull. In fact, *Courageous* was a light boat, quite conservative in her lines and very elegant. She was one of the first Twelves to have a computer system installed on board enabling tuning and sail testing. The defence trials were raced between *Courageous*, *Heritage*, *Intrepid* and *Valiant*. The first skipper was Bob Bavier, replaced by Ted Hood later in the trial period; Dennis Conner was the starting helmsman, marking the start of his long career with the America's Cup. She was appointed official defender after beating *Intrepid* in the races which resembled the battle between *Columbia* and *Vim* in the 1958 selection trials. *Courageous* defeated the Australian *Southern Cross* in the America's Cup. In the same year she won the Chandler Hovey Gold Bowl (NYYC). According to Olin Stephens, Ted Hood discovered in 1977 that *Courageous*'s displacement was less than the one shown on the rating certificate by 1700lbs. This meant that in her rating certificate 35 cm. should have been added to her length and around 9 sq.m. to her the sail area

1977 - 1979 Kings Point Fund, Inc. US Merchant Marine Academy; home port: Kings Point, NY. In 1977 she was altered by Frederick E. Hood and Sparkman & Stephens to comply to the new 12 Metre rule. The main winches were placed on deck, some 850 kilos were added to the ballast, the rudder was moved forward to reduce the waterline. In the 1977 trials, with Ted Turner as skipper, she outperformed the other contenders, *Independence* and *Enterprise*. In the match she won easily: four races to none against Alan Bond's *Australia*. With this victory, she became the third Twelve, after *Columbia* and *Intrepid,* to have successfully defended the Cup. In 1977, she won the Chandler Hovey Gold Bowl again

1979 - 1980 R.E. "Ted" Turner III; new name: *Courageous II*; home port:

Atlanta, GA; altered in 1980, she participated in the 24th America's Cup defender trials against *Freedom* and *Clipper*

1981 David Vietor and Leonard Greene, head of the People to People Sports Committee

1982 - 1983 Defender/Courageous Group (People to People Sports Committee). She entered unsuccessfully the defender trials for the 25th America's Cup. In 1983 she won the Lipton Memorial Trophy (NYYC)

1984 - 1985 Courageous Synd. Inc. (David Vietor and Leonard Greene); new names: *Courageous III* and *IV*; home port: Short Beach, CT. She was altered with a new winglet keel that was modified several times in a campaign to send *Courageous* to Australia in 1987 as a challenger. In 1986, she was next to last in the Fremantle World Championship but, under the name of *Courageous IV*, none of the alterations could make her a winner in the challenger trials

1993-1994 Courageous Sailing Centre; new name: *Courageous*; home port: Cambridge, MA. The Centre was founded and based at the Boston Navy Yard to assist wheelchair-bound people in learning to sail

1996 US 26 Corporation; home port: Wilmington, DE

Since 1997 The Museum of Yachting; home port: Newport, RI. She was donated by Leonard Greene to the museum and has undergone a restoration programme

▪ CRUSADER

DESIGNER: *Ian Howlett*
BUILDER: *Cougar Marine*
YEAR: *1985*
CONSTRUCTION: *aluminium alloy*
FIRST OWNER: *British America's Cup Challenge, PLC*
FIRST NAME: *Crusader I*
FIRST COUNTRY: *Great Britain*
HOME PORT: *London*
FIRST SAIL NUMBER: *K24*
OTHER NAMES: *White Crusader (1986)*
CURRENT LOCATION: *Ipswich (GB)*
CONDITION: *at her best*
FURTHER DETAILS AND HISTORY: Built according to the Third Int. Rule America's Cup. Owners and history:

1985 - 1986 British America's Cup Challenge, PLC (Graham Walker); name: *Crusader I*; home port: London. *Crusader I* was the first boat built for the 26th America's Cup in 1987. Howlett carried out an extensive research programme with models at the Wolfson Unit at the University of Southampton to create a relatively conservative project. The syndicate decided to build another boat which was more radical but which had worse results than *Crusader I*

1986 - 1987 British America's Cup Challenge, PLC (Graham Walker); new name: *White Crusader*

Since 1993 Richard Matthews; new name: *Crusader*; home port: Ipswich

▪ CRUSADER II (HIPPO)

DESIGNER: *David H.J. Hollom*
BUILDER: *Cougar Marine*
YEAR: *1986*
CONSTRUCTION: *aluminium alloy*
FIRST OWNER: *British America's Cup Challenge, PLC*

FIRST NAME: *Crusader II (Hippo)*
FIRST COUNTRY: *Great Britain*
HOME PORT: *London*
FIRST SAIL NUMBER: *K 25*
OTHER NAMES: *White Crusader II*
CONDITION: *reported to have been broken up*
FURTHER DETAILS AND HISTORY: Built according to the Third Int. Rule America's Cup. Owners and history:
1986 British America's Cup Challenge, PLC (Graham Walker); name: *Crusader II*, home port: London. *Crusader II* was the second boat built for the British challenge for the 26th America's Cup 1987. She was a more radical design than the previous boat with long overhangs and a winged canard keel which gave her the *"Hippo"* nickname. The first tests were carried out with simulated wave motion in the ship model basin of the Teddington Nautical Maritime Institute
1986 - 1987 British America's Cup Challenge, PLC (Graham Walker); name: *White Crusader II*; although shipped to Fremantle, she did not race in the Louis Vuitton Cup in 1986
1994 Chris Freer; new name: *Crusader II*; home port: Southampton; reported to have been broken up

■ DEFENDER

DESIGNER: *David R. Pedrick - design n. 20*
BUILDER: *Newport Offshore Ltd.*
YEAR: *1982*
LENGTH OVERALL: *19.53 m.*
LENGTH AT WATERLINE: *13.56 m.*
BEAM: *3.76 m.*
DRAFT: *2.67 m.*
DISPLACEMENT: *24.05 tons*
SAIL AREA: *167 sq.m.*
CONSTRUCTION: *aluminium alloy*
FIRST OWNER: *Defender Courageous Gr., People to People*
FIRST NAME: *Defender*
FIRST COUNTRY: *U.S.A.*
HOME PORT: *Newport, RI*
FIRST SAIL NUMBER: *US 33*
CURRENT LOCATION: *West Palm Beach, FL (U.S.A.)*
CONDITION: *sailing, good*
FURTHER DETAILS AND HISTORY: Built according to the Third Int. Rule America's Cup. Owners and history:
1982 - 1983 Defender/Courageous Group, People to People Sports Committee; name: *Defender*; home port: Newport. She was designed for light weather sailing using computer calculations and hydrodynamic tests carried at the Stevens Institute. She was altered in 1983 by David Pedrick. She entered, with Tom Blackaller as skipper, in the defender trials for the 25th America's Cup in 1983 racing against *Liberty* and *Courageous*. She did not succeed as she was short of speed
1986 *Heart of America* challenge. She was trial horse for *Heart of America*
1986 Brian Mock; home port: Newport Beach, CA; engine installed in 1989
1993 - 1994 B. Sheryl Geddes and Lance Brush; home port: Palo Alto, CA
1996 Lawrence R. Spira, MD; home port: Santa Monica, CA
Since 2000 Ken Carrico, West Palm Beach, FL

■ EAGLE

DESIGNER: *Johan Valentijn*
BUILDER: *Williams & Manchester Shipyard*
YEAR: *1986*
CONSTRUCTION: *aluminium alloy*
FIRST OWNER: *Eagle Challenge*
FIRST NAME: *Eagle*
FIRST COUNTRY: *U.S.A.*
HOME PORT: *Newport Beach, CA (U.S.A.)*
FIRST SAIL NUMBER: *US 60*
CONDITION: *bare hull*
FURTHER DETAILS AND HISTORY: Built according to the Third Int. Rule America's Cup. Owners and history:
1986 - 1987 Eagle Challenge; name *Eagle*; home port: Newport Beach, CA. Challenger to the 26th America's Cup in 1987 in Fremantle, skipper Rod Davis. No significant result
1993-1994 Don Oakes; home port: Portland, OR. Yacht was stripped of all hardware. Many parts were reused on *Lionheart* (rig, sails, winches, etc.)

■ EASTERNER

DESIGNER: *C Raymond Hunt & F.C. Williams Association*
BUILDER: *James E. Graves Inc.*
YEAR: *1958*
LENGTH OVERALL: *19.94 m.*
LENGTH AT WATERLINE: *14.35 m.*
BEAM: *3.66 m.*
DRAFT: *2.79 m.*
DISPLACEMENT: *27.8 tons*
SAIL AREA: *179 sq.m.*
CONSTRUCTION: *double-planked mahogany on oak frames*
FIRST OWNER: *Easterner Syndicate*
FIRST NAME: *Easterner*
FIRST COUNTRY: *U.S.A.*
HOME PORT: *Marblehead*
FIRST SAIL NUMBER: *US 18*
OTHER NAMES: *Newsboy (1969)*
CURRENT LOCATION: *Jamestown, RI (U.S.A.)*
CONDITION: *sailing, good*
FURTHER DETAILS AND HISTORY: Built according the Third Int. Rule America's Cup
Owners and history:
1958 - 1966 Easterner Syndicate (Chandler Hovey); name: *Easterner*; home port: Marblehead, MA. Built for the Chandler Hovey family (already owner of the J-Class *Rainbow* and *Weetamoe*), she entered in the 1958, 1962 and 1964 defender trials for the 17th and 18th America's Cup. Although the boat had a good potential as she was considered the fastest of the 1958 Twelves, due to lack of crew and helmsmanship (Chandler Hovey was on the tiller with a crew formed of mostly family members), she competed unsuccessfully and was eliminated in the first round of trials. Winner in 1962 of the Astor Cup (NYYC) and in 1964 of the Queen's Cup (NYYC)
1967 - 1968 John K. Baillie & Phyllis D. Baillie; Marblehead, MA and Los Angeles, CA

1968 - 1995 John K. Baillie; new name: *Newsboy*; home port: Newport Beach (California)

Since 1995 SASA Charters, Inc. (Arthur Schlossmann); home port: Jamestown, RI. Yacht rebuilt at the Brooklin Boat Yard and Cove Haven Marina with a major structural restoration including reframing, refastening and refinishing

■ ECOSSE

DESIGNER: *Gary Mull*
BUILDER: *Robert E. Derecktor, Inc.*
YEAR: *1986*
LENGTH OVERALL: *20.12 m.*
BEAM: *3.66 m.*
CONSTRUCTION: *aluminium alloy*
FIRST OWNER: *Golden Gate Challenge San Francisco*
FIRST NAME: *USA (R-1)*
FIRST COUNTRY: *U.S.A.*
HOME PORT: *San Francisco*
FIRST SAIL NUMBER: *US 61*
CURRENT LOCATION: *Montecarlo (Monaco)*
CONDITION: *perfect condition*
FURTHER DETAILS AND HISTORY: Built according to the Third Int. Rule
Owners and history:

1986 - 1987 Golden Gate Challenge San Francisco; name: *USA (R-1)*; home port: San Francisco, CA. She was nicknamed *R-1* for *"Revolutionary"*. Her hull had a torpedo ballast keel and two rudders aft and a forward canard type. She performed well, with Tom Blackaller as skipper and Paul Cayard as tactician, in the semi-finals of the 1987 America's Cup. She was beaten by *Stars & Stripes '87* by a score of 4-0. Winner of the 1987 Lipton Memorial Trophy (NYYC)

1988 - 1989 The St. Francis 12 Foundation

1993 - 1994 Robert B. Cole; home port: Woodside, CA

1996 The St. Francis 12 Foundation; home port: San Francisco, CA

Since 2000 Irvine Laidlaw; new name: *Ecosse*; home port: Monaco

■ ENDLESS SUMMER

DESIGNER: *Warwick J. Hood*
BUILDER: *William H. Barnett Pty. Ltd.*
YEAR: *1966*
LENGTH OVERALL: *19.84 m.*
LENGTH AT WATERLINE: *14.32 m.*
BEAM: *3.68 m.*
DRAFT: *2.76 m.*
DISPLACEMENT: *28.25 tons*
SAIL AREA: *165 sq.m.*
CONSTRUCTION: *wood*
FIRST OWNER: *The "America's Cup" Challenger Syndicate*
FIRST NAME: *Dame Pattie*
FIRST COUNTRY: *Australia*
HOME PORT: *Sydney*
FIRST SAIL NUMBER: *KA 2*
OTHER NAMES: *Endless Summer (1971)*
COUNTRY: *Canada*

FURTHER DETAILS AND HISTORY: Built according to the Third Int. Rule America's Cup. Owners and history:

1966 - 1970 The "America's Cup" Challenger Syndicate (Emil Christensen); name: *Dame Pattie*; home port: Sydney, NSW. Challenger for the 20th America's Cup Match in 1967, she was designed by Warwick Hood who had worked with Alan Payne on the design of *Gretel*. She was lighter than this one and entirely built in Australia as required by the "country of origin" clause. The sails were weaved in the Australian version of Dacron called "Ka-dron". *Dame Pattie* performed well against *Gretel* but she lost zero to four to *Intrepid*

1970 - 1980 G.W. O'Brien; new name: *Endless Summer*; home port: Vancouver, BC (Canada). Altered to an ocean racer and engine installed in 1972, re-engined 1975

Since 1993 Lawrence Lambert; home port: Sidney, BC (Canada)

■ ENTERPRISE

DESIGNER: *Sparkman & Stephens - design no 2270*
BUILDER: *Minneford Yacht Yard Inc.*
YEAR: *1977*
LENGTH OVERALL: *20.15 m.*
LENGTH AT WATERLINE: *13.41 m.*
BEAM: *3.78 m.*
DRAFT: *2.74 m.*
DISPLACEMENT: *25.7 tons*
SAIL AREA: *168 sq.m.*
CONSTRUCTION: *aluminium alloy*
FIRST OWNER: *The Maritime College of Fort Schuyler Foundation*
FIRST NAME: *Enterprise*
FIRST COUNTRY: *U.S.A.*
HOME PORT: *New York*
FIRST SAIL NUMBER: *US 27*
CURRENT LOCATION: *Antibes, France*
CONDITION: *at her best*
FURTHER DETAILS AND HISTORY: Built according to the Third Int. Rule America's Cup. Owners and history:

1977 - 1980 The Maritime College of Fort Schuyler Foundation, Inc; name: *Enterprise*; home port: New York, NY. She was an improved version of *Courageous* designed by Olin Stephens, with the cooperation of David Pedrick, for the 23rd America's Cup. Skipper was Lowell North and a fight started between the two sailmakers, Ted Hood being the skipper of *Independence*, the other defender candidate. It was also the first time that computers were used systematically in the design of sails. In the defender trials she was beaten by *Courageous*. Altered in 1979 by Sparkman & Stephens, she was the trial horse for *Freedom* in 1980. In 1977 she won the Caritas Cup (NYYC) and was co-winner with *Independence* of the Lipton Memorial Trophy (NYYC). In 1980 she won the Caritas Cup again

1981 Italian Challenge America's Cup Syndicate; home port: Porto Cervo. *Enterprise* was bought for around $300.000 as trial horse for *Azzurra* and point of reference for the Vallicelli design

1984 BNZ Challenge; charter for Worlds; Sardinia

1986 - 1987 Challenge Kis France; home port: La Rochelle (France). Trial horse for *French Kiss* in 1986. Due to the financial problems of the syndicate, *Enterprise* was seized and was bought by Chantiers Tréhard

Since 1996 Antibes Marine Chantiers; home port: Antibes. She has undergone a complete restoration and was again racing in 2000

■ FRANCE I

DESIGNER: *André Mauric*
BUILDER: *Herman Egger, Chantier AFCA*
YEAR: *1970*
LENGTH OVERALL: *19.13 m.*
LENGTH AT WATERLINE: *14.40 m.*
BEAM: *3.76 m.*
DRAFT: *2.57 m.*
DISPLACEMENT: *27.45 tons*
SAIL AREA: *165 sq.m.*
CONSTRUCTION: *wood*
FIRST OWNER: *L'Ass. Fr. pour la Coupe de l'Amérique*
FIRST NAME: *France*
FIRST COUNTRY: *France*
HOME PORT: *Hyères*
FIRST SAIL NUMBER: *F 1*
CURRENT LOCATION: *Brest (France)*
CONDITION: *good, sailing*
PRESENT OWNER: *French Navy*
FURTHER DETAILS AND HISTORY: Built according to the Third Int. Rule America's Cup. Owners and history:
1970 - 1976 Association Française pour La Coupe de l'Amérique (AFCA) (Marcel Bich); name: *France*; home port: Hyères. *France* represented the first of four attempts by Baron Bich to win the America's Cup. After the 1967 Cup, he started the organisation of a French challenge: L'Association Française pour la Coupe de l'Amérique (AFCA). As trial horses he bought *Kurrewa V*, *Sovereign* and *Constellation*. He asked to Britton Chance and Egger to construct *Chancegger* to be used to test the new *France*. Despite the important financial input, the results were not encouraging: *France* was beaten by *Gretel* by four-zero. If the hull was a quick one, rigging, sails and the crew were very different the Australians. She competed unsuccessfully again in the challenger trials of 1974 and 1977
1977 - 1980 Same owner; new name: *France I*; altered in 1977
Since 1986 Ecole Navale de la Marine Française; home port: Brest

■ FRANCE II (PROJECT)

DESIGNER: *Paul Elvstrom & Jan Kjaerulff*
BUILDER: *Hermann Egger, Chantier AFCA*
YEAR: *1973*
LENGTH OVERALL: *19.27 m.*
LENGTH AT WATERLINE: *13.94 m.*
BEAM: *3.83 m.*
DRAFT: *2.74 m.*
DISPLACEMENT: *26.05 tons*
SAIL AREA: *166 sq.m.*
CONSTRUCTION: *aluminium alloy*
FIRST OWNER: *L'Ass. Fr. pour la Coupe de l'Amérique*
FIRST NAME: *France II*
FIRST COUNTRY: *France*
HOME PORT: *Hyères*
FIRST SAIL NUMBER: *none issued*
FURTHER DETAILS AND HISTORY: Designed according to the Third Int. Rule America's Cup. Owners and history:

1973 L'Association Française pour la Coupe de l'Amérique. This *France II* is not to be confused with the *France II* actually built and completed for A.F.C.A. in 1977. This yacht was to be an aluminium yacht but construction was stopped during the setting-up of her frames. The framing was subsequently destroyed. The project was a radical one with a bulb designed by Paul Elvstrom, asked in 1971 by Baron Bich to form a new crew, and the Danish designer Jan Kjaerulff. The project was suddenly interrupted when Baron Bich had to face the objections from French opinion makers who did not want a French challenger designed by a non French citizen

■ FRANCE II

DESIGNER: *André Mauric*
BUILDER: *Pontarlier*
YEAR: *1977*
LENGTH OVERALL: *19.13 m.*
LENGTH AT WATERLINE: *13.94 m.*
BEAM: *3.86 m.*
DRAFT: *2.79 m.*
FIRST OWNER: *L'Ass. Fr. pour la Coupe de l'Amérique*
FIRST NAME: *France II*
FIRST COUNTRY: *France*
HOME PORT: *Hyères*
FIRST SAIL NUMBER: *F 2*
FURTHER DETAILS AND HISTORY: Built according to the Third Int. Rule America's Cup
Owners and history:
1977 L'Association Française de la Coupe de l'Amérique; name: *France II*; home port: Hyères. Designed by Mauric for the 1977 challenge, she suffered from so many changes and modifications that the designer rejected her. *France II* was so slow that the old *France I* was chosen to race *Australia*. There was no contest and *Australia* won by a score of 4-0
1994 *France II* was transformed into a cruising yacht with rich interiors of solid wood
1996 She took part in some races for the European Cup but she didn't qualify

■ FRANCE III

DESIGNER: *J.W. Vallentijin & Zonen*
BUILDER: *C. N. A. 80*
YEAR: *1979 February*
LENGTH OVERALL: *19.91 m.*
LENGTH AT WATERLINE: *14.22 m.*
BEAM: *3.71 m.*
DRAFT: *2.74 m.*
CONSTRUCTION: *aluminium alloy*
FIRST OWNER: *L'Ass. Fr. pour la Coupe de l'Amérique*
FIRST NAME: *France III*
FIRST COUNTRY: *France*
HOME PORT: *Hyères*
FIRST SAIL NUMBER: *F 3*
CURRENT LOCATION: *Brest, France*
CONDITION: *good*
PRESENT OWNER: *French Military Navy*

FURTHER DETAILS AND HISTORY: Designed according to the Third Int. Rule America's Cup
Owners and history:

1979 L'Association Française pour La Coupe de l'Amérique; name: *France III*; *France III* was the evolution of the challenger *Australia* in whose project Valentijn co-operated with Ben Lexcen. It was the first success of Baron Bich. *France III* won by a score of 4-3 against the British *Lionheart*. Later she lost to *Australia* by a score of 4-1. At the end of the race Baron Bich announced his retirement from the America's Cup

■ FREEDOM

DESIGNER: *Olin J. Stephens - design no 2368*
BUILDER: *Minneford Yacht Yard Inc.*
YEAR: *1979 June*
LENGTH OVERALL: *18.97 m.*
LENGTH AT WATERLINE: *13.76 m.*
BEAM: *3.73 m.*
DRAFT: *2.74 m.*
DISPLACEMENT: *25.95 tons*
SAIL AREA: *168 sq.m.*
CONSTRUCTION: *aluminium alloy*
FIRST OWNER: *The Maritime Coll. of Fort Schuyler Foundation Inc.*
FIRST NAME: *Freedom*
FIRST COUNTRY: *United States*
HOME PORT: *Newport*
FIRST SAIL NUMBER: *US 30*
CURRENT LOCATION: *Newport (U.S.A.)*
CONDITION: *perfect condition*
FURTHER DETAILS AND HISTORY: Built according to the Third Int. Rule America's Cup
Owners and history:

1979 - 1980 The Maritime College of Fort Schuyler Foundation, Inc. SUNY; name: *Freedom*; home port: Newport. *Freedom* was the last Twelve designed by Olin Stephens with the cooperation of Bill Langan. Her hull lines were inspired by *Enterprise*, while work was done to reduce the pitch and the windage of the hull with a very reduced freeboard. *Freedom* was skippered by Dennis Conner and dominated the defender trials on *Clipper* and *Courageous*. In the America's Cup match she beat *Australia* 4-1. In 1980 she won the Chandler Hovey Gold Bowl (1980)
1983 Freedom Campaign '83 SUNY at Ft. Schuyler. Altered by Sparkman & Stephens in 1982. Trial horse: *Liberty* in 1983
1985 Consorzio Italia (?)
1986 - 1987 Challenge Kis France; home port: La Rochelle (France). Trial horse: *French Kiss* in 1986
1995 - 2000 François Fontes; home port: Montpellier (France)
Since June 2000 Freedom Foundation, LLC (Ernest K. Jacquet); home port: Newport, RI

■ FRENCH KISS

DESIGNER: *P. Briand, P. Perrier, D. Chaumette*
BUILDER: *Alubat*
YEAR: *October 17 1985*
LENGTH OVERALL: *19.20 m.*

BEAM: *3.60 m.*
DISPLACEMENT: *24.05 tons*
SAIL AREA: *160 sq.m.*
CONSTRUCTION: *aluminium alloy*
FIRST OWNER: *Challenge Kis France/Clipper's & Associés*
FIRST NAME: *French Kiss*
FIRST COUNTRY: *France*
HOME PORT: *La Rochelle*
FIRST SAIL NUMBER: *F 7*
CURRENT LOCATION: *Marina di Carrara (Italy)*
CONDITION: *perfect condition*
PRESENT OWNER: *Corrado Fratini*
FURTHER DETAILS AND HISTORY: Built according to the Third Int. Rule America's Cup
Owners and history:

1985 - 1987 Challenge Kis France/Clipper's & Associés; name: *French Kiss*; home port: La Rochelle. *French Kiss* was the only Twelve, out of two designed, built for the 1987 America's Cup. The budget was in the region of US$9.000.000 entirely covered by the photographic Kis Company. The leading men of the project were Philippe Briand for the design, Marc Pajot as manager and skipper. The computer research for the project was done by Dassault under the direction of Philippe Perrier and Daniel Chamette with no tests in tanks or wind tunnels just flow and pressure simulations. *French Kiss* was both original and highly efficient in winds over 15 knots. She was the big surprise in the challenger trials for her speed, the only weak point being her reliability. She was fifth in the 1986 World Championship and she entered in the challenger's Semi-finals where she was beaten by *New Zealand*
1987 - 1994 STCA - home port: St. Tropez
1995 - 1999 Codara S.A. (Albert Khodara); home port: Marseille (France). She was again tuned up at the top with new sails and the original equipment was updated. She won several races on the Mediterranean circuit: the 1996 Coppa d'Europa and St. Tropez Rolex Cup. In 1997 she was second in Coppa d'Europa but she won the Rolex Cup again. She was third in the 1999 World Championship and won the 2000 St. Tropez Cup

■ GRETEL

DESIGNER: *Alan Payne*
BUILDER: *Lars Holvorsen Sons. Pty. Ltd.*
YEAR: *February 19 1962*
LENGTH OVERALL: *21.16 m.*
LENGTH AT WATERLINE: *13.84 m.*
BEAM: *3.58 m.*
DRAFT: *2.67 m.*
DISPLACEMENT: *26.7 tons*
SAIL AREA: *171 sq.m.*
CONSTRUCTION: *wood on steel frames*
FIRST OWNER: *Sir Franck Packer, Australian ACCA*
FIRST NAME: *Gretel*
FIRST COUNTRY: *Australia*
HOME PORT: *Sydney*
FIRST SAIL NUMBER: *KA1 - F5*
CURRENT LOCATION: *North Queensland (Australia)*

CONDITION: *sailing*
COUNTRY: *Australia*
FURTHER DETAILS AND HISTORY: Built according to the Third Int. Rule America's Cup
Owners and history:
1962 - 1973 Sir Franck Packer, Australian America's Cup Challenge Association; name: *Gretel*; home port: Sydney. In 1959 Sir Franck Packer, an Australian newspaper magnate, chartered *Vim* for four years and took her to his country for an Australian challenge for the 1962 America's Cup. In that period, there were no limitations in the Deed of Gift export of technologies and materials and Packer sent for Alan Payne at the Stevens Institute at Hoboken to work on the design of a new challenger. *Gretel* was based on the lines of *Vim*, carefully analysed, and on the American calculations and measurements from the Stevens Institute which were accessible to Payne. One major innovation was the possibility of linking the winches of the genoa sheets and have the four gears operated by the winchman's foot pedal. Such a possibility increased the efficiency while tacking. *Gretel* competed successfully against *Weatherly*: the races were very close and the Australians were even able to win a race finally losing by a score of 4-1. The Americans won due to a greater efficiency of the crew and greater experience rather than having a better boat. As a consequence, it was decided to prevent the future challengers from accessing any kind of American technology. *Gretel* was altered by Payne in 1966 and 1967 and she was the trial horse to *Dame Pattie* for the 1967 America's Cup and for *Gretel II* for the following match
1973 - 1974 Yanchep Estates Pty. Ltd.; home port: Perth and Yanchep
1975 The Southern Cross America's Cup Challenge Association, Ltd. She was the trial horse for *Southern Cross*
1976 - 1979 Gretel Syndicate; home port: Yanchep, WA (1976 and 1977), Port Melbourne, Victoria & Sydney, NSW
1980 Disappeared of Lloyd's Register
1993-1994 Operated as a charter vessel in North Queensland

■ GRETEL II

DESIGNER: *Alan Payne*
BUILDER: *W.H. Barnett*
YEAR: *1970*
LENGTH OVERALL: *19.81 m.*
LENGTH AT WATERLINE: *14.02 m.*
BEAM: *3.66 m.*
DRAFT: *2.74 m.*
SAIL AREA: *187 m.*
FIRST OWNER: *Sir Francis Packer*
FIRST NAME: *Gretel II*
FIRST COUNTRY: *Australia*
HOME PORT: *Sydney*
FIRST SAIL NUMBER: *KA 3*
FURTHER DETAILS AND HISTORY: Built according to the Third Int. Rule America's Cup
Owners and history:
1970 Sir Francis Packer; name: *Gretel II*; home port: Sydney

■ HEART OF AMERICA

DESIGNER: *Gretzky, Graham, MacLane, Schlageter*

BUILDER: *Merrifield-Roberts, Inc.*
YEAR: *May 8 1986*
CONSTRUCTION: *aluminium alloy*
FIRST OWNER: *Heart of America Challenge*
FIRST NAME: *Heart of America*
FIRST COUNTRY: *U.S.A.*
HOME PORT: *Newport, RI*
FIRST SAIL NUMBER: *US 51*
CURRENT LOCATION: *Turkey*
FURTHER DETAILS AND HISTORY: Built according to the Third Int. Rule America's Cup
Owners and history:
1986 - 1987 Heart of America Challenge; name: *Heart of America*; home port: Newport, RI. Challenger of the 26th 1987 America's Cup representing the Chicago Yacht Club with skipper Harry C. "Buddy" Melges. She was designed by a design team formed by James Gretzky, Scott Graham, Duncan Maclane and Eric Schlageter who was more famous for small ocean racers. Her lines are very close to the ones of *French Kiss* with a high bow, low freeboard and a large stern. The keel is similar to the one of *Australia II*.
? US 12 Metre San Diego, Inc; home port: La Jolla, CA
Since 1993 in Turkey

■ HERITAGE

DESIGNER: *Charles E. Morgan Jr. - design no 3603*
BUILDER: *Morgan Yacht Corp.*
YEAR: *1970*
LENGTH OVERALL: *19.20 m.*
LENGTH AT WATERLINE: *14.40 m.*
BEAM: *3.78 m.*
DRAFT: *2.84 m.*
DISPLACEMENT: *29.8 tons*
SAIL AREA: *164 sq.m.*
CONSTRUCTION: *double planked on laminated oak and ash frames*
FIRST OWNER: *Heritage Syndicate Charles E. Morgan Jr.*
FIRST NAME: *Heritage*
FIRST COUNTRY: *U.S.A.*
HOME PORT: *St. Petersburg, FL*
FIRST SAIL NUMBER: *US 23*
CURRENT LOCATION: *Marblehead, USA*
CONDITION: *altered to IOR rating*
PRESENT OWNER: *Jeffrey Barrows*
FURTHER DETAILS AND HISTORY: Built according to the Third Int. Rule America's Cup. Owners and history:
1970 - 1973 Heritage Syndicate, Charles E. Morgan Jr.; home port: St. Petersburg, FL. Charles E. Morgan was a renowned designer, yacht builder, sailmaker and ocean racer. To enter as a challenger in the America's Cup he sold his business, Morgan Yachts in order to finance his campaign. *Heritage* was a splendid Twelve, inspired by *Intrepid*, but with a more wetted surface and displacement. She had never been competitive
1973 - 1975 Florida Institute of Technology; home port: Melbourne and St. Petersburg, FL
1976 Disappeared off record
1976 Yacht hull substantially altered to IOR rating; Don Wildman; home

port: Chicago, IL
1985 Sea Scouts, Boy Scouts of America
Since 1993 HYC, Inc. (Jeffrey G. Barrows); home port: Salem, MA; rig altered to auxiliary sloop and an engine installed

■ HISSAR
DESIGNER: *Laurie Davidson, Bruce Farr, Ron Holland*
BUILDER: *Marten Marine*
YEAR: *January 8 1986*
LENGTH OVERALL: *19.99 m.*
LENGTH AT WATERLINE: *14.02 m.*
BEAM: *4.02 m.*
DRAFT: *2.74 m.*
CONSTRUCTION: *glassfibre composite glass reinforced plastic*
FIRST OWNER: *NZ America's Cup Challenge Trust*
FIRST NAME: *New Zealand*
FIRST COUNTRY: *New Zealand*
HOME PORT: *Auckland*
FIRST SAIL NUMBER: *KZ 5 - J 5 - US 62*
OTHER NAMES: *Nippon (1992) - Cannonball (1993) - Fury (1995)*
CURRENT LOCATION: *Newport, RI (U.S.A)*
CONDITION: *very good, sailing*
PRESENT OWNER: *Edgar Cato*
FURTHER DETAILS AND HISTORY: Built according to the Third Int. Rule America's Cup. Owners and history:
1986 - 1987 NZ America's Cup Challenge Trust; name: *New Zealand*; home port: Auckland. The budget for the New Zealander challenge was for $15.000.000 and the Syndicate was chaired by Sir Michael Fay, a rich merchant banker. He decided to get together the three leading *New Zealand* designers to realise the first of a long-lasting challenge for the Cup. First, two models were created of *Victory '83* and *Australia II* (it was said that the lines of *Australia II* were acquired by the New Zealanders). Tests are run at the Wolfson Institute at Southampton University and five other models were designed and their tank test data verified with computer analysis. The fifth model was chosen as a good heavy weather performer on which the first two Twelves were designed: *KZ 3* and *KZ 5*. Both were identical and, after long consultations with Lloyd's, they were built. This was the first time in the International Rule history, that glassfibre composite was used (hence the nickname of "plastic fantastics"). The advantage was to have much stiffer boats, estimated by Laurie Davidson in the order of 20 times that of aluminium with no flexing in the hull – especially in the mast region where the shrouds are attached. From the results of the two Twelves, *KZ 7* took shape after much more testing and other models. Special attention was devoted to the keel design for which exhaustive tests were conducted in wind tunnels. *New Zealand KZ 5* was the second of the two "plastic fantastics" trial horses for *KZ 7* in view of the challenger trials. In 1986 she was second in the fifth Twelve Metre World Championship
1992 - 1993 Nippon Yacht Club; new name: *Nippon*; home port: Tokyo (Japan); new sail number: J 5
1993 - 1995 Charles A. Robertson; new name: *Cannonball*; home port: Old Saybrook, CT (USA); new sail number: US 62 in 1994. She was altered at Pilot's Point (Westbrook, CT)

1995 - 2000 Paul Campbell, Jr; new name: *Fury*; home port: Boston, MA and New York, NY
Since 2000 Edgar Cato; new name: *Hissar*; home port: Newport, RI

■ IKRA
DESIGNER: *David Boyd*
BUILDER: *Alexr. Robertson & Sons (Y. Builders) Ltd.*
YEAR: *1964 May*
LENGTH OVERALL: *21.06 m.*
LENGTH AT WATERLINE: *13.93 m.*
BEAM: *3.81 m.*
DRAFT: *2.67 m.*
DISPLACEMENT: *27.27 tons*
SAIL AREA: *175 sq.m.*
CONSTRUCTION: *wood on steel frames*
FIRST OWNER: *Frank W. & John H. Livingston*
FIRST NAME: *Kurrewa V*
FIRST COUNTRY: *Great Britain*
HOME PORT: *Greenock*
FIRST SAIL NUMBER: *K 3*
OTHER NAMES: *Levrier de Mer (1972) - Ikra (1974)*
CURRENT LOCATION: *Antibes, France*
CONDITION: *very good*
PRESENT OWNER: *Jean Rédélé*
FURTHER DETAILS AND HISTORY: Built according to the Third Int. Rule America's Cup. Owners and history:
1964 - 1966 Frank W. & John H. Livingston (Owen Aisher, Mgr.); name: *Kurrewa V*; home port: Greenock. She was built for the 1964 19th match by the two Livingston brothers in order to have a second British challenger. In order to save time and money, instead of organising a new syndicate, David Boyd was requested to design a second Twelve sister ship to *Sovereign* with slight differences in the keel and in the rigging. She was built at the same yard using *Sovereign's* framework. She was faster than *Sovereign* but using Hood sails was forbidden in the match as they were not of British manufacture. In the final trials *Sovereign* prevailed and was the British challenger
1967 John M. Livingstone
1968 - 1975 Robert Laforest; new name: *Levrier de Mer* (1970); home port: Greenock, Asnières and Sandbank. She was one of the Twelves bought by Baron Bich in his campaign for the America's Cup and she was trial horse of *France* in 1970
Since 1976 Jean Rédélé; new name: *Ikra*; home port: Antibes. She was modified for cruising with a shorter mast and boom and a new interior layout. *Ikra* was also known as the challenger of the yacht *Pride* in the race which became known as Nioulargue regatta in St. Tropez

■ INDEPENDENCE
DESIGNER: *Frederick E. Hood - design no 691*
BUILDER: *Minneford Yacht Yard*
YEAR: *1976 July*
LENGTH OVERALL: *19.34 m.*
LENGTH AT WATERLINE: *13.77 m.*
BEAM: *3.73 m.*
DRAFT: *2.69 m.*

DISPLACEMENT: *25.1 tons*
SAIL AREA: *174 sq.m.*
CONSTRUCTION: *aluminium alloy*
FIRST OWNER: *Kings Point Fund, Inc.*
FIRST NAME: *Independence*
FIRST COUNTRY: *U.S.A.*
HOME PORT: *Kings Point, NY*
FIRST SAIL NUMBER: *US 28*
CONDITION: *redesigned and rebuilt as Clipper*
FURTHER DETAILS AND HISTORY: Built according to the Third Int. Rule America's Cup. Owners and history:
1976 - 1979 Kings Point Fund, Inc.; name: *Independence*; home port: Kings Point, NY. She was the second Twelve designed by Hood after *Nefertiti*. Hood had been the skipper of *Courageous*, winner of the 1974 America's Cup and, Olin Stephens not being available, decided to design his own Twelve. A big fight was dominating the cup between the two leading sailmakers: Ted Hood with *Independence* and Lowell North with *Enterprise*. *Independence* was not chosen as the defender, *Courageous* winning the defender trials co-winner with *Enterprise* of the 1977 Lipton Memorial Trophy (NYYC)
1980 R.E. "Ted" Turner; the yacht completely redesigned and rebuilt as a Clipper

■ INTREPID

DESIGNER: *Olin J. Stephens - design no 1834*
BUILDER: *Minneford Yacht Yard - construction no 75*
YEAR: *1967 May*
LENGTH OVERALL: *19.66 m.*
LENGTH AT WATERLINE: *14.27 m. (1967) - 14.75 m. (1970)*
BEAM: *3.68 m.*
DRAFT: *2.78 m. (1967) - 2.82 m. (1970)*
DISPLACEMENT: *27.9 tons (1967) - 30.55 tons (1970)*
SAIL AREA: *164 sq.m. (1967) - 161 sq.m. (1970)*
CONSTRUCTION: *double-planked mahogany on white oak frames*
FIRST OWNER: *Intrepid Syndicate*
FIRST NAME: *Intrepid*
FIRST COUNTRY: *United States*
HOME PORT: *New York*
FIRST SAIL NUMBER: *US 22*
OTHER NAMES: *Windancer*
CURRENT LOCATION: *Newport, RI (U.S.A.)*
CONDITION: *very good*
PRESENT OWNER: *John P. Curtin Jr*
FURTHER DETAILS AND HISTORY: Built according to the Third Int. Rule America's Cup. Owners and history:
1967 - 1971 Intrepid Syndacate; name: *Intrepid*; home port: New York, NY. *Intrepid* was one of those few projects that made yachting history and, more importantly, the history of the Twelve Metre Class. She was undoubtedly a breakthrough yacht. Stephen's aim was to reduce the wetted surface by cutting away the keel at the after end and redistributing the saved volume in the afterlines of the hull. Tests at the Hoboken tank confirm the validity of his ideas and *Intrepid* was the best result which could be imagined. Not only were her hull lines completely innovative, she also had the first fin and skeg configuration with a trim tab at the aft end

of the keel combined with the rudder with the same steering mechanism. Moreover, the deck layout was new with the crew off the deck and the winches and related mechanism below decks. This solution meant that the boom was lowered towards the deck with greater stability. Painstaking attention was directed to save any waight, which was not structural so to increase the ballast to a maximum. The accommodation in the boat was reduced to a minimum. The rig too was innovative with the bending boom and the higher part of the mast made of titanium. New sails were cut and she was a splendid success. There was no competition in the America's Cup: *Intrepid* was the defender and outclassed *Dame Pattie* by a score of 4-0. For the 1970 America's Cup match she was modified by Britton Chance and her keel redesigned and recast. She was given a longer waterline, a reduced wetted area and the weight increased. For the second time she won the Cup match by a score of 4-1 over *Gretel II*. Winner of the Chandle Hovey Gold Bowl (NYYC) in 1967 and 1970 winner of the Caritas Cup (NYYC) in 1970
1971 - 1974 International Oceanographic Foundation; home port: Miami, FL. Winner of the Caritas Cup (NYYC) in 1974; winner of the Lipton Memorial Trophy (NYYC) in 1974
1975 Intrepid West; home port: Seattle, WA
1975 - 1976 Seattle Sailing Foundation (according to American Lloyd's)
From 1973 to 1976 Intrepid/West & Seattle Sailing Foundation
1977 - 1978 Robert H. Fendler
1978 - 1980 Pierre G. Goemans (resident in Monaco Principality and owner, on behalf of the French challenge, also of *Sovereign* and *Constellation*)
1979 L'Association Française pour La Coupe de l'Amérique (AFCA) (Marcel Bich)
? New name: *Windancer*; home port: Luskegon, MI. She was taken to Lake Champlain for charter
1993 - 1996 Intrepid Sailing Inc; new name: *Intrepid*; home port: Seekonk, MA. After 1994 she was run aground on the Nantucket breakwater
Since 1996 Intrepid Charters LLC (John P. Curtin, Jr.); home port: Newport, RI. She was completely rebuilt under the direction of Herb Marshall and George Hill at Brewer's Cove Haven Marina in Barrington, RI. She had a new deck and deckbeams, new floor timbers, new ring frames, new bottom planking and a new ballast keel

■ ITALIA I

DESIGNER: *Giorgetti e Magrini*
BUILDER: *Cantieri Baglietto*
YEAR: *1985 August*
LENGTH OVERALL: *19.65 m.*
BEAM: *3.64 m.*
DISPLACEMENT: *25.12 tons*
SAIL AREA: *165 sq.m.*
CONSTRUCTION: *aluminium alloy*
FIRST OWNER: *Consorzio Italia*
FIRST NAME: *Italia I*
FIRST COUNTRY: *Italy*
HOME PORT: *Genova*
FIRST SAIL NUMBER: *I 7*
CURRENT LOCATION: *Lymington*

CONDITION: *perfect condition*

FURTHER DETAILS AND HISTORY: Built according to the Third Int. Rule America's Cup. Owners and history:

1984 - 1987 Consorzio Italia; name: *Italia I*; home port: Genova. *Italia I* was the first of two Twelves designed by Giorgetti & Magrini for the 26th 1987 America's Cup. The budget was twelve billion Italian lire covered by ten sponsors. Five models on a 1:3 scale were tested at Wageningen and the research continued at the ship model basin at Trieste with models on a scale of 1:10, while the aircraft company Aermacchi assisted with her wind tunnel and computer centre. Organising problems and the ones related to *Italia II*, dropped during her launch, did not allow the Consorzio to achieve good results: *Italia I* scored eighth at the 1986 World Championship and achieved modest results in the Louis Vuitton Cup. *Italia II* did not even enter the Louis Vuitton Cup

1988 - 1995 Luigi Scappa; home port: Lecco (Lake Como, Italy)

1995 - 1999 Corrado Fratini; home port: Marina di Carrara. *Italia I* was restored, an engine was installed and she entered the Mediterranean Twelve regattas. In 1996 she was second behind *French Kiss* in the Coppa del Mediterraneo and in the Europe Cup. In 1997 she won the Europe Cup and she was second in the Itma and Aive Cups. In 1999 she was second, behind *Kiwi Magic*, in the World Championship

Since 2000 Don J.L. Wood; home port: Lymington (UK)

■ ITALIA II

DESIGNER: *Giorgetti & Magrini*
BUILDER: *Cantieri Ferri*
YEAR: *June 1986*
CONSTRUCTION: *aluminium alloy*
FIRST OWNER: *Consorzio Italia*
FIRST NAME: *Italia II*
FIRST COUNTRY: *Italy*
HOME PORT: *Genova*
FIRST SAIL NUMBER: *I 9*
CURRENT LOCATION: *Adriatic Sea*
CONDITION: *sailing, but not good*
PRESENT OWNER: *Renaissance School*
COUNTRY: *Italy*

FURTHER DETAILS AND HISTORY: Built according to the Third Int. Rule America's Cup
Owners and history:

1986 - 1987 Consorzio Italia; name: *Italia II*; home port: Genova (Italy). *Italia II* was the second Twelve built for the 1987 America's Cup by Consorzio Italia. She represented an evolution of the *Italia I* design after tests on about ten models in the Wageningen tests tank. She was supposed to be a much faster boat but she was dropped on her keel and sank when launched. She was rebuilt and shipped to Fremantle in September 1986 too late to be tuned up for the challenger's trials. She did not race in the Louis Vuitton Cup

1986 - 1996 Intermarine; home port: La Spezia. She was laid up in a shed, for sale

1996 - 2000 Francesco Menconi; home port: Marina di Carrara. She was launched again, but not well mantained. She was used for daily charter

Since 2000 Renaissance School; home port: somewhere in the Adriatic Sea; she is being used for training in a sailing school

■ KIWI

DESIGNER: *Laurie Davidson, Bruce Farr, Ron Holland*
BUILDER: *McMullen & Wing*
YEAR: *1985 December*
LENGTH OVERALL: *19.99 m.*
LENGTH AT WATERLINE: *14.02 m.*
BEAM: *4.02 m.*
DRAFT: *2.74 m.*
CONSTRUCTION: *glassfibre composite; glass reinforced plastic*
FIRST OWNER: *NZ America's Cup Challenge Trust*
FIRST NAME: *New Zealand*
FIRST COUNTRY: *New Zealand*
HOME PORT: *Auckland*
FIRST SAIL NUMBER: *KZ 3 changed to J 3 in Japan*
OTHER NAMES: *Nippon Challenge (1992) - Kiwi (2000)*
CURRENT LOCATION: *Melbourne (Australia)*
CONDITION: *very good, sailing*
PRESENT OWNER: *Michael G. Smith*

FURTHER DETAILS AND HISTORY: Built according to the Third Int. Rule America's Cup
Owners and history:

1986 - 1987 NZ America's Cup Challenge Trust; name: *New Zealand*; home port: Auckland. The budget for the New Zealander challenge was $15.000.000 and the syndicate was chaired by Sir Michael Fay, a rich merchant banker. He decided to put together the three leading *New Zealand* designers to realise the first of a long-lasting challenge for the Cup. First, two models were created of *Victory '83* and *Australia II* (it was said that the lines of *Australia II* were acquired by the New Zealanders). Tests were run at Wolfson Institute at Southampton University and five other models were designed and their tank test data verified with computer analysis. The fifth model was chosen as a good heavy weather performer on which the first two Twelves were designed: *KZ 3* and *KZ 5*; both were identical and, after long consultations with Lloyd's, they were built. This was the first time in the International Rule history the 12M were built in glassfibre composite (hence the nickname of "plastic fantastics"). The advantage was to have much stiffer boats, estimated by Laurie Davidson in the order of 20 times more than aluminium with no flexing of the hull and especially in the mast region where the shrouds are attached. From the results of the two Twelves, *KZ 7* took shape after much more testing and other models. Special attention was devoted to the keel design for which exhaustive tests were conducted in wind tunnels. *New Zealand KZ 3* was one of the two "plastic fantastics". She was the first glassfibre Twelve ever built and a trial horse for *KZ 7* in view of the challenger trials. She was placed seventh in the 1986 fifth Twelve Metre World Championship

1992 - 1998 Nippon Yacht Club; new name: *Nippon Challenge*; home port: Tokyo (Japan); new sail number: J 3

Since 1998 Michael G. Smith; new name: *Kiwi*; home port: Melbourne; sail number: back to the original *KZ 3*

■ KOOKABURRA I

DESIGNER: *Iain Murray & John Swarbrick*
BUILDER: *Parry Boat Builders*
YEAR: *1985 February*
LENGTH OVERALL: *20.22 m.*

LENGTH AT WATERLINE: *13.41 m.*
BEAM: *3.80 m.*
DRAFT: *2.64 m.*
DISPLACEMENT: *23.3 tons*
SAIL AREA: *168 m.*
CONSTRUCTION: *aluminium alloy*
FIRST OWNER: *Taskforce '87 America's Cup Defence Ltd.*
FIRST NAME: *Kookaburra I*
FIRST COUNTRY: *Australia*
HOME PORT: *Perth*
FIRST SAIL NUMBER: *KA 11*
CURRENT LOCATION: *Melbourne (Australia)*
CONDITION: *good, sailing*
FURTHER DETAILS AND HISTORY: Built according to the Third Int. Rule America's Cup. Owners and history:
1985 Taskforce '87 America's Cup Defence Ltd. (Kedvin Parry); name *Kookaburra I*; home port: Perth, WA. This was the first out of three (plus one project) *Kookaburras* built by Taskforce '87 managed by Iain Murray. There was no lack of money: Murray could organise his own sail loft, yard, workshop and a large shed where the yachts could be hauled out. One distinctive point was the computer performance monitoring gear housed below decks in watertight Plexiglas cases aboard each of the three boats. The computer monitored and recorded a host of critical performance functions and they were interfaced by similar gear aboard the tender and the mainframe located in the Taskforce '87 headquarters. *Kookaburra's* projects were inspired by *Australia II* with quite innovative ideas coming from Murray and Swarbrick. Alan Payne was called to cooperate on the winglet keel shapes. The three yachts were distinguished for their elegance, long overhangs and more freeboard than the traditional boats. *Kookaburra I* would not participate in the defenders trials
1993 - 1994 Kookaburra Challenge Pty, Ltd.; home port: Newport, NSW
Since 1996 Michael Smith; home port: Melbourne. She is currently used for sailing and charter. She also appeared as the feature yacht in the movie *Wind*

■ KOOKABURRA II

DESIGNER: *John Swarbrick*
BUILDER: *Parry Boat Builders*
YEAR: *1985 December*
LENGTH OVERALL: *20.12 m.*
LENGTH AT WATERLINE: *13.68 m.*
BEAM: *3.79 m.*
DRAFT: *2.68 m.*
DISPLACEMENT: *24.65 m.*
SAIL AREA: *164 sq.m.*
CONSTRUCTION: *aluminium alloy*
FIRST OWNER: *Taskforce '87 America's Cup Defence, Ltd.*
FIRST NAME: *Kookaburra II*
FIRST COUNTRY: *Australia*
HOME PORT: *Perth*
FIRST SAIL NUMBER: *KA 12*
FURTHER DETAILS AND HISTORY: Built according to the Third Int. Rule America's Cup. Owners and history:
1985 - ? Taskforce '87 America's Cup Defence, Ltd. (Kevin Parry); name:

Kookaburra II; home port: Perth. She was the second out of three (plus one project) *Kookaburras* built by Taskforce '87 managed by Iain Murray. There was no lack of money: Murray could organise his own sail loft, yard, workshop and a large shed where the yachts could be hauled out. One distinctive point was the computer performance monitoring gear housed below decks in watertight Plexiglas cases aboard each of the three boats. The computers monitored and recorded a host of critical performance functions and they were interfaced by similar gear aboard the tender and the mainframe located in the Taskforce '87 headquarters. *Kookaburra's* projects were inspired by *Australia II* with quite innovative ideas coming from Murray and Swarbrick. Alan Payne was called to cooperate on the winglet keel shapes. The three yachts were distinguished by their elegance, long overhangs and more freeboard than the traditional boats. *Kookaburra II's* design had been realised by Swarbrick before the one for *K1* and only built when the decision was taken to have a second yacht. It came about after a survey conducted at the NSMB at Wageningen based on 24 drawings and dozens of models. The model of *K II* was successfully tested against the one of *KI*; *K II* was easy to sail although not so fast close to the wind as *KI* but much more stable. In spite of the disappointment and disagreement of her designer, *K III* was chosen. However, *Kookaburra II* performed well in the defender trials of the 1987 America's Cup and was third behind *Kookaburra III* and *Australia IV*
1993 - 1994 Kookaburra Challenge Pty, Ltd.; home port: Newport, NSW

■ KOOKABURRA III

DESIGNER: *Iain Murray & John Swarbrick*
BUILDER: *Parry Boat Builders*
YEAR: *August 1986*
CONSTRUCTION: *aluminium alloy*
FIRST OWNER: *Taskforce '87 America's Cup Defence Ltd.*
FIRST NAME: *Kookaburra III*
FIRST COUNTRY: *Australia*
HOME PORT: *Perth*
FIRST SAIL NUMBER: *KA 15*
CURRENT LOCATION: *unknown*
FURTHER DETAILS AND HISTORY: Built to the Third Int. Rule America's Cup. Owners and history:
1986 - 1987 Taskforce '87 America's Cup Defence Ltd. (Kevin Parry); name: *Kookaburra III*; home port: Perth. This was the third out of the three (plus one project) *Kookaburras* built by Taskforce '87 and managed by Iain Murray. There was no lack of money. Murray could organise his own sail loft, yard, workshop and a large shed where the yachts could be hauled out. One distinctive point was the computer performance monitoring gear housed below decks in watertight Plexiglas cases aboard each of the three boats. The computers monitored and recorded a host of critical performance functions and they were interfaced by similar gear aboard the tender and the mainframe located in the Taskforce '87 headquarters. *Kookaburra's* projects were inspired by *Australia II* and innovative ideas came from Murray. Alan Payne was called to cooperate on the winglet keel shapes. The three yachts were distinguished for their elegance, long overhangs and more freeboard than the traditional boats. It was doubtful if *K III* was a faster and more handy boat then *K II*. She won the defender trials for the 26th 1987 America's Cup by beating *Australia IV* by a score of 6-0. Iain Murray was skipper and Peter Gilmour the

starting helmsman. In the America's Cup Match she lost by a score of 4-1 against Dennis Conner's *Stars & Stripes*: the Cup went back to the States
1993 - 1994 Kookaburra Challenge Pty, Ltd; home port: Newport, NSW

■ KOOKABURRA (PROJECT)

DESIGNER: *John Swarbrick*
BUILDER: *not built*
YEAR: *1987*
LENGTH OVERALL: *21.18 m.*
LENGTH AT WATERLINE: *13.60 m.*
BEAM: *3.79 m.*
DRAFT: *2.68 m.*
SAIL AREA: *167 sq.m.*
FIRST OWNER: *Taskforce '87 America's Cup Defence Ltd.*
FIRST NAME: *Kookaburra*
FIRST COUNTRY: *Australia*
HOME PORT: *Perth*
FIRST SAIL NUMBER: *no sail number issued*
FURTHER DETAILS AND HISTORY: Designed according to the Third Int. Rule America's Cup. Owners and history:
1987 Taskforce '87 America's Cup Defence Ltd. (Kevin Parry); project, not built

■ LIBERTY

DESIGNER: *Johan Valentijn*
BUILDER: *Newport Offshore Ltd.*
YEAR: *1983 June*
LENGTH OVERALL: *19.37 m.*
LENGTH AT WATERLINE: *13.70 m.*
BEAM: *3.70 m.*
DRAFT: *2.67 m.*
DISPLACEMENT: *24.35 tons*
SAIL AREA: *168 sq.m.*
CONSTRUCTION: *aluminium alloy*
FIRST OWNER: *Freedom Camp. '83 SUNY at Ft. Schuyler*
FIRST NAME: *Liberty*
FIRST COUNTRY: *U.S.A.*
HOME PORT: *New York, NY*
FIRST SAIL NUMBER: *US 40*
FURTHER DETAILS AND HISTORY: Built according to the Third Int. Rule America's Cup
Owners and history:
1983 Freedom Campaign '83 SUNY at Ft. Schuyler; name: *Freedom*; home port: New York, NY. She was the third Twelve to be designed for the Freedom Campaign, the others having been *Magic* and *Spirit of America*. Her design came off the table of Johan Valentijn with direct involvement of Dennis Conner, who was the skipper. After the first confrontation with the other two boats, she was faster but she had difficulty beating *Freedom*, despite her stern being shortened by two feet and the mast and keel moved forward by the same proportions. She was chosen as defender as she was designed from the outset to allow reballasting. In order to alter the characteristics slightly between races, *Liberty* could be tuned to varying weather conditions by changing the displacement, choosing the sails previously adapted for each configuration and being re-rated before racing.

However, *Liberty* lost the 1983 25th America's Cup to *Australia II* by a score of 3-4. For the first time in 132 years the Cup went out of the United States. Winner of the Chandler Hovey Gold Bowl 1983 (NYYC)
1986 - 1988 Sail America Foundation; home port: San Diego, CA. Trial horse to *Stars & Stripes '87*
1988 - 1989 America's Cup Organising Committee; home port: San Diego
Since 1989 sold to Japan, owner not known

■ LIONHEART

DESIGNER: *Ian Howlett*
BUILDER: *Joyce Bros. Marine*
YEAR: *1979 April*
LENGTH OVERALL: *19.43 m.*
LENGTH AT WATERLINE: *14.94 m.*
BEAM: *3.73 m.*
DRAFT: *2.82 m.*
DISPLACEMENT: *29.1 tons*
SAIL AREA: *170 sq.m. - 224 sq.m. - 222 sq.m. (1980)*
CONSTRUCTION: *aluminium alloy*
FIRST OWNER: *British Industry 1500 Club*
FIRST NAME: *Lionheart*
FIRST COUNTRY: *Great Britain*
HOME PORT: *Hamble*
FIRST SAIL NUMBER: *K 18*
OTHER NAMES: *Lionheart of Wessex (1980) - Lionheart (1991)*
CURRENT LOCATION: *U.S.A.*
CONDITION: *perfect condition*
FURTHER DETAILS AND HISTORY: Built according to the Third Int. Rule America's Cup. Owners and history:
1979 - 1980 British Industry 1500 Club (J. Anthony J. Boyden); name: *Lionheart*; home port: Hamble. She was the first Twelve designed by Howlett. She was a heavy displacement yacht with the main sections of the hull quite similar to the ones of *Mariner*. The most innovative device for which she was marked from the other Twelves was a bendy mast which increased the sail area by nearly 7%. She proved to be very fast in a straight line but with a lack of manoeuvrability in comparison to the other Twelves. In the 1980 24th America's Cup Challenger Trials, she was beaten by *France III* after a close fight
1980 British Industry 1500 Club (J. Anthony J. Boyden); new name: *Lionheart of Wessex*
1981 - 1983 Victory '83 Challenge (Peter de Savary). Altered in 1982, she was trial horse to *Victory '82* and *Victory '83*
? - 1991 Intrepid Marketing Inc. (Joe Krawczyk); home port: Seekonk, MA (USA)
1991 - 2001 Harry H. Graves; new name: *Lionheart*; home port: ?

■ MAGIC

DESIGNER: *Johan Valentijn*
BUILDER: *Custom Marine & Pilots Point Marina*
YEAR: *1982 April*
LENGTH OVERALL: *18.59 m.*
LENGTH AT WATERLINE: *13.24 m.*
BEAM: *3.79 m.*

DRAFT: *2.62 m.*
DISPLACEMENT: *22.5 m.*
SAIL AREA: *155 sq.m.*
CONSTRUCTION: *aluminium alloy*
FIRST OWNER: *Freedom Camp. '83 SUNY Fort Schuyler*
FIRST NAME: *Magic*
FIRST COUNTRY: *U.S.A.*
HOME PORT: *New York*
FIRST SAIL NUMBER: *US 38*
CURRENT LOCATION: *The Netherlands*
CONDITION: *unknown*
FURTHER DETAILS AND HISTORY: Built according to the Third Int. Rule America's Cup
Owners and history:
1982 - 1983 Freedom Campaign '83; SUNY Fort Schuyler; name: *Magic*; home port: New York. She was one of two Twelves ordered by Dennis Conner for the 25th America's Cup. While Bill Langan with *Spirit of America* designed a traditional Twelve, Johan Valentijn was requested to design a radical boat on the edge of the rule and design parameters; *Magic* was very short and light and out of rating.
She was a total disappointment and was sold to fund a third boat which became *Liberty*
1986 Eagle Syndicate. She was altered and given a winglet keel for a better righting moment and she was used as a trial horse for *Eagle* in 1986
1988-1989 California International Leasing Co.
? Sailing California, Inc.
1993 - 1994 J.P.W.S. Hin/Teylinger; home port: Vogelenzag (Holland)
Since 1995 Club Ardennen

■ MARINER

DESIGNER: *Britton Chance Jr*
BUILDER: *Robert E. Derecktor Yacht Yard*
YEAR: *1974 May*
LENGTH OVERALL: *18.77 m.*
LENGTH AT WATERLINE: *14.43 m.*
BEAM: *3.55 m.*
DRAFT: *2.79 m.*
DISPLACEMENT: *29.85 tons*
SAIL AREA: *162 sq.m.*
CONSTRUCTION: *aluminium alloy*
FIRST OWNER: *Kings Point Fund Inc. USMMA*
FIRST NAME: *Mariner*
FIRST COUNTRY: *U.S.A.*
HOME PORT: *New York*
FIRST SAIL NUMBER: *US 25*
CURRENT LOCATION: *wrecked off Palm Beach (Florida)*
FURTHER DETAILS AND HISTORY: Built according to the Third Int. Rule America's Cup
Owners and history:
1974 - 1975 Kings Point Fund. Inc. USMMA; name: *Mariner*; home port: Kings Point, NY. *Mariner*, together with *Courageous*, was the first American Twelve built in aluminium alloy. She was a revolutionary design. Britton Chance had tried to reduce, as much as possible, the wetted surface with a bow bustle, a low drag keel and a squared off termination of the hull lines, the so-called "fast back stern".
However, she was a slow Twelve creating big turbulence behind her stern. Neither Ted Turner nor Dennis Conner, both skippers of *Mariner*, could avoid her elimination from the defender trials of the 22nd America's Cup
1976 - 1989 Charles S. Conway; home port: Oyster Bay, NY
1993 - 1994 Arthur J. Kappelle; home port: New Smyrna Beach, FL
1995 reported that the yacht was converted to an IMS cruiser/racer by Derecktor Shipyard
1999 Wrecked on beach off Palm Beach, Florida

■ NEFERTITI

DESIGNER: *Frederick E. Hood*
BUILDER: *James E. Gravies, Inc. & Little Harbor Yard*
YEAR: *1962 May*
LENGTH OVERALL: *20.52 m.*
LENGTH AT WATERLINE: *13.90 m.*
BEAM: *4.04 m.*
DRAFT: *2.74 m.*
DISPLACEMENT: *24.85 tons*
SAIL AREA: *174 sq.m.*
CONSTRUCTION: *double planked mahogany on oak frames*
FIRST OWNER: *Anderson-Purcell Syndicate*
FIRST NAME: *Nefertiti*
FIRST COUNTRY: *U.S.A.*
HOME PORT: *Boston*
FIRST SAIL NUMBER: *US 19*
CURRENT LOCATION: *Newport, RI (U.S.A.)*
CONDITION: *sailing, very good*
FURTHER DETAILS AND HISTORY: Built according to the Third Int. Rule America's Cup
Owners and history:
1962 - 1968 Anderson-Purcell Syndicate; name: *Nefertiti*; home port: Boston, MA. She was the first Twelve designed by Hood and the only new defender for the Australian challenge of 1962. Her construction was indeed a fast one, her launch taking place only 96 days after the delivery of the plans to the yard.
At the time, she was the beamiest Twelve ever built, as Hood was in search of stability, and had a long foretriangle.
She was good and fast in strong winds but unfortunately the defender selection finals took place in light airs: *Weatherly* won and entered the match against *Gretel*. She won the 1962 Lipton Memorial Trophy (NYYC). Altered in 1964 by Ted Hood. In 1967 chartered by AC Challenger Syndicate as the trial horse for *Dame Pattie*
1968 - 1979 Man Johnson Co. Ltd. S.A.; home port: Piraeus (Greece)
1979 - 1995 After the 1964 America's Cup *Nefertiti* started voyages around the world that took her to Greece for charter, back to the U.S., then to the West Indies, on to Fremantle for the 1987 Cup races and then to South Africa for six years
1996 - 1998 George Hill and Herb Marshall; home port: Newport, RI (U.S.A.)
Since 1998 Nefertiti Charters LLC (Sears Wullschleger)

▪ NEW ZEALAND - "KIWI MAGIC"

DESIGNER: *Laurie Davidson, Bruce Farr, Ron Holland*
BUILDER: *Marten Marine & McMullen & Wing*
YEAR: *1986 July*
CONSTRUCTION: *glassfibre composite; glass reinforced plastic*
FIRST OWNER: *NZ America's Cup Challenge Trust*
FIRST NAME: *New Zealand "Kiwi Magic"*
FIRST COUNTRY: *New Zealand*
HOME PORT: *Auckland*
FIRST SAIL NUMBER: *KZ 7*
CURRENT LOCATION: *Punta Ala*
CONDITION: *perfect condition*
FURTHER DETAILS AND HISTORY: Built according to Third Int. Rule America's Cup
Owners and history:

1986 - 1987 NZ America's Cup Challenge Trust; name: *New Zealand*; home port: Auckland. The budget for the New Zealander challenge was $15.000.000 and the syndicate was chaired by Sir Michael Fay, a rich merchant banker. He decided to put together the three leading New Zealand designers to realise the first of a long-lasting challenge for the Cup. First, two models were created: *Victory '83* and *Australia II* (it was said that the lines of *Australia II* were acquired by the New Zealanders). Tests were run at Wolfson Institute at Southampton University and five other models were built and their tank test data verified with computer analysis. The fifth model was chosen as a good heavy weather performer on which the first two Twelves were based: *KZ 3* and *KZ 5*. Both were identical and, after long consultations with Lloyd's, they were built. This was the first time in the International Rule history that glassfibre composite had been used (hence the nickname of "plastic fantastics"). The advantage was to have much stiffer boats, estimated by Laurie Davidson in the order of 20 times than more aluminium with no flexing in the hull – especially the mast region where the shrouds were attached. From the results of the two Twelves, *KZ 7* took shape after much more testing and other models. Special attention was devoted to the keel design for which exhaustives tests were conducted in wind tunnels. *New Zealand KZ 7* was nicknamed *"Kiwi Magic"* and profited from the experience of *KZ 3* and *KZ 5* during the 1996 World Championship. She had an innovative deck layout and two cockpits. She was longer than the two others with a little more sheer and was a good all-round boat. During the Challenger Trials she had an impressive series of wins but in the finals she was beaten by *Stars & Stripes '87* by a score of 4-1. The skippers were Chris Dickson and Dennis Conner. *Stars & Stripes '87* won the 26th match against *Kookaburra III*
Since 1987 Sir Michael Fay
1994 She won the Sesquicentennal Regatta (NYYC) in Newport
1998 She was rented for three years to Patrizio Bertelli and she entered the Mediterranean circuit. In 1998 she won the St. Tropez Rolex Cup
1999 The Sixth Twelve Metre World Championship held in St. Tropez while she was second in the 2000 St. Tropez Cup

▪ ROYAL OAK

DESIGNER: *David H.J. Hollam*
YEAR: *1981*
FIRST NAME: *Royal Oak*

FIRST COUNTRY: *Great Britain*
FURTHER DETAILS AND HISTORY: Project - not built
No sail number authorized or issued

▪ SCEPTRE

DESIGNER: *David Boyd*
BUILDER: *Alexander Robertson & Sons Yacht Builders Ltd.*
YEAR: *1958 April*
LENGTH OVERALL: *21.00 m. - 19.81 m. (1972)*
LENGTH AT WATERLINE: *14.15 m.*
BEAM: *3.56 m.*
DRAFT: *2.76 m.*
DISPLACEMENT: *27 tons*
SAIL AREA: *172 sq.m. - 166 sq.m. (1972)*
CONSTRUCTION: *wood on steel frames*
FIRST OWNER: *Royal Yacht Squadron Syndicate*
FIRST NAME: *Sceptre*
FIRST COUNTRY: *Great Britain*
HOME PORT: *Cowes*
FIRST SAIL NUMBER: *K 17*
CURRENT LOCATION: *Preston Marina (Great Britain)*
CONDITION: *sailing, altered to a cruising yacht*
PRESENT OWNER: *The Sceptre Preservation Society*
FURTHER DETAILS AND HISTORY: Built according to Third Int. Rule America's Cup
Owners and history:

1958 - 1959 Royal Yacht Squadron Syndicate; name: *Sceptre*; home port: Cowes. *Sceptre* was the first Twelve built as a challenger for the America's Cup after the post-war decision to have the cup match raced by the Twelve Metre. David Boyd was chosen out of the four best English designers (the others being James McGruer, Charles Nicholson Jr. and Arthur Robb). *Sceptre* project was criticised from the start and her defeat confirmed the criticism: she was outclassed in the match by *Columbia* by a score of 4-0. Compared to the pre-war Twelves *Sceptre* was conceived just to race and the interior accommodation was reduced to the minimum required by the Rule. She had a very large cockpit extended to the base of the mast. This enabled her to have a weight advantage due to a smaller deck with more weight in the keel. The crew stayed in the cockpit and where they could work better and the crew weight served to lower the centre of gravity. The winch drums were on deck, with their mechanical parts underneath giving greater access and a lower centre of gravity. After the 1958 match, the large cockpits were forbidden by the Rule but some of *Sceptre*'s innovation were found again ten years later in *Intrepid*
1959 - 1972 Erik A. Maxwell. Trial horse for *Sovereign* in 1963, *Sovereign* and *Kurrewa V* in 1964, *American Eagle* and *Dame Pattie* in 1967. She was slightly modified and her performance improved well. For *American Eagle* she was a valid trial horse and hard to beat
1972 - 1973 E.A. King
1973 - 1974 I.D. MacKay; home port: Glasgow and Cowes
1975 Estate of I.D. Mackay
1976 - 1980 J.D.A. Walker
Since 1985 Sceptre Preservation Society; home port: Preston Marina. She has undergone a major refit and conversion to provide accommodation for twelve people

SOUTHERN CROSS

DESIGNER: *Miller & Whitworth*
BUILDER: *Halvorsen, Morson & Gowland*
YEAR: *1974 January*
LENGTH OVERALL: *20.45 m.*
LENGTH AT WATERLINE: *14.20 m.*
BEAM: *3.71 m.*
DRAFT: *2.74 m.*
DISPLACEMENT: *27.55 tons*
SAIL AREA: *168 sq.m.*
CONSTRUCTION: *aluminium alloy*
FIRST OWNER: *Dalhold Investments Pty. Ltd.*
FIRST NAME: *Southern Cross*
FIRST COUNTRY: *Australia*
HOME PORT: *Yanchep*
FIRST SAIL NUMBER: *KA 4*
CURRENT LOCATION: *Northern Queensland (Australia)*
CONDITION: *sailing*
PRESENT OWNER: *unknown*
FURTHER DETAILS AND HISTORY: Built according to Third Int. Rule America's Cup. Owners and history:
1974 - 1975 Dalhold Investments Pty. Ltd.; name: *Southern Cross*; home port: Yanchep. This was the first Twelve designed by Bob Miller (Ben Lexcen), already known for some successful offshore racing yachts. *Southern Cross* had a greater waterline than usual and was the first Twelve with a bow bustle that allowed her to absorb forward displacement with the advantage of reducing resistance aft; the keel design is in line with Miller's most well-known offshore designs such as *Apollo* or *Ginko*. She suffered the same problems and had poor windward stability. *Southern Cross*, skippered by Jim Hardy, was the challenger for the 22nd America's Cup after having defeated, by a score of 4-0, Baron Bich's *France I*. She lost to *Courageous*, skippered by Ted Hood by a score of 4-0. In the following years, Hood discovered that *Courageous* raced underweight by 1700lbs.
1975 - 1977 The Southern Cross America's Cup Challenge Association, Ltd.; home port: Yanchep and Fremantle, WA. In 1977, trial horse for *Australia*
1978 - 1980 Bond Corporation Pty. Ltd.; home port: Perth and Yanchep, WA
Since 1993 Charter vessel in North Queensland

SOUTH AUSTRALIA

DESIGNER: *Ben Lexcen*
BUILDER: *Steve E. Ward & Co.*
YEAR: *1985 March*
CONSTRUCTION: *aluminium alloy*
FIRST OWNER: *S. Austr. Chall. for the Defence 1987, Ltd.*
FIRST NAME: *South Australia*
FIRST COUNTRY: *Australia*
HOME PORT: *Port Adelaide*
FIRST SAIL NUMBER: *KA 8*
CURRENT LOCATION: *St. Tropez*
CONDITION: *sailing, very good*
PRESENT OWNER: *South Australia (UK) Ltd. (E. Marlin)*

COUNTRY: *Switzerland*
FURTHER DETAILS AND HISTORY: Built according to the Third Int. Rule America's Cup. Owners and history:
1985 - 1987 South Australian Challenge for the Defence 1987, Ltd.; name: *South Australia*; home port: Port Adelaide. She was a sister ship to *Australia III*, although she performed quite differently; she was very fast in light airs but the 1987 America's Cup was raced in high winds. Her results were disappointing both in the 1986 Twelve Metre World Championship and in the 1987 America's Cup defender trials
1993 - 1998 Stenungsbaden Yacht Club of Sweden; home port: Stenungsund (Sweden)
Since 1998 South Australia (UK) Ltd. (Elisabeth Marlin); home port: St. Tropez

SOVEREIGN

DESIGNER: *David Boyd*
BUILDER: *Alexander Robertson & Sons(Y. Builders) Ltd.*
YEAR: *June 6 1963*
LENGTH OVERALL: *21.08 m.*
LENGTH AT WATERLINE: *13.91 m.*
BEAM: *3.81 m.*
DRAFT: *2.71 m.*
DISPLACEMENT: *28.38 tons*
SAIL AREA: *175 sq.m.*
CONSTRUCTION: *wood*
FIRST OWNER: *J. Anthony J. Boyden*
FIRST NAME: *Sovereign*
FIRST COUNTRY: *Great Britain*
HOME PORT: *Greenock*
FIRST SAIL NUMBER: *K 12*
CURRENT LOCATION: *Antibes, France*
CONDITION: *perfect conditions*
PRESENT OWNER: *Jean-Claude Perdriel*
FURTHER DETAILS AND HISTORY: Built according to the Third Int. Rule America's Cup
Owners and history:
1963 - 1965 J. Anthony J. Boyden; name: *Sovereign*; home port: Greenock. She was built for the second post-war British challenge but again her design was conservative and *Sovereign* even had problems beating the old *Sceptre*. She won the British trials against *Kurrewa V* but she lost the Match to *Constellation* by a score of 4-0 with big gaps of twenty minutes. *Sovereign*'s poor performance was not only due to Boyd's design but also she suffered from poor quality sails and the inexperience of the skipper, Peter Scott, in the choppy waters off Newport and in match racing
1965 - 1967 Pierre E. Goemans
1968 - 1971 Baron Marcel Bich; home port: Toulon and La Trinité-sur-Mer (France); *Sovereign*, together with *Kurrewa V* and *Constellation* was bought by Baron Bich for his campaign for the America's Cup
1972 - 1973 Clive D. Bourchier; home port: Chichester; engine installed in 1972
1974 - 1976 François Germain; home port: Chichester and Angers (France)
Since 1977 (?) Jean-Claude Perdriel (a well-known French press editor);

home port: Antibes (France). *Sovereign* was altered by Jacques Fauroux with a new interior layout and a suspended rudder. In 1985, according to AIVE Rules, she was restored to her original condition apart from the hull shape. She regularly entered the Mediterranean races for the Twelve Metre Class. She was first in the Twelve Vintage class in the 1999 World Championship

■ SPIRIT OF AMERICA

DESIGNER: *Sparkman & Stephens - design no 2420*
BUILDER: *Newport Offshore, Ltd*
YEAR: *1982 April*
LENGTH OVERALL: *19.64 m.*
LENGTH AT WATERLINE: *13.84 m.*
BEAM: *3.78 m.*
DRAFT: *2.72 m.*
DISPLACEMENT: *25.5 tons*
SAIL AREA: *164 sq.m.*
CONSTRUCTION: *aluminium alloy*
FIRST OWNER: *Freedom Camp.'83 SUNY at Fort Schuyler*
FIRST NAME: *Spirit of America*
FIRST COUNTRY: *U.S.A.*
HOME PORT: *New York, NY*
FIRST SAIL NUMBER: *US 34*
CURRENT LOCATION: *Hilton Head (U.S.A.)*
CONDITION: *sailing, good*
PRESENT OWNER: *S & M, Inc.*
FURTHER DETAILS AND HISTORY: Built according Third Int. Rule America's Cup
Owners and history:
1982 - 1983 Freedom Campaign '83 SUNY at Fort Schuyler; name: *Spirit of America*; home port: New York. Designed by Bill Langan for the Defender Trials of the 1983 America's Cup. She was a slow boat and she did not enter the trials. She was redesigned and rebuilt as *Stars & Stripes '83*

■ STARS & STRIPES '83

DESIGNER: *B. Chance Jr., B. Nelson, D. Pedrick*
BUILDER: *Geraghty Marine*
YEAR: *1985 October*
LENGTH OVERALL: *19.50 m.*
LENGTH AT WATERLINE: *13.84 m.*
BEAM: *3.65 m.*
DRAFT: *3.63 m.*
SAIL AREA: *164 sq.m.*
CONSTRUCTION: *aluminium alloy*
FIRST OWNER: *Sail America Foundation*
FIRST NAME: *Stars & Stripes*
FIRST COUNTRY: *U.S.A.*
HOME PORT: *San Diego*
FIRST SAIL NUMBER: *US 53*
CURRENT LOCATION: *Hilton Head Island, U.S.A.*
CONDITION: *sailing, good*
PRESENT OWNER: *S & M, Inc*
FURTHER DETAILS AND HISTORY: Built according to the Third Int. Rule

America's Cup
Owners and history:
1985 - 1987 Sail America Foundation; name: *Stars & Stripes '83*; home port: San Diego. Sail America Foundation represented the New York Yacht Club's effort to win back the America's Cup in the 1987 26th match in Fremantle. Dennis Conner was the skipper and helmsman and had no involvement in the design of the four *Stars & Stripes* Twelves. The design team was formed by Britton Chance, Bruce Nelson and David Pedrick. The budget was estimated at over $16.000.000 (including over $1.000.000 for sails created by North Sails and Sobstad). The training course was at Molokai Channel (Hawaii). The trial horse was *Liberty*. *Stars & Stripes '83* was the first of the four Twelves and she was the ex *Spirit of America* completely redesigned by the Sail America design team and rebuilt at Geraghty Marine in San Diego
1988 - 1989 America's Cup Organising Committee
1993 - 1996 Intrepid Sailing Inc. (Joseph G. Krawczyk); home port: Seekonk, MA
Since 1996 S & M, Inc.; home port: Hilton Head Island, SC

■ STARS & STRIPES '85

DESIGNER: *B. Chance, B. Nelson, D. Pedrick*
BUILDER: *Robert E. Derecktor, Inc.*
YEAR: *1985 August*
LENGTH OVERALL: *20.12 m.*
BEAM: *3.66 m.*
CONSTRUCTION: *aluminium alloy*
FIRST OWNER: *Sail American Foundation*
FIRST NAME: *Stars & Stripes '85*
FIRST COUNTRY: *U.S.A.*
HOME PORT: *San Diego*
FIRST SAIL NUMBER: *US 54*
FURTHER DETAILS AND HISTORY: Built according to the Third Int. Rule America's Cup
Owners and history:
1985 - 1987 Sail America Foundation; name: *Stars & Stripes '85*; home port: San Diego. Sail America Foundation represented the New York Yacht Club's effort to win back the America's Cup in the 1987 26th Match in Fremantle. Dennis Conner was the skipper and helmsman and had no involvement in the design of the four *Stars & Stripes* Twelves. The design team was formed by Britton Chance, Bruce Nelson and David Pedrick. The budget was estimated at over $16.000.000 (including over $1.000.000 for the sails made by North Sails and Sobstad). The training course was at Molokai Channel (Haway). The trial horse was *Liberty*. *Stars & Stripes '85* was the second of the four Twelves and she proved immediately superior to *S&S '83* which was faster than *Liberty*
1988 America's Cup Organising Committee
Since 1988 Pier 39 Yacht Club; home port: Tokyo Bay (Japan)

■ STARS & STRIPES '86

DESIGNER: *B. Chance Jr., B. Nelson, D. Pedrick*
BUILDER: *Robert E. Derecktor, Inc.*
YEAR: *1986 February*
LENGTH OVERALL: *20.24 m.*
BEAM: *3.68 m.*

CONSTRUCTION: *aluminium alloy*
FIRST OWNER: *Sail America Foundation*
FIRST NAME: *Stars & Stripes '86*
FIRST COUNTRY: *U.S.A.*
HOME PORT: *San Diego*
FIRST SAIL NUMBER: *US 56*
CURRENT LOCATION: *St. Maarten, U.S.A.*
CONDITION: *sailing, very good*
PRESENT OWNER: *International Yacht Leasing Agency, Inc.*
FURTHER DETAILS AND HISTORY: Built according to the Third Int. Rule America's Cup
Owners and history:
1986 - 1987 Sail America Foundation; name: *Stars & Stripes '86*; home port: San Diego. Sail America Foundation represented the New York Yacht Club's efforts to win back the America's Cup in the 1987 26th Match in Fremantle. Dennis Conner was the skipper and helmsman and had no involvement in the design of the four *Stars & Stripes* Twelves. The design team was formed by Britton Chance, Bruce Nelson and David Pedrick. The budget was estimated at over $16.000.000 (including over $1.000.000 for the sails made by North Sails and Sobstad).
The training course was at Molokai Channel (Hawaii). The trial horse was *Liberty*. *Stars & Stripes '86* was the third of the four Twelves and she differed from the first two by having a radical keel and more sail area
1996 Kona Kai Resort Associates
? up to present International Yacht Leasing Agency, Inc. The yacht was leased to Colin Percy at St. Maarten where she was chartered daily together with *Canada I*, *True North IV* and *V, Stars & Stripes '87*. The boat was original with no engine and all the original hardware.
The only thing that has changed is the cut of the main and furling jib. The dacron and rod rigging has been replaced and once a year she was re-rigged again for a major race

■ STARS & STRIPES '87

DESIGNER: *B. Chance, B. Nelson, D. Pedrick*
BUILDER: *Robert E. Derecktor, Inc.*
YEAR: *1986 July*
LENGTH OVERALL: *20.12 m.*
BEAM: *3.66 m.*
CONSTRUCTION: *aluminium alloy*
FIRST OWNER: *Sail America Foundation*
FIRST NAME: *Stars & Stripes '87*
FIRST COUNTRY: *U.S.A.*
HOME PORT: *San Diego*
FIRST SAIL NUMBER: *US 55*
CURRENT LOCATION: *St. Maarten, NA, U.S.A.*
CONDITION: *sailing, very good*
PRESENT OWNER: *International Yacht Leasing Inc.*
FURTHER DETAILS AND HISTORY: Built according to the Third Int. Rule America's Cup
Owners and history:
1986 - 1987 Sail America Foundation; name: *Stars & Stripes '87*; home port: San Diego. Sail America Foundation represented the New York Yacht Club's efforts to win back the America's Cup in the 1987

26th Match in Fremantle. Dennis Conner was the skipper and helmsman and had no involvement in the design of the four *Stars & Stripes* Twelves. The design team was formed by Britton Chance, Bruce Nelson and David Pedrick. The budget was estimated at over $16.000.000 (including over $1.000.000 for the sails made by North Sails and Sobstad). The training course was at Molokai Channel (Hawaii). The trial horse was *Liberty*.
Stars & Stripes '87 was the last of the four Twelves and she was a refinement of the earlier ones
1988 - 1989 America's Cup Organising Committee
1992 - 1994 George F. Jewett, Jr.; home port: St. Francisco, CA
1996 Dennis Conner Sports, Inc.; home port: San Diego.
? up to present International Yacht Leasing Agency, Inc; home port: St. Maarten, NA. The yacht was leased to Colin Percy at St. Maarten where she was chartered daily together with *Canada I*, *True North IV and V*, *Stars & Stripes '87*. The boat was original with no engine and the original hardware. The only thing changed was a cut down main and furling jib. Dacron sails and rod rigging were replaced. Once a year she was re-rigged again for a major race

■ STEAK 'N' KIDNEY

DESIGNER: *Peter Cole*
BUILDER: *Consolidated Marine*
YEAR: *1986 April*
CONSTRUCTION: *aluminium alloy*
FIRST OWNER: *Eastern Australia America's Cup Defence*
FIRST NAME: *Steak 'n' Kidney*
FIRST COUNTRY: *Australia*
HOME PORT: *Sydney*
FIRST SAIL NUMBER: *KA 14*
CURRENT LOCATION: *Sydney*
COUNTRY: *Australia*
FURTHER DETAILS AND HISTORY: Built according to the Third Int. Rule America's Cup
Owners and history:
1986 - 1987 Eastern Australia America's Cup Defence; name: *Steak 'n' Kidney*; home port: Sidney, NSW. The final design of *Steak 'n' Kidney* was the product of 22 hull shapes and 11 winged keel variations. She was a powerful boat. She scored the last position in the defender trials of the 26th America's Cup
Since 1988 Syd Fischer; home port: Sydney

■ SWISSMADE

DESIGNER: *Jean Grobety*
YEAR: *1984*
LENGTH OVERALL: *19.6 m.*
LENGTH AT WATERLINE: *13.75 m.*
BEAM: *3.95 m.*
DRAFT: *2.70 m.*
SAIL AREA: *162 sq.m.*
FIRST OWNER: *Ass. Suisse pour La Coupe de l'Amérique*
FIRST NAME: *Swissmade*
FIRST COUNTRY: *Switzerland*
FURTHER DETAILS AND HISTORY: project; not built

■ TRUE NORTH

DESIGNER: *Steve Killing*
BUILDER: *Crockett-McConnel, Inc.*
YEAR: *1985 June*
LENGTH OVERALL: *19.84 m.*
LENGTH AT WATERLINE: *13.64 m.*
BEAM: *3.79 m.*
DRAFT: *2.67 m.*
SAIL AREA: *167 sq.m.*
CONSTRUCTION: *aluminium alloy*
FIRST OWNER: *True North Yachting Challenges, Inc.*
FIRST NAME: *True North*
FIRST COUNTRY: *Canada*
HOME PORT: *Halifax, NS*
FIRST SAIL NUMBER: *KC 87*
CURRENT LOCATION: *St. Maarten (Netherland Antilles)*
CONDITION: *modified for charter*
FURTHER DETAILS AND HISTORY: Built according to the Third Int. Rule America's Cup
Owners and history:
1985 - 1986 True North Yachting Challenges, Inc.; name: *True North*; home port: Halifax, NS
1986 - 1987 Canada's Challenge '87. She competed in the 12 Metre World Championship in Fremantle in February 1986. The True North Challenge of Canada subsequently combined their America's Cup challenge effort with that of the Secret Cove Challenge, also of Canada, and the decision was made not to use *True North* but to compete with *Canada II*
Since 1993 Colin Percy, 12 Metre Challenge; home port: St. Maarten, NA. Together with other Twelves, she has been used for day charter in St. Maarten

■ TRUE NORTH II

DESIGNER: *Steve Killing*
BUILDER: *Crockett-McConnell, Inc.*
YEAR: *1985*
LENGTH OVERALL: *20.50 m.*
LENGTH AT WATERLINE: *14.02 m.*
BEAM: *3.79 m.*
DRAFT: *2.68 m.*
SAIL AREA: *164 sq.m.*
CONSTRUCTION: *aluminium alloy*
FIRST OWNER: *True North Yachting Challenges, Inc.*
FIRST NAME: *True North II*
FIRST COUNTRY: *Canada*
HOME PORT: *Halifax*
FIRST SAIL NUMBER: *not authorised or issued*
CURRENT LOCATION: *St. Maarten (Netherland Antilles)*
CONDITION: *transformed for charter*
FURTHER DETAILS AND HISTORY: Built according to the Third Int. Rule America's Cup
Owners and history:
1985 - 1993 True North Yachting Challenges, Inc.; name: *True North II*; home port: Halifax. In 1986 the yacht that became *True North II* was under construction. This construction was halted in March 1986 when

the True North Challenge of Canada combined with the Secret Cove Challenge. The unfinished yacht was later purchased for competition (1993) and used for day charter in the Netherlands Antilles. She has not completed post-construction measurement or Lloyd's survey under the 12 Metre Rule

■ USA (E-1)

DESIGNER: *Gary Mull*
BUILDER: *Stephens Marine*
YEAR: *1985 August*
CONSTRUCTION: *aluminium alloy*
FIRST OWNER: *Golden Gate Challenge*
FIRST NAME: *USA (E-1)*
FIRST COUNTRY: *U.S.A.*
HOME PORT: *San Francisco*
FIRST SAIL NUMBER: *US 49*
CURRENT LOCATION: *Woodside, CA, U.S.A.*
CONDITION: *not known*
FURTHER DETAILS AND HISTORY: Built according to the Third Int. Rule America's Cup
Owners and history:
1985 - 1987 Golden Gate Challenge; name: *USA (E-1)*; home port: San Francisco, CA. She was the first of two Twelves built by the Challenge, nicknamed *"E-1"* for *"Evolutionary"*, in view of the 1987 America's Cup
Since 1988 Robert B. Cole; home port: Woodside, CA (U.S.A.)

■ UWA

DESIGNER: *P. Petterson, L. Wiklund & S. Westerdahl*
BUILDER: *Enoch & Elfstedt A.B.*
YEAR: *1976 September*
LENGTH OVERALL: *19.50 m.*
LENGTH AT WATERLINE: *13.95 m.*
BEAM: *3.72 m.*
DRAFT: *2.72 m.*
DISPLACEMENT: *25.3 tons (1976) - 26,05 tons (1980)*
SAIL AREA: *162 sq.m. (1977) - 174 sq.m. (1980)*
CONSTRUCTION: *aluminium alloy*
FIRST OWNER: *Sverige Syndicate*
FIRST NAME: *Sverige*
FIRST COUNTRY: *Sweden*
HOME PORT: *Goteborg*
FIRST SAIL NUMBER: *S 3 - G 5*
OTHER NAMES: *Blue Magic or Blaupunkt (1986)*
CURRENT LOCATION: *Germany*
CONDITION: *sailing*
FURTHER DETAILS AND HISTORY: Built according to the Third Int. Rule America's Cup
Owners and history:
1976 - 1978 Sverige Syndicate; name: *Sverige*; home port: Goteborg. Challenger for the 23rd 1977 America's Cup. Under the ensign of the Royal Goteborg Yacht Club, a large group of Swedish industries supported the project of the Syndicate having among the members King Gustav, Christer Salen and Pelle Petterson himself. Models were tested at the Experimental Tank of Goteborg with the assistance of the Volvo

calculations centre. *Sverige* had some peculiarities: foot-pedal coffee grinders, a double tiller and the bow design where the centreline is flat at the waterline reducing its length. She was a light displacement yacht. She performed well in the challenger trials losing the final to *Australia*

1978 - 1979 Pelle Petterson, Lars Wiklund & Stellan Westerdahl

1979 - 1980 Swedish Challenge to the America's Cup, Inc.

In April 1980 she was altered by Pelle Petterson at Eriksberg Shipyard for the occasion of the 24th 1980 America's Cup.

The hull lines were modified with a new keel, stern and bow; the sail area was increased and also her displacement. The results were disappointing and Sweden declined to enter the America's Cup following modifications

1986 12 ER Syndikat EV; new name: *Bluemagic* or *Blaupunkt*; home port: Travemunde (Germany)

Since 1987 Jurgen Rohl; new name: *UWA*; home port: Hamburg; engine installed; new sail number: G 5

■ VALIANT

DESIGNER: *Olin J. Stephens - design no 1978*
BUILDER: *Robert E. Derecktor Yacht Yard, Inc.*
YEAR: *1970 May*
LENGTH OVERALL: *19.63 m.*
LENGTH AT WATERLINE: *14.53 m.*
BEAM: *3.66 m.*
DRAFT: *2.76 m.*
DISPLACEMENT: *32.35 tons*
SAIL AREA: *163 sq.m.*
CONSTRUCTION: *triple planked mahogany, laminated oak frames*
FIRST OWNER: *12 US/24 Syndicate*
FIRST NAME: *Valiant*
FIRST COUNTRY: *U.S.A.*
HOME PORT: *New York*
FIRST SAIL NUMBER: *US 24*
CURRENT LOCATION: *Marblehead*
CONDITION: *perfect condition*
FURTHER DETAILS AND HISTORY: Built according to the Third Int. Rule America's Cup
Owners and history:

1970 - 1972 12 US/24 Syndicate (Robert W. McCullough); name: *Valiant*; home port: New York, NY. She was one of the so-called jumbo Twelves and the heaviest ever built. Stephens considers her as the "poorest" he had ever designed. She entered the 1970 defender trials and she was second to *Intrepid*. She won the 1970 Lipton Memorial Trophy (NYYC)

1973 Brown University; home port: Providence, RI

1974 Kings Point Fund USMMA; home port: Kings Point, NY. In 1974 she entered the defender trials of the 1974 22nd America's Cup. As the trial horse of *Mariner*, she was modified by Britton Chance in order to incorporate in her hull the same "fast back"

1978 William Edwards; home port: St. Petersburg, FL; engine installed in 1978

1988-1989 Charles W. Kem; home port: Long Beach, CA

1993 - 2001 Paul G. Gregory III; home port: Marblehead,MA

■ VICTORY '82

DESIGNER: *Edward Dubois*
BUILDER: *William A. Souter & Son*
YEAR: *1982 April*
LENGTH OVERALL: *19.96 m.*
LENGTH AT WATERLINE: *13.85 m.*
BEAM: *3.76 m.*
DRAFT: *2.72 m.*
DISPLACEMENT: *25.55 tons*
SAIL AREA: *168 sq.m.*
CONSTRUCTION: *aluminium alloy*
FIRST OWNER: *Victory Syndicate (Peter De Savary)*
FIRST NAME: *Victory '82*
FIRST COUNTRY: *Great Britain*
HOME PORT: *Burnham on Crouch (Great Britain)*
FIRST SAIL NUMBER: *K 21*
CURRENT LOCATION: *Burnham on Crouch*
CONDITION: *sailing, very good*
FURTHER DETAILS AND HISTORY: Built according to the Third Int. Rule America's Cup
Owners and history:

1982 - 1983 Victory Syndicate (Peter de Savary); name: *Victory '82*; home port: Burnham on Crouch. She was the first yacht ordered by Peter De Savary for the 1983 25th America's Cup. Her design was tested at the Wolfson tank of University of Southampton. Her results were not very encouraging and De Savary commissioned a new Twelve, *Victory '83*, from Ian Howlett

1983 - 1993 Home port: Falmouth

Since 1993 Roy Hart

■ VICTORY '83

DESIGNER: *Ian Howlett*
BUILDER: *Fairey Allday Marine*
YEAR: *1982*
LENGTH OVERALL: *19.81 m.*
BEAM: *3.76 m.*
DISPLACEMENT: *25.2 tons*
SAIL AREA: *198 sq.m.*
CONSTRUCTION: *aluminium alloy*
FIRST OWNER: *Consorzio Victory*
FIRST NAME: *Victory '83*
FIRST COUNTRY: *Great Britain*
FIRST SAIL NUMBER: *K 22*
CURRENT LOCATION: *Cogolin (Italy)*
CONDITION: *excellent*
FURTHER DETAILS AND HISTORY: Built according to the Third Int. Rule America's Cup
Owners and history:

1982 - 1984 Victory Syndicate; name: *Victory '83*. She was the second 12 Metre ordered by Peter de Savary for the English challenge in 1983. She won the defender trials over the other 12 Metre *Victory '82*. *Victory* was very fast and seaworthy although she had to change crew and helmsmen. No doubt she was the fastest 12 Metre yacht until the coming of the wing keels. *Victory* lost the challenger trials by a score of 1-4 versus *Australia II*

1985 - 1987 Consorzio Italia; home port: Genova. She was bought by the Consorzio Italia for US$500.000 and used as the trial horse for the America's Cup Challenge in 1987. Under Italian flag she won the World Championship in Porto Cervo, Sardinia, with Flavio Scala at the helm

1988 Giovanni Gini; home port: Lecco. In 1996 she joined the fleet in the Tirrenian Sea, taking part in the European Class Regatta and other regattas of the Class

■ WEATHERLY

DESIGNER: *Philip L. Rhodes - design no. 676*
BUILDER: *Luders Marine Construction Co. - no. 989*
YEAR: *1958*
LENGTH OVERALL: *21.00 m.*
LENGTH AT WATERLINE: *13.84 m.*
BEAM: *3.55 m.*
DRAFT: *2.74 m.*
DISPLACEMENT: *26.6 tons (1958) - 25.65 tons (1962)*
SAIL AREA: *sq.m. 173 (1958) - sq.m. 178 (1962)*
CONSTRUCTION: *double planked mahogany on oak frames*
FIRST OWNER: *Weatherly Syndicate*
FIRST NAME: *Weatherly*
FIRST COUNTRY: *U.S.A.*
HOME PORT: *New York*
FIRST SAIL NUMBER: *US 17*
CURRENT LOCATION: *Newport, RI (U.S.A.)*
CONDITION: *sailing, very good*
FURTHER DETAILS AND HISTORY: Built according to the Third Int. Rule America's Cup
Owners and history:
1958 - 1965 Weatherly Syndicate: Henry D. Mercer, Arnold D. Frese & Cornelius S. Walsh (Mercer Syndicate); name: *Weatherly*; home port: New York, NY. She was one of three boats built for the 1958 Cup Defence. She was solidly built, with extensive use of laminated mahogany in the keel, the stem and the stern pieces. At her best in light airs. The laminated construction was approved by Lloyd's as the scantling rules do not mention such type of construction for which Luders is well known. After demonstration and discussions by Al Masson, who was in charge of construction and arrangement plans, the modification was accepted. In the defender trials she was eliminated, but four years later both Rhodes and Luders collaborated in radical interventions: the stern was cut; weight reduced above deck and the wetted surface reduced by the hull; about 1000 lbs were stripped off the structure and transferred to a redesigned ballast keel. The boat increased her speed, but the decisive element was the new skipper, Bus Mosbacher. *Weatherly* won the defender trials and the Cup Match by a score of 4-1 although the race is remembered among the most exciting of *Gretel*'s achievements. *Weatherly* won the Queen's Cup (NYYC) and the Chandler Hovey Gold Bowl in 1959, 1960, 1961 and 1962. Winner of the 1961 Astor Cup
1966 - 1971 U.S. Merchant Marine Academy; home port: King's Point, NY. She was donated by Henry Mercer to be used as a training boat by the Merchant Marine cadets. Trial horse for *Columbia* in 1967 and for *Valiant* in 1970
1971 - 1974 Douglas E. Jones; home port: King's Point, NY, and

Menomonee, WI. She was again altered to race in the Great Lakes and she won the Mackinac Race and then one in Puget Sound
1975 Disappeared off record
1975 - 1981 Lynn Summers & Alan Buchanan; home port: Seattle
1981 - 1986 Seattle Council Boy Scouts of America
Since 1986 Weatherly, Inc. (George Hill); home port: Newport, RI. She was sailed from Seattle to Florida via the Panama Canal. There, she fell from a crane on her bow and suffered from severe damage to her stem planking and frames and to her rig. With a stay-sail and a storm trysail from the mast stub to steady her, *Weatherly* was motored to Newport for a complete restoration by her new owner

■ WHITE STREAK

DESIGNER: *Charles E Morgan Jr.*
YEAR: *1963*
FIRST OWNER: *Homer Denius*
FIRST NAME: *White Streak*
FIRST COUNTRY: *U.S.A.*
FURTHER DETAILS AND HISTORY: Hull only partially built. No sail number authorised or issued

■ WINDROSE

DESIGNER: *Britton Chance, Jr.*
BUILDER: *Chantier Naval Hermann Egger*
YEAR: *1969*
LENGTH OVERALL: *19.13 m.*
LENGTH AT WATERLINE: *14.40 m.*
BEAM: *3.76 m.*
DRAFT: *2.57 m.*
DISPLACEMENT: *27 tons*
SAIL AREA: *165 sq.m.*
CONSTRUCTION: *wood*
FIRST OWNER: *L'Assoc. Fran. pour La Coupe de l'Amérique*
FIRST NAME: *Chancegger*
FIRST COUNTRY: *France*
HOME PORT: *Hyères*
CURRENT LOCATION: *The Netherlands*
CONDITION: *unknown*
FURTHER DETAILS AND HISTORY: Built according to the Third Int. Rule America's Cup
Owners and history:
1969 - 1975 L'Association Française pour La Coupe de l'Amérique (AFCA) (Marcel Bich); name: *Chancegger*; home port: Hyères. She was the first Twelve built for Baron Bich's French campaign for the America's Cup. Her name came from the designer (Chance) and the builder (Egger) joined together. In order to profit from the American experience of Britton Chance at Sparkman & Stephens, Baron Bich ordered an experimental boat to be used as an example for the AFCA official designer, André Mauric and as trial horse for the French – designed Twelve
1976 - 1979 Baron Marcel Bich
1980 Romke de Vries; home port: Amsterdam; Swiss Challenge SORC (Pierre Fehlmann)

3. Index of Yacht Names

The list includes the names of every Twelve Metre yacht.
They are listed in alphabetical order,
and the present name is given only when the yacht is still in existence.

▬ ADVANCE
PRESENT NAME: ADVANCE
FIRST NAME: ADVANCE
OTHER NAMES:
SAIL NUMBER: KA 7

▬ AILE
PRESENT NAME: WINGS
FIRST NAME: WINGS
OTHER NAMES: MOHITA II
SAIL NUMBER: K 15

▬ ALACHIE
PRESENT NAME:
FIRST NAME: ALACHIE
OTHER NAMES:
SAIL NUMBER:

▬ ALANNA
PRESENT NAME: BLUE MARLIN
FIRST NAME: HURRICANE
OTHER NAMES:
SAIL NUMBER: K 2 - K 10 - K 17

▬ ALEXANDRA III
PRESENT NAME:
FIRST NAME: SKUM III
OTHER NAMES: SYRIN
SAIL NUMBER:

▬ ALKOR II
PRESENT NAME: CLYMENE
FIRST NAME: CLYMENE
OTHER NAMES: MOYANA V
SAIL NUMBER: K 10

▬ AMERICA II
PRESENT NAME: AMERICA II
FIRST NAME: AMERICA II
OTHER NAMES:
SAIL NUMBER: US 42

▬ AMERICA II
PRESENT NAME: AMERICA II
FIRST NAME: AMERICA II
OTHER NAMES:
SAIL NUMBER: US 44

▬ AMERICA II
PRESENT NAME: FIDDLER
FIRST NAME: AMERICA II
OTHER NAMES:
SAIL NUMBER: US 46

▬ AMERICAN EAGLE
PRESENT NAME: AMERICAN EAGLE
FIRST NAME: AMERICAN EAGLE
OTHER NAMES: WAR BABY, GOLDEN EAGLE
SAIL NUMBER: US 21

▬ AMITY
PRESENT NAME:
FIRST NAME: MOYANA
OTHER NAMES:
SAIL NUMBER: K 3 - K 5

▬ ANITA
PRESENT NAME: ANITA
FIRST NAME: ANITA
OTHER NAMES:
SAIL NUMBER: G 2

▬ ANITRA
PRESENT NAME: ANITRA
FIRST NAME: ANITRA
OTHER NAMES:
SAIL NUMBER: US 5

▬ AQUITAINE
PRESENT NAME: FRANCE II
FIRST NAME: FRANCE II
OTHER NAMES:
SAIL NUMBER: F 2

▬ ARROW
PRESENT NAME:
FIRST NAME: FIGARO IV
OTHER NAMES: SYLVANA, SOLVEIG II
SAIL NUMBER: N 6

▬ ARROW XVI
PRESENT NAME:
FIRST NAME: NARGIE
OTHER NAMES: MALVA
SAIL NUMBER:

▬ ARUNDEL
PRESENT NAME:
FIRST NAME: TYCOON
OTHER NAMES: TRULL, ZIO
SAIL NUMBER: US 3

▬ ASCHANTI
PRESENT NAME:
FIRST NAME: ASCHANTI
OTHER NAMES:
SAIL NUMBER: G 3

▬ ATALANTA
PRESENT NAME:
FIRST NAME: ATALANTA
OTHER NAMES:
SAIL NUMBER: K 5

▬ AUSTRALIA
PRESENT NAME: AUSTRALIA
FIRST NAME: AUSTRALIA
OTHER NAMES: TEMERAIRE
SAIL NUMBER: KA 5

AUSTRALIA II
PRESENT NAME: AUSTRALIA II
FIRST NAME: AUSTRALIA II
OTHER NAMES:
SAIL NUMBER: KA 6

AUSTRALIA III
PRESENT NAME: AUSTRALIA III
FIRST NAME: AUSTRALIA III
OTHER NAMES:
SAIL NUMBER: KA 9

AUSTRALIA IV
PRESENT NAME: AUSTRALIA IV
FIRST NAME: AUSTRALIA IV
OTHER NAMES:
SAIL NUMBER: KA 16

AZZURRA
PRESENT NAME: AZZURRA
FIRST NAME: AZZURRA
OTHER NAMES:
SAIL NUMBER: I 4

AZZURRA II
PRESENT NAME: AZZURRA II
FIRST NAME: AZZURRA II
OTHER NAMES: FRITZZ
SAIL NUMBER: I 8 - G 6

AZZURRA III
PRESENT NAME: AZZURRA III
FIRST NAME: AZZURRA III
OTHER NAMES: FRATZZ
SAIL NUMBER: I 10 - G 7

AZZURRA IV
PRESENT NAME: AZZURRA IV
FIRST NAME: AZZURRA IV
OTHER NAMES:
SAIL NUMBER: I 11

BACCARAT
PRESENT NAME:
FIRST NAME: JAVOTTE
OTHER NAMES: BETTY II, BEDUIN II
SAIL NUMBER:

BARCAROLLA
PRESENT NAME:
FIRST NAME: HEIRA II
OTHER NAMES: NANETTE II, MARIELLA, TOVE LILIAN
SAIL NUMBER:

BARRANQUILLA
PRESENT NAME: BARRANQUILLA
FIRST NAME: PRINCESS SVANIVET
OTHER NAMES: IRENE, SILVERVINGEN X
SAIL NUMBER: S 2 - K 22

BEDUIN
PRESENT NAME: DANSEUSE
FIRST NAME: BEDUIN
OTHER NAMES: MAUD III, GADIE, DANSEUSE III
SAIL NUMBER: E 7

BEDUIN II
PRESENT NAME:
FIRST NAME: JAVOTTE
OTHER NAMES: BACCARAT, BETTY II
SAIL NUMBER: E 5

BETTY II
PRESENT NAME:
FIRST NAME: JAVOTTE
OTHER NAMES: BACCARAT, BEDUIN II
SAIL NUMBER:

BLAUPUNKT
PRESENT NAME: UWA
FIRST NAME: SVERIGE
OTHER NAMES: BLUE MAGIC
SAIL NUMBER: S 3 - G 5

BLOODHOUND
PRESENT NAME: BLOODHOUND
FIRST NAME: BLOODHOUND
OTHER NAMES:
SAIL NUMBER:

BLUE MAGIC
PRESENT NAME: UWA
FIRST NAME: SVERIGE
OTHER NAMES: BLAUPUNKT
SAIL NUMBER: S 3 - D 5

BLUE MARLIN
PRESENT NAME: BLUE MARLIN
FIRST NAME: HURRICANE
OTHER NAMES: ALANNA
SAIL NUMBER: K 2 - K 10 - K 17

BONITA
PRESENT NAME: VINETA
FIRST NAME: FIGARO
OTHER NAMES: FIGARO II
SAIL NUMBER: E 10

BRAND IV
PRESENT NAME:
FIRST NAME: BRAND IV
OTHER NAMES: ISLA II, DORA III, RAGNA III, ELMARI, SOLVEIG I
SAIL NUMBER:

CALEDONIAN
PRESENT NAME:
FIRST NAME: CALEDONIAN
OTHER NAMES:
SAIL NUMBER:

CANADA I
PRESENT NAME: CANADA I
FIRST NAME: CANADA I
OTHER NAMES:
SAIL NUMBER: KC 1

CANADA II
PRESENT NAME: CANADA II
FIRST NAME: CANADA II
OTHER NAMES:
SAIL NUMBER: KC 2

CANNONBALL
PRESENT NAME: HISSAR
FIRST NAME: NEW ZEALAND KZ5
OTHER NAMES: NIPPON, FURY
SAIL NUMBER: KZ 5 - J 5 - US 62

CANTITOE
PRESENT NAME:
FIRST NAME: MAGDA XI
OTHER NAMES:
SAIL NUMBER: N7 - US7

CAPRICE
PRESENT NAME:
FIRST NAME: ROLLO
OTHER NAMES:
SAIL NUMBER:

CERIGO
PRESENT NAME:
FIRST NAME: CERIGO
OTHER NAMES:
SAIL NUMBER: K12 - B1 - F 2

CHALLENGE 12
PRESENT NAME: CHALLENGE 12
FIRST NAME: CHALLENGE 12
OTHER NAMES:
SAIL NUMBER: KA 10 - F 5

CHALLENGE FRANCE
PRESENT NAME: CHALLENGE FRANCE
FIRST NAME: CHALLENGE FRANCE
OTHER NAMES:
SAIL NUMBER: F 8

CHANCEGGER
PRESENT NAME: WINDROSE
FIRST NAME: CHANCEGGER
OTHER NAMES:
SAIL NUMBER:

CHARLOTTE II
PRESENT NAME: GLEAM
FIRST NAME: GLEAM
OTHER NAMES:
SAIL NUMBER: US 11

CINTRA
PRESENT NAME: CINTRA
FIRST NAME: CINTRA
OTHER NAMES: CINTRO
SAIL NUMBER:

CINTRO
PRESENT NAME: CINTRA
FIRST NAME: CINTRA
OTHER NAMES:
SAIL NUMBER:

CLIPPER
PRESENT NAME:
FIRST NAME: CLIPPER
OTHER NAMES:
SAIL NUMBER: US 32

CLYMENE
PRESENT NAME: CLYMENE
FIRST NAME: CLYMENE
OTHER NAMES: MOYANA V, ALKOR II
SAIL NUMBER: K10

CLYTIE
PRESENT NAME:
FIRST NAME: WAIANDANCE
OTHER NAMES: COTTON BLOSSOM III, NIGHT WIND
SAIL NUMBER: US 1

COLUMBIA
PRESENT NAME: COLUMBIA
FIRST NAME: COLUMBIA
OTHER NAMES:
SAIL NUMBER: US 16

INDEX OF YACHT NAMES

CONSTELLATION
PRESENT NAME:
FIRST NAME: CONSTELLATION
OTHER NAMES:
SAIL NUMBER: US 20

COPEJA
PRESENT NAME:
FIRST NAME: SKEAF IV
OTHER NAMES: STERNA, FREYA, EMMELINE, MAID OFASTOLAT, CYMBELINE, GIFT OF THE WIND
SAIL NUMBER:

CORONA
PRESENT NAME:
FIRST NAME: CORONA
OTHER NAMES: HAWAII VI, OSLO, STORMSVALA
SAIL NUMBER:

CORSARA
PRESENT NAME: CORSARA
FIRST NAME: LA SPINA
OTHER NAMES: LA VESPA
SAIL NUMBER: I 1

COTTON BLOSSOM III
PRESENT NAME:
FIRST NAME: WAIANDANCE
OTHER NAMES: CLYTIE, NIGHT WIND
SAIL NUMBER: US 1

COURAGEOUS
PRESENT NAME: COURAGEOUS
FIRST NAME: COURAGEOUS
OTHER NAMES: COURAGEOUS II, COURAGEOUS III, COURAGEOUS IV
SAIL NUMBER: US 26

COURAGEOUS II
PRESENT NAME: COURAGEOUS
FIRST NAME: COURAGEOUS
OTHER NAMES: COURAGEOUS III, COURAGEOUS IV
SAIL NUMBER: US 26

COURAGEOUS III
PRESENT NAME: COURAGEOUS
FIRST NAME: COURAGEOUS
OTHER NAMES: COURAGEOUS II, COURAGEOUS IV
SAIL NUMBER: US 26

COURAGEOUS IV
PRESENT NAME: COURAGEOUS
FIRST NAME: COURAGEOUS
OTHER NAMES: COURAGEOUS II,COURAGEOUS III
SAIL NUMBER: US 26

CRUSADER
PRESENT NAME: CRUSADER
FIRST NAME: CRUSADER I
OTHER NAMES: WHITE CRUSADER
SAIL NUMBER: K 24

CRUSADER I
PRESENT NAME: CRUSADER
FIRST NAME: CRUSADER I
OTHER NAMES: WHITE CRUSADER
SAIL NUMBER: K 24

CRUSADER II
PRESENT NAME:
FIRST NAME: CRUSADER II
OTHER NAMES: WHITE CRUSADER II
SAIL NUMBER: K 25

CYGNE
PRESENT NAME:
FIRST NAME: CYGNE
OTHER NAMES: ELLA, MARIA
SAIL NUMBER:

CYMBELINE
PRESENT NAME:
FIRST NAME: SKEAF IV
OTHER NAMES: STERNA, FREYA, COPEJA, EMMELINE, MAID OF ASTOLAT, GIFT OF THE WIND
SAIL NUMBER:

CYRA
PRESENT NAME:
FIRST NAME: CYRA
OTHER NAMES: LUCELLA, ELFE II, ELSA
SAIL NUMBER:

DAME PATTIE
PRESENT NAME: ENDLESS SUMMER
FIRST NAME: DAME PATTIE
OTHER NAMES:
SAIL NUMBER: KA2

DANSEUSE
PRESENT NAME: DANSEUSE
FIRST NAME: BEDUIN
OTHER NAMES: MAUD III, GADIE, DANSEUSE III
SAIL NUMBER: E 7

DANSEUSE III
PRESENT NAME: DANSEUSE
FIRST NAME: BEDUIN
OTHER NAMES: MAUD III, GADIE,
SAIL NUMBER: E 7

DAVO II
PRESENT NAME:
FIRST NAME: DAVO II
OTHER NAMES:
SAIL NUMBER:

DAVO III
PRESENT NAME:
FIRST NAME: DAVO III
OTHER NAMES: WULP, NOORDSTER III
SAIL NUMBER:

DEFENDER
PRESENT NAME: DEFENDER
FIRST NAME: DEFENDER
OTHER NAMES:
SAIL NUMBER: US 33

DESIREE
PRESENT NAME: DESIREE
FIRST NAME: SIBYLLAN
OTHER NAMES: SIROCCO, SCIROCCO, DUX, MARISETTA, VALERIA
SAIL NUMBER:

DEVONIA
PRESENT NAME:
FIRST NAME: DEVONIA
OTHER NAMES:
SAIL NUMBER:

DIVA III
PRESENT NAME: VEMA III
FIRST NAME: VEMA III
OTHER NAMES: VARG VI, LAKME VI
SAIL NUMBER: N 11

DORA II
PRESENT NAME:
FIRST NAME: BRAND IV
OTHER NAMES: ISLA II, RAGNA III, ELMARI, SOLVEIG I
SAIL NUMBER:

DORIS
PRESENT NAME:
FIRST NAME: DORIS
OTHER NAMES:
SAIL NUMBER: K2 - F2

DUX
PRESENT NAME: DESIREE
FIRST NAME: SIBYLLAN
OTHER NAMES: SIROCCO, SCIROCCO, MARISETTA, VALERIA
SAIL NUMBER:

EAGLE
PRESENT NAME: EAGLE
FIRST NAME: EAGLE
OTHER NAMES:
SAIL NUMBER: US 60

EASTERNER
PRESENT NAME: EASTERNER
FIRST NAME: EASTERNER
OTHER NAMES: NEWSBOY
SAIL NUMBER: US 18

ECOSSE
PRESENT NAME: ECOSSE
FIRST NAME: USA (R-1)
OTHER NAMES:
SAIL NUMBER: US 61

ELEKTRA
PRESENT NAME:
FIRST NAME: FIGARO III
OTHER NAMES: IRINA III, MARJANA
SAIL NUMBER: N 1

ELFE II
PRESENT NAME:
FIRST NAME: CYRA
OTHER NAMES: LUCELLA, ELSA
SAIL NUMBER:

EILEEN
PRESENT NAME: EILEEN
FIRST NAME: EILEEN
OTHER NAMES:
SAIL NUMBER: E 21

ELLA
PRESENT NAME:
FIRST NAME: CYGNE
OTHER NAMES: MARIA
SAIL NUMBER:

ELMARI
PRESENT NAME:
FIRST NAME: BRAND IV
OTHER NAMES: ISLA II, DORA III, RAGNA III, SOLVEIG I
SAIL NUMBER:

ELSA
PRESENT NAME:
FIRST NAME: CYRA
OTHER NAMES: LUCELLA, ELFE II
SAIL NUMBER:

EMILIA
PRESENT NAME: EMILIA
FIRST NAME: EMILIA
OTHER NAMES:
SAIL NUMBER:

EMMELINE
PRESENT NAME:
FIRST NAME: SKEAF IV
OTHER NAMES: STERNA, FREYA, COPEJA, MAID OF ASTOLAT, CYMBELINE, GIFT OF THE WIND
SAIL NUMBER:

ENDLESS SUMMER
PRESENT NAME: ENDLESS SUMMER
FIRST NAME: DAME PATTIE
OTHER NAMES:
SAIL NUMBER: KA 2

ENTERPRISE
PRESENT NAME: ENTERPRISE
FIRST NAME: ENTERPRISE
OTHER NAMES:
SAIL NUMBER: US 27 - I 3

ERNA SIGNE
PRESENT NAME: ERNA SIGNE
FIRST NAME: ERNA SIGNE
OTHER NAMES: VOGUE, MARJORIE
SAIL NUMBER: E 8

ESTRILDA
PRESENT NAME:
FIRST NAME: MOYANA II
OTHER NAMES: WESTWARDHO, MAHARANA, SAGRACE
SAIL NUMBER: K 8 - K 14

EVAINE
PRESENT NAME: EVAINE
FIRST NAME: EVAINE
OTHER NAMES:
SAIL NUMBER: K 2

FARAWAY
PRESENT NAME:
FIRST NAME: NORESCA
OTHER NAMES:
SAIL NUMBER: K 9

FIDDLER
PRESENT NAME: FIDDLER
FIRST NAME: AMERICA II
OTHER NAMES:
SAIL NUMBER: US 46

FIGARO
PRESENT NAME: VINETA
FIRST NAME: FIGARO
OTHER NAMES: FIGARO II, BONITA
SAIL NUMBER: E 10

FIGARO II
PRESENT NAME: VINETA
FIRST NAME: FIGARO
OTHER NAMES: BONITA
SAIL NUMBER: E 10

FIGARO III
PRESENT NAME:
FIRST NAME: FIGARO III
OTHER NAMES: ELEKTRA, IRINA III, MARJANA
SAIL NUMBER: N 1

FIGARO IV
PRESENT NAME:
FIRST NAME: FIGARO IV
OTHER NAMES: ARROW, SYLVANA, SOLVEIG II
SAIL NUMBER: N 6

FIGARO VI
PRESENT NAME:
FIRST NAME: FIGARO VI
OTHER NAMES: SILVERVINGEN
SAIL NUMBER: N12

FLICA
PRESENT NAME: FLICA
FIRST NAME: FLICA
OTHER NAMES:
SAIL NUMBER: K 16

FLICA II
PRESENT NAME: FLICA II
FIRST NAME: FLICA II
OTHER NAMES:
SAIL NUMBER: K 14

FOXHOUND
PRESENT NAME:
FIRST NAME: FOXHOUND
OTHER NAMES: FOXHOUND OF LEPE
SAIL NUMBER:

FOXHOUND OF LEPE
PRESENT NAME:
FIRST NAME: FOXHOUND
OTHER NAMES:
SAIL NUMBER:

FRANCE
PRESENT NAME: FRANCE I
FIRST NAME: FRANCE
OTHER NAMES:
SAIL NUMBER: F 1

FRANCE I
PRESENT NAME: FRANCE I
FIRST NAME: FRANCE I
OTHER NAMES:
SAIL NUMBER: F 1

FRANCE II
PRESENT NAME: FRANCE II
FIRST NAME: FRANCE II
OTHER NAMES: AQUITAINE
SAIL NUMBER: F 2

FRANCE III
PRESENT NAME: FRANCE III
FIRST NAME: FRANCE III
OTHER NAMES:
SAIL NUMBER: F 3

FRATERNITAS
PRESENT NAME: FRATERNITAS
FIRST NAME: VIVO VIII
OTHER NAMES:
SAIL NUMBER: E 20

FRATZZ
PRESENT NAME: AZZURRA III
FIRST NAME: AZZURRA III
OTHER NAMES:
SAIL NUMBER: I 10 - G 7

FREEDOM
PRESENT NAME: FREEDOM
FIRST NAME: FREEDOM
OTHER NAMES:
SAIL NUMBER: US 30

FRENCH KISS
PRESENT NAME: FRENCH KISS
FIRST NAME: FRENCH KISS
OTHER NAMES:
SAIL NUMBER: F 7

FREYA
PRESENT NAME:
FIRST NAME: SKEAF IV
OTHER NAMES: STERNA, COPEJA, EMMELINE, MAID OF ASTOLAT
SAIL NUMBER:

FRISCO VI
PRESENT NAME:
FIRST NAME: RHONA
OTHER NAMES: HEI II
SAIL NUMBER: K 7 - N 10

FRITZZ
PRESENT NAME: AZZURRA II
FIRST NAME: AZZURRA II
OTHER NAMES:
SAIL NUMBER: I 8 - G 6

FURY
PRESENT NAME: HISSAR
FIRST NAME: NEW ZEALAND KZ5
OTHER NAMES: NIPPON, CANNONBALL
SAIL NUMBER: KZ 5 - J 5 - US 62

GADIE
PRESENT NAME: DANSEUSE
FIRST NAME: BEDUIN
OTHER NAMES: MAUD III, DANSEUSE III
SAIL NUMBER: E 7

GALATEA
PRESENT NAME:
FIRST NAME: GALATEA
OTHER NAMES:
SAIL NUMBER:

GAVOTTE III
PRESENT NAME: THEA
FIRST NAME: SANTA
OTHER NAMES: NINA, TENDEREN III
SAIL NUMBER: N 4 - D 1

GHISLAINE
PRESENT NAME:
FIRST NAME: GHISLAINE
OTHER NAMES:
SAIL NUMBER:

GIFT OF THE WIND
PRESENT NAME:
FIRST NAME: SKEAF IV
OTHER NAMES: STERNA, FREYA, COPEJA, EMMELINE, MAID OF ASTOLAT, CYMBELINE
SAIL NUMBER:

GLEAM
PRESENT NAME: GLEAM
FIRST NAME: GLEAM
OTHER NAMES: CHARLOTTE II
SAIL NUMBER: US 11

GOLDEN EAGLE
PRESENT NAME: AMERICAN EAGLE
FIRST NAME: AMERICAN EAGLE
OTHER NAMES: WAR BABY
SAIL NUMBER:

GRETEL
PRESENT NAME: GRETEL
FIRST NAME: GRETEL
OTHER NAMES:
SAIL NUMBER: KA 1 - F 5

GRETEL II
PRESENT NAME: GRETEL II
FIRST NAME: GRETEL II
OTHER NAMES:
SAIL NUMBER: KA 3

GURI
PRESENT NAME: GURI
FIRST NAME: GURI
OTHER NAMES:
SAIL NUMBER:

HAWAII VI
PRESENT NAME:
FIRST NAME: CORONA
OTHER NAMES: OSLO, STORMSVALA
SAIL NUMBER:

HEART OF AMERICA
PRESENT NAME: HEART OF AMERICA
FIRST NAME: HEART OF AMERICA
OTHER NAMES:
SAIL NUMBER: US 51

HEATHERBELL
PRESENT NAME:
FIRST NAME: HEATHERBELL
OTHER NAMES: TERESITA, MARGIT IV, YOLANDE, SYLVA
SAIL NUMBER:

HEI II
PRESENT NAME:
FIRST NAME: RHONA
OTHER NAMES: FRISCO VI
SAIL NUMBER: K 7 - N 10

HEIRA II
PRESENT NAME:
FIRST NAME: HEIRA II
OTHER NAMES: NANETTE II, MARIELLA, TOVE LILIAN, BARCAROLLA
SAIL NUMBER:

HERA
PRESENT NAME:
FIRST NAME: HERA
OTHER NAMES:
SAIL NUMBER:

HERITAGE
PRESENT NAME: HERITAGE
FIRST NAME: HERITAGE
OTHER NAMES:
SAIL NUMBER: US 23

HETI
PRESENT NAME: HETI
FIRST NAME: HETI
OTHER NAMES: TRAUM, NATHURN, SEESCHWALBE, MOBY DICK, SATURN
SAIL NUMBER: E 3

HISSAR
PRESENT NAME: HISSAR
FIRST NAME: NEW ZEALAND KZ5
OTHER NAMES: NIPPON, CANNONBALL, FURY
SAIL NUMBER: KZ 5 - J 5 - US 62

HORIZONS
PRESENT NAME: ONAWA
FIRST NAME: ONAWA
OTHER NAMES: LITHUANICA
SAIL NUMBER: US 6

HURRICANE
PRESENT NAME: BLUE MARLIN
FIRST NAME: HURRICANE
OTHER NAMES: ALANNA
SAIL NUMBER: K 2 - K 10 - K 17

IERNE
PRESENT NAME:
FIRST NAME: IERNE
OTHER NAMES: NATASCHA
SAIL NUMBER:

IKRA
PRESENT NAME: IKRA
FIRST NAME: KURREWA V
OTHER NAMES: LEVRIER DE MER
SAIL NUMBER: K 3

INDEPENDENCE
PRESENT NAME: INDEPENDENCE
FIRST NAME: INDEPENDENCE
OTHER NAMES:
SAIL NUMBER: US 28

INGA
PRESENT NAME: WESTWIND
FIRST NAME: INGA
OTHER NAMES:
SAIL NUMBER: G 1

INTREPID
PRESENT NAME: INTREPID
FIRST NAME: INTREPID
OTHER NAMES: WINDANCER
SAIL NUMBER: US 22

IRENE
PRESENT NAME: BARRANQUILLA
FIRST NAME: PRINCESS SVANEVI
OTHER NAMES: SILVERVINGEN X
SAIL NUMBER: S 2 - K 22

IRINA III
PRESENT NAME:
FIRST NAME: FIGARO III
OTHER NAMES: ELEKTRA, MARJANA
SAIL NUMBER: N 1

IRINA V
PRESENT NAME:
FIRST NAME: IRIS
OTHER NAMES:
SAIL NUMBER: K 6 - N9

IRIS
PRESENT NAME:
FIRST NAME: IRIS
OTHER NAMES: IRINA V
SAIL NUMBER: K 6

IRIS
PRESENT NAME:
FIRST NAME: IRIS
OTHER NAMES:
SAIL NUMBER: US 4

ISLA II
PRESENT NAME:
FIRST NAME: BRAND IV
OTHER NAMES: DORA III, RAGNA III, ELMARI, SOLVEIG I
SAIL NUMBER:

ISOLDE
PRESENT NAME:
FIRST NAME: ISOLDE
OTHER NAMES: SALLY ANN, PTARMIGAN, SOLILOQUY
SAIL NUMBER: US 2

ISTAR
PRESENT NAME:
FIRST NAME: SKEAF V
OTHER NAMES:
SAIL NUMBER:

ITALIA I
PRESENT NAME: ITALIA I
FIRST NAME: ITALIA I
OTHER NAMES:
SAIL NUMBER: I 7

ITALIA II
PRESENT NAME: ITALIA II
FIRST NAME: ITALIA II
OTHER NAMES:
SAIL NUMBER: I 9

IVANHOE
PRESENT NAME:
FIRST NAME: IVANHOE
OTHER NAMES:
SAIL NUMBER:

IYRUNA
PRESENT NAME:
FIRST NAME: IYRUNA
OTHER NAMES:
SAIL NUMBER: K 11

JAVOTTE
PRESENT NAME:
FIRST NAME: JAVOTTE
OTHER NAMES: BETTY II, BACCARAT, BEDUIN II
SAIL NUMBER: E 5

JENETTA
PRESENT NAME: JENETTA
FIRST NAME: JENETTA
OTHER NAMES:
SAIL NUMBER: KC 1

KAHURANGI
PRESENT NAME: KAHURANGI
FIRST NAME: KAHURANGI
OTHER NAMES:
SAIL NUMBER:

KAILENA
PRESENT NAME:
FIRST NAME: MOYANA
OTHER NAMES: MORWENNA
SAIL NUMBER: K 3

KAILUA
PRESENT NAME:
FIRST NAME: LADY EDITH
OTHER NAMES:
SAIL NUMBER:

KIWI
PRESENT NAME: KIWI
FIRST NAME: NEW ZEALAND KZ3
OTHER NAMES: NIPPON CHALLENGE
SAIL NUMBER: KZ 3 - J 3

KIWI MAGIC
PRESENT NAME: KIWI MAGIC
FIRST NAME: NEW ZEALAND
OTHER NAMES:
SAIL NUMBER: KZ 7

KOOKABURRA I
PRESENT NAME: KOOKABURRA I
FIRST NAME: KOOKABURRA I
OTHER NAMES:
SAIL NUMBER: KA 11

KOOKABURRA II
PRESENT NAME: KOOKABURRA II
FIRST NAME: KOOKABURRA II
OTHER NAMES:
SAIL NUMBER: KA 12

KOOKABURRA III
PRESENT NAME: KOOKABURRA III
FIRST NAME: KOOKABURRA III
OTHER NAMES:
SAIL NUMBER: KA 15

KURREWA V
PRESENT NAME: IKRA
FIRST NAME: KURREWA V
OTHER NAMES: LEVRIER DE MER
SAIL NUMBER: K 3

LA PINTA
PRESENT NAME:
FIRST NAME: MODESTY
OTHER NAMES: ROXANA
SAIL NUMBER: K 4

LA PINTA
PRESENT NAME: VANITY V
FIRST NAME: VANITY V
OTHER NAMES:
SAIL NUMBER: K 5

LA SPINA
PRESENT NAME: CORSARA
FIRST NAME: LA SPINA
OTHER NAMES: LA VESPA
SAIL NUMBER: I 1

LA VESPA
PRESENT NAME: CORSARA
FIRST NAME: LA SPINA
OTHER NAMES:
SAIL NUMBER: I 1

LADY EDITH
PRESENT NAME:
FIRST NAME: LADY EDITH
OTHER NAMES: KAILUA
SAIL NUMBER:

LAKME VI
PRESENT NAME: VEMA III
FIRST NAME: VEMA III
OTHER NAMES: DIVA III, VARG VI
SAIL NUMBER: N 11

LE
PRESENT NAME: LE
FIRST NAME: LE
OTHER NAMES:
SAIL NUMBER:

LEVRIER DE MER
PRESENT NAME: IKRA
FIRST NAME: KURREWA V
OTHER NAMES:
SAIL NUMBER: K 3

LIBERTY
PRESENT NAME: LIBERTY
FIRST NAME: LIBERTY
OTHER NAMES:
SAIL NUMBER: US 40

LIONHEART
PRESENT NAME: LIONHEART
FIRST NAME: LIONHEART
OTHER NAMES: LIONHEART OF WESSEX
SAIL NUMBER: K 18

LIONHEART OF WESSEX
PRESENT NAME: LIONHEART
FIRST NAME: LIONHEART
OTHER NAMES:
SAIL NUMBER: K 18

LISS V
PRESENT NAME:
FIRST NAME: MAGDA IX
OTHER NAMES: MOYANA, MOYANA II
SAIL NUMBER: E 11

LITHUANICA
PRESENT NAME: ONAWA
FIRST NAME: ONAWA
OTHER NAMES: HORIZONS
SAIL NUMBER: US 6

LITTLE ASTRA
PRESENT NAME:
FIRST NAME: LITTLE ASTRA
OTHER NAMES:
SAIL NUMBER: K 18

LOBITO
PRESENT NAME: OSTWIND
FIRST NAME: SPHINX
OTHER NAMES:
SAIL NUMBER: G 4

LUCELLA
PRESENT NAME:
FIRST NAME: CYRA
OTHER NAMES: ELFE II, ELSA
SAIL NUMBER:

LUCILLA
PRESENT NAME:
FIRST NAME: LUCILLA
OTHER NAMES:
SAIL NUMBER: K 17

LUCIE VIII
PRESENT NAME: MAGNOLIA
FIRST NAME: MAGDA VIII
OTHER NAMES:
SAIL NUMBER: E 4

MAGDA IX
PRESENT NAME:
FIRST NAME: MAGDA IX
OTHER NAMES: MOYANA, MOYANA II, LISS V
SAIL NUMBER: E 11

MAGDA VIII
PRESENT NAME: MAGNOLIA
FIRST NAME: MAGDA VIII
OTHER NAMES: LUCIE VIII
SAIL NUMBER: E 4

MAGDA XI
PRESENT NAME:
FIRST NAME: MAGDA XI
OTHER NAMES: CANTITOE
SAIL NUMBER: N 7 - US 7

MAGIC
PRESENT NAME: MAGIC
FIRST NAME: MAGIC
OTHER NAMES:
SAIL NUMBER: US 38

INDEX OF YACHT NAMES

MAGNOLIA
PRESENT NAME: MAGNOLIA
FIRST NAME: MAGDA VIII
OTHER NAMES: LUCIE VIII
SAIL NUMBER: E 4

MAHARANA
PRESENT NAME:
FIRST NAME: MOYANA II
OTHER NAMES: WESTWARD HO, ESTRILDA, SAGRACE
SAIL NUMBER: K 8 - K 14

MAID OF ASTOLAT
PRESENT NAME:
FIRST NAME: SKEAF IV
OTHER NAMES: STERNA, FREYA, COPEJA, EMMELINE, CYMBELINE, GIFT OF THE WIND
SAIL NUMBER:

MALVA
PRESENT NAME:
FIRST NAME: NARGIE
OTHER NAMES: ARROW XVI
SAIL NUMBER:

MARGIT IV
PRESENT NAME:
FIRST NAME: HEATHERBELL
OTHER NAMES: HEATHERBELL, TERESITA, MARGIT IV, YOLANDE, SYLVA
SAIL NUMBER:

MARIA
PRESENT NAME:
FIRST NAME: CYGNE
OTHER NAMES: ELLA
SAIL NUMBER:

MARJANA
PRESENT NAME:
FIRST NAME: FIGARO III
OTHER NAMES: ELEKTRA, IRINA III
SAIL NUMBER: N 1

MARIANNE
PRESENT NAME:
FIRST NAME: MARIANNE
OTHER NAMES:
SAIL NUMBER:

MARIELLA
PRESENT NAME:
FIRST NAME: HEIRA II
OTHER NAMES: NANETTE II, TOVE LILIAN, BARCAROLLA
SAIL NUMBER:

MARILINE
PRESENT NAME: MARILINE
FIRST NAME: SKEAF
OTHER NAMES: TREUDEUTSCH
SAIL NUMBER:

MARINA
PRESENT NAME:
FIRST NAME: MARINA
OTHER NAMES:
SAIL NUMBER: K 6

MARINER
PRESENT NAME: MARINER
FIRST NAME: MARINER
OTHER NAMES:
SAIL NUMBER: US 25

MARISETTA
PRESENT NAME: DESIREE
FIRST NAME: SIBYLLAN
OTHER NAMES: SIROCCO, SCIROCCO, DUX, VALERIA
SAIL NUMBER:

MARJORIE
PRESENT NAME: ERNA SIGNE
FIRST NAME: ERNA SIGNE
OTHER NAMES: VOGUE
SAIL NUMBER: E 8

MARY II
PRESENT NAME:
FIRST NAME: SKEAF II
OTHER NAMES:
SAIL NUMBER:

MAUD III
PRESENT NAME: DANSEUSE
FIRST NAME: BEDUIN
OTHER NAMES: BEDUIN, DANSEUSE, DANSEUSE III, GADIE
SAIL NUMBER: E 7

MIQUETTE
PRESENT NAME: MIQUETTE
FIRST NAME: MIQUETTE
OTHER NAMES:
SAIL NUMBER: K 14 - X 1

MITENA
PRESENT NAME: MITENA
FIRST NAME: MITENA
OTHER NAMES:
SAIL NUMBER: US 10

MOBY DICK
PRESENT NAME: HETI
FIRST NAME: HETI
OTHER NAMES: TRAUM, NATHURN, SEESCHWALBE, SATURN
SAIL NUMBER: E 3

MODESTY
PRESENT NAME:
FIRST NAME: MODESTY
OTHER NAMES: ROXANA, LA PINTA
SAIL NUMBER: K 4

MOHITA
PRESENT NAME: WINGS
FIRST NAME: WINGS
OTHER NAMES: AILE
SAIL NUMBER: K 15

MORWENNA
PRESENT NAME:
FIRST NAME: MOYANA
OTHER NAMES: KAYLENA
SAIL NUMBER: K 3

MOUCHETTE
PRESENT NAME:
FIRST NAME: MOUCHETTE
OTHER NAMES:
SAIL NUMBER:

MOUETTE
PRESENT NAME:
FIRST NAME: MOUETTE
OTHER NAMES:
SAIL NUMBER: K15

MOYANA
PRESENT NAME:
FIRST NAME: MOYANA
OTHER NAMES: MORWENNA, KAYLENA
SAIL NUMBER: K 3

MOYANA
PRESENT NAME:
FIRST NAME: MOYANA
OTHER NAMES: AMITY
SAIL NUMBER: K3 - K5

MOYANA
PRESENT NAME:
FIRST NAME: MAGDA IX
OTHER NAMES: MOYANA II, LISS V
SAIL NUMBER: E 11

MOYANA II
PRESENT NAME:
FIRST NAME: MAGDA IX
OTHER NAMES: MOYANA, LISS V
SAIL NUMBER: E 11

MOYANA II
PRESENT NAME:
FIRST NAME: MOYANA II
OTHER NAMES: WESTWARD HO, MAHARANA, ESTRILDA, SAGRACE
SAIL NUMBER: K 8 - K 14

MOYANA V
PRESENT NAME: CLYMENE
FIRST NAME: CLYMENE
OTHER NAMES: ALKOR II
SAIL NUMBER: K 10

NANETTE II
PRESENT NAME:
FIRST NAME: HEIRA II
OTHER NAMES: MARIELLA, TOVE LILIAN, BARCAROLLA
SAIL NUMBER:

NAAGH
PRESENT NAME:
FIRST NAME: NAAGH
OTHER NAMES:
SAIL NUMBER:

NARGIE
PRESENT NAME:
FIRST NAME: NARGIE
OTHER NAMES: MALVA, ARROW XVI
SAIL NUMBER:

NATASCHA
PRESENT NAME:
FIRST NAME: IERNE
OTHER NAMES:
SAIL NUMBER:

INDEX OF YACHT NAMES

NATHURN
PRESENT NAME: HETI
FIRST NAME: HETI
OTHER NAMES: TRAUM,
SEESCHWALBE, MOBY DICK, SATURN
SAIL NUMBER: E3

NEFERTITI
PRESENT NAME: NEFERTITI
FIRST NAME: NEFERTITI
OTHER NAMES:
SAIL NUMBER: US 19

NEREUS
PRESENT NAME: NORTHERN LIGHT
FIRST NAME: NORTHERN LIGHT
OTHER NAMES:
SAIL NUMBER: US 14

NEW ZEALAND KZ5
PRESENT NAME: HISSAR
FIRST NAME: NEW ZEALAND KZ5
OTHER NAMES: CANNONBALL, FURY,
NIPPON
SAIL NUMBER: KZ 5 - J 5 - US 62

NEW ZEALAND KZ3
PRESENT NAME: KIWI
FIRST NAME: NEW ZEALAND KZ3
OTHER NAMES: NIPPON CHALLENGE
SAIL NUMBER: KZ 3 - J 3

**NEW ZEALAND
"KIWI MAGIC"**
PRESENT NAME: NEW ZEALAND
"KIWI MAGIC"
FIRST NAME: NEW ZEALAND "KIWI
MAGIC"
OTHER NAMES:
SAIL NUMBER: KZ 7

NEWS BOY
PRESENT NAME: EASTERNER
FIRST NAME: EASTERNER
OTHER NAMES:
SAIL NUMBER: US 18

NIGHT WIND
PRESENT NAME:
FIRST NAME: WAIaNDANCE
OTHER NAMES: CLYTIE, COTTON
BLOSSOM III
SAIL NUMBER: US 1

NINA
PRESENT NAME: THEA
FIRST NAME: SANTA
OTHER NAMES: TENDEREN II,
GAVOTTE II
SAIL NUMBER: N 4 - D 1

NIPPON
PRESENT NAME: HISSAR
FIRST NAME: NEW ZEALAND KZ5
OTHER NAMES: CANNONBALL, FURY
SAIL NUMBER: KZ 5 - J 5 - US 62

NIPPON CHALLENGE
PRESENT NAME: KIWI
FIRST NAME: NEW ZEALAND KZ3
OTHER NAMES:
SAIL NUMBER: KZ 3 - J 3

NORDSTER III
PRESENT NAME:
FIRST NAME: DAVO III
OTHER NAMES: WULP
SAIL NUMBER:

NOREEN
PRESENT NAME:
FIRST NAME: TATJANA
OTHER NAMES:
SAIL NUMBER: K 2

NORESCA
PRESENT NAME:
FIRST NAME: NORESCA
OTHER NAMES: FARAWAY
SAIL NUMBER: K9

NORSAGA
PRESENT NAME: TRIVIA
FIRST NAME: TRIVIA
OTHER NAMES: TRIVIA OF GOSPORT,
PHOENIX
SAIL NUMBER: K10-N16-US16

NORTHERN LIGHT
PRESENT NAME: NORTHERN LIGHT
FIRST NAME: NORTHERN LIGHT
OTHER NAMES: NEREUS
SAIL NUMBER: US 14

NYALA
PRESENT NAME: NYALA
FIRST NAME: NYALA
OTHER NAMES:
SAIL NUMBER: US12

ONAWA
PRESENT NAME: ONAWA
FIRST NAME: ONAWA
OTHER NAMES: HORIZONS,
LITHUANICA
SAIL NUMBER: US 6

ORNSAY
PRESENT NAME:
FIRST NAME: ORNSAY
OTHER NAMES:
SAIL NUMBER:

OSLO
PRESENT NAME:
FIRST NAME: CORONA
OTHER NAMES: HAWAII VI,
STORMSVALA
SAIL NUMBER:

OSTWIND
PRESENT NAME: OSTWIND
FIRST NAME: SPHINX
OTHER NAMES: LOBITO
SAIL NUMBER: G4

PHOENIX
PRESENT NAME: TRIVIA
FIRST NAME: TRIVIA
OTHER NAMES: TRIVIA OF GOSPORT,
PHOENIX
SAIL NUMBER: K10-N16-US16

PRINCESS SVANIVET
PRESENT NAME: BARRANQUILLA
FIRST NAME: PRINCESS SVANIVET
OTHER NAMES: IRENE,
SILVERVINGEN X
SAIL NUMBER: S 2 - K 22

PTARMIGAN
PRESENT NAME:
FIRST NAME: ISOLDE
OTHER NAMES: SALLY ANN,
SOLILOQUY
SAIL NUMBER: US 2

RAAK
PRESENT NAME: RAAK
FIRST NAME: RAAK
OTHER NAMES: ULLABRAND IV, VICI
SAIL NUMBER: E 15

RÁFAGA
PRESENT NAME:
FIRST NAME: RÁFAGA
OTHER NAMES:
SAIL NUMBER:

RAGNA III
PRESENT NAME:
FIRST NAME: BRAND IV
OTHER NAMES: ISLA II, DORA III,
ELMARI, SOLVEIG I
SAIL NUMBER:

RHONA
PRESENT NAME:
FIRST NAME: RHONA
OTHER NAMES: FRISCO VI, HEI II
SAIL NUMBER:

ROLLO
PRESENT NAME:
FIRST NAME: ROLLO
OTHER NAMES: CAPRICE
SAIL NUMBER: E 8

ROMEO
PRESENT NAME: HETI
FIRST NAME: HETI
OTHER NAMES: TRAUM, NATHURN,
SEESCHWALBE, MOBY DICK, SATURN
SAIL NUMBER: E 3

ROXANA
PRESENT NAME:
FIRST NAME: MODESTY
OTHER NAMES: LA PINTA
SAIL NUMBER: F 2

ROYAL OAK
PRESENT NAME:
FIRST NAME: ROYAL OAK
OTHER NAMES:
SAIL NUMBER:

SAGRACE
PRESENT NAME:
FIRST NAME: MOYANA II
OTHER NAMES: WESTWARD HO,
MAHARANA, ESTRILDA
SAIL NUMBER: K 8 - K 14

SALLY ANN
PRESENT NAME:
FIRST NAME: ISOLDE
OTHER NAMES: PTARMIGAN, SOLILOQUY
SAIL NUMBER: US 2

SANTA
PRESENT NAME: THEA
FIRST NAME: SANTA
OTHER NAMES: TENDEREN III, GAVOTTE III, NINA
SAIL NUMBER: N 4 - D 1

SATURN
PRESENT NAME: HETI
FIRST NAME: HETI
OTHER NAMES: TRAUM, NATHURN, SEESCHWALBE, MOBY DICK
SAIL NUMBER: E3

SCEPTRE
PRESENT NAME:
FIRST NAME:
OTHER NAMES:
SAIL NUMBER: K 17

SCHWANHILD
PRESENT NAME:
FIRST NAME: SCHWANHILD
OTHER NAMES:
SAIL NUMBER:

SCIROCCO
PRESENT NAME: DESIREE
FIRST NAME: SIBYLLAN
OTHER NAMES: SIROCCO, DUX, MARISETTA, VALERIA
SAIL NUMBER:

SEESCHWALBE
PRESENT NAME: HETI
FIRST NAME: HETI
OTHER NAMES: TRAUM, NATHURN, MOBY DICK, SATURN
SAIL NUMBER: E3

SEVEN SEAS
PRESENT NAME: SEVEN SEAS OF PORTO
FIRST NAME: SEVEN SEAS
OTHER NAMES: SUNDAY
SAIL NUMBER: US 9-P 1-K 26

SEVEN SEAS OF PORTO
PRESENT NAME: SEVEN SEAS OF PORTO
FIRST NAME: SEVEN SEAS
OTHER NAMES: SUNDAY
SAIL NUMBER: US 9-P 1-K 26

SIBYLLAN
PRESENT NAME: DESIREE
FIRST NAME: SIBYLLAN
OTHER NAMES: SIROCCO, SCIROCCO, DUX, MARISETTA, VALERIA
SAIL NUMBER:

SILVERVINGEN X
PRESENT NAME: BARRANQUILLA
FIRST NAME: PRINCESS SVANIVET
OTHER NAMES: IRENE
SAIL NUMBER: S 2 - K 22

SIROCCO
PRESENT NAME: DESIREE
FIRST NAME: SIBYLLAN
OTHER NAMES: SCIROCCO, DUX, MARISETTA, VALERIA
SAIL NUMBER:

SKEAF
PRESENT NAME: MARILINE
FIRST NAME: SKEAF
OTHER NAMES: TREUDEUTSCH
SAIL NUMBER:

SKEAF II
PRESENT NAME:
FIRST NAME: SKEAF II
OTHER NAMES: MARY II
SAIL NUMBER:

SKEAF III
PRESENT NAME:
FIRST NAME: SKEAF III
OTHER NAMES:
SAIL NUMBER:

SKEAF IV
PRESENT NAME:
FIRST NAME: SKEAF IV
OTHER NAMES: STERNA, FREYA, COPEJA, EMMELINE, MAID OF ASTOLAT, CYMBELINE, GIFT OF THE WIND
SAIL NUMBER:

SKEAF V
PRESENT NAME:
FIRST NAME: SKEAF V
OTHER NAMES: ISTAR
SAIL NUMBER:

SKUM III
PRESENT NAME:
FIRST NAME: SKUM III
OTHER NAMES: ALEXANDRA III, SYRIN
SAIL NUMBER:

SOLILOQUY
PRESENT NAME:
FIRST NAME: ISOLDE
OTHER NAMES: PTARMIGAN, SALLY ANN
SAIL NUMBER: US 2

SOLVEIG II
PRESENT NAME:
FIRST NAME: BRAND IV
OTHER NAMES: ISLA II, DORA III, RAGNA III, ELMARI
SAIL NUMBER:

SOLVEIG II
PRESENT NAME:
FIRST NAME: FIGARO IV
OTHER NAMES: ARROW, SYLVANIA
SAIL NUMBER: N 6

SOUTH AUSTRALIA
PRESENT NAME: SOUTH AUSTRALIA
FIRST NAME: SOUTH AUSTRALIA
OTHER NAMES:
SAIL NUMBER: KA 8

SOUTHERN CROSS
PRESENT NAME: SOUTHERN CROSS
FIRST NAME: SOUTHERN CROSS
OTHER NAMES:
SAIL NUMBER: KA 4

SOVEREIGN
PRESENT NAME: SOVEREIGN
FIRST NAME: SOVEREIGN
OTHER NAMES:
SAIL NUMBER: K 12

SPHINX
PRESENT NAME: OSTWIND
FIRST NAME: SPHINX
OTHER NAMES: LOBITO
SAIL NUMBER: G 4

SPIRIT OF AMERICA
PRESENT NAME:
FIRST NAME: SPIRIT OF AMERICA
OTHER NAMES:
SAIL NUMBER: US 34

STARS & STRIPES '83
PRESENT NAME: STARS & STRIPES '83
FIRST NAME: STARS & STRIPES '83
OTHER NAMES:
SAIL NUMBER: US 53

STARS & STRIPES '85
PRESENT NAME: STARS & STRIPES '85
FIRST NAME: STARS & STRIPES '85
OTHER NAMES:
SAIL NUMBER: US 54

STARS & STRIPES '86
PRESENT NAME: STARS & STRIPES '86
FIRST NAME: STARS & STRIPES '86
OTHER NAMES:
SAIL NUMBER: US 56

STARS & STRIPES '87
PRESENT NAME: STARS & STRIPES '87
FIRST NAME: STARS & STRIPES '87
OTHER NAMES:
SAIL NUMBER: US 55

STEAK 'N' KIDNEY
PRESENT NAME: STEAK 'N' KIDNEY
FIRST NAME: STEAK 'N' KIDNEY
OTHER NAMES:
SAIL NUMBER: KA 14

STERNA
PRESENT NAME:
FIRST NAME: SKEAF IV
OTHER NAMES: FREYA, COPEJA, EMMELINE, MAID OF ASTOLAT, CYMBELINE, GIFT OF THE WIND
SAIL NUMBER:

STIARNA
PRESENT NAME:
FIRST NAME: STIARNA
OTHER NAMES:
SAIL NUMBER:

STORM
PRESENT NAME: STORM
FIRST NAME: STORM
OTHER NAMES:
SAIL NUMBER: E 31

STORMSVALA
PRESENT NAME:
FIRST NAME: CORONA
OTHER NAMES: HAWAII VI, OSLO
SAIL NUMBER:

SUNDAY
PRESENT NAME: SEVEN SEAS OF PORTO
FIRST NAME: SEVEN SEAS
OTHER NAMES:
SAIL NUMBER: US 9-P 1-K 26

SVERIGE
PRESENT NAME: UWA
FIRST NAME: SVERIGE
OTHER NAMES: BLUE MAGIC, BLAUPUNKT
SAIL NUMBER: S 3 - G 5

SYLVA
PRESENT NAME:
FIRST NAME: HEATHERBELL
OTHER NAMES: TERESITA, MARGIT IV, YOLANDE
SAIL NUMBER:

SYLVANA
PRESENT NAME:
FIRST NAME: FIGARO IV
OTHER NAMES: ARROW, SOLVEIG II
SAIL NUMBER: N 6

SYMRA
PRESENT NAME:
FIRST NAME: SYMRA
OTHER NAMES:
SAIL NUMBER: N 2

SYRIN
PRESENT NAME:
FIRST NAME: SKUM III
OTHER NAMES: ALEXANDRA III
SAIL NUMBER:

TATJANA
PRESENT NAME:
FIRST NAME: TATJANA
OTHER NAMES: NOREEN
SAIL NUMBER: K 2

TEMERAIRE
PRESENT NAME: AUSTRALIA
FIRST NAME: AUSTRALIA
OTHER NAMES:
SAIL NUMBER: KA 5

TENDEREN III
PRESENT NAME: THEA
FIRST NAME: SANTA
OTHER NAMES: GAVOTTE II, NINA
SAIL NUMBER: N 4 - D 1

TERESITA
PRESENT NAME:
FIRST NAME: HEATHERBELL
OTHER NAMES: MARGIT IV, YOLANDE, SYLVA
SAIL NUMBER:

THEA
PRESENT NAME: THEA
FIRST NAME: SANTA
OTHER NAMES: NINA, TENDEREN III, GAVOTTE III
SAIL NUMBER: N 4 - D 1

TITANIA
PRESENT NAME:
FIRST NAME: TITANIA
OTHER NAMES:
SAIL NUMBER:

TOMAHAWK
PRESENT NAME: TOMAHAWK
FIRST NAME: TOMAHAWK
OTHER NAMES:
SAIL NUMBER: K13

TOVE LILIAN
PRESENT NAME:
FIRST NAME: HEIRA II
OTHER NAMES: NANETTE II, MARIELLA, BARCAROLLA
SAIL NUMBER:

TRAUM
PRESENT NAME: HETI
FIRST NAME: HETI
OTHER NAMES: NATHURN, SEESCHWALBE, MOBY DICK, SATURN
SAIL NUMBER: E 3

TREUDEUTSCH
PRESENT NAME: MARILINE
FIRST NAME: SKEAF
OTHER NAMES:
SAIL NUMBER:

TRIVIA
PRESENT NAME: TRIVIA
FIRST NAME: TRIVIA
OTHER NAMES: NORSAGA, PHOENIX, TRIVIA OF GOSPORT
SAIL NUMBER: K10-N16-US16

TRIVIA OF GOSPORT
PRESENT NAME: TRIVIA
FIRST NAME: TRIVIA
OTHER NAMES: NORSAGA, PHOENIX
SAIL NUMBER: K10 - N16 - US16

TRULL
PRESENT NAME:
FIRST NAME: TYCOON
OTHER NAMES: ARUNDEL, ZIO
SAIL NUMBER: US 3

TRUE NORTH
PRESENT NAME: TRUE NORTH
FIRST NAME: TRUE NORTH
OTHER NAMES:
SAIL NUMBER: KC 87

TRUE NORTH II
PRESENT NAME: TRUE NORTH II
FIRST NAME: TRUE NORTH II
OTHER NAMES:
SAIL NUMBER:

TYCOON
PRESENT NAME:
FIRST NAME: TYCOON
OTHER NAMES: ARUNDEL, ZIO, TRULL
SAIL NUMBER: US 3

ULL II
PRESENT NAME:
FIRST NAME: ULL II
OTHER NAMES:
SAIL NUMBER:

ULLABRAND IV
PRESENT NAME: RAAK
FIRST NAME: RAAK
OTHER NAMES: VICI
SAIL NUMBER: E 15

USA (E-1)
PRESENT NAME: USA (E-1)
FIRST NAME: USA (E-1)
OTHER NAMES:
SAIL NUMBER: US 49

USA (R-1)
PRESENT NAME: ECOSSE
FIRST NAME: USA (R-1)
OTHER NAMES:
SAIL NUMBER: US 61

UWA
PRESENT NAME: UWA
FIRST NAME: SVERIGE
OTHER N.: BLUE MAGIC, BLAUPUNKT
SAIL NUMBER: S 3 - G 5

VALERIA
PRESENT NAME: DESIREE
FIRST NAME: SIBYLLAN
OTHER NAMES: SIROCCO, SCIROCCO, DUX, MARISETTA
SAIL NUMBER:

VALIANT
PRESENT NAME: VALIANT
FIRST NAME: VALIANT
OTHER NAMES:
SAIL NUMBER: US 24

VANITY
PRESENT NAME:
FIRST NAME: VANITY
OTHER NAMES:
SAIL NUMBER: K 1

VANITY V
PRESENT NAME: VANITY V
FIRST NAME: VANITY V
OTHER NAMES: LA PINTA
SAIL NUMBER: K 5

VARG VI
PRESENT NAME: VEMA III
FIRST NAME: VEMA III
OTHER NAMES: DIVA III, LAKME VI
SAIL NUMBER: N 11

VARUNA
PRESENT NAME: VARUNA
FIRST NAME: WHITE HEATHER
OTHER NAMES:
SAIL NUMBER:

VEMA III
PRESENT NAME: VEMA III
FIRST NAME: VEMA III
OTHER NAMES: VARG VI, DIVA III, LAKME VI
SAIL NUMBER: N 11

VERONICA
PRESENT NAME:
FIRST NAME: VERONICA
OTHER NAMES:
SAIL NUMBER: K10

VICI
PRESENT NAME: RAAK
FIRST NAME: RAAK
OTHER NAMES: ULLABRAND IV
SAIL NUMBER: E 15

VICTORIA
PRESENT NAME:
FIRST NAME: VICTORIA
OTHER NAMES:
SAIL NUMBER:

VICTORY '82
PRESENT NAME: VICTORY '82
FIRST NAME: VICTORY '82
OTHER NAMES:
SAIL NUMBER: K 21

VICTORY '83
PRESENT NAME: VICTORY '83
FIRST NAME: VICTORY '83
OTHER NAMES:
SAIL NUMBER: K 22 - I 6

VIM
PRESENT NAME: VIM
FIRST NAME: VIM
OTHER NAMES:
SAIL NUMBER: US 15

VINETA
PRESENT NAME:
FIRST NAME: FIGARO
OTHER NAMES: FIGARO, FIGARO II, BONITA
SAIL NUMBER: E 10

VIVO VIII
PRESENT NAME: FRATERNITAS
FIRST NAME: VIVO VIII
OTHER NAMES:
SAIL NUMBER: E 20

VOGUE
PRESENT NAME: ERNA SIGNE
FIRST NAME: ERNA SIGNE
OTHER NAMES: MARJORIE
SAIL NUMBER: E 8

WAIANDANCE
PRESENT NAME:
FIRST NAME: WAIANDANCE
OTHER NAMES: CLYTIE, NIGHT WIND, COTTON BLOSSOM III
SAIL NUMBER: US 1

WAR BABY
PRESENT NAME: AMERICAN EAGLE
FIRST NAME: AMERICAN EAGLE
OTHER NAMES: GOLDEN EAGLE
SAIL NUMBER: US 21

WEATHERLY
PRESENT NAME: WEATHERLY
FIRST NAME: WEATHERLY
OTHER NAMES:
SAIL NUMBER: US 17

WESTRA
PRESENT NAME:
FIRST NAME: WESTRA
OTHER NAMES:
SAIL NUMBER: K 4

WESTWARD HO
PRESENT NAME:
FIRST NAME: MOYANA II
OTHER NAMES: MAHARANA, ESTRILDA, SAGRACE
SAIL NUMBER: K 8

WESTWIND
PRESENT NAME: WESTWIND
FIRST NAME: INGA
OTHER NAMES:
SAIL NUMBER: G 1

WHITE CRUSADER
PRESENT NAME: CRUSADER
FIRST NAME: CRUSADER I
OTHER NAMES:
SAIL NUMBER: K 24

WHITE CRUSADER II
PRESENT NAME:
FIRST NAME: CRUSADER II
OTHER NAMES:
SAIL NUMBER: K 25

WHITE HEATHER
PRESENT NAME: VARUNA
FIRST NAME: WHITE HEATHER
OTHER NAMES:
SAIL NUMBER:

WHITE STREAK
PRESENT NAME:
FIRST NAME: WHITE STREAK
OTHER NAMES:
SAIL NUMBER:

WINDANCER
PRESENT NAME: INTREPID
FIRST NAME: INTREPID
OTHER NAMES:
SAIL NUMBER: US 22

WINDROSE
PRESENT NAME: WINDROSE
FIRST NAME: CHANCEGGER
OTHER NAMES:
SAIL NUMBER:

WINGS
PRESENT NAME: WINGS
FIRST NAME: WINGS
OTHER NAMES: MOHITA II, AILE
SAIL NUMBER: K 15

WULP
PRESENT NAME:
FIRST NAME: DAVO III
OTHER NAMES: NOORDSTER III
SAIL NUMBER:

YATSET
PRESENT NAME:
FIRST NAME: YATSET
OTHER NAMES:
SAIL NUMBER:

YOLANDE
PRESENT NAME:
FIRST NAME: HEATHERBELL
OTHER NAMES: TERESITA, MARGIT IV, SYLVA
SAIL NUMBER:

ZELITA
PRESENT NAME:
FIRST NAME: ZELITA
OTHER NAMES:
SAIL NUMBER: K 9

ZINITA
PRESENT NAME:
FIRST NAME: ZINITA
OTHER NAMES: ZINITA OF CHICHESTER
SAIL NUMBER: K 8 - N 8

ZINITA OF CHICHESTER
PRESENT NAME:
FIRST NAME: ZINITA
OTHER NAMES: ZINITA
SAIL NUMBER: K 8 - N 8

ZIO
PRESENT NAME:
FIRST NAME: TYCOON
OTHER NAMES: ARUNDEL, TRULL
SAIL NUMBER: US 3

ZORAIDA
PRESENT NAME:
FIRST NAME: ZORAIDA
OTHER NAMES:
SAIL NUMBER: K 8

BIBLIOGRAPHY

A.I.V.E., *I Dodici, cenni storici sulla classe 12 Metri S.I.*, 1997
BADMINTON LIBRARY, Vol. I and 2, Ashford Press Publishing, 1985
R.N. BAVIER JR, *A View from the Cockpit*, Dodd, Mead & Company, New York, 1965
BEKEN OF COWES, *1897-1914*, Cassel & Co., 1966
– *1919-1939*, Cassel & Co., 1969
– *The America's Cup*, Collins Harvill, 1990
– *A Hundred Years of Sail*, Harvill Press, 1996
J. BERTRAND, *Born to Win*, Hearst Marine, New York, 1985
L. BONTEMPELLI, *Luna Rossa*, Prada America's Cup, Milan, 2000
BOTTINI, CRANE, STANNARD, *From Newport to Perth*, Nautical Books, London, 1986
F. CHEVALIER, J. TAGLAND, *America's Cup Yacht Designs, 1851-1986*, Paris, 1987
D. CONNER, *No Excuse to Lose: Winning Yacht Races*, W.W. Norton & Co., New York, 1978
– *A Manual of Yacht and Boat Sailing*, Horace Cox, 1891
S. DOMIZLAFF, *Abeking and Rasmussen, an Evolution in Yacht Building*, Delius Klasing, 1996
J. EASTLAND, *Great Yachts and their Designers*, Adlard Coles Nautical, London, 1987
T. FAIRCHILD, *The America's Cup Challenge: there is no second*, Nautical Books, 1983
B. FISHER, *12-Metre Images*, Pelham Books, London, 1986
U. FOX, *Second Book*, Peter Daviers, London, 1946
– *Sail and Power*, Peter Daviers, London, 1948
– *Racing, Cruising and Design*, Peter Davies, London, 1948
– *Thoughts on Yacht and Yachting*, Peter Davies, London, 1952
– *Sailing Boats*, Newnes, London, 1959
H.C. FOLKHARD, *The Sailing Boat*, London, 1906
C. FREER, *The Twelve-Metre Yacht*, Nautical Books, London, 1986
R.E. FROUDE, *Yacht Racing Measurements Rules, and the International Conference*, Institution of Naval Architects, 1906
B. HECKSTALL-SMITH, *The Helmsman's Handbook*, Horace Cox, 1908, 1912
– *The Britannia and her Contemporaries*, Methuen & Co. Ltd., 1929
R. HENDERSON, *Philip L. Rhodes and his Yacht Designs*, Int. Marine, Camden, 1993
L.F. HERRESHOFF, *The Common Sense of Yacht Design*, The Rudder Publishing, 1946
J.H. ILLINGWORTH, *La Coppa America*, Mursia, Milan, 1992
P. JOHNSON, *Yacht Rating*, Bucksea Guides, 1997
T. JONES, *Challenges 77. Newport and the America's Cup*, W.W. Norton & Co., New York, 1978
D. KEMP, *Yacht Architecture: a Treaty*, Horace Cox, 1885
F.S. KINNEY, R. BOURNE, *The Best of the Best*, W.W. Norton & Co., New York, 1996
M. KLUDAS, *Im Zwolfer-Rausch*, Meer & Yachten
J. LAMMERTS VAN BUEREN, *The Great Eights*, Yachting Library, Milan, 2000
M. LEVITT, *Le vele più famose del mondo*, Yachting Library, Milan, 1999
LLOYD'S REGISTER OF YACHTING, 1905-1980
MCCALLUN FIFE MAY, *Fast and Bonnie*, John Donald Publishers Ltd., Edinburgh, 1998
C. MITCHELL, *Summer of the Twelves*, Charles Scribner's Sons, New York, 1959
A. MORGAN ET AL., *America's Cup '87, Sail of the century*, Sheridan House, 1987
F. PACE, *Charles E. Nicholson and his Yachts*, Adlard Coles Nautical, 2000
J. PARKINSON JR, *The History of the New York Yacht Club*, The New York Yacht Club, New York, 1975
D. PHILLIPS-BIRT, *Sailing Yacht Design*, Int. Marine Publishing Co., 1971
– *The Cumberland Fleet*, The Royal Thames Yacht Club, London, 1978
R. RAYNER, *The Story of the America's Cup*, David and Charles, 1996
B. ROBINSON, *Legendary Yachts*, David McKay Company Inc., New York, 1978
C. SCIARRELLI, *Lo Yacht*, Mursia, Milan, 1988
O.J. STEPHENS II, *All This and Sailing, Too*, Mystic Seaport, Mystic, 1999
P.W. STEPHENS, *Traditions and Memories of American Yachting*, Wooden Boat, 1989
B. STANNARD, *Ben Lexcen: the Man, the Keel and the Cup*, Faber and Faber, London, 1984
A. VINER, *A History of Rating Rules for Yachts*, National Maritime Museum, London, 1979
R. VOLMER, *Unsere Zwolfer*, Freundeskreis Klassische Yachten, June 7th, 1997
YACHT CLUB ARGENTINO, *La istoria de los primeros 100 años 1883-1983*

MAGAZINES AND PERIODICALS
Classic Boat - Le Yacht, 1898-1938 - *Rivista Nautica*, 1906, 1907, 1910, 1911 - *The Yachtsman*
Wooden Boat - Yachting - Yachting Gazette, 1900-1907 - *Yachting Monthly - Yachting World*

ACKNOWLEDGEMENT

Any history of the 12 Metre, no matter how thoroughly researched, is certain to be revised. New information will be found. Missing yachts will be located. New owners and restoration projects will return derelicts to their former beauty. And some yachts will be lost forever by neglect and accident. Nevertheless, it is our hope that this book will excite interest in the 12 Metre, and the faithful preservation of these lovely yachts for generations of sailors to come.

After many years of independent research, the authors are grateful for the fortunate circumstance that led to our collaboration, and perhaps a better book than each might have done alone. Although we have tried to be thorough, we thank those who will point out the inevitable errors so that we can correct them in the future.

We are also indebted to many people for their assistance in our research and preparation. First and foremost to the Associazione Italiana Vele d'epoca, the Yacht Club Italiano, and the New York Yacht Club for the use of their libraries; and to Olin Stephens, not only for writing the Introduction, but also for sharing his wealth of information and experience.

We also thank Bob Tiedemann, who has been an advocate for the preservation and use of 12 Metres for nearly 30 years, Chris Ennels and Monika Kludas for their contribution on the Scandinavian and German Twelves, and encouragement from John Lemmerts van Beuren of the 8 Metre Association, and Gary Jobson who always asked "When will the book be finished?"

To our publisher, Fabio Ratti, and the staff of Ratti Editoria and Adlard Coles Nautical, our thanks for their encouragement and advice while pressing for completion at the earliest possible date.

And finally to all 12 Metre owners and the International Twelve Metre Association, not only for the information they have supplied, but also for the commitment they have made to preserve the 12 Metre. Without them there would be little to write about.

Luigi Lang   *Wm. H. Dyer Jones*
Genoa, Italy   *Newport, Rhode Island*